How Our Garden Grows

Gardening and
Northern

Mary Ellen Connelly

May Ellen Connelly

Illustrations by Linda Shields
Cover Design by Nathan Holman

Plants rule and shade all my motions and thinking. Through a greater nature that folds them and me together, I am coaxed and controlled. My world-view and interpretation comes through my identification and alliance with these. Sure, they provide nearly every means of our basic existence, but my intent travels beyond their life-sustaining oxygen, food, clothing, heat and dwellings. I would be empty except for the spiritual gifts they allow me to discover by growing and observing them in and out of the boundaries of my garden.

The Maria Corporation
dba Perennial Passion
The Plant Lovers' Nursery...*Rare Finds*
1510 West 51st Street
Sioux Falls, South Dakota 57105
Telephone 605.335.3526; Fax 605.335.2215
Email perennialpassion@home.com

Library of Congress Control Number: 2001 129122
ISBN: 0-9713540-0-6

Connelly, Mary Ellen
How Our Garden Grows

Printed in the United States by Morris Publishing
3212 East Highway 30 • Kearney, NE 68847
1-800-650-7888

Table of Contents

How Our Garden Grows
Mary Ellen Connelly

Introduction

Perennials are the focus of this, my first, book. That I could be inclusive with this category was an illusive idea. Here I've written about 1200 plants; there are tens of thousands more that could be included. Every year dozens of new plants are introduced to the marketplace from selections from breeding or rediscovered native plants that come into favor and are now considered "worthy." Older, out-of-favor plants are reintroduced as they cycle back into popularity. It has always surprised me how many of this vast selection of perennials really are adaptable or hardy to our locale. I've also included a few, of what I consider indispensable, self-sowing annuals, biennials, half-hardy perennials, woody sub-shrubs and fall planted bulbs that can add great diversity and dynamics to gardens.

I've included some essays about my state...my geographical state, South Dakota, that is...my reverence for soil, soil pH, how to plant a tree on a compacted site, and my opinions on the terrible effects of soil compaction and the stripping away of topsoil by builders. The tidbits and leftovers section addresses many areas of gardening and offer many tips.

Since venturing into this realm of writing, I originally had organized and planned to finish this book in 1998, then 1999, then the millennium, and now 2001. From the beginning I wanted to include all potentially hardy plants, perennials, shrubs, trees, vines and herbs, and then finish up with tender annuals, tropicals and half-hardy perennials. This proved to be a task too great for me to complete for a single book. In order to finally reach some sort of closure, I had to fix a new mark, finish with perennials for now, close the cover, quit the Mac, and get to the printer. In the not-so-distant future I would like to finish the rest of the categories.

To all of you miracle workers who have made my dreams come true and Perennial Passion Nursery a reality, thank you from the bottom of my soiled soul. Thanks to:
Sparky, otherwise known as Paul, my greatest enabler.
My children, Alex, Sam, Liz, Maggie and Suzie. They call me Earth Mother and I like that.
Mom and Dad, siblings and in-laws.
Lori, Sue, Jeff and Linda, the regular sidekicks at the nursery, and all the other people who have helped over the past twelve summers...sales people, planters and potters, weeders and waterers...you are all indispensable. We could not have grown without you!
Both loyal old and new customers, garden compatriots, all who contribute to hortomania and nourish the dream of the Plant Lovers' Nursery.
All of our friends, passionate gardeners and the original Garden Groupies, Linda, Lynne, Sunni, Marianne, Mary, Kay, Bev.
Linda Shields for her original drawings.
Nathan Holman for the original cover design.
Dr. Caroline Geyer for editing the larger portions of the book, the genera summary descriptions and my five essays at the beginning of the book. (Blame me for the errors that are bound to spring up in the species descriptions, but please be kind).
The Culligan Water Conditioning and Minnehaha Ice and Recreation associates.

The Objectives of PERENNIAL PASSION

EVANGELIZE about the diversity of plant life. Create awareness and interest in plants of all types and functions-- perennials, herbs, annuals, vines, shrubs, trees, woodland, prairie, drought-tolerant, moisture-loving--the entire spectrum. ("Know your plants!" charged great plantsman, Allan Bloom. We heeded.)

MINIMIZE Pareto's Principle. The observation, "domination of the significant few," acknowledged by an Italian named Pareto, has been coined the Pareto Principle, which describes the fact that 90 percent of any activity revolves around only 10 percent of the possible items involved. Applied to plant selection this principle means that about 10 percent of potentially suitable plants are planted 90 percent of the time. Often only a few different plants will dominate landscaping in a given region. Observe the South Dakota landscapes that are commanded by Spiraea, Potentilla, juniper and ash.

EMPHASIZE the importance of soil preparation. (Dirt's a four letter word.) "The soil, the basis of a successful garden should first receive your thought. Even more than receiving your thought, it should receive your respect, and then you must learn to know it." (*Garden Making and Keeping*, Hugh Findlay, 1932.) Practice and educate about good plant culture including organic amendments, proper watering and integrated pest management. Use chemicals as a last resort.

RECOGNIZE sound design principles to build strong gardens. Remember that "Strength Comes From Green - A Chloroborealis!" Teach about contrasts of foliage texture, color, form and habit.

IMPROVISE a peaceful repose where plants and people can connect. Enable tip-toeing through the tulips in OUR GARDEN where we carry out our own trials on unusual plants. Since we grow these plants ourselves, we can advise of their preferred culture to enable them to survive and thrive in South Dakota

My Sense of Place
The Northern Plains Region

My Place in the Plains

As an immigrant offspring, I've clung to a simple heritage, the great granddaughter of two homesteading families that added to the South Dakota eastern prairie, the names Schlund, from Schleswig Holstein of northern Germany and Schau (now Scott) from the island of Bornholm of Denmark. But then, as with many families, there are sketchy rumors of royalty on our family tree. The connections our family supposedly has to the "your highness set" are the king's daughter and gardener who ran away to garden together forever in happy bliss!

I have a 1950s aerial view of the pastoral Schlund homestead, six miles north of Mt. Vernon, South Dakota, where Grandma and Grandpa farmed, gardened, preserved and prospered for most of their adult lives. I look down on the neat furrows of the newly planted garden, where we later rooted out potatoes and onions. The mulberry trees are nearby along with the old yellow rose shrub and evenly placed peony bushes. Grandpa is still in the seat of his dusty little Ford tractor. My eyes can barely focus on the tiny light dot that is the straw hat he is wearing. Just in time for an airborn inspection, he has finished his disking maneuvers through the orchard. For many decades before, approval had been given from above.

Their farm was the nearly self-sufficient operation typical of the early homesteaders, where much of their own fruit, vegetables, flour, eggs, chicken and pork were raised and processed, using many of the same practices brought over from the "old country" by their parents.

Escaping from town on the back of my horse, Champ, to the lane that led to their big red barn was like going through the restorative passage to Shangri-la. There I could spend mornings awakening to roosters' crows and searching for the mother cat's latest secret hiding place for her kittens. My cuddling hands and face ached to hold and feel their silky, squirmy bodies.

Claiming and cleaning out the brooder house was a chore we eagerly accepted to make way for a summer-long playhouse. But we had to wait until baby chicks, earlier delivered in cheeping, perforated cardboard boxes, had outgrown it. Even the big chickens were small enough to allow intimacy with little people. Sometimes while I was in the chicken house picking eggs, a hen would slowly ease herself up and I would be spellbound while watching the shelled essence of a baby chick, slide slowly out of the "part that goes over the fence last" (Grandma's expression) and hear its gentle thump against the straw-lined box. I looked forward to the day when I could have the daring that Grandma showed. (One might say I was *egged-on*). Oblivious to pecks and scolding, she could calmly grab their fresh daily genesis while the chickens were still *in* their nests.

On spring Sunday nights, just before heading back to town time, we could watch Uncle Billy pull baby piglets, easing the mother pig's stress and saving a few from being smashed by her huge portly body.

Most of my young life's lessons were learned right there in touch with the earth, encircled by that big old farm yard with all its little buildings with their secrets to explore. That tiny dot of existence spread out into the great big world through concentric rings of farm yards, shelter belts, country schoolyards, pastures and fields, rows of fence and power posts, grimy gravel grids, little towns and county seats.

When younger, I often imagined what life would have brought me if these old timers could have just kept going, a little more to the west so I could have grown up in real horse country, or a few hundred more miles to Colorado, near the mountains where I eventually adventured to college. Many of us left South Dakota for awhile, not intending to come back to live. But with chromosomes laden with the soil, grit, prairie fields of chlorophyll, leaves, stems, flowers, weather, sunshine and scents of the prairie, it's hard to resist the magnet of the land, people, security and past. Our roots run deep and I'm glad we've returned to raise our families with some of the same values and conditions in which we felt secure.

To all of you beloved angels, blessed spirits of natives and newcomers, those gone before and those who remain with us on this beloved prairie earth, these words and this growing life is dedicated.

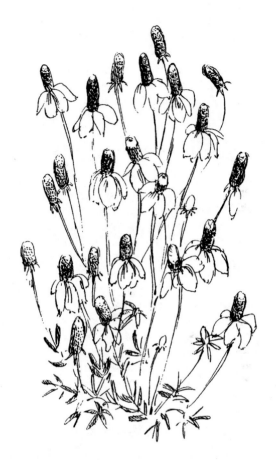

The Beautiful State in Which I Live

South Dakota, the unique and beautiful state in which I live, is located on the planet with the loveliest name, Earth. There it spreads its land mass, in the exact center of the Northern Great Plains, the prairie region of the United States on the North American Continent. It shares unitary location, environment and culture with the adjoining areas of North Dakota, Minnesota, Nebraska, Iowa and eastern Wyoming and Montana.

<u>Herstory</u> Mother Earth's "herstory" among these northern longitudes and latitudes includes the covering and receding of the waters of oceans. While the oceans covered this region, sedimentary layers of soil and grit were pressed and bonded together as sandstone, shale and limestone in the western parts of South Dakota. In

southeastern parts, where I grew up and continue to live and garden, the distinct weimereiner-pink stone named Sioux quartzite, just beneath diamonds on the hardness scale, is easily observed as prominent outcroppings of the natural terrain. It has been dated to over one billion years old. Significant historical buildings, walls, terraces and remnant cobblestone streets proudly display quartzite stones, hand-chiseled to fit their positions. Early settlers carefully extracted them from a number of quarries that operated in the early 20th century.

The oceans finally disappeared the last time that land heaved upward, and 60 million years ago, a warm and damp climate supported a subtropical forest within the imaginary lines of my State.

After the Black Hills burst from its subterranean anchor and heaved upward to command the western plains in what is now western South Dakota, the climate changed drastically. Pushed by prevailing westerly winds, air was forced up and over the new low mountains. There it cooled and dropped its moisture at the higher altitudes instead of sharing it further along the way as clouds drifted east. The subtropical forest soon dried up and the grasslands emerged.

From the new mountains the rains washed debris that found its way to the adjacent plains directly east. There it settled as alluvium deposits. Though not strictly desert, the flat land just east of the Black Hills receive much less moisture than those in the far eastern part of the state, a couple hundred miles farther down from prevailing westerly winds.

In eastern South Dakota, from one million years to a few thousand years ago, sheets of ice began to advance and retreat and formed the Missouri River at their western edges. Caches of gravel and stone were buried throughout the area. The alternating freezing and thawing of the earth frees this indigenous field stone that was used in earlier days to build foundations and walls and is finding new popularity for use in dry-set retaining walls.

<u>Climate</u> For the past 5000 years, the climate here has been relatively stable. The length of the growing season averages from 160 days in the southeast to 130 days in the north. The Black Hills has fewer, approximately 100 growing days.

Average temperatures of 10 to 20 degrees Fahrenheit in January and 70 to 80 degrees for July hide the bitter truth. Temperatures can drop to below -30 degrees Fahrenheit in winter. Wind chills that combine the effects of air temperature and wind velocity can make it feel like minus 80 degrees. Combine this brutality with open, sometimes-

snowless winters, and plant tissues sense no mercy! Desiccation sets in quickly.

But then we and the plants count our blessings when mild winters grace us and move the mercury above the zero degree mark or way higher to the balmy 50, 60 or even 70 degree calibration as we have seen.

What is truly remarkable, flabbergasting, unbelievable, and amazing is that the diversity of our weather can hand us all of the above described conditions in a single winter season! In early November, 1998, we experienced a relentless snowstorm that left deep, moisture-laden, heavy snow that damaged many a limb. After that system finished up, we returned to beautiful fall weather and enjoyed record temperatures well into the twelfth month. But during that same remarkable December, we watched as the star magnolia, *Magnolia stellata*, tricked into believing winter had left for good, began to swell and open her flower buds ever so slightly.

That year winter came again for real by the end of December with a bitter cold period, well below zero, with little to no snow cover, that lasted until the middle of January. The rest of the normally winter months of February and March were mild, and the not-so-deep-this-time frost had breathed its last steamy breath by mid February, and nearly everyone predicted an early spring (novices often do).

April, which offers promises it never keeps, slowed things down as usual, and in the end nearly every spring thing bloomed right on schedule--including the star magnolia! It never ceases to amaze me that the plants seem to know the future and pace themselves accordingly.

Spring Our early springs cold-tease and torment us all. The Aprils that we long for often disappoint. Springs flash by like a too-soon, Fourth of July explosion. May can be cool and rainy and zap us with a few more frost-filled nights or gives us record high temperatures. We don't just garden in South Dakota, we garden all-at-once!

Summer Summer steps up quickly. It is short and beautiful. Rainfall, however, is not always dependable, and there are often prolonged periods of drought.

Autumn In my State autumn is beyond description, my favorite time of the year. September might just be the best garden planning and planting month. Seeds and plants of hope are tucked into the soil to be realized the following spring. Roots of plants nestle cozily in warm soil that has been heated through by hot summer days, and with their heads breathing free in cool air above, they store energy for the onslaught ahead. We can all relate to that.

<u>Prairie Designations</u> Geographically diverse, the center of South Dakota is smack in the middle of the grassland region. Its eastern end is located near deciduous forests that spread into Minnesota, and its western opposite joins with the Rocky Mountain coniferous forests that spread into Wyoming and Montana. Because of the variety of ecosystems, the natural vegetation is more diverse than that of neighboring states. Over 1500 different plant species have been identified.

My State is often divided into the designations of short-grass prairie, mid-grass prairie and tall-grass prairie. The short-grass area in the western third has the lowest precipitation of 14-16 inches of moisture. Here dominate shorter grama and buffalo grass and forbs that are grazed by cattle and sheep.

The mid-grass prairie in the central third of the state flanks both shores of the Missouri River and grows little bluestem, side oats grama and needle grass and more forbs. Today this area is mostly used for grazing or growing wheat because of steep rolling hills and high-alkaline, clay soils.

The tall-grass prairie, once dominated by big blue stem, Indian and switch grass, existed in the eastern third of South Dakota, where today's geometric grids of cultivated fields now rule. Prairie grasses had grown and decayed for centuries before the European farmers arrived in the late 1800s, creating the mineral, clay soils that grow well their fellow monocots, corn. This is the area of greatest precipitation, averaging 26 inches. Small shallow lakes, prairie potholes, and sloughs dot northeast and eastern South Dakota and support many plants that have adapted to standing water, marsh areas, and the transitional areas between wet and dry prairie.

As farmers settled west of Iowa and Minnesota, row crops like corn declined in per-acre yield. Silo phallics, which allow one to note farmsteads from a distance, were spaced farther apart, and by the time furrows reached an imaginary line near Mt. Vernon, where I grew up and about where the mid-grass prairie begins, one could pretty much depend on not-always-reliable yields. In past especially dry years, dry-land crops of cane and milo were substitutes for corn, assuring there would at least be winter feed for livestock. My dad calls the Aurora County line, three miles to the west, the "jumping –off point." It was hard enough to farm where we lived and even harder as one plowed west.

Too-far-west-to-farm was the land west of Kadoka, the short-grass prairie where my paternal grandfather attempted to homestead in the early 1900s. A few summers ago, Dad found the well that was

abandoned by Grandpa Emerson after a brief, not-so-prosperous, sod-house existence. The land had been turned back to federal grazing long ago.

Trees on the Prairie

Cottonwood and peach-leaf willow trees flourish along the streams and undeveloped rivers throughout my State, and there are natural oak, ash and basswood forests in the east. Coniferous forests of spruce and pine are found in the Black Hills, but the only native evergreen east of the Missouri River is *Juniperus virginiana*, the eastern red cedar.

Soiled

There is a force that pulls me towards soil, but not like that of gravity or the one-foot-in-the-grave kind, though my skin and muscles certainly do sag in that direction more each year. As if to the priesthood, I am called by this rich substance. It is tenacious, resolute. The reminders never fade completely. They flow back in cycles like spring floods, high water that comes over the tops of my boots, soak me cold and uncomfortable until I react. I sit down to take time to remove those boots, dry off and examine those soiled, souled soles.

"Say, 'Soil;' dirt's a dirty word!" reads the short expression on the button I pin to my shirt. But looking up thesaurus substitutes for the word, "soil," arouses in me thought-provoking agitation about how our English language fails to elevate the value of this precious substance.

The word, "soil," used as a noun, it suggests, can be substituted with the apparently neutral words earth, dirt, clay, dry land, dust, homestead, region, spread and terra firma. But read on! "Soil," as a verb, offers these options: to make dirty, bedraggle, befoul, besmirch, contaminate, crumb, debase, defile, degrade, dirty, discolor, disgrace, foul, grime, maculate, mess, muck and muss up, muddy, pollute, shame, smear, smudge, spatter, spoil, spot, stain, sully, taint, tar and tarnish.

Looking up the word, "dirt," as a noun, gives me these innocuous choices: clay, dust, earth, loam, real estate and terra firma. But the synonyms defile with crud, dreck, dregs, excrement, feculence, filth, filthiness, gook, ground, gunk, mire, muck, mud, rottenness, scuz, sleaze, slime, smudge, smut, soil, stain and tarnish. (By now you are probably thinking, "Overkill! Spare me!" But thanks for letting me make my point!)

"Earth," the loveliest of all words, is exempt from blasphemy in my references. If vowels and consonants are formed slowly and carefully as one inhales and exhales, it resonates like breath itself, "Eaarrrtthh." It could be the sound of the first-drawn breath of a newborn or the last sigh of a creature leaving life as we know it.

Why is soil, wherein lies the essential elements of the earth, the life-giving substance that nourishes all of the world and its creatures, disparaged with all these opposite and negative oxymora? I wonder: Do other languages promote the same negative connotations of soil as does ours? Has the concept of soil as unclean or tainted been perpetuated because of a religious teaching that the devil lives "down there?" Did early white assemblers of English dictionaries have an anti-dark prejudice that has been handed down and left unchallenged? Did a super-clean existence or pristine mentality cause them to recoil at the concept of dirt?

I can think of more compelling words and phrases to describe the product and action of soil. When I go to the garden to "soil myself," I am grounded, rejuvenated, connected, real and relaxed, and come-clean in the process. I could be tan, dark-skinned, ruddy complected, unclean, barefoot on the beach, and...never anal-retentive! Once my hands are "dirty," I am meditated, naturalized and in-touch with the earth, literally. After all, I come from soil, and I will become soil.

How Delicious

My adult children tease, "Mom still plays in the dirt!" I've never really moved beyond the mud pie days. My friend and playmate, Faith and I stirred them up. We would sprinkle the rich, dark cakes with sugary sands of time and frost them with the petals of hollyhocks and asters and the "banana" seed clusters from native box elder trees, regular landscape plants that mostly volunteered here and there in our small town. If we couldn't get our younger

siblings to taste them, we would pretend by smacking our lips and licking our fingers saying, "How delicious!"

I suppose our naiveté kept us from understanding then that the metaphor we were playing out was real; we were kneeling at the foot--sole, soul, soil--of the food chain. The chemical combinations we were playing with, the minerals, humus and wet ions of water, along with miraculous sunlight, carbon dioxide and oxygen, can explode seed into dynamic pieces of edible chlorophyll, not to mention colorful, sumptuous and sexy reproductive parts. For us they grow milk, meat, eggs and cheese, fabrics of wool, cotton, flax, hemp and mulberry leaves that are digested by worms into silk. The synthetic plastics that make so many of the materials of our modern world have their origins in soil. There is the furniture we sit, sleep, eat on and store in, and the fossil fuels that provide energy to travel, cook and heat and cool our buildings.

Soil Sense

The depth of the mineral   topsoils in the fields of Minnehaha County ranges from four or more feet in valleys, on gentle slopes or near river bottoms where erosion has helped it to accumulate, to a few inches on steep slopes and at the tops of hills from where it has eroded over the years. An average would be 18 inches to over 24 inches (Munk).

My friend, Linda, and I have shared a concern about the way soil is managed, compacted and somehow depleted during construction projects. We both live in houses built in the pre-1950s where there is deep topsoil supporting mature trees, landscapes and healthy gardens. She called one day and asked me to accompany her to check out a house lot; maybe they would build a new home. I grabbed my spade and off we went. There, after blunt attempts to determine a layer of topsoil, we were flabbergasted to find no topsoil on this lot whatsoever! It had been graded smooth with barely a ripple of contour, who knew when or by whom? The asking price of this lot was over $50,000. To replace the rich topsoil to compare with that in her older neighborhood, the cost would be more thousands of dollars.

After this experience, Linda pursued the question, "Is there an ordinance that requires notification of property soil conditions to potential buyers of such property? Are any soil standards required?" Here is Sioux Falls City Commissioner, Casey Murschel's reply to the question.

It has taken me awhile to research your question on topsoil.   The City Subdivision Ordinance and Engineering Design Standards do not address requirements for topsoil. Grading and drainage plans are required for any new subdivision, however they do not specify a depth of cover material. I am informed that an ordinance requiring a specific depth of topsoil would be extremely difficult to enforce. Therefore, potential buyers are responsible for negotiating with the seller or builder issues such as final grading and soil cover before a purchase agreement is signed. This may not be the answer you were hoping for, but I am glad you asked the question (Murschel).

A problem we detect is that these potential buyers, the inexperienced and sometimes experienced, don't know the questions to ask or what to expect when pursuing the purchase of property or negotiating with contractors. What is the agenda when negotiating? Must one negotiate to keep the indigenous topsoil, that which naturally originated with and belongs to the property? Who advocates for the soil?

Some owners of newly built houses had anticipated the damage inflicted on their soils by the construction development process. But for others it was an abrupt and unwelcome surprise. They weren't aware of the results of heavy equipment stripping away the natural topsoil. They hadn't been alerted that only four to six inches would be added back, often moved in from somewhere else to be spread over the compacted subsoil of their site. They assume, as I have, that the experts know what is best; surely the land would be left in good condition after construction because everyone knows that the natural next step after building is the planting of trees, shrubs, flowers and gardens.

Even I, who assume a modest few years of experience don't always know how to proceed. I thought I had soil-sense when my husband and I built the Culligan building. There was beautiful, deep and rich, sandy clay loam, dream soil for the display garden we planned to grow alongside our adjoining nursery, Perennial Passion. Our plans were repeated more than once to both the main contractor and the grading sub-contractor. With hindsight, though, I never noticed anyone taking notes and there was no written agreement. All the topsoil remained on site as I had requested. Yet when I came to the site one morning to interrupt the final soil-work process, I was mortified to see sticky, yellowish, gumbo-like fill being spread about. My stomach did flip-flops; the message had never been carried down through the ranks. Why was I sickened? I had big plans for this garden; I knew we would be experimenting with many unusual plants and I wanted the best possible growing conditions.

> "Simply put, planting a specimen (plant) in
> inadequate soil...reduces its adaptability." (Sabuco 14).

The most frustrating fact is that the maiming of soil, the stripping of soil, the compaction of soil could be kept at a minimum if one would plan ahead with prevention tactics. But don't depend entirely on your

contractor to monitor your prevention measures. Regardless of his or her good intentions, expediency and cost often win out, and things get done that are difficult and expensive to undo.

Attitudes

There are two different attitudes towards soil and there is a conflict of interest between them. There is that of the farmer, gardener, homeowner who value soil as the product of nature, the useful and indispensable habitat in which to grow crops, trees and other ornamental plants. The value of their property is directly related to the condition of their soil, and they describe it in terms of longevity and productivity. Compaction is a negative term for this group for it squeezes the air from the soil that is necessary for plants to live and thrive (Brady).

On the other side, engineers and construction-related occupations regard soil over the short term, the immediate use it has to them. For them, compaction is a post construction requirement. They classify soils in terms of their ability to support building foundations or highway construction. An engineering testing group, ASTM sets standard procedures and percentages for compaction, and the standard proctor test assures the high density compaction determined to best-support foundations, sidewalks and driveways. They quantify compaction with a measurement of bulk density. Up to 95% bulk density may be specified, the same as an extremely low percentage of pore space for air or water and the constriction at which hardly any roots will grow—anaerobic soil (Brady).

Topsoil

Topsoil that has developed over subsoil is the main location for root development and elongation and provides the medium to carry nutrients and water to plant roots. It is the area that gets plowed, cultivated, landscaped, fertilized and planted.

Thin Topsoil - Poor Subsoil Conditions

"The productivity of a soil is determined in no small degree by the nature of its subsoil. The permeability and chemical nature of the subsoil influences the surface soil in its role as a medium for plant growth." (Brady).

Sometimes we hear, "You don't need deep topsoil; a few inches will support basic things such as sod. Many commonly used landscape plants will survive the soil conditions left at new sites," or, "When soil is removed from a site, there never seems to be enough to fill the space back up again," or, "It is customary to put only four to six inches of topsoil back onto a new construction site." (My reply to these scenarios, "Customary, schmutztomary!")

Here is a list of problems when planting in subsoil and shallow topsoil.

- Planting into highly alkaline subsoil reduces the range of plant adaptability; most plants grow best at pH around neutral or slightly less (acid).

- Diversity of plants is limited. Because of poor subsoil conditions and shallow replacement topsoil on new sites, homeowners and others are limited to planting the handful of common plants that is seen on every other new landscape.

- Subsoil accumulates the iron, aluminum oxides, clays, gypsum, and calcium and contains very little organic matter. Sometimes free calcium is found which indicates and contributes to heightened alkalinity.

- Shrubs grown in two or more gallon containers have roots developed to a 10 to 12 inch depth and these are planted directly into subsoil.

- Anchoring roots of a two-inch caliper tree are already developed at two or more feet and feeder roots adapt in the aerated upper ten to twelve inches of topsoil, if it is available.

- The physical compaction of the subsoil makes it difficult for roots to push through even if the availability of nutrients is satisfactory.

- More water is required by turf grass when grown on minimal topsoil underlain by hard impenetrable subsoil. Sometimes it runs off between the layers. (One is sometimes able to observe it flowing over curbs and into storm sewers.)

Amending Soil - Raising the Organic Component of Mineral Soils

Though I've gardened all my life, when younger, someone else cultivated or manured the garden space. Then, in the late 60's, as a newlywed starting my very own garden, an aunt and uncle told me that after ten years of soil amending around their new-in-the-50's home, they were finally getting it right. At first the concept of amending seemed overwhelming to someone who was twenty-something! Ten years seemed like an eternity. What about all those years in between? Now I know that even baby steps yield great results.

The good news is that compacted or depleted soils can be revived and replenished. The key ingredients needed to enable this process are time, freeze-thaw cycles, and inorganic and organic amendments. Together they open up soil structure, creating perfect pore space to absorb and retain air and water, allow for proper drainage and give resistance to compaction.

Organic amendments such as compost have many advantages for soil. They increase the growing ability of sandy soil, increase the drainage of clay soil, encourage beneficial insects, bacteria and earthworms, slow down leaching and keep water and nutrients in place and available to the plant over a longer period of time.

Many gardeners have finally "arrived" in this category. Their spades now glide easily, as if greased, into near-ideal soil. They may have started with marginal soil, but after consistent amending, they have realized garden utopia--balanced organic matter and introduction of bacteria and their fellow organisms, the lively little germ gems that will decompose these additives into parts that can be used in the plants' growth processes. It will not easily be blown or washed away.

Soil Amendment Suggestions

When adding to soil, use a mixture of amendments instead of a single type. Here are some ideas: decomposed food scraps, compost, buckwheat hulls, rotted sawdust, straw, marsh hay, shredded bark, cocoa bean hulls, cottonseed, cottonseed hulls, ground peanut shells, conifer and pine needles, mushroom compost, peat moss, decomposed manure and saw dust, alfalfa meal or pellets, fish meal, pine bark, rotting leaves, diatomaceous earth, mycorrhizal fungi, ground corn cobs, fenugreek, discarded leather shoes, boots, and belts, composted vegetable and animal household wastes. I bury fish, banana peels and coffee grounds directly into the garden. Beneficial inorganic amendments are coarse sand, pea rock, crushed quartzite or other rock that is indigenous to the region.

Growing cover crops such as annual legumes fix nitrogen back to soil. 'Nitro' is an annual alfalfa from the University of Minnesota that grows late into fall and fixes 50% more nitrogen than the perennial types.

Once established, most organic soils are adequately fertile and can be replenished. Don't get carried away using too much chemical nitrogen around most perennials because you will just encourage their competition--weedy grasses that pig-out on the stuff.

What is Soil?

Soil is really tiny little pieces of rock that have been broken down by the crushing of glacier movement, the freeze-thaw cycle, soil and wind erosion, and the action of lichens and mosses. These pieces grade downward in size from large, coarse gravel and round and fractured fine sands that are visible to the naked eye; very fine silt particles that are visible with a microscope, and the tiniest flat platelets of clay adhering tightly together that are visible with an electron microscope. Soil covers the earth in a thin layer and to plants contributes

mechanical support, heat, air, water and nutrients, everything except light.

Decayed organic matter and the ubiquitous tiny lives within bring it to life, give it soul--soil-soul, souled soil. In a well-choreographed scheme, these microscopic protozoa, nematodes, algae, fungi, molds, mycorrhizae, actinomycetes and bacteria feed, digest, grow and reproduce on the organic material around them, changing the nutrients into forms that can be taken up by tiny root hairs. One acre teams with up to three billion in number, two tons in weight, of microscopic simple-celled plants and animals (Brady). After time spent weeding and planting one's palms will be coated with these tiny microbes that continue a great mission. Their value cannot be overemphasized. They are our friends. Sharing this planet, they have worked for hundreds of thousands of years decomposing the remains of dead animal and plant matter into humus, the most-useful byproduct of all. Larger organisms, insects, worms and grubs are their assistants.

Soil Variation

Like people, no two soils are exactly alike, even when gathered from the same garden. Most contain all of the main ingredients mentioned above, maybe in balanced proportions; but most of the time, one ingredient will dominate.

Clay soil particles are flat, coin-like spheres, near molecular in size and many times smaller than sand or silt. They feel greasy or slippery and are attracted to each other. Soil with a high volume of clay compacts easily and sticks together when squeezed into a ball. The flat shapes stick together like stacks of pancakes and do not allow many air pores. Though it can slowly soak up a lot of water, up to eight times more than sandy soil, when saturated, it also drains slowly. It is slow to dry out once saturated and difficult to till or work into a loose structure. Plants can meet their demise in clay soil by either of two extremes, drowning or drying up.

In early spring when well-saturated by winter snow melt, it is slow to warm up. Once warmed, though, it stays warm and is good for growing late season crops. Nutrients remain in clay soil much longer and there is little leaching. The pH tends to be neutral or alkaline, pH 7 and above. Its heavy weight supports large trees and shrubs. Pure clay veins are sought after by ceramic artists.

Silt particles are fine as talcum powder, many times smaller than sand particles but larger than clay particles. Too much silt can present problems in soils similar to those with too much sand. It is found where it has accumulated for hundred of centuries, settled to the bottoms of now-dry, large bodies of water or in low-lying areas that

are frequently flooded by rivers. It is fertile and good garden soil if amended with organic material to open pores for water and air.

Sandy soils drain and dry out quickly. Water and nutrients rush through and are not long-available for plant roots to take them up. This quick leaching of nutrients contribute to the depletion of nitrogen, phosphorus, potassium and trace minerals from soils. When rubbing it between the palms of hands one can detect the gritty, grainy texture. It is easy to till because particles are much larger than clay and they are either round or fractured and do not stick together or become compacted. It dries up and warms up early in the spring, much to the liking of plants, like thymes, that love these conditions; but most plants will be continually hungry and thirsty when growing here. Later in the warmer part of the growing season, it is difficult to keep sandy soils watered enough for most crops but can be wonderfully productive with the addition of organic matter.

Organic particles of soil
- are the source of the nutrients phosphorus, sulfur and nitrogen,
- are the main source of energy for soil microorganisms,
- are made up of two parts from the action of microbes, the varying stages of breakdown as they consume the organic matter and the resulting humus from microbial digestive action,
- along with nitrogen, are directly related to a soil's ability to produce crops,
- are easily   easily depleted by crops or by leaching and need management practices to replenish it,
- create a loose and open soil texture,
- increase the amount of water soil can hold,
- provide chemical stability to soil and half the chemical reactions.

Mineral Soils Compared with Organic Soils

Mineral soils such as those in which we garden in South Dakota are the most abundant and contribute the greatest number of acres to agriculture. They are more compact because of a low, 1-10 percent volume of organic matter and subsequent small pore size that holds less volume of air but a higher volume of water and minerals. Though the organic component of mineral soils is the lowest of all components, it plays the primary role in bringing about change in soil properties and effecting plant growth.

Far-more productive organic soil , not found in South Dakota, may contain 90 - 95 percent organic matter but there are fewer acres in production. Especially valued for fresh-market vegetable crops in regions such as eastern U.S., it retains two to four times its weight in moisture, is easy to cultivate, is very porous allowing air and microbial and other animal activity, and has over-all good physical condition.

Ideal Soil – Mineral or Organic

Ideal composition of an organic soil solids is 40% sand, 40% humus or organic matter, and 20% clay. It holds moisture well yet allows good drainage so plants won't drown. Nutrient leaching is kept at a minimum. In mineral soils such as ours in southeastern South Dakota, 50% solids of which 45% are the mineral components of clay, sand and silt and 5% the organic component, is considered good. In either mineral or organic soils, the ideal pore space for 25% penetration of water and 25% of air for a total of 50% of total soil volume is provided. These percentages are important requirements for plant viability (Sabuco, Evers).

Soil Air

Soil oxygen has overwhelming importance to the growth of most plants and ways must be found to facilitate its supply.

Without soil air
- the growth of plants is effected, especially the roots.
- plants are not as able to absorb available nutrients and manufacture hormones and food. There may be an abundance of the preferred elements in the soil, but plants cannot utilize them profitably without oxygen.
- the absorption of water is decreased. There is an irony that an oversupply of water in soil can actually reduce the amount of water absorbed by plants because the necessary oxygen, replaced by water, is not available.
- inorganic compounds can form that are toxic to plant growth.
- necessary bacteria, insects and worms cannot survive.

20% of air space is the minimum required for root elongation and health and adaptability of plants and to allow natural air exchange from the atmosphere into the soil. When reduced to 12 - 15%, new root growth is inhibited; at 5 - 10% they may grow existing roots but not new ones. There is no growth at near-anaerobic conditions of 2%. (Patterson)

The typical construction site today has 10% or less air penetration and water, not air, will dominate what pore space is available. Many urban soils are as dense as concrete. Reestablishing aerobic conditions is difficult once a site is compacted (Evers).

Compaction and low porosity is further complicated by limiting top soil to a shallow four to six inches. Root systems that can't penetrate the tight layer of subsoil are restricted, and they can't be expected to effectively absorb sufficient moisture and nutrients to provide normal plant growth.

The Common Nutrients in Soil

Of the seventeen elements for plant nutrition, carbon, hydrogen, oxygen and sometimes nitrogen are provided by air and water. The other 14 are provided through the soil. Six macro nutrients are nitrogen, phosphorus, potassium, calcium, magnesium and sulfur. Eight micro nutrients, usually available in organic soils, are iron, manganese, zinc, boron, copper, chlorine, cobalt, and molybdenum.

Nitrogen (symbol N) Without nitrogen no plant growth takes place. Low nitrogen symptoms are stunted, sickly plants with pale leaves. With adequate nitrogen, dark green foliage grows and matures quickly. Too much nitrogen and a plant may grow and grow and delay flowering at the expense of excess foliage. It can push a plant to grow to a point of exhaustion. Some natural sources of nitrogen are fish emulsion, manure and blood meal. The nitrogen in fresh manure and urine is chemically hot and will burn foliage, turn it yellow, and maybe even kill a plant. Over-application of nitrogen from granular fertilizer produces the same results. Nitrogen is easily lost from oxidation, leaching or plant uptake.

Phosphorus (symbol P) Phosphorus gives plants resistance to diseases and especially boosts fibrous and lateral root strength, flowering, and seed and fruit quality. Too much phosphorus slows down cell division and plants stop growing or maturing, and may show a purple coloration to the underside of their leaves. Bone meal and ground rock phosphate are sources of phosphorus. Though this element is often available in soils, its complex compounds keep it from being available to plants. It is most-available at soil pH of 6.5 and less available at pH above 7 and is somewhat stationary in soils, migrating very little.

Potassium (symbol K) Without potassium, no photosynthesis can be conducted. It gives plants energy to fight off diseases. Look for yellow spots and blotches and browning leaf margins when there is not enough. Compost, granite dust, manure, green sand, seaweed and wood ashes are all natural sources of potassium. It is usually plentiful in all except sandy soil. Mineral soils such as we experience are usually high in total potassium but not always soluble or available to plants.

Chemical Fertilizers and Pesticides

Chemical fertilizers may provide a quick fix for plants, but in the absence of organic matter, they leach out of the soil. Studies have shown that in some cases insects will attack a chemically fertilized plant before it will an organically maintained plant. Chemical fertilizers can alter the diversity of bacteria and pesticides can kill and inhibit bacteria and other organisms in soil.

A Summary of Soil pH

PH is the number given to compare the quantity of the two ions of water in a solution, the negative-charged hydroxide ions (OH) and positive-charged hydrogen ions (H), in a solution. Soils, soup, juice, vinegar, food, any solution with water has a pH level.

When the pH is 7, the solution is neutral and neither ion dominates.

When the pH is less than 7, the positive-charged hydrogen ion dominates and the solution is described as acid. When it is lowered one whole number to pH 6, a solution has 10 times the number of hydrogen ions and one-tenth the number of hydroxide ions than it did when neutral. Once pH is lowered to 5, the solution has 100 times more hydrogen ions than it did at neutral 7. It is far more difficult to lower the pH of soil from 6 to 5 than it is to lower it from 7 to 6.

As the pH increases above 7, the same rules apply. Now the negative hydroxide ion dominates and the solution becomes alkaline. A pH of 8 has 10 times more negative ions and one-tenth the positive ions than neutral 7 does. A pH 9 has 100 times more negative ions than neutral 7.

It is much harder to raise the pH from 8 to 9 than it is to raise it from neutral 7 to 8.

	Low pH	High pH
Described as	acid, sour	alkaline, basic, base, sweet
Number value	Below pH 7	Above pH 7
Climate	high precipitation and humidity	lower precipitation and humidity
Leaching	high precipitation results in leached soils; alkalinity leached away	lower precipitation, less leaching; alkalinity remains
Organic structure of soil	high organic content, soil with more decomposed animal and plant material	low organic content, soil with less decomposed animal and plant material
Mineral content of soil	low mineral content	high mineral content

"Soils are the way they are largely because of water. Soils are made of mineral and organic matter in various stages of decomposition. The mineral fraction of soil is usually base (alkaline). The organic fraction is usually acidic. The West has alkaline soils because a lack of water creates a lack of vegetation and, therefore, humus. Also, the soils are never leached. The East has acid soil due to excessive moisture, which leaches the baser (alkaline) elements from upper soil horizons and the constant influx of humus from all the plants decays acidly" (Sabuco 19).

Typical South Dakota soils have a pH between 6.5 and 7.5. In Sioux Falls they average 6.9 - 7.2, with some around 6.5. Even in eastern South Dakota, native deciduous forests such as Cactus Heights or Newton Hills are not appreciably acid. (These are generalizations and many exceptions will exist. No two soils are exactly the same.)

In South Dakota, where soils tend to be already near neutral or higher, liming is rarely or never necessary, though one may find occasional individual situations in which lime could be beneficial to homeowners. Lowering pH (increasing the acidity) in areas of low precipitation and alkaline soils like in the Northern Plains is difficult. In any situation, never add lime before first doing a soil test (Munk).

With today's construction practices of hauling away the deeper topsoil that originated on a site and replacing it with fewer inches of topsoil that may have originated somewhere else, plant roots often end up in the more alkaline subsoil, creating a less-than-ideal foundation for plant roots. Sometimes the calcium associated with high alkalinity is found separating from the subsoil solution in pure form (Munk).

Checking for pH
It's easy to have soil pH checked and confirmed when in doubt. The best source for information about your soils is from local and state horticulture and agriculture extension experts: Steve Munk at Minnehaha County Extension, 220 West 6th St., Sioux Falls, S. D. 57104, telephone 605-367-7877, and Dave Graper, South Dakota State University Extension Horticulture Specialist, Brookings, S. D. The SDSU Agriculture Extension Specialists are an entomologist, plant pathologist, agronomist or soil expert, and weeds specialist also located in Brookings, S.D.

Plants and pH
Vegetables and many plants grow best at a neutral 7 pH or slightly lower, 6.0 - 6.8 pH. At either extreme, above 8 and below 5.5, nutrient availability is diminished to most plants.

Alkalinity
I've collected hundreds of gardening books over the years. It took me a while to figure out that the advice from authors of these books varies widely based on the area in which they live. Before following recommendations in any garden book, check to see where the author has garnered his or her experience. Many garden in states that are far to the south and east of us, often with very different, acid soils.

I'm sure my old neighbors who annually dusted lime over the soil near their Clematis were following instructions from one of these. Clematis prefer slightly-acid soils, and one may need to add lime in areas of the country that have very low pH (high acid). But in South Dakota, adding lime to soils that already tend towards alkalinity isn't recommended. And don't assume that because you have a mature pine tree growing in the midst of these neutral to alkaline Northern Plains, that the soil beneath is now appreciably acid, although that pine would prefer such an environment and will gradually change it by littering with acid-aiding needles and branches.

Acidity
At our nursery, Perennial Passion, most pH inquiries are about how to acidify soil for adaptable ericaceous (acid-loving) plants, such as hardy azaleas, blueberries and hydrangeas. In his book "The Best of the Hardiest," John Sabuco states that it is a myth that these plants need a very low pH of 4 to 5.5. Here are excerpts from his convincing position:

> I can't tell you how often I have seen the gyrations gardeners go through trying to produce this condition [soils with low pH, high acid conditions]....This is the case with the nationwide slaughter of Rhododendrons each year by well-meaning gardeners....They ultimately poison their prize plants with repeated doses of dilute acids and sulfates....The pH at which most nutrients are most available is 6.5....A stable pH of 6.0 or 6.5 is far better for a Rhododendron than a changeable pH of

4.0 to 5.5....This is probably true for most ericaceous [acid-loving] plants (p. 14).

Sabuco provides some of the best practical, candid and easy-to-understand information on climate, plant adaptability, watering, soils and pH. Great reading, one of my favorites and I recommend to all. And since I've been quoting so much from this book, it is important that I point out that though this author writes from a home base of Illinois, his information on pH and clay soil amendments are applicable to our area.

Changing the pH of Soil
It is difficult to lower the pH of the high mineral, clay soils such as those found in southeastern S. D. It is not as simplistic as assuming or guessing at the pH and then randomly adding acid to lower it. One must consider the original pH, the amount of natural rainfall and supplemental irrigation, and the organic and mineral structure of the soil.

First, confirm the existing pH. If it already falls into a range of 6 to 6.5, don't lower it any further. Instead, work on providing other ways to simulate the natural, forest-floor environment of acid-loving plants. Create entire beds, not individual planting holes, of loose, highly organic, consistently moist and well-drained soils that allow broad and shallow rooting, traits of most acid-loving plants. Amend with a combination of organic materials to increase the friability of the soil. Yes, if you use only peat moss, the pH will decrease, but as it decomposes it will fluctuate up and down. The goal is a steady environment for the plants, not an erratic one.

If an azalea or other acid-friendly plant is purchased in a nursery container, one can bet it has been grown in an organic soil mix to enable shallow roots to penetrate and stabilize both physically and nutritionally. Such a plant is short-lived in home landscapes if it has been dropped into a small tight hole like a cork in a bottle. If no incentive is given for it to extend and establish its broad, shallow root structure, within very few years the plant will begin to decline and eventually die. This is just one example that demonstrate the extreme importance soils play in aiding in the adaptability or hardiness of a plant. Sometimes soil conditions are more important than climate.

The following directions from Sabuco are the best organic methods I've read about how to attain and maintain a stable, lowered pH for ericaceous plants in clay soils:

1. Till the soil loosely in spring, leaving large lumps and clods, to nine inches.
2. Incorporate many different types of humus into the soil--leaves, sticks, twigs, bark, anything except ash and maple leaves. Start with a layer of eight- to ten-inches deep, then work it in gently.
3. Incorporate one pound per square foot of alfalfa pellets into the soil.
4. Till this in loosely to nine inches deep.
5. Cover with four to six inches of coarse pine bark chips.
6. Let it lie fallow for one year.
7. Repeat the above process, tilling the pine bark chips into the soil in the first go through.
8. This year plant three cheap ericaceous plants (blueberries are usually reasonable) per 200 square feet for establishment of mycorrhiza in the soil. Expect these to die.
9. Let it lie fallow for another year.
10. The following spring should be wonderfully productive. Till in the pine bark chips once and again and plant away!
11. Mulch with pine bark, shredded bark or wood to a depth of six inches.
12. Add to the mulch every year. (p.19).

Sabuco continues that the "pH will remain stable to falling in a range of 5.5 to 6.5. The mycorrhiza will be well-established. Water this bed well; its soil structure will be porous. My bed raised almost two feet during this process. I had to surround it in wood to hold the soil in place. Many years of beautiful flowers and fruit have come from this bed. It was worth the wait."

A soil-modification method that I have half-way practiced after recommendation by mentor, Betty Ann Addison of Rice Creek Gardens in Blaine, Minnesota, is to gather and spread two feet of oak leaves over a chosen garden spot. (No need to remove turf; its dead blades and roots will contribute to the overall organic matter after being suffocated by the additions.) Weight them down with branches and allow to lie fallow for two years. Spade or till in. When I started this project, the usual lazy gardener in me reared its impatient head.

The Hosta and shade garden I was preparing was to undulate around mature fir and spruce trees. I raked out a six-inch layer of needles from beneath the spruces and gathered bags of oak leaves from nearby Sherman Park, spreading them over the needles, a mere twelve inches rather than the two feet recommended. (Enough of dragging those bags, already!). After only one year, the following late summer, I spaded them in and by fall began planting. I know now that there was probably depletion of nitrogen because of this fresh, partially composted material, but everything flourished and by the second year the condition of that space was to die for!! I can easily weed the area with a hand trowel and, when slightly moist, ease out dandelion roots with my bare fingers. I've never checked for pH in this area.

Another way to lower acidity for acid-loving plants is to add elemental sulfur along with organic amendments. It is four or five times more effective than ferrous sulfate, inexpensive and easy to find. Brady in *Nature and Property of Soils*, recommends 1- 2 pounds of sulfur per 100 square feet for each 1/2 unit of pH to be lowered in a medium textured soil. Because sulfur doesn't migrate well through the soil, it must be spaded and stirred in manually. Broadcasting it over the ground or attempting to water it in won't work. Follow a sulfur application by mulching with acid-based organic materials, such as pine needles or bark, leaf mold, tan bark or sawdust. Farm manure may be alkaline and offset some of the acid amendments.

Many sources recommend the simple addition of acid-based fertilizer to lower pH, a quick high for the plants, but no long-term solution. Again, this does not provide a stable environment but rather, a weak and vacillating one. Since my goal is to provide conditions to aid the adaptability of plants in our fluctuating and often rugged winter climate, I want to use the best methods to help them survive, rather than use expedient, short-term approaches.

Hydrangea and pH

Those beautiful blues of certain Hydrangea blossoms are determined by soil pH. Well-acidified soil allows blue shades; slightly acid, neutral and alkaline soil accompanies most pink shades. (Some cultivars are selected because they retain pink color even in acid soils.)

Most of the lovely, large and billowy, pastel-colored flowers, shown so often in garden magazines, can range only to the south of us, at best zone 5, beyond our limitations of winter extremes. But for determined gardeners, many of the non-hardy selections adapt well

to large-container culture, where the soil condition is easy to modify and maintain. Store them during the winter in a heated garage or root cellar, out of the freeze-thaw cycle, for following years' performances.

When choosing pink or blue-flowered cultivars to plant directly outdoors, seek out those that bloom on current year's growth, such as *H. 'Piamina'*, *'Nikko Blue'* or *'All Summer Beauty'*. Most, if not all, of the cream, white and salmon-colored *H. paniculata* and *arborescens* cultivars are easy to grow and hardy here.

Pink Shades of Hydrangea
Pink shades are easy and automatic for us because of our near neutral to slightly acid, mineral, soil.

Blue Shades of Hydrangea
The blue shades take a little more effort.
- First confirm existing soil pH.
- Follow Sabuco's directions on page 26 and 27.
- Follow Brady's sulfur additive directions on page 28.
- If growing non-hardy selections in containers, the four square feet of soil in a container that measures two feet square would require 1.28 - 2.56 oz. sulfur to lower one whole pH point.
- Fertilize with nitrate-based fertilizer. Make sure the middle number, the phosphate level, is low. Avoid higher phosphate levels from bonemeal and super phosphate.

More on pH
- High alkalinity interferes with iron uptake by some plants, like pin oaks, causing iron chlorosis. The trace minerals, manganese and zinc, are also less available.
- To remedy problems in soils with very high pH, provide a layer of sulfur and a porous ground cloth barrier over the old soil, and then add non alkaline soil over the top. The barrier will keep worms from blending the lower alkaline soil with the new soil.
- Irrigating with alkaline water may eventually raise soil pH. But sometimes extra watering, even when alkaline, induces more leaching of chemicals in soil and may actually lower pH.
- If liming is necessary, Sabuco recommends the use of bonemeal instead of lime or dolomitic lime. Bonemeal causes a slower, more stable increase in pH, leaches more slowly and will last seven to ten years (in Illinois).
- From an Internet chat line: Aluminum sulfate has a negative reaction in the soil. The sulfur portion does lower the pH, but the

aluminum bonds with nitrogen, creating aluminum nitrate, robbing the soil of available nitrogen. Overuse may result in aluminum toxicity.

Another contributor, probably from the south or southeast, recommended cotton seed meal because it acidifies well and is inexpensive. (Apply in cool or cold weather because it attracts flies with its strong odor.)

Ground slate is a long-lasting acidifier that is difficult to locate.

Vinegar, which is acetic acid, will lower soil pH, as will other acids.

- Deciduous elm or ash leaves are basic, and these forest floors are more alklaline, while oak leaves contribute to acidity. The soil of natural coniferous forests of pine and other evergreen trees tends to be acid.

In Sioux Falls there is no ordinance to protect soils and existing trees from construction compaction and damage. Nor is there any requirement to notify property owners of the potential for such damage (Murschel).

Soil Compaction and Other Negative Impacts of Construction

Early traffic on the Northern Plains was the footfalls of Native American people, hunters and gatherers who settled in one location or nomads who followed food sources and seasons. There were the larger cohabitants, buffalo, elk, and deer, and after the 14th century, *equus*, the horse. Myriads of deeply rooted, happy plants adapted with ecotypes in all non or lightly trodden areas. Native plant parts provided food, medicine, tools, shelter, and more that enhanced the comfort and content of the lives of native people.

Along came the newcomers: foreign explorers and settlers by the then-seemed masses, light-weight at first with horse and oxen power to pull equipment for plowing and farming the centuries-old sod. Inventions of the steam and gasoline powered tractor soon followed. Since the decade of the 40s, our equipment has grown mightier yet. Now, instead of using a small-field tractor, we drive over root zones

and new construction sites, pillaging the ground with up to ten-ton equipment, the same that could be used for constructing highways and streets designed to carry 20+ ton tractor trailers.

During the post-war era of the late 40s and early 50s, construction of housing subdivisions maintained the deep topsoil around houses. Compare that to today's practice of scraping away topsoil and often hauling it off-site. Where before early inhabitants found an average of 18- to 24-inches of topsoil, today four- to six-inches are spread back in preparation for turf, trees, shrubs, perennials and gardens.

Today subsoil is often recontoured to adapt to the design of a structure rather than having the structure designed to match existing contours of a site. Once the earth movers are finished with the preliminaries, building contractors and subcontractors continue the demise and compaction by having or taking the liberty to maneuver over all parts of the site, regardless of conditions, wet or dry. *It is a foreign field. What roots will interpret this as soil? Which will go there, grow there?*

Effects of Soil Compaction on Existing Trees

God forbid there be existing trees on a site as just described. The proficiency of a tree's feeder roots is now bankrupt as the air and moisture are squeezed out of soils. In a strangle-hold, the trees quickly succumb to trauma and distress. Sooner or later the top growth will be on the skids, a reflection of the deteriorating roots. With such limited roots, trees cannot manufacture enough energy to sustain existing leafy growth or put on new growth. Instead of prospering, leaves and branches begin to die back; the tree slowly but surely declines and eventually dies.

Sometimes it may take up to five-years or longer for a mature tree to kick the bucket after a single drive-by with a heavy piece of equipment. No, we can't see the damage, but imagine the stress of these plants as their roots are squeezed and tortured within the soil around them.

In one originally wooded neighborhood of mature native trees, the new residents of brand new houses were overheard saying, "When the people move in, the oaks move out." It was a sorry lesson to see a towering bur oak tree, for example, now encased within a narrow, six-foot median surrounded on both sides by fresh blacktop, lose its 60' crown within two years. Other trees, closer to the houses, died a slower death, taking a year or two longer before being cut up and hauled away to the dead-tree cemetery in the open hearses of tree-

removal. These home sites originally had great value because of natural woods and stately, mature trees that were now being chopped down. So sad that no one knew to take timely measures to protect them.

In addition to the maneuvering of heavy front-end loaders and graders, lighter vehicles such as one-ton trucks, pickups, and even cars are guilty. Lighter equipment, such as skid loaders or the old-model small cub cadet or ford tractors, can also mistreat if soil is worked when wet.

Other Negative Impacts of Construction

Accompanying soil compaction are these practices that exacerbate the problems of existing trees and soils:

- Change of soil surface gradation alters long-established drainage patterns and existing trees, and other plants receive less than the accustomed moisture or languish and eventually drown in standing water or poorly drained areas.
- Feeder and anchor roots may be cut or trunks and branches may be wounded.
- Chemicals can wash off from the equipment of subcontractors, such as painters and masons if cleaned on site.
- Stockpiling topsoil higher than six-feet smothers and depletes necessary bacteria and other organisms. The soil at the bottom of 20-foot piles is essentially sterile (Ball).

Planting on Compacted Sites

Usually occurring hand-in-hand, the two greatest causes of death of newly planted plants are

- The absence of aerobic soil conditions (availability of oxygen, carbon dioxide and other gasses that make up air); *roots won't grow where air can't go.* The topsoil volume and condition of a typical landscape site in the 1990s is not much better than that of a reclaimed strip mine (Evers).
- Lack of drainage. Soils must drain well. Most plants die from over-watering and drowning than from being under-watered (Evers).

Prevention of Construction Damage

The good news amidst all the previous gloom and doom of construction damage, is that with foresight, counter tactics, determination and commitment, damage to trees and property can be prevented or, at least, reduced. It is ultimately the property owner or a hired specialist who will be the ones to follow through and monitor

regularly during the construction process to make sure that exact specifications are met (Prosser). Don't depend on a contractor to do this for you.

Practice These Pre-construction Preventative Measures

- Limit all construction equipment and vehicles to designated access areas.
- Erect a stable, strong fence to keep equipment and debris away and to protect a radius around existing trees, using the following formulation by Dr. John Ball, SDSU professor and certified arborist. The diameter of the trunk in inches multiplied times 1.5 equals the radius measured in feet that should be protected. For example: If a tree has a trunk diameter of 24", multiply 24 x 1.5. Protect 36' from the trunk in all directions. Within this designated root zone there should be
  - no driving of any vehicle;
  - no piling of trash or debris;
  - no raising or lowering the soil elevation by over-filling or piling of soil or excavation material;
  - no scraping away of soil; and
  - no excessive foot traffic, especially when wet.
- Improve the health of existing trees before construction begins by mulching with wood chips over the root zone, provide an adequate water supply and aerate deeply if already compacted (Ball).

Mitigation of Compacted Soil and Tree Damage

If the damage has already been done and one is faced with trees in declining states of shock, what are the options for restorative techniques? How soon should one act? Within weeks, months or years? How will newly planted trees and other plants perform?

Practice these post construction measures as soon as possible:

- Allow trees to adjust and stabilize in the post-construction soil condition.
- Do not encourage new growth until roots recover. Withhold nitrogen fertilizer from construction-effected trees. Since pruning can prompt new growth, do not prune trees in areas of compaction for at least a year (Ball).
- Compaction is eventually mitigated by nature's repeated freeze-thaw cycle, which aerates soil over time, but the actual duration

required for recovery varies. Soil will begin to open up after the first winter, improving annually, but for complete recovery some advise that it may take up to ten-years or more! It will depend on the severity of the original damage and measures used to speed up the aeration process, such as uses of organic and inorganic amendments, plowing, tilling, hand spading and other manual methods (Evers).

- Mulching every year with organic materials such as shredded bark will hasten the remediation of damage. Be sure to keep mulch away from the base of the trunk.

- Trench for renewed aeration, using the same calculation for protection of root zones of trees. Dig between the root flare, starting three feet from the base of the tree, and radiate out with four to seven trenches dug twelve-inches deep. Backfill with original soil or amend with compost. For more detail on this process, contact John Ball, SDSU professor and State Forester (Ball).

- In selected areas where landscape or gardens are to be planted, break up compacted substructure and bring in amended soil--one-third heavy black soil, one-third humus and one-third sand--and create eight-inch to two-feet high, raised or bermed areas. (Do not build these raised areas from the subsoil of swimming pool or basement excavation.) This healthy solution offers varied undulations and elevations for interesting design while retaining opportunities such as dry-set stone or sod walls.

- In turf areas, make subsoil more penetrable by cultivating or cross ripping deeply in both directions to a depth of 12- to 18-inches, blending the topsoil that is there (usually only four- to six-inches in a suburban development) with the subsoil clay. Then rototil this mixture deeply with a lightweight tractor tiller (Evers).

- Add enough good, new topsoil so that after it settles (allow for up to 40% decrease in volume due to settling), there will be six- to twelve-inches remaining. Sometimes on new sites, irrigation water will penetrate the shallow topsoil/turf layer, but then flow on top of the impenetrable compacted subsoil beneath (Evers).

- Additives such as coarse sand, gravel, or gypsum may help by creating air spaces and improving drainage. These non-soluble substances need to penetrate into the soil so that roots can discover their benefits. Adding unblended large pockets or layers of these coarser amendments may allow perched soils or water tables. Without pressure, water can stubbornly sit or perch in areas of fine or

clay soil and not percolate naturally into areas of coarse soil (Sabuco).

-   Do not work soil when it is too wet, or the result will be an uneven texture and hard clumps. When you squeeze a fistful of soil together in the palm of your hand and it remains in a sticky muddy ball, it is too wet. Soil should be friable and crumble through your fingers (Evers, Ball).

If I were to build a house today, I would
-   measure and check depth of topsoil in several parts of a development *before* purchasing real estate. Test for pH levels and soil profile at a number of different sites. If there is suspect history or other things that indicate contaminating substances, check for those that may be indicated, i.e., fuels, pesticides, lead. Based on what is found in the soil study, adjust final topsoil depth to a minimum of 24 inches, using the techniques listed above under "Mitigation of Compacted Soil and Tree Damage."
-   design a prairie-style house tucked into the existing terrain. If drainage modification is needed, then contouring would be done with a small lightweight tractor. Soil work would not proceed until site is dry, probably best in late summer or fall.
-   procure a signed contract with contractor and subcontractors with exact requirements to be met and allow recourse if the specifications are not complied with.
-   protect existing tree root zones with a sturdy temporary fence using John Ball's specifications on page 32 and 33.
-   limit compaction areas to one, or maybe two, access points to construction. These would be at the same location as the future driveway, a patio, or other later-added construction. Separate these areas from off-limits areas with a substantial barrier.
-   allow no topsoil to be hauled from the site. If soil is stockpiled, piles would be no higher than six feet.
-   manure and plow as if preparing to plant a field of dreams. Consider future landscape plants, trees, shrubs and garden as important as a cash crop.
-   amend garden and landscaping areas with one-third coarse sand and gravel and a one-third mixture of organic material, including oak leaves, composted manure, old leather boots, mushroom compost, ground corn cobs, and pine bark. Use stones found on site and bring in other indigenous stone to retain changes in or contouring necessary to conform to drainage ordinances.

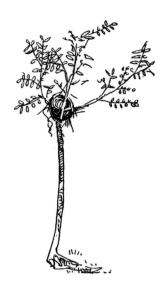

"The productivity of a soil is determined in no small degree by the nature of its subsoil." Brady

Planting Trees in Compacted Soil

Our home was built before 1950, and the site was left with the generous 18- to 24-inches of rich clay-loam soil that seemed to grow anything we gave to it. I naively thought all soil was this great; or if it looked good on the surface, it must be good below.

My initiation into the world of compacted and less-than-ideal soil began many years ago, when I started to plant for others. I had heard lectures and laments about post-construction soil conditions but didn't realize how bad it could get. To plant the smaller perennials and flowering shrubs we had then wasn't too tricky. When it wasn't feasible to amend entire beds or if we were just interspersing our plants into an existing landscape, we would just dig out a few gallons of poor subsoil from an individual planting hole, blend it with amendments, tuck in the plant, mulch with wood chips and haul away whatever soil was left over. It was like leaving behind a perennial mine field that would later explode into color! We weren't solving the overall compaction problem, but at least we knew that each of our plants would be able to root well into its own little microcosm. (Knowing now that water is reluctant to migrate from tight soils into loose soils, this practice would be best followed using drought-tolerant plants or where there is supplemental irrigation.)

But I've witnessed large trees being planted on compacted sites; for example, eight-foot pines with three-foot diameter, 400+ pound rootballs that have been squeezed into holes just barely wide enough, the-not-so-desirable "perfect fit." Sometimes the hole depth would be over-estimated and dug a detrimental inch or more deeper than optimum. The hard-to-maneuver rootball would then be precariously lowered into the hole, and the original soil surface of the rootball would end up an inch or more below grade, deep into compacted subsoil. With the trees and balls weighing as much as they did, there was not much allowance for adjustment after they had been sunk, short of lifting them with the help of equipment, but events usually didn't progress that far.

On the other hand, I've observed planting holes sometimes dug a little shallower than calculated, and the rootball would sit perched slightly above grade. These were the lucky ones, the ones that had a chance to keep their noses above water, literally. Their roots would be able to survive with access to the air in soil above grade that would not become waterlogged.

Since then tree planting specifications for compacted and non-compacted sites have changed drastically and have been carefully spelled out.

Out-of-date Tree Planting Practices
- A hole is dug 50% wider or less than the diameter of the rootball.
- The sides of the hole are usually vertical, straight up and down, forcing roots to circle on compacted sites.
- Six-inches of soil is loosened in the bottom of the hole.
- The top of the rootball is level with grade.
- The backfill is amended then with sand and organic matter.

Today's Tree Planting Recommendations
- Dig a hole two- to three-times wider than the root diameter of the rootball.
- Dig hole shallower than the depth of the rootball on compacted sites. If location is well-drained, dig the same depth as the rootball.
- Slant the sides of the hole so it will be wider at the top than at the bottom. This will help to divert roots upwards to the more-aerated surface. Score and break up the sides of these holes.
- On compacted sites Norm Evers, SDSU horticulture instructor, states that he doesn't recommend digging the rootball into the subsoil

at all. He sets the rootball directly on top of the compacted subsoil and berms soil up around the ball. Other sources recommend perching the top of rootball at least three-inches above final grade. Mound soil up around ball. Tree will appear as if growing from a low hummock.

- Or plant in a 15- to 24-inch berm to place rootballs up and away from the threat of drowning or existing in poor-quality subsoils. Trees can be planted singly or grouped as a community on these elevations, creating a natural, colonized setting.

- Amending is not necessarily beneficial in clay soils, but may be in sandy soils.

- Remove all turf competition and mulch three- to four-times the diameter of the rootball with two- to three-inches of wood chips or other organic matter. Mulch should not come into contact with the trunk. To avoid rotting and discourage rodents, keep mulch six-inches (twelve-inch diameter) from the trunk above the root/trunk collar or the graft.

Watering Newly Planted Trees

Newly planted trees can die from insufficient watering, but most die from over-watering. On compacted sites many trees die from what is termed "the bathtub effect." Trees may be planted too deeply and over-watered in subsoil that will not drain, creating a soggy bathtub for its roots and drowning it.

Always check with a trowel before irrigating new plantings. Water only when the top six- to eight-inches is dry, and then add only enough to saturate this top tier of soil. Besides keeping the root area moist, be sure to water a few feet away from the tree base to encourage roots to stretch to get a footing in surrounding soil.

Turf Control Around Newly Planted Trees

Observing grass growing right up to the base of nearly every tree planted in residential lawns and parks, one would think no one knew or had ever been taught that grass is an oxygen, water and food-grubbing rival of trees. Grass roots dominate and use up the water and nutrients from the upper few inches of the soil profile, the exact area where a tree's essential feeder roots need to be.

Broadleaf perennials such as Solomon's seal, Canadian ginger or Astilbe usually cohabit well with trees, share in the soil's nutrition and do not deplete the necessary elements from the area.

Tidbits and Leftovers

On Amending When adding organic amendments, use a combination of peat moss, compost, rotted manure, pine bark, pine mulch, pine or spruce needles, or rotting leaves. Quickly decomposing materials and fresh manure can burn plant leaves, turn them yellow and kill the plant.   Adding non-composted amendments will occupy bacteria, which will use up available nitrogen in the soil.   Supplemental nitrogen may be necessary during this period.   See more organic amendments on page 17.

When adding sand to mineral soils like those in South Dakota, work in a minimum of 25% of the volume and add organic amendments at the same time. Amending clay soil with too little sand may do more harm than good and can turn the combination to a brick-like consistency with increased compaction and decreased drainage.

On Annuals Many common annuals, like marigolds and petunias, will bloom in a six pack of 1" plugs in as little time as six weeks. They provide the hungered-for color in early season, are the easiest for growers to profit from, and are the most predominant types seen in the hundreds of hoop houses erected in every other commercial parking lot from April to late June.   Many are designated by mass merchandising discount stores as loss-leaders, sold at cost or slightly above or even given away as a way to get people into businesses to purchase the profitable items like drugs and cosmetics.

Lots of experienced gardeners seek out new and unusual annuals or tropical plants not found or given away at every supermarket. These tender plants are harder to find because they won't bloom quickly or easily in small packs, needing several more weeks in a 4" or larger pot.   There are many possibilities such as Heliotrope, Brazilian button flower, Angelonia, tall Ageratum, Gomphrena, Mexican sunflower, castor bean plant and more.

On Banana Peels ' Banana peels quickly break down and provide potassium for the soil. One source claims that aphids are repelled if peels are placed at base of plants such as roses.

On Butterfly Gardening

Butterfly Nectar Plants - Perennials

Achillea	Yarrow
Agastache	Anise Mint, Anise Hyssop
Anthemis	Marguerite Daisy
Asclepias	Butterfly Milkweed
Aster	Aster, Michaelmas Daisy
Buddleia	(half-hardy shrub) Butterfly Bush
Caryopteris	(half-hardy shrub) Blue Beard, Spirea
Centaurea	Perennial Bachelor's Button
Centranthus	Jupiter's Beard, Red Valerian
Cephalaria	Giant Scalehead, Yellow Scabiosa
Coreopsis	Tickseed
Dianthus	Pinks, Carnation
Echinacea	Purple Coneflower
Eupatorium	Joe Pye Weed, Snakeroot, Smokeweed
Gaillardia	Blanket Flower
Helenium	Helen's Flower, Sneezeweed
Helianthus	Sunflower
Heliopsis	False Sunflower
Hibiscus	Rose Mallow
Inula	Sword Leaf, Sunwheels
Kalimeras	Orphanage Plant, Oriental Aster
Knautia	Red Scabiosa
Lavandula	(half-hardy perennial) Lavender
Liatris	Gayfeather, Blazing Star
Lilium	True Lily, Asiatic, Oriental, other
Limonium	Perennial Statice
Lobelia	Cardinal Flower
Malva	Mallow, Miniature Hollyhock
Monarda	Bee Balm
Nepeta	Catmint
Origanum	Oregano
Phlox pilosa	Downy Phlox
Phlox other	Meadow, Garden
Porteranthus	Bowman's Root, Indian Physic
Rudbeckia	Black Eyed Susan
Scabiosa	Pincushion Flower
Sedum spectabile	Tall Sedum

Solidago	Golden Rod
Solidaster	Asterago
Thymus	Thyme
Trollius	Globeflower
Verbena hastata	Blue Vervain
Veronica	Speedwell
Veronicastrum	Culver's Root

Butterfly Nectar Plants – Annuals or Tenders

Antirrhinum	Snapdragon
Aster	Aster
Centaurea	Bachelor Button, Annual, Biennial
Cosmos	Cosmos
Gomphrena	Globe Amaranth
Heliotrope	Heliotrope
Helianthus	Sunflower
Limonium	Annual Statice
Lobelia	Lobelia
Lobularia	Alyssum)
Nicotiana	Tobacco Plant
Petunia	Petunia
Phlox	Phlox
Rosmarinus	Rosemary
Scabiosa	Pincushion Flower, Annual
Salvia farinaceae	Sage, Mealy Cup
Salvia officinalis	Sage, Culinary
Tagetes	Marigold
Tithonia	Mexican sunflower
Verbena boniarensis	Peruvian Verbena
Zinnia	Zinnia

Caterpillar Food Plants - Perennials

Anaphalis	Pearly everlasting
Artemisia ludoviciana	Wormwood or Mugwort
Asclepias	Butterfly milkweed
Aster	Aster
Cassia	Senna
Helianthus	Sunflower
Humulus lupulus	Hops
Malva	Mallow, Miniature Hollyhock

Caterpillar Food Plants – Annuals or Tenders

Anthriscus	Chervil
Angelica	Wild Parsley, Dong Quai
Anethum	Dill

Coriandrum	Coriander
Foeniculum	Fennel
Passiflora	Passion Flower Vine
Petroselinum	Parsley
Ruta graveolens	Rue
Viola odorata	Violet
Viola pedata	Violet

Shrubs and Trees

Buddleia (half-hardy shrub)	Butterfly Bush
Caryopteris (half-hardy shrub)	Blue Beard, Spirea
Cornus	Dogwood Shrubs
Salix	Willow for roosting
Robinia	Black Locust for roosting
Spirea	Bridal Veil and summer blooming
Syringa	Lilac
Viburnum	Arrowwood, Cranberry Bush, Lantana, etc.
Wiegela	Cardinal Shrub

For successful butterfly gardens provide

- feeding places for both larvae and adults. Provide a continuum of color and food by using a variety of plants so that something attractive to butterflies is in bloom all season long. A common characteristic of these plants might be their purple, red, yellow and orange flowers that have short tubular flowers with shapes that are easy for butterflies to light upon.
- sunny warm places such as rocks or stepping stones that soak up heat.
- sheltering places like willow trees and others with deeply-furrowed bark.
- watering places like shallow puddles.
- pesticide-free zones so these good insects won't be killed with poisonous chemical use.
- observing places, where you can sit back and watch them mystify and captivate!

On Canna Bulbs Allow tops to freeze with first hard frost; then dig and dry for a few days. Store cool but above 40 degrees in moist peat.

On Chemicals One is careful how one treats what is valued; tiny grains of soil are like multitudinous little diamonds in the rough. Never indiscriminately broadcast chemicals over large areas. Use non-toxic home remedies, or handpick easily managed insect infestations after positively identifying them as truly harmful. More often than not, once damage of a plant is observed, the harmful insect has already moved on and spraying becomes a moot issue. If poisonous chemicals are warranted, carefully use them in quarantined spots and protect your skin and lungs.

Spot control or hand pull weeds. In landscape or garden areas, top dress yearly with compost or wood mulch and a combination of other organic amendments to control weed seed germination.

On Creeping Charlie Killer 10 oz. of Twenty Mule Team Borax, sodium terraborate, in 4 oz. of warm water, diluted to make 2.5 gallons is a solution not well-tolerated by creeping charlie and recommended by Iowa State University to kill this weed. Measure very carefully, for if mixed too strong, it could kill the grass too. Try on a small, sample area first to make sure you have blended an accurate dilution. After waiting a few days to observe the results of the test plot, spray evenly over 1000 square feet of lawn. Since this treatment doesn't break down and can build up in soil, limit to one application a year and apply in only two consecutive years. Because it works best at warm temperatures, May or June applications are recommended in our climate. It is also more effective when soil moisture is average or better so that plants are actively growing.

On Drainage Soil's ability to drain well is as important as the nutrition it supplies. To check for drainage in an area, dig holes two to three feet deep and fill completely with water; then time how long it takes for this water to drain away. If gone in one-half hour, soil is too porous, probably too sandy, and does not retain moisture long enough. Water standing and taking four hours or more indicates a poorly drained site and many plants planted here, especially certain trees, will drown.

On Earthworms One of God's greatest gift to gardeners, the androgynous earthworm, aerates soil by crawling through and leaving spaces for air and water while consuming organic matter and leaving their rich waste called worm cones or castings. They bring lower soil to the surface and pull organic matter below. Sometimes people wonder where their wood mulch has disappeared to often assuming that it has blown away. But if there is no physical barrier like plastic or cloth between the mulch and the soil, the disappearing mulch can be attributed to the worms that are digesting and carrying it down into their tunnels. An early experience with Grandpa Schlund, as we would prepare to go fishing in Firesteel Creek, north of Mt. Vernon, was helping with the digging and plucking of plenteous earthworms from soil that had been overlaid with the daily coffee grounds.

Having abundant worms in your soil is a good sign that the soil is healthy and organic; 100 to 1000 pounds of worms per acre is common in arable soils or 500 worms per square meter on non-compacted grassland soils, such as those found in our midst.

One of Darwin's greatest contributions to science was his great volumes of research about the great volumes of earthworm cones or castings (as much as 16,000 pounds per acre) left on the soil surface, though few people know of him other than for theories of evolution.

Lumpy and rough, uneven lawn surfaces are blamed on worm populations, but these usually occur in new developments where only a few inches of topsoil is replaced and where there is very little organic matter in topsoil and subsoil. Healthy lawns supported by healthy soils do not have these problems. There are no approved chemicals to destroy earthworm populations; their benefits have long been recognized.

Post-construction, compacted subsoil with a few inches of topsoil is not the preferred environment of earthworms. If only a few inches of penetrable soil is available, they can be killed by sudden frosts or flooding because they cannot burrow far enough to escape these conditions.

On Extension, the SDSU Extension Service I recently took a tiny spider to the SDSU Minnehaha County Cooperative Extension Service for identification. There it squirmed under a strong lens while I got to view its multiple eyes and count its eight legs. Steve Munk, our local extension agent, reconfirmed my opinion that this guy, as with most spiders, are beneficial to most plants and that I shouldn't overreact and automatically blast the poor thing to death with unnecessary chemicals.

I wish I would take time to seek out the expertise of the County Extension Office more often. They provide up-to-date, locally applicable information on most everything that is related to horticulture, agriculture and home economics. And if they don't know the answer, they will provide reference to someone who does.

But then, there is this problem with the title of this institution! First, I've always considered the name, SDSU Minnehaha (or substitute your county name here) County Cooperative Extension Service, as ambiguous and hard to explain--an extension of what? And then, there is that long title that can barely be completed in one breath, and never can I remember it long enough to find it in the phone book. And just where would one find it in the phone book anyway, might I ask?

Before all this extension business started, President Abraham Lincoln, through the Morrill Act of 1862, set aside land in each state as an agriculture experiment station for research that would affect food, fiber and nutrition. From this, our state universities, "land-grant" colleges, were born. But while the researchers were spinning away behind their ivy-covered walls, there was no channel by which this locally pertinent information could be disseminated to benefit the general public.

Finally in 1914, the Smith-Lever Act created the Cooperative Extension Service to be associated with each U.S. land-grant college. Now this research-based information could be "extended to" and improve the quality of life of the general public. The cooperative part refers to the cooperation of local, state and federal governments in funding this "extension" or outreach of information.

It is unique because there is an extension agency that is customized to the needs of each state and county, and each agency has contact and ties with those in all other states, access across the nation. Each provides different services that include, but are not limited to, printed research-based information through brochures, fact sheets and newsletters; troubleshooting and problem solving; horticulture and agriculture pest identification and disease control; and now, access through the internet.

The S.D. Extension web site address at SDSU is www.abs.sdstate.edu/, and here you can find links to the county web sites.

The Master Gardener Program is another means by which the outreach and objectives of the Extension Agency are met. Participants take part in a 50-hour crash course in horticulture and then donate 50 hours in return to the extension service. Minnehaha and other S. D. counties have active Master Gardeners Associations which donate time through annual plant sales and garden tours, maintenance of extension office gardens, youth outreach projects, staffing an information booth at the Home and Garden Expo and more. The Minnehaha Group currently meets the second Saturday of every month at the Minnehaha County Extension Office in Sioux Falls.

I first learned about the program by reading an article in a periodical back in the early 80s. Looking for something just like what was described, I called our local extension office and inquired about becoming a Master Gardener. At the time, S. D. was not offering this program and few knew that it was begun in a northwestern state in the 70s. But that year it happened to be offered in southwestern Minnesota, and I was allowed to participate in those lectures by

driving over the border to nearby Windom and later volunteering here in Minnehaha County.

On The Genius of Genus, Speaking the Language of Plant The binomial nomenclature that simplifies the organization of plants into groups consists most obviously of a genus name and a species name. A genus is a broad group of plants with similar botanical physiology and anatomy. (If the car manufacturer name, Ford, were a genus name, always capitalized, then various species of Fords would be taurus, mustang, escort, etc., never capitalized.) Thankfully, at least in those countries whose language is based on the Roman language, Latin has been sustained as the somewhat-universal language of Plant.

When pronouncing Latin botanical names:

- Words with three syllables or more--the accent is usually (but not always) the third syllable from the end of a word.   Example: *Cam PAN u la* (reminder - SYL la ble.)

- Words with two syllables--the accent is usually on the first syllable. Example: *LYCH nis, AS ter, BRI za, CAL la* (reminder - AC cent).

- Exceptions are plentiful. Obvious familiar root words and names of people are maintained intact. Example: *co to ne AS ter.*

On Hands Try these two recipes for chapped hands:

2 oz. lanolin

1 egg yolk

1 tablespoon honey

Add oatmeal to thicken into a paste. Apply to hands and cover with cotton gloves overnight.

Melt together:

2 tablespoons cocoa butter

2 tablespoons beeswax

Add 2 tablespoons almond oil

Use lavender or tea tree essential oil with either of the above recipes for healing.

On Hardiness_ There are many variables that affect a gardener's introduction of new or uncommon plants, or those of purported marginal hardiness. All of the following must be considered when adapting new plants to a new culture:

Soil conditions

Drainage in both winter and summer

Summer temperature

Wind

Position - south facing hills, north slope or south slope

Snow cover
Humidity
Cloud cover; winter sunlight on evergreens
Maturity of plant when planted
Elevation
Length of growing season - long enough to store energy or too
long so that it depletes energy. (Sabuco, Evers)

Many plants not considered hardy for our area will easily adapt well to older neighborhoods. I've always assumed this is because of the protection offered by mature trees and buildings from winter cold, winter sun, and summer and winter winds. I know now that the most important reason why plants adapt well in these neighborhoods is because of the rich, indigenous, non-compacted soils.

On Manure Tea Watering containers and gardens with manure tea is an easy organic way to fertilize and amend the soil. Fill an old fabric bag or pillowcase with well rotted cow manure, and use it like a giant tea bag, submerging it in a garbage can of water. Allow to steep for a week, then "pour tea" over plant roots and dig the leftover manure into the soil.

On Mole Matters These soft little subterranean critters
- are protected in some states; you need a permit to kill them.
- are nearly blind.
- aerate and blend soil which improves plant growth.
- feed mainly on grubs and insects.
- may disturb or break plant roots during their forages for food.
- leave annoying ridges and tunnels that can be easily treated by tamping back down or rolling over with lawn rollers.
- are rarely diverted by noises, windmills or other vibrating action used to scare, juicy fruit gum to gum up their innards, or broken glass. And seldom are they killed by using knife-like traps or starving when harsh chemicals are used to kill their food supply.
- may be repelled to your neighbor's yard by the smell of this non-toxic solution: Mix 1/8 cup of castor oil, 1 gallon of water, and a few drops of dish washing detergent and spray over 300 square feet area (Nursery Retailer, 1998).

On Native Plants To where is a plant really native anyway? All the major crops and most ornamental plants grown in the United States have arrived from outside the boundaries of North America.

On Nitrogen, When not Accessible Non-composted organic matter-- like leaves, mulch and grass clippings--incorporated into soil ties up available nitrogen, and plants may actually appear to decline or

slow down in growth. It may be necessary to add supplemental nitrogen during this time.

On Oak Leaves Don't withhold oak leaves, pine needles and pine bark on the assumption that they will overly acidify your soil. These organic amendments will do wonders to increase the friability of heavy clay loam, alkaline and mineral soil. Oak leaves provide one of the best winter mulches because they do not compact when wet like most other deciduous tree leaves do. In Sioux Falls, we gather them from the city parks that are near the Big Sioux River.

On Organic Gardening Gardening without chemicals comes first to mind when discussing organic gardening. It also means gardening in sync with nature, to duplicate what would occur if we humans weren't around to meddle. Diversity, natural cycles and soils enhanced with natural organisms is promoted. Organic gardening is based on management practices that restore, maintain, and enhance ecological harmony. Natural, organic-based applications such as insecticidal soaps, Bacillus thuringinensis (BT), pyrethrum and rotenone may be condoned, but most man-made chemical products used to fertilize or to kill weeds and insects are not used.

On Pelargonium Geraniums Saving and reusing geranium roots from year to year is easy.
- Pull roots and all from the soil while keeping roots intact and attached.
- Cut back by one-half and remove all flowers and most of the soil. Place several loosely together into a garbage bag, roots first.
- Store cool, dark, dry, not below 45 degrees or above 60 degrees F. Roots will shrivel from dehydration.
- When the calendar is turned to February or March, remove from bag and soak in root starter (1 Tbls. for 3 gallons water) for 24 hours. You will be able to observe the stems and roots swelling back to their original sizes and begin to green up.
- Plant into a good soil mix in a pot large enough to match the root size, but not too big.
- Allow to dry out almost completely between waterings. Dormant plants such as these require very little water until they begin to produce leaves.
- Heat will boost them, so place in a warm window, over a heat mat, near a register, or on top of the refrigerator.
- Prune and shape stems and then begin to pinch for fullness as new growth begins.
- Turn them frequently as they reach for the sun.

- After 8-12 weeks, when flower buds appear, begin to fertilize at one-quarter strength, every other time you water.
- Geraniums bloom best when in a pot by themselves, with no companions or competitors.

On Powdery Mildew of Roses
2 tsp. baking soda
2 tsp. ultra fine horticulture oil
1 gallon water
Spray weekly to prevent mildew

This recipe from Cornell University specifically recommends this amount of baking soda and no more. Higher quantities of baking soda and oil can cause leaf damage. An Oregon State University test had good results with water and ultra fine oil alone with no additive of baking soda. They used 2.5 Tbls. of Sun Spray oil per gallon of water. This is not effective for black spot fungus (Sunset Magazine).

On Pre-emergents Carefully scrutinize the label on pre-emergent products such as Preen on your perennial beds. These products often affect the fibrous root systems of certain perennials and annuals. They have been shown to create a balling effect at the tips of tiny roots, similar to the result when the tip of a plastic fiber passes through a small flame. Small, immature plants are most affected and may seem stunted or be slow to establish. Mature perennials that have well-established root systems, the woody roots of trees and shrubs, and turf grass are better able to withstand the effects of these chemicals.

If you depend on the flowering of self-sowing annuals, biennials and perennials to provide diversity and complexity in the garden, as we do at Perennial Passion, pre-emergents would never be used. They inhibit the germination of desirable seed such as our Verbena boniarensis, as well as undesirable seed such as crabgrass.

A natural organic product, corn gluten meal, will inhibit seed germination. A recent *Minnesota Horticulture Magazine* advises applying it in early May and mid August for best results. With continued use over time, weed problems are fewer and fewer. An added benefit is that it will contribute nitrogen to the soil.

On Repellents for Rabbit and Deer We've all felt a fondness for the innocent little creatures that share our neighborhoods. But how do you react when you look out of your window one morning, and there in bold, broad morning light are those, cute little animals--contentedly eating the buds from your new and probably-rare plant, or from one your best friend just shared with you, or maybe it is the one you

dragged halfway across the country, or the last in line of plant-family heirlooms?! The love and work and the effort and the cost you just went to--and, and, and--you have just lost it with those #@XX*# animals!!!!

A new product called Plant Pro-Tec Garlic Units kept rabbits away from the tulips in Perennial Passion's garden in spring, 2000. It is also supposed to keep deer at bay. According to the package the garlic odor is most effective on sunny warm days. (What about the cool, dark nights?) Each 3.5-inch long unit looks like a sawed off green pencil. It contains a combination of garlic oil and chili pepper ingredients that is activated when located. There is a clip attached so one can hang it into shrubs, trees and lower near tulips, annuals and perennials.

We've gathered some concoctions to use to repel animals:

Murphy's Oil Soap Recipe
 1 tablespoon dish washing liquid
 1/4 cup Murphy's Oil Soap
 1 gallon water
 1 tablespoon cayenne pepper or tobasco sauce
 Shake well and spray. Stronger concentrations of soap can cause leaves to yellow and die. Use only the amount suggested. (John Ball, State Forester, just advised that rabbits may actually develop a taste for hot sauce.)

Rotten Egg Recipe
 1 gallon water
 1 tsp. liquid detergent
 1/3 cup of milk
 1 beaten egg
 1 tsp. cooking oil
 Strain and put in sprayer bottle and allow to ferment at room temperature for several days, the longer the stronger (S.D. Horticulture Newsletter).

- Repellents that include bitrex are purportedly non-toxic and needed only once per season.
- Grandma used snuff to ward off rabbits.
- Blood meal, human hair, fox urine, human urine and strong smelling soap hung by the bar in trees or shrubs or cut into slivers around the bases of small plants are other remedies about which people report varying results.
- Strong-smelling substances will deter most animals because the odor interferes with their primary defense system, their sense of smell.

Hold a potent bar of soap up to your pet's nose and you'll see what I mean!

- Rabbits usually won't walk through chicken wire or other mesh that lies right on the ground surrounding the area that is being protected.

The following recipe was recommended to deter deer, slugs and insects from Hosta and other plants.

2 cups water
1 - 2 cups green onion or chives tops
2 cloves garlic
3 whole old eggs with shells
Pulverize for 2 minutes in blender or food processor
Add to a pail and dissolve strong bar soap into it.
Add 1 - 2 tablespoons of any of these: ground red pepper, hot sauce, cumin, mustard or any spicy or smelly non-toxic ingredient.

Make ahead and allow it to sour well. Humans will not detect the odor once it dries, but more odor-sensitive animals will. The bottom precipitate of shells and onion skin can be placed around the base of Hosta.

Insect Repellents
Insect repellent for plants:
1/4 tsp. liquid dish soap
1 tablespoon vinegar
1/4 tsp. ground red pepper
1 clove pulverized garlic
1 quart water
Pulverize in a blender or food processor, strain through a paper filter and spray on leaves.

Insecticidal Soap for Plants
4 cloves fresh garlic
1/2 tsp. vegetable oil
1/2 tsp. liquid dish soap
1 quart water

Adding soap helps to blend oil and water by breaking the surface tension of the water. It will then not draw up into little beaded droplets but will, rather, spread and adhere to leaves and stems. When sprayed onto the body of an insect, the oil will clog its pores and smother it.

Garlic will repel insects such as aphids if applied before infestation occurs.

<u>Insect Repellent Recipe for Humans and Animals</u>
Gnat repellent
1 cup water
1 cup Skin So Soft
2 cups white vinegar
1 tablespoon eucalyptus oil

<u>Recipe for Plant Tonic</u>
1 gallon water
1 tsp. baking powder
1 tsp. Epson salts
1 tsp. salt peter
1/2 tsp. of household ammonia

Spray plants once a month for best results (S.D. Horticulture Newsletter adaptation of Jerry Baker recipes).

On Slugs If you are a Hosta grower, you shudder at the sound of a simple four-letter word, s-l-u-g. These little, slimy, shell-less snails love the same environment as do Hosta and savor their juicy, tender leaves. Unsightly holes remain after their nighttime forages. Mature plants and those with the thickest leaves show the least damage.

There are a number of controls recommended. Gritty substances such as crushed egg shells, fractured rock or sand, copper scraps or shavings, coffee grounds, rice hulls, cocoa shells, and wood ashes spread around the base of leafy clumps discourage slimy bellies, and a copper band encircling the plant's base might keep them from oozing near to the plant. (Read more about wood ashes in the next topic.) Beer traps are often advertised for sale, but I wonder how many gardeners, poorer but wiser, have caught on to this unreliable and hard-to-monitor process. There are chemical methods using pellets or gels containing metaldehyde which we try to avoid because of potential harm to birds and other animals that may eat dead or dying slugs.

Oat bran is recommended to thwart snails by interfering with their digestion. Could it work on slugs?

On Slug Treatment with Ashes Repeated use of ashes has a liming effect and will raise the pH to make soil more alkaline, but in small amounts can contribute beneficial potassium to the soil. If the pH is below 6.5, up to 10 pounds of ashes for 100 square feet of garden area can be applied. Because of their accumulative effect, do not apply every year. Never apply them near ericaceous, acid-loving, plants such as azaleas or blueberries. (Gerwing)

On Soil Tests A number of different soil tests are conducted by the Plant Science Department, Box 2207A, Ag Hall 07, South Dakota State University, Brookings, SD 57007, telephone 605-688-4766. (They also test for feed, fertilizer and pesticide residue and purity of water used for livestock and human consumption.) Pick up sample bags and instructions at the Minnehaha County Extension Office, 220 West 6th St., Sioux Falls, SD 57104, telephone 605 367 7877.

On Watering Tap-rooted plants usually require less water; fibrous surface roots require more.

On Weeding Before beginning to weed an area, top dress first with an inch or more of compost. Then as one digs and pulls weeds, always with a trowel, air and compost tumble together into crevices and blend with the soil. No need to create a perfect homogeneous mixture here. Just give it a little start and the earthworms, bacteria, fungi, insects and animals will continue the mixing and aerating process.

On Weight - Plant Weight A single seed is placed in the ground, and in a few weeks one could harvest pounds of fruit! Plants do seem to miraculously appear from very little. Though observed daily, the concept is still hard for me to truly grasp. Have you ever wondered what contributes to all that bulk or volume? Surprisingly, 94-99 percent of plant leaves, fruit and roots is made from the carbon, hydrogen and oxygen from water and invisible air. Though only one-half to six percent comes from soil nutrients, it is this portion that is the most important in initiating and sustaining plant growth (Brady).

On Weight - Human Weight From humans, 30 to 45 minutes of gardening burns 150 calories or about the same as walking two miles in 30 minutes.

On Xeriscaping Defined as "the creative landscaping for water and energy efficiency," xeriscaping promotes the use of these horticulture principles:
- Good landscape planning and design
- Appropriate turf areas
- Efficient irrigation
- Use of soil amendments
- Use of mulches
- Incorporation of low-water-use plants into the landscape
- Appropriate maintenance of plants and irrigation systems

Key

Genus
Description of Genus

Key to Perennials

Species
Cultivar   Flowering Period   Height
Common Name
Perennial, Biennial, etc.   ○ ◑ ●   NEW IN   Year First Acquired
                                                GARDEN Year Planted
Flower Color   Light Requirement
Description of individual species or cultivar

Key to Hosta

Species
Cultivar
Hosta Foliage Color
Hosta Foliage Other, Sun and Slug Tolerance
Flower Color   Flowering Period   Height
Individual Plant Descriptions

Key to Hemerocallis

Species
Cultivar   Foliage hardiness   Flowering Period   Height

                                                NEW IN   Year First Acquired
Flower color   Flower shape   GARDEN Year Planted
Individual Plant Descriptions

Light Requirement	Flowering Period	
○ Sun, at least one-half day	spr Spring	fall Autumn
◑ Part shade to part sun	esu Early summer	LB Long blooming
● Part shade to shade	msu Mid summer	ext Extended bloom
	lsu Late summer	rpts Repeat bloom

NEW IN: Year First Acquired
Usually the year in which we first purchased and began to grow and sell this
plant, either at Perennial Passion Nursery, the Nursery Garden, or at our home
garden.

GARDEN: Year Planted
Usually the year in which we first planted this in the Perennial Passion Nursery
Garden. Prior to 1993, the year planted at our home garden.

ACHILLEA

The yarrows make up a wide-ranging native genus that thrives on neglect and is indispensable in today's gardens. Ranging from heights of four inches to four feet, ornamental species and cultivars contribute grand foliages and flowers. Most plants are sturdy; some are invasive; all are carefree and sun loving. Other than requiring good drainage, they aren't fussy about soils and are drought resistant once established, a xeriscaping plant.

Foliage is deeply divided, almost fern-like for some, often very silvery with a spicy aroma.

Flowers are unique. Packed tightly into flat, broad clusters are tiny ray or pistillate female flowers in colors of pink, white, yellow and red. The tiny, middle, disk flowers, predominantly yellow, are both male and female. Excellent vase flowers, dried or fresh, are provided to us by these plants. A cut flower tip: do not cut stems until pollen is visible. Deadhead regularly, and flowers repeat all summer on most cultivars. They provide a valuable nectar source for butterflies.

The newer Galaxy hybrids are a result of crossing A. millefolium, a Northern Plains native, and A. taygetea. They have larger flower heads and stronger stems. Some of the millefolium species are invasive; site them carefully.

'Anthea'

Fernleaf Yarrow, Milfoil	msu-Isu LB	24"
Perennial, Containers ○	NEW for us in	97
Primrose and creamy yellow	In our GARDEN	97

Numerous gleaming flower heads, 3-4" across, on sturdy stems provide distinctive contrasts with soft, ferny silver foliage. New hybrid in early 1990's from Blooms of Bressingham Gardens, England. More vigorous than A. 'Moonshine'. Honors: Exceptional field rating in 1997 Michigan trials, Penn State Top 20 Perennial Performers.

'Colorado'

Yarrow	msu-Isu LB	34"
Perennial ○	NEW for us in	00
Pastel mixture	In our GARDEN	

Vigorous, mixed colors. Honors: High marks in '97 Michigan trials, Penn State Top 20 Perennial Performers.

 55

'Credo'

Yarrow	msu-Isu LB 36"
Perennial ○	NEW for us in 98
Soft yellow, fragrant	In our GARDEN

This will be a future staple of the perennial border because of long blooming, fragrant, beautiful flower color and strong stems for cutting. An A. millefolium and filipendulina cross by the German grower, Pagels. A fragrant, light-yellow form of A. 'Coronation Gold'.

'Orange Queen'

Fernleaf Yarrow, Milfoil	msu-Isu LB 24"
Perennial ○	NEW for us in 98
Dark russet red	In our GARDEN

Inviting warm color, more intense than that of A. 'Terra Cotta'. A favorite combination is this color with blue flowers of Salvia, Campanula, Russian sage, Erigeron and Delphinium. Any or all will do. Dark green, disease free ferny foliage and reliable reblooming.

'Terra Cotta'

Fernleaf Yarrow, Milfoil	msu-Isu LB 24-36"
Perennial, Containers ○	NEW for us in 97
Dark rusty pink matures to red orange	In our GARDEN 97

Flowers emerge as a dark peach blend and gradually lighten to the color of a terra cotta pot. Excellent silver foliage provides additional contrast. A favorite of ours, again combined with blue flowering perennials. A German introduction. Honors: Cut Flower Association special designation.

'Walter Funke'

Yarrow	msu-Isu LB 24"
Perennial ○	NEW for us in 98
Brick red	In our GARDEN

Strong and compact plant could be called an improved and shorter A. 'Fireland'. Foliage has silver highlights.

clypeolata x taygetea
'Moonshine'

Fernleaf Yarrow, Milfoil	msu-Isu LB 24-30"
Perennial, Containers ○	NEW for us in 91
Bright, clear sulphur yellow	In our GARDEN 95

Deservedly popular; outstanding in both foliage and flower with silver, feathery leaves and bright flowers to cut and dry. Deadhead for prolonged bloom. Originated at the Blooms of Bressingham Nursery in northern England. Honors: High ratings in field trials.

filipendulina x
'Schwellenberg'

Fernleaf Yarrow, Milfoil	msu-Isu LB 24"
Perennial, Containers ○	NEW for us in 96
Dark golden yellow	In our GARDEN

An outstanding new introduction combining silvery foliage of A. 'Moonshine' with deep gold of A. 'Coronation Gold'. No staking needed, compact and sturdy, won't flop. Deadhead for continued bloom.

 56

millefolium
'Fireland', 'Feuerland'

Fernleaf Yarrow, Milfoil
Perennial ○
Brilliant cardinal red

msu-lsu LB   36"
NEW for us in   96
In our GARDEN

Very bright red, flat topped blossoms age to an apricot yellow. This extra tall German selection has sturdy stems and won't flop.

millefolium
'Sawa Sawa'

Fernleaf Yarrow, Milfoil
Perennial ○
Deep clear pink

msu-lsu LB   24-30"
NEW for us in   97
In our GARDEN   97

Long, full flowering appearance and excellent cut flower production. Deadheads do not dominate the plant at any time. Edging ahead of A. 'Lilac Beauty', this one has darker flowers. This was still blooming in 12/99! Honors: Very high ratings in Midwest trials.

millefolium
'Snow Sport'

Fernleaf Yarrow, Milfoil
Perennial ○
White masses

msu-lsu LB   18-30"
NEW for us in   96
In our GARDEN   96

Best white blooming yarrow, repeatedly inquired of in our garden. Masses of snowy brightness and fine, filigree foliage. Trim back flowers and foliage by one-half in midsummer, and yarrows will perform a second act by late season.

millefolium x
'Hope', 'Hoffnung'

Fernleaf Yarrow, Milfoil
Perennial ○
Peach, yielding to antique yellow

msu-lsu LB   18-24"
NEW for us in   93
In our GARDEN

Very large blooms of antique yellow with hint of peach prompt the same senses as does antique fabric, aged, worn, warm. German Galaxy hybrid of improved A. millefolium. Honors: High ratings in field trials.

millefolium x
'Paprika'

Fernleaf Yarrow, Milfoil
Perennial ○
Bodacious ruby red, yellow center

msu-lsu LB   18"
NEW for us in   93
In our GARDEN

German Galaxy hybrid selected for color with punch on a strong growing plant. Tough and undemanding as are all Achillea. Provide good drainage and plenty of sunshine.

millefolium x
'Salmon Beauty'

Fernleaf Yarrow, Milfoil
Perennial ○
Large, salmon heads

msu-lsu LB   36"
NEW for us in   98
In our GARDEN

German Galaxy selection. Remove spent flowers of all yarrows to promote continued flowering.

millifolium
'Summer Pastels'
Fernleaf Yarrow, Milfoil

Perennial ○

Mixed, warm colors, reds, pinks

msu-lsu LB 24'

NEW for us in 0C

In our GARDEN

Warm red and pink, long blooming combination on a compact plant. This and all other yarrows make excellent plants for South Dakota. Site this one carefully because of potential invasiveness. Honors: 1990 All American Selection, Best seller in '97 by "GMpro Magazine."

ptarmica
'Ballerina'
Sneezewort, Yarrow

Perennial ○

White

msu LB 9-12"

NEW for us in 94

In our GARDEN

Don't be disarmed by the common name sneezewort. Unique yarrow with non dissected, fine foliage. High ratings and excellent for cutting; cuts can substitute for baby's breath. Cultivars of this group are usually better than the ordinary species.

ptarmica
'The Pearl'
Sneezewort, Yarrow

Perennial ○

White, semi double, airy

esu-msu LB 18-24"

NEW for us in 94

In our GARDEN 97

Blooms heavily with double flowers, excellent for cutting. For many years, one of the most popular cultivars and always gets high ratings in trials. Spreads rapidly, not an uncommon trait for yarrow.

sibirica, kamtschaticum
Kamtschaticum 'Love Parade'
Sneezewort, Yarrow

Perennial ○

Soft pink

msu 12-18"

NEW for us in 00

In our GARDEN

Classy in flower and in leaf with shiny, dark green foliage with serrated margins. Newly introduced from eastern Russian Kamtschatka Peninsula. Flat topped blossoms for cutting.

 58

ACONITUM

Despite centuries-old warnings of the poisonous properties of all parts of all Aconitum species, especially the roots, this genus contains excellent plants for the garden. Do not plant near food crops and use gloves or wash hands after handling or cutting. Knowing that deer and rabbits avoid eating plants in this genus is a pretty strong indication that lessons have been well-learned in the animal kingdom.

Sturdy flowers with enlarged, hood-shaped sepals (resembling monks' hoods) grow up and down stalks (racemes) to 3' tall or more. Most species produce flowers in late summer to fall, some in midsummer. Much-sought-after blue flowers dominate this genus, but white, rose, yellow and bicolors are also found. All are excellent providers of long-lasting cut flowers. Lustrous, desirable foliage adds to these plants' overall excellent quality.

General cultural requirements are full sun to part shade, moist, well-drained soil and cool nights. Plant where they are to remain; they dislike transplanting. Propagation is best by division in fall or early spring.

anthora
Pyrenees Monkshood, Helmet Flower   msu   24-36"
Perennial   ○ ●   NEW for us in 98
Pale yellow   In our GARDEN

Uncommon in the market place, yellow flowered monkshood is one of nature's original European species.

cammarum x
'Eleanor'
Monkshood   msu   36-42"
Perennial   ○ ●   NEW for us in 98
White, blue edge   In our GARDEN

Unusual, strong white helmets with dainty blue edge, an improvement over A. 'Bicolor'. Stems are shorter and more branching than the species resulting in shrubby plants, growing as wide as they are tall. Deer resistant and vigorous.

carmichaelii
'Barker'
Azure Monkshood   msu-lsu   24-36"
Perennial   ○ ●   NEW for us in 96
Deep blue   In our GARDEN

Thick textured foliage and stems give sturdiness without staking. Moisture and afternoon shade conditions are desirable.

carmichaelii, fischeri

Azure Monkshood | lsu-fall | 18-24"
Perennial   **O ●** | NEW for us in | 98
Lavender blue | In our GARDEN

One of the last of monkshoods to bloom in the fall. Thick, lustrous stems and leaves do not require staking.

henryi
'Spark's Variety'

Common Blue Monkshood | msu-lsu | 36-60"
Perennial   **O ●** | NEW for us in | 95
Deep blue purple | In our GARDEN

Beautiful flowers in dark, purplish blue with rich, glossy foliage are stunning on this tall plant, which is one of the showiest of monkshood. Prefers partially shaded site and rich soil and probably will require support. All parts poisonous; wash hands after handling or wear gloves. Excellent in masses. Late to emerge from the soil in spring and one of the late-flowering species.

lamarckii (lycotocum)
ssp. neapolitanum

Yellow Monkshood | msu | 36-60"
Perennial   **O ●** | NEW for us in | 98
Soft creamy yellow | In our GARDEN

Branched stems of soft-yellow, midsummer helmets are as easy to grow in the woodland as the blue forms. Sometimes listed under the species pyrenaicum or barbatum.

napellus
'Blue Valley'

Autumn Monkshood | | 36"
Perennial   **O ●** | NEW for us in | 00
Dark blue | In our GARDEN

Another excellent napellus cultivar to compete with some of the older, but still reliable, monkshoods.

napellus
'Newry Blue'

Monkshood | | 36"
Perennial   **O ●** | NEW for us in
Dark blue | In our GARDEN

Considered by many to be a choice cultivar of A. napellus.

napellus, autumnale, californicum

Autumn Monkshood | msu-lsu | 6"
Perennial   **O ●** | NEW for us in | 94
Mid blue | In our GARDEN | 94

An easy monkshood to grow, but most of them are. Excellent cut flowers and fine garden plants. All parts poisonous.

napellus, autumnale, californicum
'Alba'
Common White Monkshood msu-lsu   36-48"
Perennial   ◐ ● NEW for us in   99
Lovely, pure white In our GARDEN

Helmet-like flowers appear in abundance on sturdy, branched stalks that need no staking. Remove flowers when spent. Very poisonous, wash hands after handling. Easy to grow.

napellus x. stoerkianum
'Bicolor'
Autumn Monkshood msu   36-48"
Perennial   ◐ ● NEW for us in   96
Blue violet and white hoods In our GARDEN

Helmet flowers on a shrubby plant as tall as it is wide. Deer resistant, easy and long-lived, all parts poisonous.

septentrionale
'Ivorine'
Monkshood msu   24"
Perennial   ◐ ● NEW for us in   96
Dense, creamy white In our GARDEN   96

The compact, unique and best white form of Aconitum with very dense, heavily branched spikes. A Blooms of Bressingham introduction from England from whom always come reliable choices. Earliest monkshood to flower, throughout June in our garden. Elegant and rare.

ADENOPHORA

A genus similar to *Campanula*.

lilifolia
Ladybells, Lilyleaf spr-esu   24"
Perennial   ◐ ● NEW for us in   97
Pale lavender blue In our GARDEN

Old fashioned, charming and popular wildflower. Stalks of bell-shaped, fragrant flowers in early summer. Best massed and naturalized as it probably will self-sow. Kidney-shaped, basal leaves are often mistaken for those of Campanula.

AEGOPODIUM

podagraria
'Variegatum'
Snow On The Mountain, Bishop's Weed esu-msu   9-12"
Perennial   ○ ◐ ● NEW for us in   80
Creamy white In our GARDEN   85

Pretty, tough, fast spreading, variegated groundcover, grown for foliage effect. Site carefully and keep isolated so it will not visually and physically overpower other desirable garden plants. Easily divided and propagated, start with a few and end up with a few hundred!

AGASTACHE

foeniculum x rugosum
'Blue Fortune'

Anise Hyssop   esu-lsu LB   24-36"
Perennial   ○   NEW for us in   97
Dark blue   In our GARDEN   97

All the way from Rotterdam to Sioux Falls, this wonderful newcomer has become a long-blooming staple in our garden with long-lasting, dark, blue-lavender spikes from June to fall. Licorice scented foliage tastes like licorice, too. Use as flavoring for beverages and fruit and to scent potpourri. Butterflies are seduced by the flowers. Drought-tolerant plant, use for xeriscaping.

AJUGA

Bugleweeds perform with showy, small flowers that grow up and down terminal spikes in spring. Many cultivars are available, displaying a variety of beautiful foliage colors, variegations and textures. Growing in mounded rosettes, they make excellent groundcovers under appropriate conditions.

Sometimes during naked winters (those without snow cover), extremely cold air will desiccate (like freezer burn) these plants beyond recovery. Grow them as a broad-leaf evergreen and provide areas with winter shade and protection, obtained by planting to the north of coniferous trees and shrubs or providing a blanket of loose-fitting leaves. Crown rot, aphids and mildew will occasionally take their toll. Soil should be enriched and humusy. Propagate them easily by division in early spring.

'Royalty'

Bugleweed   spr-esu   4"
Perennial, Groundcover   ○ ●   NEW for us in   98
Blue on short spikes   In our GARDEN

Very dark purple, almost black, mature foliage. Crisp thick leaves have deeply ruffled and scalloped margins. Blue flowers on short spikes provide a beautiful contrast.

reptans
'Catlin's Giant'

Bugleweed   spr-esu   9"
Perennial, Groundcover   ○ ●   NEW for us in   95
Deep blue spikes   In our GARDEN

Larger, purple leaved plant with bright flower spikes. Fast growing groundcover in mounded rosettes that looks like it's been given growth hormones! Prosper best if provided winter cover and good soil.

reptans
'Jungle Beauty Improved'

Bugleweed
Perennial, Groundcover ◯ ●
Deep blue

spr-esu   12-15"
NEW for us in 95
In our GARDEN

Stunning, larger-than-normal, purple-tinted foliage, dark-blue flower spikes up to 15". Donated to the U.S. National Arboretum by Beth Chatto, English nurserywoman, in 1987. Handsome groundcover in shade; provide winter shade as well.

ALCEA (ALTHAEA)

Though many hollyhocks are perennials, it is convenient to classify them as biennials since most are short lived. Some may even bloom the first year from seed and can be treated as annuals. A gardener may need to plant them for a couple of consecutive years to establish them. In the first year following germination, a leafy basal rosette (don't mistake this for some non-flowering weed and pull it out), will develop. The second year's growth and arousal results in elongation and blooming of the upright flower stalks. Eventually colonies will establish and new plants will bloom every year.

Tall, vertical accents, their lovely, 4-5" blossoms remind most of us of our youth, and its flowers are the first to come to mind when considering an old-fashioned garden. They are commonly viewed naturalized near farm buildings (especially outhouses), and fences and up and down alleyways in old neighborhoods. Butterflies will manage to find them wherever they put down roots.

Susceptible to rust fungus, lower leaves may quickly become brown and unsightly. Hide this defect behind other plantings. Once germinated, they are drought tolerant.

rosea
'Chater's Double Mix', Powderpuff

Hollyhock
Perennial, Biennial   ◯
Mixed, red, pink, yellow, maroon

msu   60-72"
NEW for us in 96
In our GARDEN

Fully double mixed colors, but one color per plant (we are often asked if multiple colors appear on one plant), of red, yellow, white, pink flowers grow up and down tall stalks.

rosea
'Nigra'

Hollyhock
Perennial, Biennial   ◯
Dark maroon red, nearly black, single

msu   60-72"
NEW for us in 96
In our GARDEN

Bold, beautiful and mysterious, striking upright thrust, very dark and shiny, single flowers. Allow to self-sow and do not cultivate until emerging seedlings are detected the following spring.

 63

rosea
Scarlet, red

Hollyhock   msu   60-72"
Perennial, Biennial   ○   NEW for us in   96
Scarlet red singles   In our GARDEN

Single flowering, tall hollyhocks in pure red color. Drought tolerant.

rosea
'The Watchman'

Hollyhock   msu   72"
Perennial, Biennial   ○   NEW for us in   99
Maroon to black   In our GARDEN

Single, shiny, dramatic, very dark flowers.

rosea, ficifolia
'Single Mix'

Hollyhock   msu   60-72"
Perennial, Biennial   ○   NEW for us in   89
Mixed colors   In our GARDEN

Still room for the nostalgic, single, mixed varieties. Not true perennials. Allow to bloom and self-sow at least two subsequent years to set up self perpetuating colonies.

rugosa

Russian Hollyhock   msu-fall LB   60-72"
Biennial, Perennial   ○ ◉   NEW for us in   00
Single yellow   In our GARDEN

Tall, old fashioned single yellow that blooms over a long period. Some of these classic old forms are often overlooked in favor of new introductions, but this is such a reliable old thing, blooms forever and has less trouble with notorious lower leaf rust problems that accompany most hollyhocks. Hairy stems support 5-lobed leaves.

 64

ALCHEMILLA

Always on my top ten list, the genus Alchemilla gives us great perennials, indispensable for foliage strength, with the added attribute of lovely, chartreuse-yellow, apetalous (no petals) sprays in June that are excellent for cutting and drying. When dried, they provide the same texture as baby's breath. Rounded, pleated and serrated leaves catch droplets of water. "Its leaves are like an umbrella turned inside out and they are hairy, holding raindrops in their center, but with a light-reflecting air bubble trapped underneath, that winks and sparkles with contagious glee." (Christopher Lloyd, "Foliage Plants").

Grow in sun or shade, but provide extra moisture in full sun. Plant in drifts to get full visual impact from these captivating, charming, old-fashioned plants. My favorite uses are tucking them near dark green yew shrubs and lining garden pathways, where they will spill over and soften any edges. The chartreuse flowers are nearly an exact color match to the foliage of Veronica trehanii, the gold or yellow variegation of many Hosta or Polemonium 'Brise de Anjou'. Other plants that produce large yellow flowers repeat the color as well.

Different species exist with differing stature and applications, expanding garden design options. All divide easily in spring before blooming, and they will moderately self-sow.

After the first showy blossoming begins to taper off by the end of June, cut back leaves and flowers to within 2" of soil (if you can bear to) and this plant will start all over with fresh, new leaves and rebloom again later in the summer. From where does it get all that energy?! It must have extremely energy-efficient leaves and a highly capable, root-storage system.

alpina

Mountain Lady's Mantle	esu, rpts 6"
Perennial, Containers ○ ◑ ●	NEW for us in 93
Foamy, chartreuse yellow	In our GARDEN 97

A favorite and desirable, compact, neat form for partially shaded rock gardens or small areas where diminutive scale is desirable. 2" leaves are glossy with distinct thread-like, silver edge, and flowers are foamy sprays of yellow.

erythropoda

Lady's Mantle
Perennial   ○ ◐ ●
Foamy, chartreuse yellow

esu, rpts   6-9"
NEW for us in   93
In our GARDEN   93

Same foliage impact on a compact form, less than one-half the size of A. mollis or vulgaris, but larger than A. alpina. This adds a subtle, silver edged leaf. We love any and all lady's mantles, because their excellent foliage contrasts well with all other plants.

mollis
'Auslese'

Lady's Mantle
Perennial   ○ ◐ ●
Billowy, chartreuse yellow sprays

esu, rpts   18"
NEW for us in   96
In our GARDEN

Lacy, foamy flowers are held more upright over the lovely clumps of pleated foliage.

mollis
'Thriller'

Lady's Mantle
Perennial   ○ ◐ ●
Foamy, chartreuse yellow spray

esu-rpts   18"
NEW for us in   96
In our GARDEN

Long a favorite genus, lady's mantle sources are moving into new and diverse cultivars. Most still closely resemble the original species. A. 'Thriller' supports its foamy flowers erect over basal leaves. Honors: Penn State Top 20 Perennial Performers.

mollis (vulgaris)

Lady's Mantle
Perennial   ○ ◐ ●
Foamy, chartreuse yellow

esu, rpts   18"
NEW for us in   92
In our GARDEN   93

The most commonly used, yet still-excellent species. Honors: 20 Top Selling Perennials of '95.

monticola

Lady's Mantle
Perennial   ○ ◐ ●
Yellow sprays

esu, rpts   12"
NEW for us in   96
In our GARDEN   97

Uncommon species planted beneath our office arbor. At first glance, not significantly different than other compact species of lady's mantle.

xanthochlora

Lady's Mantle
Perennial   ○ ◐ ●
Yellow sprays

esu, rpts   12"
NEW for us in   96
In our GARDEN   97

Uncommon species planted beneath our office arbor but has grown strong since '97. At first glance, not significantly different than other compact species of lady's mantle.

ALLIUM

The ornamental onions from the genus, Allium, provide all kinds of easy and undemanding design possibilities. Choose them for palette or palate--color or taste. Little miniatures with outstanding foliage, like A. senescens 'Glauca', can be tucked into rock gardens or border an herb garden. Giant four foot tall selections, like A. 'Globemaster', steal the show while revealing their hues. True chives and garlic chives are culinary delights.

Many are planted as fall bulbs, blooming in spring and early summer with foliage that disappears by midsummer like that of tulips. Others maintain narrow spears of ornamental foliage throughout the summer.

In all species, hundreds of flowers sparkle around a globular shape, ranging from one to twelve inches in diameter. All are excellent for cutting and many dry perfectly, some retaining their colors. This may go without saying, but onions do have their own distinct aroma, and these pretty relatives share this trait.

Caution is to be advised since a few are invasive through abundant self-sowing; otherwise most increase at a desirable rate by duplicating underground bulbs. All can be propagated by division or seed.

'Globemaster'

Ornamental Onion	esu	36-48"
Perennial, Fall Bulb ○ ●	NEW for us in	94
Glowing lavender purple	In our GARDEN	94

This Allium captures more attention than any of the other fall planted bulbs in our garden. Thick and rigid, 3-4' flower stalks stand tall and strong, topped with 6-12" balls of tiny purple florets that look fresh for three to four weeks in June. It blooms in two stages, and it is the second flush of florets that is sterile and lasts the longest, providing excellent cut fresh or dried flowers. Foliage maintains its chlorophyll and doesn't whither and disappear until flowers begin to fade. This is unlike A. giganteum's foliage, which begins to dry as soon as flowers begin to open. A cross between A. maclenni or giganteum and A. christophii.

aflatunense

Persian Onion	spr-esu	30"
Perennial, Fall Bulb ○ ●	NEW for us in	88
Bright lilac purple	In our GARDEN	92

These onions bloom in May and can be interplanted with later emerging perennials such as daylilies and sedum. Flowers dry perfectly to shape, but lose their purple color to a light tan. Foliage will dry, whither, and disappear like that of tulip foliage. Plant in fall in sweeps of five or more. Similar to A. giganteum but about one half the scale. (The species name, afllatunense, only rhymes with flatulence.) Plant as fall bulbs.

 67

aflatunense
'Purple Sensation'
Ornamental Onion
Perennial, Fall Bulb ○ ●
Vivid dark purple

spr-esu 30"
NEW for us in 92
In our GARDEN 92

Plant bulbs in fall for showy, vivid purple, 4" spheres in May, held aloft by strong stems. Use for fresh cut or dried flowers. Flower skeletons turn wheat colored and dry perfectly.

atropurpuream
Ornamental Onion
Perennial, Fall Bulb ○ ●
Wine purple

spr-esu 30"
NEW for us in 92
In our GARDEN

Excellent as long-lasting fresh and dried cuts. Flower skeletons dry perfectly, fading to a natural tan. May blooming along with late, lily-flowering tulips.

azureum, caeruleum
Ornamental Onion
Perennial, Fall Bulb ○ ●
Cornflower blue

esu-msu 24"
NEW for us in 94
In our GARDEN 94

Small compact heads of a most beautiful, smoky cornflower blue color, excellent for cutting. Bloom June or July after being planted as fall bulbs. Foliage whithers after flowering, and bulbs go into dormancy.

beesianum
Ornamental Onion
Perennial ○ ●
Dark lavender blue

msu 6-8"
NEW for us in 96
In our GARDEN 97

Mini-sparkler in our widow's walk section. This tiny onion plant glows when chive-like flowers are open in midsummer. One of finest rock garden Allium. Combine with other tiny plants that suit its scale like prostrate Veronica and Thymus. Foliage remains visible throughout the summer and does not recede into dormancy like fall-planted Allium.

carinatum ssp. pulchellum
Ornamental Onion
Perennial, Bulb ○ ●
Lavender sprays

esu-msu 18-24"
NEW for us in 95
In our GARDEN 94

Very interesting Japanese form of the ornamental onion. Stamens and sepals curve and reflect, creating movement and fireworks! Flower form appears to explode from effects of many individual tiny flowers as they dangle and twist from their origin. Small Allium are easy to propagate by regular division of small underground bulbs.

cepa proliferum
Egyptian Tree Onion
Herb, Perennial ○ ●
Bulblets borne at tips of foliage

esu 36"
NEW for us in 95
In our GARDEN

Interesting, underused ornamental onion, with bulblets developing at the top of the strappy tubular foliage. As a true perennial onion, bulbs can be dug up in spring, harvested and stored, and will develop a stronger taste with time. Beware of self-sowing aggressiveness.

christophii, albopilosum

Star of Persia, Downy Onion
Perennial, Fall Bulb   ○ ●
Silver blue

esu   12-18"
NEW for us in   89
In our GARDEN   96

One of the most ornamental and favorite Allium, and among the best for cutting and drying, with large, 6-12" heads. Tiny, starry, silvery-purple flowers create a wide sphere, and appear to orbit together around the center. They will dry perfectly to a golden color and keep for years. This is not tall like some of the other fall bulbs that have been described. Flowers seem huge and a bit out of scale compared to its short stature. Foliage disappears after blooming. Plant in fall as dormant bulbs.

flavum

Ornamental Onion
Perennial   ○ ●
Bright, cheery yellow

esu   12-18"
NEW for us in   97
In our GARDEN   97

Hundreds of tiny, yellow, chive-like flowers group together on a rounded umbel above blue-green foliage. Like most Allium, these can be tucked in most anywhere.

giganteum

Ornamental Onion
Perennial, Fall Bulb   ○ ●
Sparkling purple

esu   36-48"
NEW for us in   88
In our GARDEN

One of the tallest member of the genus (except for A. 'Globemaster'), 3-4' feet, with 5+" umbels that contain over one thousand individual, deep-purple florets. Large strap-like foliage soon disappears, even before flowering is complete. These are heavy feeders; use a slow release bulb booster that is low in nitrogen. Plant in fall to bloom in June.

karataviense

Ornamental Onion
Perennial, Fall Bulb, Containers   ○ ●
Silver white

esu   10-12"
NEW for us in   90
In our GARDEN

Glaucous blue, wide, soft leaves form a short plant. Stubby stems parade large, silvery-white flowers in early summer. One of the best Allium for container culture and short foliage effects.

moly
'Jeanine'

Lily Leek, Ornamental Onion
Fall Bulb   ○ ●
Bright yellow

esu   10-15"
NEW for us in   97
In our GARDEN   97

Taller, compact and robust improvement on the moly species. Combine with silvery lamb's ears.

moly luteum

Lily Leek, Ornamental Onion
Perennial, Fall Bulb   ○ ●
Cheery yellow

esu   10-15"
NEW for us in   89
In our GARDEN

A small colonizing, old fashioned Allium with starry yellow clusters. Grown since 1596 in Europe for good luck and prosperity. Great for edging or groundcover.

multibulbosum, nigra

Ornamental Onion   esu   24-36"
Perennial, Fall Bulb   ○ **○**   NEW for us in   92
Greenish white with red center   In our GARDEN   93

Hundreds of tiny flowers make up beautifully shaped, 3-4", oval flower heads. This white counterpart to Allium aflatunense blooms later, in early June and is very long-lasting as a cut flower. Plant in fall as dormant bulbs.

neopolitanum, cowanii

'Neopolitanum'

Ornamental Onion   esu   15-20"
Perennial, Fall Bulb   ○ **○**   NEW for us in   89
White   In our GARDEN

Multitudes of tiny white flowers form a mounded umbel atop 15-20" stems. Sweet fragrance, rather than onion odor, is a surprise.

oreophilum, ostrowskianum

Ornamental Mountain Onion   esu   10-15"
Perennial, Fall Bulb   ○ **○**   NEW for us in   89
Rich rose   In our GARDEN

One of finest dwarf Allium for rock gardens, borders and naturalizing. 2" wide umbels of small florets have an unusual, pleasant fragrance. Usually planted in the fall as dormant bulbs.

schoenoprasum

'Schnittlauch'

Chives   esu   9-12"
Perennial   ○ **○**   NEW for us in   96
Lavender pom poms   In our GARDEN

A vigorous grower and ornamental culinary selection. Who has never cooked with chives?

senescens

'Glauca'

Curly Garlic Chives, Ornamental Onion   msu-lsu   9-12"
Perennial   ○ **○**   NEW for us in   90
Pale, lavender pink balls   In our GARDEN   93

My favorite little onion plant. Each narrow, quite blue leaf makes a full twist, giving the entire plant spiral movement. The small plants are great for edging and focal points in herb gardens and provide equal effect in the perennial garden. Strong onion flavor is added to salads by using a few flowers. This reliable plant has never self-sown in our garden. A cherished gift of many years ago from a garden mentor, Stella. Many plants have been named for her; look for the latin word "stellata."

spherocephalum

Drumstick Allium, Ornamental Onion

Perennial, Fall Bulb   ○ ●

Rich, dark, reddish-purple ovals

esu-msu   24"

NEW for us in 94

In our GARDEN 94

One of the best onion flowers for cutting and drying. Dark florets are densely packed onto 2" wide, slightly oval heads. When picked early, they dry perfectly retaining their rich purple color. Foliage is unobtrusive, hardly noticed, and cohabits well in densely planted situations. In fall, squeeze ten or fifteen tiny bulbs together into small open spots, and repeat throughout the garden for best effect. By late June they disappear into dormancy, and you'll miss their vivid purple splashes. They multiply rapidly but are not invasive, and you'll eventually have plenty to share.

stellatum

Pink Prairie Onion

Prairie Perennial   ○ ●

Deep pink

msu   9-18"

NEW for us in 96

In our GARDEN

Oodles of starry flowers on round umbels are native to eastern Great Plains. Best to cut flowers before they scatter seed throughout your garden. Self-sowing Allium such as this or A. tuberosum and A. schoenoprasum should raise red flags of caution!

tanguticum

Ornamental Onion

Perennial, Bulb   ○ ●

Purple globes

msu   18"

NEW for us in 93

In our GARDEN 94

Strong, upright foliage retains healthy appearance and provides great contrasts with other foliages all summer. Abundant, 2" purple globes cut and dry well. Excellent in herb gardens.

thumbergii
'Ozawas'

Ornamental Onion

Perennial, Bulb   ○ ●

Red violet

lsu-fall   9-12"

NEW for us in 96

In our GARDEN 95

Summer's swan song, this small-scale Japanese mountainous species is one of the last plants to flower in fall. Autumn and early winter frost accessorize it well, while its leaves turn a pumpkin color. Triangular-shaped, shiny, onion-like leaves.

tuberosum

Garlic Chives, Ornamental Garlic or Onion

Perennial, Herb   ○ ●

Lovely white spheres

lsu   12-24"

NEW for us in 95

In our GARDEN

Lovely tall white-blooming onion for late summer and fall herb garden. Be forewarned!! Do not allow seed to fall or an eternal battle will ensue--and the onion bulbs will win! Use pretty, edible flowers in chicken salad and egg dishes. Leaves, with mild garlic flavor, may be substituted for chives.

 71

ALTHEA

officinalis

Marshmallow Plant   msu   48-60"
Herb, Biennial   ◯   NEW for us in   97
Pale pink   In our GARDEN   94

Marshmallows, originally a medicinal candy, were made of the powdered root from this hollyhock relative combined with sugar and water, and used as an immune system stimulant and cough suppressor. This biennial has self-sown abundantly in our garden, and at one time was an extensive colony.

ALYSSOIDES

utriculata

Bladder Pod   spr-esu   24-36"
Perennial   ●   NEW for us in   94
Bright yellow, dried seed pods   In our GARDEN   97

Bladder-like, half-inch seed pods develop from showy, yellow flower clusters of early spring or summer. Foliage is a dark, rich green. Grows naturally on rocky ledges. Excellent choice for cut or dried flowers.

AMORPHA

Leadplant is one of the few native woody plants found in the northern Great Plains. Divided silvery foliage is soft and hairy, a lovely contrast to the pretty blue flowers, a combination that makes this shrubby plant easy to pick out when looking over native stands of forbs and grasses. The pea-like flowers have showy orange anthers and are fragrant.

In controlled gardens, remove attractive seed pods that form before they burst and self-sow too aggressively. Leave them for a naturalized, prairie garden.

Native Indians call this plant *zitka' tacan*, which means "the bird's wood" or "the bird's tree," because it provides a woody perch for birds in the mostly treeless prairie.

It is a legume from the greater pea family and makes the ground where it grows more fertile because it can fix nitrogen to the soil. As a native prairie plant, it is naturally drought tolerant.

canescens

Leadplant   esu-msu   12-24"
Prairie Perennial   ◯ ●   NEW for us in   93
Lavender blue   In our GARDEN

This outstanding, nitrogen-fixing prairie native can grow in sandy soil. Most prairie companions are herbaceous, but this is a small woody plant. Honors: Nebraska Great Plants for the Great Plains selection

nana

Fragrant False Indigo
Prairie Perennial ○ ◉
Lavender blue

esu-msu   12-36"
NEW for us in 94
In our GARDEN

Long flowering in early summer.

AMSONIA

Amsonia is a North American genus that provides a few excellent species for the garden. Pale blue, starry flowers become them in early summer, and the golden yellow glow of their fall color is a distinctive, identifying feature. Though taking their time to become established, once done, they are a resilient, low maintenance specimen that will self-sow and be drought-tolerant and dry-shade tolerant. All thrive in full sun or part shade and have few, if any, pest problems.

hubrichtii

Threadleaf Amsonia, Ark. Bluestar
Perennial ○ ◉
Steel blue heads

esu   36-48"
NEW for us in 98
In our GARDEN 97

This new plant has invitingly soft, extra fine, needle-like foliage and blooms in early summer with clusters of steely blue flowers. The yellow fall color of the foliage lights up the garden; it is worth growing this plant for this reason alone. Use at the back of the border or as a hedge. Hardiness always listed by catalogs for zone 5 or more southernly, but has been a gallant performer both here and in Minnesota. Cut new growth back a little in spring for a bushier, more compact plant. Honors: 1999 Kentucky Theodore Klein Award.

tabernaemontana

Bluestar, Willow Amsonia
Perennial ○ ◉ ●
Pale blue

esu   36-48"
NEW for us in 93
In our GARDEN

The commonly found species on the market. Alternate leaf arrangement upon long willow-like stalks provide blue-green color, compelling with early summer blue flowers. This will self-sow when met with ideal conditions. Fall color is lovely. Dry shade tolerant.

ANAPHALIS

margaritaceae

Pearly Everlasting
Prairie Perennial ○
Silvery white, yellow centers

msu-lsu   24"
NEW for us in 89
In our GARDEN

Cherished for fuzzy, silvery leaves, late bloom and white flower clusters that are perfect for cutting and drying. Well-drained soil essential. Keep tomentose (hairy or fuzzy) foliage dry to avoid rotting.

 73

ANEMONE

Anemone is a broad-ranging genus providing flowering plants that fill many niches- -from little, early blooming, soon-to-be-dormant woodland plants to the tall, splendid Japanese types, that are showy fall-bloomers. We've been trialing some of the late-blooming ones in South Dakota and though indications are positive, have not made a firm conclusion about their adaptability.

What appear to be showy flower petals are actually colorful sepals. They are mostly borne singly or in lax clusters on long stalks. Most have basal foliage, leaves that are palmately lobed or toothed. Some may be slightly invasive.

Propagation is best by division or root cuttings.

japonica hybrida
'Whirlwind'

Japanese Anemone | lsu-fall 48-60"
Perennial ○ ● | NEW for us in 98
Pristine white | In our GARDEN

Brightens and colonizes late summer woodlands with 4" semi double flowers. Until '98, because of zone suggestions, I had avoided the Japanese hybrids (except for the very hardy A. tomentosa), but Marianne made me fall for this. Seeing this in bloom was worth any risk. We'll update later.

sylvestris

Snowdrop Anemone | spr-esu 8-12"
Perennial ○ ● | NEW for us in 95
White single | In our GARDEN 95

I think only of one garden when visions of this plant emerge in my head--that of Marianne, where it has naturalized its 1.5-2", simple and pretty flowers as promised. Interesting fuzzy fruit follows. To duplicate this picture, one must provide light soil and partial shade. This one, the species, is as pretty as the cultivars.

tomentosa (vitifolia)
'Robustissima'

Hardy Grapeleaf Anemone | lsu-fall LB 36-48"
Perennial ○ ○ ● | NEW for us in 92
Mauve pink, yellow centers | In our GARDEN 97

Because garden books recommended this Chinese native plant for zone 5 or warmer, we guardedly introduced it to S.D. ten years ago. It has proven to be one of our favorite, vigorous, carefree plants, excellent for cutting, a premier choice for late-season flowers. (Goes-to-show, you can't believe everything you read.) Provide rich, well-drained soil. From northern China. Do you believe me?

 74

ANEMONELLA

thalictroides

Rue Anemone   spr-esu LB   8-10"
Perennial   ○ ●   NEW for us in   94
Charming, pure-white, pink tinge   In our GARDEN

Charming, simple, little tuberous woodland plant with small and delicate blooms for a long period in early spring. Foliage turns dormant as summer dryness ensues. Once it is gone, don't forget where it is sleeping. Prefers soil like that of a deciduous woods.

ANGELICA

Where does one begin to describe a plant such as Angelica, that simultaneously imparts inspiration, rapture, and secrets to the universe? One recent summer day a female swallowtail butterfly flitted about, weaving through the large stalks of this plant, occasionally lingering or lighting here, then there, not an uncommon sight in our garden. Then, as I watched, she arched her soft body and the narrow, egg-laying end squeezed out a tiny, glistening, opal ova that I could still see with my naked eye. One at a time, one per lighting, her progeny were gently attached to an umbel stalk about 1/4" from the beginning of the leaf whorl, a food source immediately available when the tiny, tiny larvae would wriggle free a few days hence. I waxed with awe at a wonder that has been occurring for thousands of years, and not until now had I been the chosen one.

archangelica

Angelica   msu   60-72"
Biennial, Short-lived Perennial, Herb   ○ ● ●   NEW for us in   94
Greenish-white, 3-6" umbels   In our GARDEN   94

All parts aromatic, culinary, and ornamental on an erect and imposing form. It gives an all-green architectural effect in the border and a bold cut flower. You can extend longevity of this short-lived biennial or perennial by pruning back before seed formation but then you will miss the beautiful umbels. This is a highly regarded native of Europe where, along roadside fields they towered over our heads. Pre-history reputation as a food and medicinal plant. Tolerates moisture.

atropurpurea

Angelica   72"
Biennial, Short-lived Perennial, Herb   ○ ● ●   NEW for us in   00
                                    In our GARDEN   00

How I love Angelica and, oh goody, another one to plant! A repeat of the dramatic purple stems of A. gigas but produces white umbels instead of red ones.

gigas

Angelica, Dong Quai
Biennial, Short-lived Perennial, Herb ○ ◐ ●
Deep reddish purple

esu-msu 48-60"
NEW for us in 95
In our GARDEN 96

Exciting bold foliage, unique purple baseball sized flower heads carry tiny near-white flowers at great heights, visited by hundreds of tiny bees, wasps and flies of varying species. Ornamental, imposing, tropical appearing leaves and form. Treat as a short-lived, self-sowing biennial that tolerates extra moisture. Remove large seed umbels to extend its life, if you can. Emerges very early in spring. It's easy to observe the female swallowtail butterfly dotting tiny eggs from the end of her body onto parts of this plant. Soon after we always find the bright yellow and black larvae lunching voraciously as their bodies rapidly increase in size. Recently immigrated from Korea.

ANTENNARIA

dioica

Pussy Toes
Perennial, Containers ○
Light green, pink tips

esu-msu 2-8"
NEW for us in 94
In our GARDEN 93

Flowers resembling your kitty's toes appear atop little stalks up to 8" in early season. Silvery ground-hugging rosettes sparkle and brighten the rest of the year. With stoloniferous habit (creeping with spreading roots like grass does), it fills in rapidly. Tolerant of poor soil but must have good drainage such as that provided in rock gardens. Drought tolerant and native to the Black Hills.

ANTHEMIS

Anthemis--desirable, long-blooming, daisy-like plants--work well in perennial borders or as groundcovers in difficult areas. Once beginning to bloom in early summer, they continue most of the warm part of the season if spent flowers are removed. Its cheery and bright flowers are excellent as cut flowers.

Foliage is fragrant, finely cut and silvery. Plants may be short-lived but under good conditions will self-sow. If extended flowering exhausts the plant, which it may, prune severely and new basal growth will develop. Divide every couple of years; it will spread quickly.

Alkaline, well-drained soil is preferred and most are drought tolerant.

tinctoria
'E.C. Buxton'

Marguerite Daisy
Perennial ○
White, gold center

esu-lsu LB 24"
NEW for us in 99
In our GARDEN

They just keep getting better! Opens to a pale yellow that fades to white when fully emerged. Foliage is silvery-blue and contrasts beautifully with the white flowers.

 76

tinctoria
'Kelwayi'

Hardy Golden Marguerite Daisy

Perennial, Groundcover ○ ●

Bright lemon yellow daisies

esu-lsu LB   24-36"
NEW for us in 93
In our GARDEN 94

These are bushy plants with strong stems. Filigree leaves have woolly undersides and are deeply dissected. Prune after flowering for renewed growth and flowers. Plant near blue-flowering Veronica, Platycodon, Jacob's ladder, Russian sage, white coneflower, Solidaster and Agastache 'Blue Fortune'.

tinctoria
'Moonlight'

Hardy Golden Marguerite Daisy

Perennial, Groundcover ○ ●

Pale yellow, yellow centers

esu-lsu LB   24"
NEW for us in 93
In our GARDEN 94

Superb, long-lasting, daisy-like flowers first begin to bloom in late spring or early summer and then throughout the season. Tough foliage, long-lasting cut flowers.

AQUILEGIA

Scores of outstanding, graceful cultivars, in every height and several color contrasts, make up the columbine group. All bloom in spring or early summer; some continue to repeat off and on throughout the season. Their distinct nodding or erect flowers contain five petals, clusters of stamens, and a number of backward thrusting spurs. Sizes and colors of parts vary with the cultivar. Foliage is also lovely, with ferny, compound, bluish-green leaves that resemble those of meadowrue.

They often exhaust themselves with prolific flower production. This hard-work ethic often results in their early demise; thus, they are short-lived. Many will usually self-sow, so there are always new ones coming. Some gardeners prefer that these seedlings not intermingle and cross-pollinate with chosen cultivars.

Provide decent soil that is well drained; sandy soil is recommended. Columbines have a low heat tolerance and are usually listed as shade plants, but they do best with morning sun with shade during hot times of the day.

Yellow streaks in the leaves are often easy to detect, a result of the ever prevalent, pesky insect, the leaf miner.

'Blue Star'

Columbine

Perennial ○ ● ●

Blue, white center

esu-msu   24"
NEW for us in 98
In our GARDEN

Distinct flower has very long spurs.

 77

canadensis
'Corbett'
Wild Gold Columbine

esu-msu   12-24"

Perennial   ○ ◐ ●

NEW for us in   99

Soft butter yellow

In our GARDEN

Loaded with delicate spurred flowers in early season. From Corbett, Maryland, this has a low heat tolerance and grows in sandy soil.

chrysantha
'Yellow Queen'
Golden Columbine

esu-msu LB   30-42"

Perennial   ○ ◐ ●

NEW for us in   97

Golden yellow

In our GARDEN   97

One of best of the tall columbine species. Very long 3" spurs elongate from 2-3" flowers. These have a tall relaxed habit; no staking required if ample moisture is supplied. Reliable vigorous bloom in early summer, repeats with continued modest reblooming the rest of the year if spent flowers are removed.

clematifolia x
Clematis Columbine

esu-msu   30-36"

Perennial   ○ ◐ ●

NEW for us in   95

Mixed pink to lavender pastels

In our GARDEN   95

Starry outward facing columbine are lacking the back thrusting spurs common in most species. We grew these unusual species from seed for our garden and visitors covet their tall elegance while they are blooming. The flowers are like a little Clematis flower.

cultorum x, caerulea
'Music Hybrid Mix'
Rocky Mountain Columbine

esu-msu LB   18"

Perennial   ○ ◐ ●

NEW for us in   95

Mixed pastels

In our GARDEN

Outstanding performers and flowering heavily with intense colors and long spurs in test trials, sometimes into August. They will need adequate moisture to keep blooming. Honors: Penn State Short-Lived Outstanding Perennials.

cultorum x, caerulea
'Songbird, 'Blue Bird'
Columbine

esu-msu   24"

Perennial   ○ ◐ ●

NEW for us in   97

Light blue sepals, white petals

In our GARDEN

One of the members of the outstanding A. 'Songbird' series of columbine. All produce exceptional plants that bloom sturdily and abundantly throughout early summer.

cultorum x, caerulea
'Songbird', 'Cardinal'
Columbine

esu-msu   24-36"

Perennial   ○ ◐ ●

NEW for us in   99

Dark red violet and white

In our GARDEN

 78

cultorum x, caerulea
'Songbird', 'Dove', 'Kristall'
Columbine
Perennial ○ ◑ ●
White with blue nods and bobs
One of best white columbines.

esu-msu 24"
NEW for us in 99
In our GARDEN

flabellata
'Alba'
Japanese Fan Columbine
Perennial ○ ◑ ●
White
Charming dwarf columbine with waxy verdi leaves.

esu-msu 12"
NEW for us in 99
In our GARDEN

flabellata
'Ministar'
Japanese Fan Columbine
Perennial ○ ◑ ●
Blue and white

esu-msu 6-9"
NEW for us in 96
In our GARDEN

Still one of best dwarf, rock garden types. Leaves are thicker and darker, and plants more compact than others in the genus. Spurs end in small, spell-binding hooks. I wonder, "Why?"

hybrida x
'Biedermeier'
Nosegay Columbine
Perennial ○ ◑ ●
Blue and white

esu-msu 12"
NEW for us in 96
In our GARDEN

Called the nosegay columbine because of compactness, heavy flowering and upward facing, spurred flowers. Popular in the marketplace today.

ARABIS

Arabis, rock cresses, are mostly recommended for rock garden situations- -well-drained, sandy soil in very sunny locations; but some can manage more difficult sites. Growing into 1-2' wide mats, 6-9" high, their leaves are hairy and silvery-green. Fragrant, bright, .5-1" flowers form on trailing racemes in spring, soon after the bloom of late tulips. Propagate by stem cuttings, division or seed. Most prefer cool weather; some may "melt-out" and lose foliage and form in the heat of summer.

caucasica
'Compinkie'
Rock or Wall Cress
Perennial ○
Deep rose

spr-esu 4-9"
NEW for us in 96
In our GARDEN

Excellent rock garden plant for sunny sites with woolly and toothed, grey-green foliage. Must have well-drained soil.

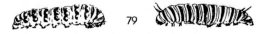

ARISAEMA

sikokianum

Snow Rice Cake Plant, Jack in the Pulpit   spr-esu   24"
Perennial   ○ ●   NEW for us in   00
Purple pulpits   In our GARDEN   00

Collectors will love this beautiful curiosity, one of the newer, unusual Asian introductions of Jack in the Pulpit that has been hardy in this area. Stiff, dark purple "pulpit" surrounds the white ball or "Jack" inside. Foliage is mottled with pewter spots. Slow to mature, but adaptable here and may even self-sow..

triphyllum

Jack In The Pulpit   spr   12-24"
Perennial   ○ ●   NEW for us in   85
Green to purple   In our GARDEN   85

Native woodland plant sparks enthusiasm whenever noticed. Unusual "Jack" (spadix) sits in its "pulpit" (spathe). Children are drawn to this plant--so are we. Large, red clusters of berries form on the spadix and are eaten by wildlife. Will spread if it likes your soils.

ARMERIA

Most of the Armeria species and cultivars are suitable for rock gardens or lining visible edges of the garden. They produce little spheres of bright colors, held on willowy leafless wands above tight little dabs of tufted foliage. The flowers, more abundant in full sun, last well as cut flowers. Seek out some of the newer introductions that bloom for most of the summer. They seem to be able to adapt to heavy clay or sandy soil.

'Joystick Lilac'

Sea Pink, Thrift   msu   15"
Perennial   ○ ◐   NEW for us in   00
Large lilac heads   In our GARDEN

Taller than many Armeria, blooming to over 1' with bright, large heads. The cultivar name is as unforgettable as the plant.

maritima

'Bloodstone'

Sea Pink, Thrift   spr-lsu LB   9"
Perennial, Containers   ○   NEW for us in   98
Intense ruby   In our GARDEN   99

Choice rock garden plant with low evergreen tufts requires sharp drainage. Some of largest flowers of the species bloom for a long time. May even be better than the desirable 'Dusseldorf Pride'. Can be forced as a flowering potted plant.

 80

maritima
'Rubrifolia'

Red Leaved Thrift
Perennial, Containers ○
Dark pink

esu   3-6"
NEW for us in 00
In our GARDEN

For well-drained rock gardens, glossy red-purple foliage makes this unique among Armeria.

maritima
'Splendens', 'Laucheana'

Sea Pink, Thrift
Perennial, Containers ○
Deep, rose red

spr-esu   6"
NEW for us in 95
In our GARDEN

One of best ornamental cultivars, splendid little plant blooms intermittently in late spring or early summer. Best in rock gardens with well-drained soil.

maritima, pseudoarmeria
'Bees Ruby'

Sea Pink, Thrift
Perennial, Containers ○
Intense dark pink

esu   15"
NEW for us in 00
In our GARDEN

Known as one of the best perfoming pseudoarmeria types. Brightest of flowers for three weeks in early summer.

ARTEMISIA

The wormwoods are an all-inclusive genus of perennials and annuals from very tall plants to diminutive rock garden types. Nearly all species are grown primarily for their beautiful foliage--finely dissected, ferny, silvery-gray, often hairy. Did I forget to mention aromatic, therapeutic and herbal? For ornamental quality, the yellow flowers are secondary for most of the species of this genus. They make excellent xeriscaping specimens because of their drought tolerance.

Of course, there has to be an exception to these broad descriptions. With opposite requirements and appearance, sometimes referred to as the "oddball Artemisia," A. lactiflora is not drought-tolerant, but prefers a moist, well-drained site in partial shade, not full sun. It is a fine perennial noted mainly for its magnificent flowering plumes that contrast richly with deep green, not silver, foliage. Beautiful and abundant small flowers come in late summer with a foamy, atmospheric presence and are excellent for cuts.

These North American native plants are also called mugwort. Some are used in Native American smudging ceremonies for healing, divining and stimulating dreams and visions.

True French tarragon is also an Artemisia.

absinthium x
'Huntington'

Absinthe, Wormwood   **48"**
Perennial, Containers   ○   NEW for us in 99
Foliage effect, yellow flowers   In our GARDEN 99

Fine, very silver, cutleaf texture that is different from A. 'Powis Castle'. Also good in containers.

absinthium x arborescens
'Powis Castle'

Absinthe, Wormwood   msu   **30"**
Perennial, Containers   ◯   NEW for us in 96
Insignificant yellow, foliage effect   In our GARDEN

Outstanding bushy and feathery foliage. Hardiness and beauty combined. One of finest cultivars. Best in the south. For trial in Sioux Falls. Sterile, uniform plants. Drought tolerant. Honors: 1999 Oklahoma Proven Selection.

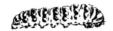 

dracunculus
'Sativa'

True French Tarragon   36"
Perennial, Herb   ○   NEW for us in 85
Foliage effect, minor flowers   In our GARDEN 85

This is the true French tarragon, not the often substituted weak-scented
Russian type. Usually perennial for us, even carrying over well in pots during
most winters. Large plant, use the tender new growth when cooking. True
French tarragon's licorice-like flavor is very popular for cooking with chicken
and fish, flavoring vinegars and sauces such as be'arnaise, tartar and
hollandaise, as an essential ingredient in the blend, fines herbes, and added to
Herbes de Provence. Try it with tomatoes and other vegetables, soups and
eggs. Infusions or tinctures provide a general tonic; it is high in iodine and
vitamins A and C.

lactiflora

White Mugwort   lsu-fall LB   48-60"
Perennial   ○ ◑ ●   NEW for us in 93
Creamy white, fragrant   In our GARDEN

This little known, outstanding favorite to brighten shady places, is the
opposite one among Artemisia. It has fragrant flowers, dark-green foliage, and
different culture requirements. Provide it with a little extra moisture. In late
summer, foamy flowers site well behind Hydrangea 'Annabelle'.

lactiflora
'Guizho'

White Mugwort   lsu-fall LB   48"
Perennial   ○ ◑ ●   NEW for us in 96
Creamy white, fragrant   In our GARDEN 97

We loved this unusual species anyway, and then along comes this refined
cultivar from England, enhancing all attributes. Fragrant, late bloomer for
shade and a little more moisture. Myriads of small flowers contrast beautifully
with black-green foliage. Form is open and sparse and does not get as bushy
as the species.

ludoviciana
'Silver King'

White Sage, Wormwood   msu   48"
Perennial   ○   NEW for us in 98
Foliage effect, some yellow flowers   In our GARDEN

Grown for frosted, deep silver, nearly white foliage with fine, cloud-like
texture. Excellent foliage for fresh or dried cuts. Harvesting too early results in
drooping tips; harvesting at the same time as flowers start to open is the
best time. Another cultivar of the King Ludoviciana artemisia. See other
descriptions with the same species.

ludoviciana
'Valerie Finnis'

White Sage, Wormwood, Mugwort   msu-lsu 24-36"
Herb, Prairie Perennial ○   NEW for us in 95
Foliage effect, some yellow flowers   In our GARDEN

A cultivar of one of the best silver foliaged plants. This species grows from Canada through the Northern Plains down to the Texas coast and Louisiana. (In French "Louisiana" is translated as "Ludoviciana," the origin of the French name, Ludwig (Louis). It must have been he, King Ludvig, who sold the vast French holding, the Ludoviciana Purchase, to the United States. At that time, and for centuries before and after, this native American plant was used by Native American people for spiritual rituals.

ludoviciana or albula
'Silver Queen'

White Sage, Wormwood, Mugwort   msu 24-36"
Perennial, Herb, Containers ○   NEW for us in 85
Whitish yellow   In our GARDEN

Few flowers but, oh, that silver foliage! Leaf margins have jagged edges. Shorter plant than A. 'Silver King'. This is an aggressive plant. Fresh and dried foliage has long had herbal uses.

pontica

Roman Wormwood   msu 12-18"
Perennial, Herb, Containers ○   NEW for us in 90
Yellow   In our GARDEN 85

Eventually spreads into a dense cover of silver, upright feathery stems and leaves. Though this colonizing trait is manageable, it's best to site with long-term plan in mind.

schmidtiana
'Silver Mound', 'Nana'

Silvermound Artemisia, Wormwood, Mugwort msu 12-15"
Perennial, Herb, Containers ○   NEW for us in 93
Foliage effect, some yellow flowers   In our GARDEN

Perfectly mounded, cushion-like, silver-soft accent plant for landscapes and gardens. May "melt-out" (collapse and lose its shape and some foliage) in late summer in overly fertile and moist soils. Prune in early summer to force shorter, sturdier bush and keep dry to hold shape. Honors: 20 Top Selling Perennials of '95.

stellerana

Old Woman or Beach Wormwood, Hardy Dusty Miller, msu 6"
Perennial, Herb, Containers ○   NEW for us in 90
Foliage effect, minor flowers   In our GARDEN

Excellent silver foliage for trailing and contrast along the front of the border. Tomentose, scalloped leaves need excellent drainage. Place mulch or gravel under leaves to separate them from heavy, wet soils. Blends beautifully with glossy, dark-red and green leaved sedum selections. See also, A. stellerana 'Silver Brocade'.

stellerana
'Silver Brocade'

Old Woman or Beach Wormwood, Hardy Dusty Miller, Dunesilver   msu   6"
Perennial, Containers   ○   NEW for us in 93
Yellow   In our GARDEN 95

Newest improved cultivar of A. stellerana. Felted leaves trail and grow into mats. Everything looks good with this plant. Allow to grow into lower branches of Rosa 'Champlain' for a perfect combination. First introduced by U of British Columbia. Honors: Canada Ornamental Plant Foundation (COPF) Selection.

ARUNCUS

aethusifolius

Korean Goatsbeard   esu-msu   12"
Perennial   ○ ●   NEW for us in 00
White   In our GARDEN

A true miniature goatsbeard for moist shade, rock garden or front of shady border. Mounds of leaves support plumes on short red stalks that appear like clouds hanging over the dark foliage.

dioicus

Goatsbeard   esu   36-60"
Perennial   ○ ●   NEW for us in 85
Creamy white   In our GARDEN 85

Like a giant white Astilbe, goatsbeard grows in full, moist shade. Enjoy white flowers in June and pretty foliage, shrub-like in stature, the rest of the season. Long-lived in my shade garden for over 15 years, where it receives little supplemental moisture or care but can tolerate wet soils.

dioicus
'Kneiffi'

Goatsbeard   esu   36"
Perennial   ○ ●   NEW for us in 95
Creamy white   In our GARDEN

This provides a tall, finely dissected, delicate form. Foliage is lacy and needle-like. Plants are not bushy like the species. For best effect, plant a few close together. Moist shade and woodland soil provide the best culture.

 85

ASARUM

The woodland gingers spread slowly to make excellent groundcovers in shady locations with humus-rich soil. Though not the true culinary, therapeutic, tropical ginger, a lovely, though faint, ginger-like smell wafts up from the roots when divided or transplanted.

Many are evergreen with enticing, very dark and shiny, leathery, green leaves. Gingers need some special conditions starting with winter shade, snow or leaf cover. Rich, consistently moist soil is a must to keep these plants vigorous, though even then they seem to grow at a snail's pace.

Most reliable for the northern plains is herbaceous A. canadense, Canadian ginger. For us, over the past two decades, it has spread by rhizomes from a meager half-dozen fat but dormant buds, layered just beneath the soil surface in late fall, to a lush broad patch, now purposely limited to a 12' diameter. Modest self-sowing has also been apparent in our garden.

Intriguing brown, barrel-shaped flowers are not obvious because they are borne out of sight, on the ground, beneath the glossy, heart-shaped leaves. There they are pollinated by insects, animals and fairies that live under the leaf canopy playing hide and seek among the ginger trunks.

Plant established potted plants carefully in spring, or even better, as we did so many years ago, dormant rhizomes with attached fat buds in late fall. Position them horizontally in loosened good soil, with roots reaching down and buds barely covered. Water well and pray for snow.

canadense

Canadian Ginger	spr-esu	6-9"
Perennial, Groundcover	NEW for us in	80
Hidden little brown jugs	In our GARDEN	97

Observe pairs of leaves as they emerge in spring, first clasped together, then slowly unfurling, a dance in slow motion. Heart-shaped, 6-7" leaves have lovely, delicate green sheen. A couple of hours of direct sun over our ginger patch prompted the idea to interplant true Asiatic lilies with this herbaceous groundcover. The upright lilies present a great vertical form emerging from the carpeting ginger.

europeaum

European Ginger	spr-esu	6-8"
Perennial, Groundcover	NEW for us in	95
Brown purple jugs	In our GARDEN	

Rich, dark-green, glossy evergreen and, yes, hardy ginger. Adaptable if proper culture is provided - humus-rich soil that is slightly damp and well-drained, and loose winter cover to protect from the desiccating winter sun.

 86

ASCLEPIAS

Handsome native plants are often neglected, but butterfly milkweed is getting a lot of attention in these days of renewed interest in nature, gardening, and, in the 90s, bold color!

Both foliage and flowers have great value in the garden. Plants are sturdy with thick blue-green foliage topped with colorful and complex flowers. Flowers normally occur over a long period, up to six weeks. They make good vase cuts, and cutting mature flowers will prompt the plant to continue blooming for a few more weeks. Leave some flowers to set seed inside of crisp and crusty, ornamental seed pods. Memories still linger of blowing seeds free as children and later spraying the pods gold for garish, more-is-better, 70s arrangements.

Some tolerate moist soil, but we've observed them in dry locations. Some are drought-tolerant. Allow plants to dry out well between waterings. Long, carrot-like tubers reach down a foot or more into the soil and will rot if allowed to stand in water-logged soil before late-emerging foliage has a chance to get up and get going. This is one of the last plants to emerge in the spring; be patient.

All attract butterflies, and A. tuberosa is an indispensable link in the life cycle of the Monarch butterfly. The larvae, or caterpillars, eat the leaves, and the adult butterflies feed on the flower pollen and nectar.

Aphids sometimes unite en masse on stems. Clean them off with a sliding and slippery pinch of thumb and forefinger or spray with a hard stream of water.

incarnata

Swamp or Butterfly Milkweed

Prairie Perennial ○

Dusty pink

NEW for us in 97

In our GARDEN

One of best milkweeds for the garden. The incarnata species will tolerate moist soils. Flat clusters of bright pink flowers are slightly fragrant. Unopened flower heads have appearance, texture and taste of cauliflower. In ecology class we gathered them for raw snacks. I have recently read that an occasional taste is not harmful, but eating several may be.

incarnata

'Cinderella'

Swamp Milkweed

Prairie Perennial ○

Abundance of rose pink heads

esu-msu   24-36"

NEW for us in 95

In our GARDEN

One of best and easiest milkweeds for the garden with flowers and foliage to attract butterflies and their larvae, and beautiful 3" fluffy white seed pods in fall. Form and texture is bushy and leafy. This is grown as a commercial cut flower in Holland and is noninvasive. Honors: 20 Top Selling Perennials of '95.

 87

incarnata
'Ice Ballet'
Swamp or Butterfly Milkweed | msu-lsu   24-36"
Prairie Perennial   ○ | NEW for us in   95
Bright white with attractive seed pods | In our GARDEN

Long-lasting, up to six weeks, beautiful, waxy, white flowers on this fascinating, new, German adaptation of a prairie plant. Tolerates moist areas. Useful and attractive, one of best milkweeds for the garden. Honors: 20 Top Selling Perennials of '95.

incarnata
'Soulmate'
Swamp Milkweed | esu   36-48"
Prairie Perennial   ○ ● | NEW for us in
Dark rose | In our GARDEN

Some of the best milkweeds for the garden are in this genus, and this is a very new introduction. Butterflies love this too. When cutting stems for cut flowers, abundant milky sap will exude. You can seal cut end with a flame to stop the flow, place in warm water and then refrigerate overnight for longest-lasting flowers. It prefers moist soil.

tuberosa
Butterfly Milkweed, Pleurisy Root | esu-msu   24-36"
Prairie Perennial   ○ | NEW for us in   85
Vibrant orange | In our GARDEN

If you like hot colors, you'll love this showy plant. The leaves are the food source for the Monarch butterfly larvae, vital to its survival, and flowers provide food for mature butterflies. (When birds feed on the Monarch, they experience poisoning and vomit for up to 30 minutes.) Tolerates moist sites but also drought tolerant. Honors: Nebraska Great Plants for the Great Plains selection, 20 Top Selling Perennials of '95.

verticillata
Milkweed | esu-msu   12-18"
Perennial   ○ | NEW for us in
White | In our GARDEN

Most delicate appearing of all milkweeds with long and narrow, needle-like leaves. White flowers have a delicate sweet fragrance. Side branches develop over the summer and keep flowers available for butterfly forages. Fall colored foliage of orange and yellow combine with decorative seed capsules that split open to reveal silvery seeds. Native to eastern and central U.S. Somewhat invasive by underground runners but easily pulled.

 88

ASPARAGUS

officinalis
'Pseudoscaber'

Veil of Lace, Lacy Veil   36-60"
Perennial   ○ ●   NEW for us in 93
Foliage effect, minor flowers   In our GARDEN 95

Winter hardy, feathery foliage and branching. Since '92 it has consistently
wintered over for us in pots under cover, and one large specimen happily
returns year after year in the garden. Grow it woven into bold leaved plants.
Flowers are barely visible and hardly worth mentioning.

ASTER

Hundreds of species and cultivars make up the Aster genus. In
addition to the many worthy natives of New England and New York
Asters, selections and hybrids have been named and introduced since
1890. Heights range from tiny, 6-12" miniatures up to towering 6-7'
giants, providing many design opportunities for their use.

Most love sun and there are some fine, little-known, shade-loving
species as well. They enjoy rich soil and long summer days in the
north. Moisture requirements vary. Many are drought tolerant after
established. Some of the cultivars are susceptible to powdery
mildew; the species are more resistant.

Their primary purpose, blooming, comes forth in needy, late summer
or fall seasons, via a wide range of colors reflected from single and
double, large and tiny, daisy-like flowers.

Pinching back 2-3" of the terminal growth from each stem before
June 15 encourages compact and dense plants. To rejuvenate, divide
every two to four years for they spread rapidly. Avoid root virus
problems with stem cuttings.

Asters provide food for fall-lingering butterflies, and we love them
also as flowers for cutting. We couldn't garden without them.

'Melba'

Michaelmas Daisy   lsu-fall   12-18"
Perennial   ○ ●   NEW for us in 97
Rose pink   In our GARDEN

Fine semi double flower on a compact plant.

cordifolius

Blue Wood Aster   lsu-fall   24-36"
Perennial   ○ ● ●   NEW for us in 98
Pale blue violet, near white   In our GARDEN

These are native to the open woodlands, thus tolerant of light, dry shade.
Dense clouds of small flowers are held on loose, graceful sprays. Heart-shaped
leaves are pretty. Tall plants may need staking. Combine with Hosta, Astilbe,
Cimicifuga and other shade loving plants.

 89

divaricatus, corymbosus

White Wood Aster   lsu-fall   12-30"
Perennial   ○ ◐ ●   NEW for us in 96
White, yellow or red centers   In our GARDEN 94

Handsome in foliage and flower, anticipate glistening clouds of tiny daisy-like flowers on dark purple stems that brighten shady corners from this dry-shade tolerant, North American native. A favorite combination of plantswoman, Gertrude Jekyll, was this placed adjacent to other shade-tolerant, strong foliaged plants such as Bergenia or fall blooming monkshood. Allow to naturalize because it will self-sow. We've grown this since '96 and it has wintered successfully in pots and in the garden.

ericoides
'Blue Star'

Heath Aster   lsu-fall   24-36"
Perennial   ○ ●   NEW for us in 97
Starry blue   In our GARDEN -

Charming pastel blue form of the usually white forms. Dense, bushy plants with tiny leaves support abundant small daisy stars in late summer.

ericoides
'Monte Casino'

Heath Aster   msu-lsu   12-36"
Perennial   ○ ●   NEW for us in 96
Delicate white   In our GARDEN

Tiny, airy and cloud-like, delicate daisies in countless numbers float atop stiff, many branched stems. Carefree and drought tolerant.

ericoides
'White Master', 'Sobar'

Heath Aster   lsu-fall   12-36"
Perennial   ○ ●   NEW for us in 96
Delicate white   In our GARDEN

Tiny, delicate, airy daisies in countless numbers on stiff, many branched stems. Carefree and drought tolerant. One of best heath asters. A patented Bartel Stek plant grown for the cut flower market.

fendleri

Prairie Aster   msu-lsu   4-12"
Prairie Perennial   ○ ●   NEW for us in 95
Lavender blue   In our GARDEN 96

Native, not uncommon, but still choice rock garden Aster of the Northern Plains.

fendleri
'My Antonia'

Prairie Aster   lsu-fall   10-12"
Prairie Perennial   ○ ●   NEW for us in 99
White, yellow centers   In our GARDEN

Glossy dark green, finely dissected foliage and pure white flowers with yellow centers. A namesake of the 1918 novel by Willa Cather, selected near her Nebraska birthplace. Honors: 1999 Great Plants for the Great Plains,

frikartii x
'Wonder of Staffa'

Frikart's Aster | Isu-fall   24-36"
Tender Perennial   ○ ● | NEW for us in   00
Violet-blue, gold disk center | In our GARDEN   X

Five responses to my internet question, "Has anyone had success in zone 4 with A. frikartii?" yielded unanimous "no's". Because of beautiful long bloom, these are always highly rated, but would be treated as an annual in S.D. Even where hardy, they are short lived plants. One recommendation to help over winter: never pull stalks from root or crown; always cut several inches above the soil line.

laevis

Smooth Aster | Isu-fall   48"
Prairie Perennial   ○ ● | NEW for us in   93
Lavender blue | In our GARDEN   00

Yellow centered clear lavender blue flowers seduce in September. Dark blue-green, long, narrow and smooth leaves. Attractive stems are nearly black. As with many of the species, it is disease and insect free and drought-tolerant.

laevis
'Bluebird'

Smooth Aster | Isu-fall   36-48"
Perennial   ○ ● | NEW for us in   99
Violet blue, yellow disks | In our GARDEN

This American introduction forms dense, sturdy, vase-shaped clumps with narrow, slightly shiny leaves. Small long-lasting lavender-blue flowers create lavish September displays. Wonderful in bloom even without the dark stems of other A. laevis cultivars. Drought-tolerant, disease and insect free. No mildew problems.

lateriflorus
'Prince'

Calico Aster | Isu-fall   36"
Perennial, Containers   ○ ● | NEW for us in   96
White, raspberry centered cones | In our GARDEN   97

This is covered solid with half-inch white flowers giving an airy effect in late summer or fall. Flower centers are amass with red stamens, color coordinated with foliage that is a dusky, rich, dark-plum color. Stiff branches are at near right angels to the stem. Excellent contrasts of all plant parts. An English selection of a U.S. native. Drought tolerant and one of our favorites.

laterifolius
'Lady in Black'

Calico Aster | Isu-fall   60-72"
Perennial   ○ ● | NEW for us in   98
Raspberry centered small white | In our GARDEN   99

Dark plum colored foliage like A. 'Prince', but stretches to a sturdy 4-6' tall. Unusual raspberry centered, blush-white small flowers are massed together. Many asters prefer full sun but this eastern native tolerates part shade as well. Excellent cut flower.

 91

novae angliae
'Alma Potschke'

New England Aster, Michaelmas Daisy
Perennial ○ ●
Iridescent rose pink, yellow center

lsu-fall LB 36-48"
NEW for us in 94
In our GARDEN 93

Great color breakthrough in unique iridescent pink will stop traffic for six weeks. Pinch in spring and by mid-June for bushier, mildew-resistant plants. Full name is 'Andenken an Alma Potschke', which translated means "in memory of Alma Potschke".

novae angliae
'Hella Lacy'

New England Aster, Michaelmas Daisy
Perennial ○ ●
Deep violet purple, yellow center

lsu-fall LB 36-48"
NEW for us in 95
In our GARDEN 93

Prolific bloomer, nurturing blue shades, large flower.

novae angliae
'Purple Dome'

New England Aster, Michaelmas Daisy
Perennial, Containers ○ ●
Royal purple, gold centers

lsu-fall LB 18"
NEW for us in 94
In our GARDEN 93

A solid purple dome in fall contrasts well with Solidago 'Golden Fleece' and other late blooming flowers. Because it is a naturally compact cultivar it displays well in containers. Mildew resistant and outstanding in the crowd of so many asters.

novae angliae
'Red Star'

New England Aster, Michaelmas Daisy
Perennial ○ ●
Marvelous rosy red

lsu-fall LB 12-15"
NEW for us in 94
In our GARDEN

Another excellent dwarf and an earlier, midseason bloomer that is also mildew resistant.

novae angliae
'Schone Von Dielkton'

New England Aster, Michaelmas Daisy
Perennial ○ ●
Violet

lsu-fall LB 36"
NEW for us in 98
In our GARDEN

Spreads by underground stolons into thick clumps. Always some to share.

novae angliae
'Septemberrubin', 'September Ruby'

New England Aster, Michaelmas Daisy
Perennial ○ ●
Ruby rose, gold eye

msu 24-60"
NEW for us in 00
In our GARDEN

Summer blooming aster can grow very tall in rich soils.

 92

novi belgii (dumosus)
'Alert'
New York Aster, Michaelmas Daisy
Perennial ○ ●
Deep crimson red

msu-lsu LB 12"
NEW for us in 94
In our GARDEN

Desirable compact cultivar with deep-crimson flowers. Well branched plant produces excellent cut flowers and blooms for six weeks.

novi belgii (dumosus)
'Lady in Blue'
New York Aster, Michaelmas Daisy
Perennial ○ ●
Light lavender blue

lsu-fall 12-18"
NEW for us in 01
In our GARDEN

Many semi double flowers on a compact plant.

novi belgii (dumosus)
'Nesthaekchen'
New York Aster, Michaelmas Daisy
Perennial, Containers ○ ●
Rosy pink

lsu-fall 12-15"
NEW for us in 98
In our GARDEN

Dwarf stature of this great, disease free Aster makes it excellent for container culture. It is still new and underutilized. German cultivar, 'Nesthaekchen' translated to English means "the littlest that is hooked or attached to the nest" or, in short, "the baby of the family."

novi belgii (dumosus)
'Patricia Ballard'
New York Aster, Michaelmas Daisy
Perennial ○ ●
Clear pink

lsu-fall 12-15"
NEW for us in 96
In our GARDEN

Dark-green foliage sets off lovely flowers in late summer.

novi belgii (dumosus)
'Professor Anton Kippenberg'
New York Aster, Michaelmas Daisy
Perennial ○ ●
Lavender blue with gold center

lsu-fall LB 12-18"
NEW for us in 95
In our GARDEN

Excellent semi double, dwarf cultivar, popular for many years. Called Michaelmas daisies in the British Isles because flowers emerge around the time of St. Michael's Day, Michael's Mass, Sept. 29.

novi belgii (dumosus)
'Royal Opal'
New York Aster, Michaelmas Daisy
Perennial ○ ●
Soft, gentle blue

lsu-fall 15-18"
NEW for us in 96
In our GARDEN 96

A compact, light-blue, large flowered form softens late season gardens,

 93

novi belgii (dumosus)
'Snow Flurry', 'Prostrata'
New York Aster, Michaelmas Daisy
Perennial ○ ●
Fluffy white, yellow centers

lsu-fall   18"
NEW for us in 99
In our GARDEN

Not fat, just fluffy, on plants of low stature; they glow in early fall.

novi belgii (dumosus)
'Winston Churchhill'
New York Aster, Michaelmas Daisy
Perennial ○ ●
Nearly red

msu-lsu   18"
NEW for us in 96
In our GARDEN 96

Short cultivar and earlier blooming than most. Pinch when 6" tall and again, later, to prolong blooming.

novi belgii (dumosus)
'Wood's Blue'
New York Aster, Michaelmas Daisy
Perennial, Containers ○ ●
Clean medium blue, gold center

lsu-fall   10-12"
NEW for us in 98
In our GARDEN

Excellent new, short vanguard of the Aster genus that suits container culture. Butterflies respond, of course. All 'Wood's' Aster cultivars noted for lack of fungus effects on leaves and branches that are near the ground.

novi belgii (dumosus)
'Wood's Pink'
New York Aster, Michaelmas Daisy
Perennial, Containers ○ ●
Pink, gold center

lsu-fall LB   12-18"
NEW for us in 98
In our GARDEN

Many virtues: Blooms four to six weeks, mildew and pest resistant, compact, born in the U.S.A. Slightly taller than its companion, 'Wood's Purple', but would still work well in containers.

novi belgii (dumosus)
'Wood's Purple'
New York Aster, Michaelmas Daisy
Perennial, Containers ○ ●
Purple, gold center

lsu-fall LB   16"
NEW for us in 97
In our GARDEN

Many virtues: Blooms four to six weeks, mildew and pest resistant, compact, born in the U.S.A, suitable for containers.

oblongifolius
'Raydon's Favorite'
Aster
Prairie Perennial ○ ●
Soft, medium blue

lsu-fall LB   36"
NEW for us in 97
In our GARDEN 95

Aromatic foliage to 3' produces delicate and fine, single, ray flowers in late summer and fall that smother bushy plants in a compelling medium blue. One of best, drought tolerant selections.

 94

sericeus

Silky Aster
Perennial ⭕ ⬤
Purple

Isu-fall   24"
NEW for us in   00
In our GARDEN

Lacy, daisy like flowers in late summer and fall. So named silky aster because of downy hairs that coat the small leaves.

tataricus
'Jin Dai'

Aster
Perennial ⭕ ⬤
Pale lavender clusters

msu-lsu LB   50-60"
NEW for us in   93
In our GARDEN   94

Stately, but shorter, version of Aster tataricus only reaches 4.5 to 5'. Quick colonizer with bold, large leaves that are extra dynamic when emerging in spring. Roots grow together so tightly that no weeds ever compete. Bees and butterflies are attracted to autumn flowers that form in dense rounded clusters. Brought from Jin Dai Park (meaning 'Ages of God') to Longwood Gardens in Pennsylvania and introduced by the USNA.

ASTILBE

It's hard to imagine shady gardens without crisp, bright Astilbe. The genus offers a vast selection of cultivars for our area. Beautiful plumes and elegant cut foliage create combinations that are hard to beat. They provide a broad range of heights and colors in pink, red, lavender and white shades. Feathery flower spikes make excellent cut flowers, lasting over a week in water. When left on the plants, the seed heads persist throughout the winter.

Foliage is also desirable for cutting. Glossy, rich, deeply divided leaves range in color from dark green to those that have distinct bronze and red tints. They can be sited in sun provided they are kept consistently moist. Because of their affinity for water, they can mitigate a poor drainage problem by helping to wick away accumulating water. Though they prefer moist, rich soil, they should have well-drained soil during dormancy.

They are most content if divided every third or fourth year in the spring.

'Elizabeth Bloom'

False Spirea
Perennial ⭕ ⬤ ⚫
Rich pink

esu-msu   24"
NEW for us in
In our GARDEN

Free-flowering patented Astilbe from Blooms of Bressingham in England. Abundant rich pink, feathery spikes over dark-green foliage.

 95

'Maggie Daley'

False Spirea   esu-msu   28"
Perennial   ○ ◐ ●   NEW for us in   97
Purple pink   In our GARDEN

'94 Netherlands addition has distinctive bronze foliage. It is a cross between A. 'Purpurkerze' and A. 'Mars'.

'Perkeo', 'Crispa'

False Spirea   msu-lsu   9-12"
Perennial   ○ ◐ ●   NEW for us in   99
Dark rose   In our GARDEN

Perky, tidy and small Astilbe is very different from most others and would serve well in a rock garden. Unique, rich, dark, crisp, thick foliage emerges tightly curled.

arendsii
'Erica'

False Spirea   esu-msu   36"
Perennial   ○ ◐ ●   NEW for us in   97
Clear pink plumes   In our GARDEN

Bronze, finely divided leaves.

arendsii
'Fanal' ·

False Spirea   esu-msu   18-24"
Perennial   ○ ◐ ●   NEW for us in   94
Intense, garnet red   In our GARDEN

A popular cultivar because of bronze foliage and red spire combination.

arendsii
'Glow', 'Glut'

False Spirea   esu-msu   12-18"
Perennial   ○ ◐ ●   NEW for us in   97
Intense rosy red   In our GARDEN

One of best midsummer blooming cultivars.

arendsii
'Granaat'

False Spirea   esu-msu   24"
Perennial   ○ ◐ ●   NEW for us in   95
Rose red spikes   In our GARDEN

Dark red, purplish foliage contrasts well with red plumes.

arendsii
'Greta Pungel'

False Spirea   esu-msu   36-40"
Perennial   ○ ◐ ●   NEW for us in   00
Pale pink fades white   In our GARDEN

Exceptional plant and combination of parts with distinct and unusual plume-shaped flowers and bronze tinted foliage.

 96

arendsii x
'Bressingham Beauty'

False Spirea
Perennial   ○ ◑ ●
Pure, rich salmon pink

esu-msu   36'
NEW for us in 97
In our GARDEN

Arching plumes and elegant, glossy foliage. A noted Blooms of Bressingham Nursery, English selection.

arendsii x
'Catherine Deneuve'

False Spirea
Perennial   ○ ◑ ●
Fluffy rose pink

esu   24'
NEW for us in 99
In our GARDEN 99

Compact mounds with fluffy plumes. Blooms Nursery calls it one of their stars.

arendsii x
'Cattleya'

False Spirea
Perennial   ○ ◑ ●
Bright pink

msu   36'
NEW for us in 96
In our GARDEN

Graceful showy plumes on tall plant. Excellent cut flowers last over a week in water. Of hundreds of pink selections this is still one of best.

arendsii x
'Red Light', 'Rotlicht'

False Spirea
Perennial   ○ ◑ ●
Intense red

msu   24-36"
NEW for us in 93
In our GARDEN

Intense red, feathery plumes with very shiny foliage. One of best red, medium sized cultivars.

biternata

False Spirea
Perennial   ○ ◑ ●
White

esu   36-60"
NEW for us in 98
In our GARDEN

Very tall and the only native species of eastern North America, just the way nature made it, and rarely seen in gardens. Resembles tall goatsbeard with relaxed spikes of white flowers.

chinensis
'Pumila'

False Spirea
Perennial   ○ ◑ ●
Magenta pink

msu-lsu   12-15"
NEW for us in 85
In our GARDEN 85

One of our favorite bright colored, dwarf selections will act as a moderately spreading groundcover when sited correctly. Tolerates less moisture and therefore more sun than most. Blooms later than many, usually around late July or early August. "Chinensis" means "to spread." Honors: 20 Top Selling Perennials of '95.

chinensis
'Visions'

False Spirea
Perennial ○ ◑ ●
Bright raspberry fluff

msu-lsu   12-15"
NEW for us in 98
In our GARDEN

Bronze foliage sports fragrant, luminescent, fluffy, raspberry plumes. Flowers slightly earlier than A. chinensis 'Pumila' and another excellent chinensis cultivar.

japonica
'Montgomery'

False Spirea
Perennial ○ ◑ ●
Dark salmon red

esu-msu   22"
NEW for us in 97
In our GARDEN

Bronze foliaged plant is nearly as desirable as 'Red Sentinel', and it has a heavy, broad, diamond-shaped flower stalk.

japonica x arendsii
'Deutschland'

False Spirea
Perennial ○ ◑ ●
Best, early, snow white

esu-msu   24"
NEW for us in 95
In our GARDEN 99

Some describe this as the best white, early-blooming Astilbe. Thick flowering panicles have pendant, lateral, branches.

japonica x arendsii
'Red Sentinel', 'Spartan'

False Spirea
Perennial ○ ◑ ●
Deep, brick red, full

esu-msu   24"
NEW for us in 93
In our GARDEN

Possibly the deepest red blooming selection, panicles are full and relaxed appearing. Elegant leaves have a matching bronze cast. Blooms for a long period during midsummer.

simplicifolia
'Hennie Graafland'

False Spirea
Perennial ○ ◑ ●
Delicate, clear pink

msu-lsu   12-18"
NEW for us in 94
In our GARDEN

Some have confided they actually prefer this one to the 1994 Perennial Plant of the Year, A. 'Sprite'. For the best of both, I would combine them together in a group, blending and contrasting their unique foliages and spritzy, angular flower panicles. This one has dark-green foliage with a high gloss. Honors: Holland Award of Merit.

simplicifolia
'Inshriach Pink'

False Spirea
Perennial ○ ◑ ●
Light pink

msu-lsu   10-12"
NEW for us in 99
In our GARDEN 99

Exquisite form that is nearly as good or better than A. Sprite'. Foliage is lacy, deeply cut and bronze colored.

simplicifolia
'Snow Drift'

False Spirea   esu   22"
Perennial   ○ ◐ ●   NEW for us in   97
Clear white   In our GARDEN

Another fine white flowered selection from Blooms of Bressingham in England.

simplicifolia
'Sprite'

False Spirea   msu-lsu   12-18"
Perennial   ○ ◐ ●   NEW for us in   95
Pale, shell pink   In our GARDEN

Bright, spritzy pink spikes on a dwarf, late blooming cultivar has an eye-catching appearance in midsummer. Later on, branching, spent flower stalks are still attractive. Honors: 1994 Perennial Plant of the Year, Penn. State Top 20 Perennial Performers.

ASTRAGALUS

crassicarpus

Milk Vetch, Ground Plum   12"
Prairie Perennial   ○   NEW for us in   99
Rich rosy pink, purple   In our GARDEN

Neat little plum-like pods follow the flowers on the Northern Plains native. Pea flowers indicate nitrogen-fixing plant. Provide well-drained, alkaline soil.

ASTRANTIA

We love Astrantia, prime creator of charming cottage flowers, a lovely genus of only about ten species. Only recently available, hard to find, and rarely grown in the U.S., they have been given prime attention in European gardens for decades. We've scouted out and planted different selections in our garden since 1993 as they've been available. They have proven perfectly adaptable through the last few winters that have varied from the worst recorded (lowest temperatures, highest winds, blankets of ice and snow, deepest frost penetration) to mild beyond our wildest dreams (mild temperatures, little to no snow cover, shallow frost penetration, and the mildest falls and Decembers on record in 1998 and '99).

The long-stalked, 1-1.5" flower heads grow in white, green and varying shades of pink. A center, pincushion-like umbel, packed with tiny flowers, is encompassed by a collar-like bract. It is grown commercially for the florist market because cut flowers will persist for up to two weeks in water. Just imagine how long they last uncut in your garden!

Foliage is also lovely, providing large, leafy, basal clumps, deeply cut and lobed, often toothed.

Four conditions guarantee rapidly spreading clumps and strong performing flower displays: a rich, consistently moist, well-drained site; neutral to alkaline soil; cool night temperatures; and partial shade. We have a shortage of shade in our garden at the nursery, and our earlier plantings of Astrantia are in too much sun. The original small plants have increased well, but the foliage suffers as it begins to dry and looks tattered by midsummer, though the flowers look fresh for several weeks until they begin their downward trend. Keep cutting them, and they keep on coming, blooming all summer.

major

Great Masterwort esu-lsu LB 18-30"
Perennial ○ ● ● NEW for us in 99
Greenish white, red veins In our GARDEN 95

Most common species of this subtle, relaxed and old fashioned elegant. 1.5" heads, long green bracts and pincushion-like flowers for long-lasting cut flowers.

major
'Claret'

Great Masterwort esu-lsu LB 18-30"
Perennial ○ ● NEW for us in 01
Dark red In our GARDEN

Black stems support dark red flowers.

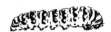 100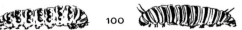

major
'Hadspen Blood'
Masterwort   esu-lsu LB   18"
Perennial   ○ ◐ ●   NEW for us in   00
Red   In our GARDEN

major
'Lars'
Masterwort   esu-lsu LB   18-30"
Perennial   ○ ◐ ●   NEW for us in   97
Greenish white, dark rose   In our GARDEN   97

Distinct, lovely, pincushion-like flowers with obvious bracts, are excellent for cutting, One cannot help but be attracted to all Astrantia and their understated beauty.

major
'Primadonna'
Masterwort   esu-lsu LB   30"
Perennial   ○ ◐ ●   NEW for us in   98
Purple   In our GARDEN

Rare strain, heavy with purple shades, excellent cut flower.

major, carniolica
'Rubra'
Dwarf Red Masterwort   esu-lsu LB   12-18"
Perennial   ○ ◐ ●   NEW for us in   95
Silver, maroon, darkest rose blend   In our GARDEN   94

The smaller species, a delicate cultivar with deeply-lobed leaves and shorter bracts. Understated elegance that establishes slowly.

major hybrida
'Rainbow'
Masterwort   esu-lsu LB   30"
Perennial   ○ ◐ ●   NEW for us in   97
White green, pink to red   In our GARDEN   97

Pretty, graceful flower with a wide color range for the garden or the vase.

major hybrida
'Rose Symphony'
Masterwort   esu-lsu LB   18-24"
Perennial   ○ ◐ ●   NEW for us in   98
Excellent rose pink   In our GARDEN   94

Demure, shy and lovely flowers, but a larger overall plant and--irresistible.

maxima
pink
Masterwort   esu-lsu LB   30"
Perennial   ○ ◐ ●   NEW for us in   99
Palest peach   In our GARDEN

All the best attributes of Astrantia with a hard to describe, unusual color of pink.

ATRIPLEX

hortensis

Self Sowing Annual, Herb, Greens ○
Foliage effect

24-36'
NEW for us in 96
In our GARDEN 96

Tender, edible greens can be ornamental too. Here they're red (red greens!) eaten raw in salads or cooked. Substitute for spinach in salads and other dishes and see if anyone notices. Self sowing annual.

AURINIA (ALYSSUM)

saxatilis

'Compacta'

Basket of Gold, Perennial Alyssum
Perennial, Subshrub ○
Saturated yellow

spr-esu 8-10'
NEW for us in 00
In our GARDEN

The intense color of this golden butterfly magnet is among the first to be seen in the garden, even from great distances. Its complement on the color wheel, rich purple, helps to calm it down a little. Effective in groups in rock gardens or bordering the garden. Prune back if it gets rangy.

saxatilis

'Golden Ball', 'Goldkugel'

Basket of Gold, Perennial Alyssum
Perennial ○
Shimmering yellow

spr-esu 6-8"
NEW for us in 00
In our GARDEN

Short and bright form of perennial alyssum that attracts butterflies.

tortuosum

Basket of Gold, Perennial Alyssum
Perennial ○
Soft yellow

esu 6-8"
NEW for us in 93
In our GARDEN 93

Silvery mats of contorted stems are completely covered with soft yellow flowers, an excellent butterfly plant for the small rock garden. For a small evergreen plant such as this, winter cover is recommended, but we have never covered it. It continues to return but hasn't increased much.

wulfenianum

Perennial Alyssum, Madwort
Perennial ○
Light golden yellow

spr-msu 9"
NEW for us in 98
In our GARDEN

Long lived prostrate clumps of silver leaves noted for rock gardens. Long-lasting flowers and reblooming attributes keep butterflies coming.

BAPTISIA

Baptisia is a genus of great-looking native plants that grow slowly into sturdy, substantial clumps. Root masses eventually become so enlarged and woody that they defy division using anything short of a small tree spade or a chain saw. The prefix "bapt" is like the word "baptise" and means "dip" in Greek. A flower extract of this plant was used in America's early days as a weak substitute for that of the better genus for blue dye, Indigofera.

Blue-green, pea-like foliage is some of the earliest to emerge in the spring. Depending on the species, foliage is soon followed by mostly blue, white or yellow, one inch, pea-like flowers on long terminal branches. Both flowers and resulting dark brown, woody, ornamental seed pods are excellent for cutting.

These plants prefer sun to partial shade, average to dry conditions, and well-drained soil. They will favor low-alkaline soils with a neutral pH and will be drought tolerant when established.

Stored seed does not germinate well. Allow ornamental pods and seeds to dry while still attached to the plant, and then sow this seed while still fresh.

alba x australis
'Purple Smoke'

False Indigo
Perennial   ○   NEW for us in   00
Smoky violet, purple eye   In our GARDEN   00

Gray-green foliage of B. alba and blue flowers of B. australis. Vigorous and quick grower. Mature plants are prolific, producing over 50 stems for cut flowers or fall-collected branches of smoky black, split dried pods. Deep rooted, tough and drought tolerant. Honors: U of Georgia Athens Better Performers.

australis

Wild Blue or False Indigo   esu-msu   36-60"
Perennial   ○   NEW for us in   89
Beautiful indigo blue, charcoal seed pods   In our GARDEN   94

For early flowering, irreplaceable blue and cut or dried specimens, this plant is not to be without. Slowly grows to bold proportions, but so, so easy for the rewards it gives.

australis
var. minor
Wild Blue or False Indigo | esu-msu   18-24"
Perennial   ○ | NEW for us in   95
Great indigo blue, dark seed pods | In our GARDEN   95

One of the loveliest and most compact in this genus. Beautiful blue, pea-like racemes in early season are followed by 2" dark dried pods. Slow to establish; start with large plants.

pendula, alba, lactea (leucantha)
White False Indigo | esu   24-36"
Perennial   ○ ● | NEW for us in   96
White with black stems | In our GARDEN   97

The hard-to-find, beautiful, white-flowered Baptisia. In early season, upright, wide clumps are topped-off with stems of iridescent white, pea-like flowers, a fabulous contrast with dark, purplish, slightly weeping stems. Finally "discovered", drought tolerant, east coast native, with subsequent increased popularity. I've listed all the confusing species that comes up for this plant in hopes they will eventually get sorted out. Honors: U of Georgia Athens Better Performers Selection.

BELAMCANDA, PARDANTHUS

Curious, exotic, red-spotted and splashed petals of warm, mostly bright orange colors are the distinctive mark of the blackberry lily, also known as leopard flower. The loose clusters of compelling flowers on forked stems remain for a brief period. Do not dismay; the flowers keep coming and the seed pods that follow are equally attractive. Later in the summer the pods split apart to reveal shiny black seeds arranged in neat order. Both flower and seed are excellent as cut specimens. The seed pod will dry for winter arrangements.

Sword-like leaves and tuberous roots resemble those of Gladioli or Iris.

Cultural requirements include Bach and sunshine, Monet and well-drained soil. Drought is tolerated once established. Presently, winter mulching is still recommended for this genus in our northern region, but after growing it for a few years, we may prove otherwise.

chinensis
Blackberry Lily, Leopard Flower, She Gan | msu-lsu   18-36"
Perennial   ○ | NEW for us in   95
Orange, maroon spotted, dried pods | In our GARDEN   99

Showy, long -asting flowers on wiry, forked stems later reveal fruit capsules that split to expose blackberry-like seed. Dry for winter arrangements. Tuberous rhizome is used in Chinese medicine as an antiviral and antifungal agent.

flava or flabellata
'Hello Yellow'
Blackberry Lily, Leopard Flower

msu-lsu   18"

Perennial   ○

NEW for us in   95

Yellow, dried seed pods

In our GARDEN

Outstanding dwarf blackberry lily that grows only to 18". Strappy leaves have a slight twist. One-day, unspotted flowers keep emerging, day after day. Shiny black seeds bulge out when seed pods split open in late summer. Cut and dry for bouquets.

BERGENIA

When "planning first in green" Bergenia is one of the first genera that comes to mind to provide always desirable foliage strength. Their handsome, glossy, thick and succulent leaves grow into large clumps that are not invasive. In flower arrangements, leaves can also provide visual strength or weight. Flowers are attractive, short clusters in pink, red or white that appear with late tulips.

At their best when ample water and some shade is supplied, their growth resembles that of large leafy cabbages, and those paddle-like leaves can reach 18" in length. Some of the finest specimens are those we've planted in local gardens and landscapes where irrigation systems sprinkle them regularly and they never are allowed to dry out. When planted in dry areas, they never really shine.

With ample snow cover, leaves remain evergreen; in open or naked winters, they may winter burn and deteriorate but reemerge in spring. The shiny, red-brown, fall leaf color blends well with other seasonal changes.

Good design uses for Bergenia cultivars are punctuating the front of the border or the ends of stair risers, tucking them into niches, or as a groundcover.

I just found out why the common name is pigsqueak. If you wet a leaf and rub it between your thumb and finger, you will hear a squealing sound. Were you hoping, too, for something a bit more profound?

'Baby Doll'
Saxifrage, Pigsqueak

spr-esu   12-18"

Perennial   ○ ◑ ●

NEW for us in   97

Baby pink deepens to rich pink

In our GARDEN

Smaller leaves and more compact in size that others. May rebloom in fall.

 105

'Winterglut', 'Winter Glow'

Saxifrage, Pigsqueak   spr-esu   12-24"
Perennial   ○ ◑ ●   NEW for us in   98
Rosy pink   In our GARDEN

Ruby winter foliage, an improvement over B. 'Rotblum'. Wonderful foliage adds weight to landscapes.

cordifolia
'Evening Glow', 'Abendglut'

Saxifrage, Pigsqueak   spr-esu   12-18"
Perennial   ○ ◑ ●   NEW for us in   96
Deep magenta   In our GARDEN

Abundant glowing, semi double flowers on multiple stalks.

cordifolia
'Perfect'

Saxifrage, Pigsqueak   spr-esu   12-24"
Perennial   ○ ◑ ●   NEW for us in   95
Lilac red stalks   In our GARDEN   95

The one that has been available for decades, and still a stalwart of the genus.

smithii x (B. newryensis)
'Bressingham White'

Saxifrage, Pigsqueak   spr-esu   12-15"
Perennial   ○ ◑ ●   NEW for us in   96
Clean, snowy white, fade to pink   In our GARDEN

A white blooming cultivar offers a change from so many rosy pink choices.

smithii x newryensis
'Silver Light', 'Silberlicht'

Saxifrage, Pigsqueak   spr-esu   12-18"
Perennial   ○ ◑ ●   NEW for us in   94
White buds change pink   In our GARDEN

Slightly different color scheme with white buds that change to light pink.

BOLTONIA

An eastern U.S. native, Boltonia is an indispensable addition to the late summer and fall garden. An aster-like perennial, it is spectacular in bloom as other plants are retiring their colors.

Flowers appear by the hundreds, three-quarter inch, daisy-like flowers, in white, pink or lavender. One mature plant will provide plenty of cut flowers while sparing enough to keep up the garden show.

The foliage resembles that of asters but has a slight bluish cast. Some cultivars grow quite tall but rarely need staking if grown in full sun.

They can tolerate a wide range of soil types, moist to dry, but probably prefer rich, moist, organic soils. They tolerate heat and humidity well and have few, if any, diseases or pests.

They bloom along with true Asters, Sedum 'Autumn Joy', Helenium, and Rudbeckia.

asteroides
'Pink Beauty'

Thousand Flowered Aster	lsu 36-48"
Perennial ○ ●	NEW for us in 94
Numerous pink daisy like	In our GARDEN 96

This plant provides a good way to introduce many late pink flowers, but it cannot compete with the performance of B. 'Snowbank'.

asteroides
'Snowbank'

Thousand Flowered Aster	lsu-fall 48-60"
Perennial ○ ●	NEW for us in 94
Abundance of glowing white	In our GARDEN 96

The name 'Snowbank' suits this plant well. Always on our most desirable, drought tolerant list. Produces hundreds, no, probably thousands of white flowers on a single plant in late season.

asteroides var. latisquama
'Nana'

Violet Boltonia, False Starwort	msu-lsu 18-24"
Perennial ○ ●	NEW for us in 94
Rosy lilac	In our GARDEN

A shorter form of Boltonia. (May be B. excisa). Abundant, billowing clouds of 1" flowers. Disease-free foliage.

BRUNNERA, ANCHUSA

For moisture retentive soil, Brunnera or Anchusa is indispensable for the lover of blue flowers. Believe the common name; once you see the flowers, you will never forget them!

Coarse, pebbly foliage is quickly forgotten when bright-blue to purplish-blue, funnel-shaped, forget-me-not flowers appear in early summer and periodically through fall for most cultivars. Plant them in full sun for quick maturation. Shear away spent flowers after each wave of bloom, then feed lightly, and water for repeat flowering. Bring indoors as cut flowers, too.

Many are biennials or short-lived perennials. The species will self-sow, but the cultivars must be propagated by root cuttings.

azurea
'Dropmore'

Forget Me Not	esu, rpts	36-48"
Perennial ○ ●	NEW for us in	90
Bright blue clusters	In our GARDEN	

Deep-blue flowers in demand and available since 1905. Sturdy, hairy leaves.

azurea
'Loddon Royalist'

Forget Me Not	esu-msu	24-36"
Perennial ○ ●	NEW for us in	94
Intense indigo blue	In our GARDEN	

Summer gardens are irresistible with the touch of intense and lovely, indigo blue that massed Anchusa provides. Branched stems bear myriads of brilliant forget-me-not-like flowers and coarse, sand papery leaves. Stake for support. Short-lived but will self-sow when happy.

capensis, azurea
'Blue Angel', 'Blue Bird'

Forget Me Not, Italian		8-10"
Perennial ○ ●	NEW for us in	95
Blue, white centers	In our GARDEN	

A shorter, more compact cultivar.

macrophylla
'Langtrees'

Forget Me Not, Alkanet		16"
Perennial ○ ●	NEW for us in	01
Unforgettable blue	In our GARDEN	

Silver leaf spots on the edges of dark green, pebbly, heart-shaped leaves. While most Brunnera require some consistent soil moisture, this one can get by with a little less.

 108

macrophylla, myosotidiflora
blue

Forget Me Not, Italian	esu	15"
Perennial ○ ●	NEW for us in	96
Light blue	In our GARDEN	96

Large, heart-shaped leaves support and surround clusters of small blue flowers. Peer deep into their centers and you'll never forget them. Requires evenly moist soils, and best in partial shade.

BUDDLEIA

Butterfly bushes must be treated as sub-shrubs in South Dakota, whereby woody stems die to the ground, and roots may remain viable when well-mulched for winter. We could treat them as perennials since they bloom on new wood. Here I would provide moist, well-drained soil to keep them healthy and vigorous and better equipped to survive winter rot. In southern climes, where reliably hardy, they can be treated as drought tolerant.

Large six to ten inch spikes hold thousands of tiny flowers with distinct stamens, which bloom continuously, attract hosts of butterflies, and are excellent for cutting. Remove spent flowers to keep plants blooming. There are many cultivars, some more exceptional than others. For best butterfly magnets, choose those that produce large quantities of nectar in dark red, pink or lavender pink colors. Cut back last year's growth in spring above emerging buds that may seem to take forever to appear. Inexperienced gardeners may want to classify these as "for-trial" plants. Siting, soil conditions, care and mulching will determine their adaptability. Michael Dirr, author of "The Woody Plants Manual," has evaluated many, and I've noted some of the ones he has praised.

davidii
'Black Knight'

Butterfly Bush	msu-lsu	36-60"
Perennial, Sub-shrub ○ ◐	NEW for us in	99
Deep violet to dark purple	In our GARDEN	

Vigorous deciduous cultivar that might be slightly hardier than others. 6-8" fragrant flower panicles, drought tolerant, and loved by butterflies. Height recommendation not valid in S.D. because it will freeze back to soil level each year. Winter mulch recommended. Introduced in 1959 and recommended by Dirr.

davidii
'Lochinch'
Butterfly Bush
Perennial, Sub-shrub ○ ●
Blue lavender, large orange eye

esu-lsu LB   36-60"
NEW for us in   96
In our GARDEN

Vigorous, large, sweet scented flowers, silvery foliage, 12" panicles, 8-10" leaves. Recommended by Dirr. Honors: Royal Horticulture Society Award of Merit.

davidii
'Nanho Blue'
Butterfly Bush
Perennial, Sub-shrub ○ ●
Mauve-blue

esu-lsu LB   36-60"
NEW for us in   01
In our GARDEN

Small grey-green leaves on compact, drought tolerant plant. Recommended by Dirr. Honors: Ohio Plant Selection Committee.

davidii
'Nanho Purple'
Butterfly Bush
Perennial, Sub-shrub ○ ●
Blue purple

msu-lsu   36-60"
NEW for us in
In our GARDEN

Compact form attracts myriads of butterflies. A drought tolerant, Dirr recommendation; for success, follow Buddleia instructions in summary above. Honors: Ohio Plant Selection.

davidii
'Pink Delight'
Butterfly Bush
Perennial, Sub-shrub ○ ●
Lavender pink

esu-lsu LB   36-60"
NEW for us in   99
In our GARDEN   99

Introduction from Holland, this is recommended by Dirr. One of best colors and nectar producers to attract the most butterflies. 12-15" panicles. Honors: 2001 Mich. Grower's Choice Award.

davidii
'Royal Red'
Butterfly Bush
Perennial, Sub-shrub ○ ●
Rich rose red

esu-lsu LB   36-60"
NEW for us in   00
In our GARDEN

20" fragrant panicles on a strong growing, drought-tolerant plant. Considered best red form, though not a true red. Recommended by Dirr. One of best colors and nectar producers to attract the most butterflies. Honors: Royal Horticulture Society Award of Garden Merit.

 110

CALAMINTHA

grandiflora
'Variegata'

Variegated Calamint, Showy Savory
Herb, Tender ○ ●
Delicate pink

msu   24"
NEW for us in   95
In our GARDEN   96

Delicate, white-splashed, mint-scented leaves are pretty with pink flowers. Provide a little afternoon shade for best variegated white and green foliage color. Contains camphor-like essential oils. According to old traditions, peppermint-flavored leaf infusion teas may ease coughs or are recommended as invigorating tonics for overall health. Fresh leaves have been used as poultices for skin bruises. Drought tolerant.

CALLICARPA

dichotoma

Purple Beautyberry
Perennial, Sub-shrub ○ ●
Glowing lilac purple fruit clusters

fall   36-48"
NEW for us in   99
In our GARDEN   99

A plant with graceful, refined texture. Arching branches reach to touch the ground while holding violet fruit clusters along the stems in late summer. Bloom on new wood from roots that may be able to survive our winter, but still for-trial here. Give best soil and care, and mulch for winter. Predicted to be a hardier serrata type because of Korean Mountains origins, from which it was gathered. Dirr exclaims, "There are few fruiting shrubs that can compete with the beautyberries in October when they are at their fruiting best. When used in mass the effect is spectacular." Honors: 1989 Philadelphia Gold Medal Award.

CALLIRHOE

alcaeoides

Pink Poppy Mallow, Wine Cups
Prairie Perennial ○ ●
Palest pink through medium pink

esu-lsu LB   4"
NEW for us in
In our GARDEN

Native to Great Plains from south to north, Texas to Dakotas.

alcaeoides
'Logan Calhoun'

White Poppy Mallow, Wine Cups
Prairie Perennial ○ ●
Glistening white

esu-lsu LB   6"
NEW for us in   00
In our GARDEN

Another excellent, flat growing, native selection that can spread up to 4'. See the description for Callirhoe involucrata.

111

involucrata

Purple Poppy Mallow, Wine Cups

Prairie Perennial ○ ●

Bright raspberry wine, white eye

esu-lsu LB   6"

NEW for us in   94

In our GARDEN   96

Basal rosettes of deeply lobed foliage yield the brightest-of-little, 1.5" flowers all summer. They can compete and mingle with grasses, using them as props to get higher in the prairie, In the garden they lay flat and trail several feet without rooting. Outstanding for northern gardens, they are drought and clay soil tolerant; use over hot facing walls. Contrasts well with colored foliaged Veronica trehannii, Artemisia stellerana and Nepeta. Still blooming in Perennial Passion's garden in '99's December. Honors: 1999 Rocky Mountain Plant Select Award.

CALYLOPHUS

Calylophus should be promising as a prairie perennial though we've only grown it since 1998. The long-blooming character attributed to it was reason enough to begin salivating over this plant. Add drought tolerance along with a tenacious personality, and I had capitulated. But everybody knows I'm easy when it comes to plants.

Sometimes listed under the genus, Oenothera, Calylophus has finer foliage and woodier stems but similar tissue-paper, yellow flowers.

lavandulifolius hartwegii

Lavender Leaved Primrose

Sub-shrub, Prairie Perennial ○

Large yellow fades to apricot

LB

NEW for us in

In our GARDEN

This is a long blooming sub-shrub of the Great Plains. Yellow flowers contrast with narrow gray-green leaves on what is technically a woody plant that has the ability to bloom on the current season's growth. Provide well-drained soil to promote dry conditions.

serrulatus

'Prairie Lode'

Dwarf Sundrops, Bellflower

Prairie Perennial ○

Bright showy yellow

spr-lsu LB   6-8"

NEW for us in   98

In our GARDEN

All summer long, yellow flowers keep coming on mat forming plants if temperatures don't heat up too much over long periods. Buds first swell like balloons with orange, rib-like streaks. Though related to prairie primrose, these flowers stay open during the daytime. Shear away old foliage in early spring, leaving crowns intact. This competes with tall plants in the prairie, but has better form in the garden.

CAMPANULA

Plant collectors, take note. Many of the 250+ species and cultivars of bellflower are garden worthy. It is impossible to list the broad descriptions and qualities of all in such a small allotted space, but we can at least scratch the surface. Many, many are adaptable to our climate; some are borderline hardy while others are downright tender and are to be used as annuals. These indispensable perennial, biennial and annual flowers provide a delicate or nostalgic, old-fashioned ambiance to the garden.

The genus name, Campanula (cam-PAN-u-la, not camp-a-NEW-la) describes a bell-like flower, which all members have, borne singly, in clusters or on a stalk. Most provide sought-after blue colors, but they may also be white or pink. They include diminutive, rock garden types to five-foot, towering spires. Some may require staking.

If you provide them neutral to alkaline, cool soils, sun or light shade and cool night temperatures under 70 degrees, they will bless you by prospering to old age.

'Mystery'

Bellflower	esu-msu	30-36"
Perennial ○ ●	NEW for us in	99
Pink	In our GARDEN	

Spidery petals on cup-shaped flowers and hairy stems and foliage rise from basal leaf rosettes. Though still "for-trial" here, couldn't leave out this out.

carpartica
'Deep Blue Clips'

Bellflower, Carpathian Harebell	esu-lsu LB	6-9"
Perennial ○ ●	NEW for us in	96
Deep, near perfect blue	In our GARDEN	

Another carpatica introduction to add to the other 'Clips' series, which have always been on our list of top perennials. Try them all, blended together; then tell me if you see any great difference between this and the old 'Blue Clips'. 2" solitary blossoms in large numbers and always in bloom. "Clip" back when first batch of flowers begin to decline; plants recover quickly with fresh new foliage and blossoms. Provide cool, noncompacted soil in full sun or part shade.

carpatica
'Blue Clips'

Bellflower, Carpathian Harebell	esu-lsu LB	6-9"
Perennial ○ ●	NEW for us in	85
Near-perfect sky blue	In our GARDEN	95

Always on our list as one of best long bloomers, maintains little cup-shaped flowers throughout the growing season. Does well in part shade at the front of the border or in rock gardens. Honors: 20 Top Selling Perennials of '95.

 113

carpatica
'White Clips', 'Weisse Clips'
Bellflower, Carpathian Harebell
Perennial ⭕⬤
Pristine white

esu-lsu LB   6-9"
NEW for us in 85
In our GARDEN

Excellent used with C. 'Blue Clips' at front of border or rock gardens. Honors: 20 Top Selling Perennials of '95.

glomerata
'Caroline'
Clustered Bellflower
Perennial ⭕⬤
Starry pink

msu   24-30"
NEW for us in 00
In our GARDEN

Bunches of beautiful star-like flowers in top-most clusters start out pink and fade to light pink or white. Flowers will last two weeks in a vase.

glomerata
'Joan Elliot'
Clustered Bellflower
Perennial ⭕⬤
Violet blue

esu-msu LB   18"
NEW for us in 96
In our GARDEN

Sturdy, short flower stalks of abundant, bright, bell-shaped flowers come from dense, basal foliage and provide excellent cut flowers. This earlier, heavy blooming, showy Campanula, one of best tall bellflowers, grows from vigorous stolons.

lactiflora
'Loddon Anna'
Milky Bellflower
Perennial ⭕⬤
Soft pink

esu-msu   42-48"
NEW for us in 97
In our GARDEN

Large columns of pink bells make wonderful cut flowers. Deadhead to prolong bloom. Desires a continuous supply of moisture with well-drained soil.

lactiflora
'Pritchard's Variety'
Milky Bellflower
Perennial ⭕⬤
Dark blue purple

esu-msu LB   36-48"
NEW for us in 97
In our GARDEN

Long blooming, abundant clusters of hundreds of large bell-shaped flowers grow on tall branching stalks when given extra moisture and well-drained soil.

lactiflora
'White Pouffe'
Milky Bellflower
Perennial ⭕⬤
Pristine white

esu-lsu   12-15"
NEW for us in
In our GARDEN

Hundreds of star-shaped flowers create a mounded white puff on a sturdy, smaller plant for over a month, if you give it extra drinks while in flower. From England's Blooms of Bressingham.

persicifolia
'Chettle Charm'

Peach Leaf or Willow Bellflower   esu-msu   36-48"
Perennial   ○ ●   NEW for us in
White, blue tinge   In our GARDEN

Delicate wiry stalks of bell flowers bloom through most of summer. Excellent cut flower from Dorset, England. Honors: Penn State Impressive Performance, COPF Introduction.

persicifolia
'Telham Beauty'

Peach Leaf or Willow Bellflower   esu-msu LB   36-48"
Perennial   ○ ●   NEW for us in 99
Light china blue   In our GARDEN 99

One of best tall bellflowers. Basal foliage, oblong leaves and tall spikes of large, bell-shaped flowers. An excellent cut flower that tolerates part shade.

persicifolia (latiloba)
blue

Peach Leaf or Willow Bellflower   esu-msu   24-36"
Perennial   ○ ●   NEW for us in 95
Light China blue   In our GARDEN

Bell-like, 1.5", flowers are broad, nearly saucer-shaped, on numerous stalks. This is an excellent garden plant that provides columns of color in the garden or for cut flowers.

portenschlagiana
'Birch Hybrid'

Dalmation Bellflower   esu   6-12"
Perennial   ○ ●   NEW for us in 96
Sea of blue   In our GARDEN

A sea of .5-1", star-shaped, blue flowers over mats of foliage in early season. A popular and choice little rock garden plant or groundcover, not too fussy about cultural requirements, but must have excellent drainage. Grown in gardens for centuries.

portenschlagiana
'Resholt Variety'

Dalmation Bellflower   esu   8"
Perennial   ○ ●   NEW for us in 98
Bright dark blue   In our GARDEN

Little clumps of cheery bells for the rock garden are as blue as any.

rotundifolia
'Olympica'

Bluebells of Scotland   msu-lsu LB   9-12"
Perennial   ○ ●   NEW for us in 97
Bright blue   In our GARDEN

One of first choices of a favorite cultivars of a favorite species. Delicate, ever popular, easy and grown for centuries. Site for good drainage; will grow in sandy soil. Many 1" bells on stalks bloom over long period.

CARYOPTERIS

These sub-shrubs or woody plants, Caryopteris, that bloom on current season's wood, have had mixed success. They will tolerate our winters better if they are mulched. They are worth the extra effort, for by the following year these plants will provide a delicate airy bonus to your fall garden. Hundreds of individual flowers will whorl around each stem, out to the tips. Sometimes the flowers of this plant are confused with the blue of Russian sage, but blue spiraea or bluebeard will be much showier very late in the season and will attract the latest butterflies and bees.

clandonensis
'Worcester Gold'

Bluebeard, Blue Mist Spiraea
Perennial, Sub-Shrub   ○ ●
Great blue

lsu-fall   24-36"
NEW for us in 98
In our GARDEN 99

Yellow-green foliage glows in sun or moonlight. Light blue flowers in late summer contrast beautifully. Loved by gardeners and butterflies. Provide afternoon shade and protection in zone 4. This plant falls under the heading "sub-shrub", also known as a "die-back shrub." It blooms on the current season's new woody growth. Honors: Grower's First Choice Liner Selection.

clanodensis
'Dark Knight'

Bluebeard, Blue Mist Spiraea
Perennial, Sub-Shrub   ○ ●
Powder blue

msu-fall LB   24"
NEW for us in 99
In our GARDEN

Fragrant deciduous sub-shrub, compact and mounding. Long-blooming once it matures by midsummer and begins to bloom on new wood. Abundant cut branches make long-lasting cuts in a vase. Honors: The Grower's First Choice Liner Selection, Cut Flower Association special designation.

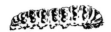 116

CENTAUREA

Out of hundreds, a dozen or more perennial and annual species of cornflower are useful in the garden and attractive to butterflies. Flowers are very pretty, albeit, unusual. The outer petals may be highly frilled and fringed. When papery, outside bracts are present, they may complement with their own frills. Some flowers resemble thistles without the deterring prickles. Flowering seasons vary with the species; some bloom in early season, others in fall.

Strong sunlight and drainage are required by all. They are drought tolerant once established and may be invasive.

If you enjoy Greek writing (like, I'm really up on my Greek literature), you may have read about this plant. A man named Chiron, unlike other wild and uncivilized Centaurs of the day, was a wise and just teacher. Upon being healed by a cornflower plant, now known by the Latin name Centaurea, he changed his life and went on to inspire many Greek heroes, one of whom was Achilles.

The annual Centaurea cyanus is the common bachelor's button.

dealbata
'Rosea'

Persian or Perennial Cornflower, Bachelor Button, Knapweed   esu   18-30"
Perennial   ○   NEW for us in 96
Lavender to rosy pink   In our GARDEN

A bright color for early season, both in the garden and as cut flowers for indoors. 2-3" fringed petals and bracts.

dealbata
'Steenbergii'

Persian Cornflower, Perennial Bachelor Button   esu LB   24-30"
Perennial   ○   NEW for us in 99
Rosy red petals with white centers   In our GARDEN

This and C. rosea are the pink forms of more common, blue perennial bachelor button, C. montana. A compact and long flowering plant.

macrocephala

Perennial Bachelor Button, Globe Centaurea   lsu   36"
Perennial   ○   NEW for us in 95
Lemon yellow   In our GARDEN

Bold, coarse, yet splendid, fall-blooming plant. Thistle-like, 3-4" yellow flowers are uniquely exotic and beautiful. Cut them to last for ten days in a vase, or dry them to last forever. This is an uncommon and late blooming contrast to the blue and pink forms of perennial bachelor button.

 117

montana
blue

Perennial Bachelor Button, Mountain Bluet, Cornflower   esu LB   12-24"
Perennial   ○   NEW for us in   95
Rich blue with reddish center   In our GARDEN   95

Lovely blue, deeply fringed, excellent cut flowers in June while many perennials are still warming-up. Watch for potential invasiveness and site accordingly.

CENTRANTHUS

ruber

Red Valerian, Jupiter's Beard   esu   18-30"
Perennial, Tender   ○   NEW for us in   00
Rosy lavender   In our GARDEN

Flowering first year from seed, one can easily replace this short-lived plant after harsh years that may test it to the max. Provide low fertility, dryness and alkaline conditions--it grows naturally on limestone cliffs. Long-lasting cut flowers and showy seed heads are reason alone to grow this plant.

CEPHALARIA

gigantia, tatarica

Giant Scalehead, Yellow Scabiosa   msu   72-90"
Perennial   ○   NEW for us in   92
Primrose yellow   In our GARDEN   92

Magnificent clumps of dark-green leaves produce tall stalks of scabiosa-like, pincushion flowers, some years reaching eight feet. Well-drained soil and adequate moisture required. Rarely found, we seed-started the plants for our entrance garden in '92. We saved seed one year but failed to bring it to germination. Writing this is a reminder that we should try a new technique, because this is a keeper.

 118

CERASTIUM

Cerastium forms thick, mat-like colonies in rock gardens and areas with good drainage and dry conditions. The fact that this plant will grow in sand is a pretty heavy hint as to its low nutrition and water needs.

Its common name, snow-in-summer, describes it well. With few exceptions, most of them have glowing, silvery, fuzzy foliage that is a cool visual relief in spring and early summer. Like most hairy-leaved plants, it abhors getting wet, and foliage will rot if not kept dry.

Here in late May, starry white, half-inch flowers sparkle against the low-growing foliage.

arvense

Starry Grasswort	esu	6"
Perennial, Groundcover ○	NEW for us in	92
White, starry	In our GARDEN	93

In Perennial Passion's garden, starry white flowers sparkle throughout the month of May along with spring bulbs and quickly cover the ground under early fern peonies. Bright-green, fine and narrow, needle-like foliage the rest of the year. Many inquire of it and we often dig to order. A native C. arvense is listed for S.D., but I've never seen it in the wild and haven't compared it to ours.

tomentosum

Snow In Summer	esu	9-12"
Perennial, Containers ○	NEW for us in	94
Bright white	In our GARDEN	99

Flowers sparkle against downy, silver that foliage spreads broadly.

tomentosum
'Yo-Yo'

Snow In Summer	spr-esu	4"
Perennial, Containers ○	NEW for us in	94
White	In our GARDEN	95

Silvery creeper covered with small white flowers in early season along with late tulips. Foliage will decline or "melt-out" during hot humid months but will reestablish in cooler weather. This cultivar supposedly flowers more freely than does the species, but I've never compared them.

CERATOSTIGMA

plumbaginoides

Leadwort, Plumbago		12-24"
Perennial, Containers ○ ●	NEW for us in	
True blue	In our GARDEN	

Underground rhizomes grow into tall groundcover. Shiny leaves have red undersides and tips, and flowers keep coming all summer. This is always listed for zone four, and I tried growing it just once many years ago but couldn't keep it going. Near-perfect-blue flowers make it worthwhile to grow this plant as an annual in containers.

 119

CHELONE

While peering closely at Chelone blossoms, I agree with its common name, turtlehead. Puffy, firm flowers resemble the shapes of reptilian heads of turtles and are attached to a rigid stalk like snapdragons. Flowers for the garden and for cutting are provided for several weeks in the cool conditions of late summer and fall by these plants. With its uncontrived presence, plants are also effective earlier in the season with shiny, dark-green opposite leaves on sturdy stalks from foliage clumps. When growth first emerges in spring, pinch tips for increased branching and bloom.

Little maintenance is required for these reliable plants, easily naturalized along the shady edges of gardens. Books recommend their use in bog gardens, standing water and acid soil. But I've grown and ignored some of them for years in my old dry-shade garden. One extreme winter set them back considerably, but they have gradually struggled to colonize again.

Among the few species there are few differences. Most are native to North America and are fed upon by late-season butterflies.

'Hot Lips'

Plumbago	lsu-fall	30"
Perennial ○ ●	NEW for us in	98
Rosy pink	In our GARDEN	

Early emerging red stems and bronze foliage turn to dark, lustrous green. Later they contrast with rosy, turtle-head flowers stationed up and down stalks. The late flowers provide food for lingering butterflies.

glabra

Turtlehead, Snakehead	lsu-fall	24-36"
Perennial ○ ●	NEW for us in	94
Lavender purple	In our GARDEN	

Late blooming plant that prefers moist sites and butterflies.

 120

CHRYSANTHEMUM

Cultivation by China and other cultures since at least 500 BC has resulted in many forms, colors and sizes of Chrysanthemum, that are popular ornamentals. Other than the most-recognized species that most people equate with "mums," cushion and other fall-blooming mums, there are at least another 100 more species. Common shasta and painted daisies are in some of these other groups. There are obviously scores more that we could be experimenting with. Any collectors in the crowd?

Most are reliable garden plants, but many of the fall-blooming ones, especially this far north, are not adapted to bloom in a shortened growing season and sometimes do not survive our winters. Others, such as the shastas, may be short-lived in South Dakota. Nearly all prefer sun. Pinch by middle-June for bushier, heavier-blooming plants.

A few years ago Chrysanthemum nomenclature was changed, dividing it further into other genera including Dendranthema, Leucanthemum and Tanacetum. But now, I guess some of these same subgroups are going back into the Chrysanthemum genus. I can't begin to keep them all straight and I have to continually refresh my memory from this list. Maybe this will help in sorting them out:

Dendranthema x grandiflorum - mum, fall-flowering mum, cushion, pompon and button mum, formerly Chrysanthemum x morifolium

Dendranthema zawadskii hybrids - hybrid red chrysanthemum, formerly Chrysanthemum x rubellum

Dendranthema weyrichii - Chrysanthemum weyrichii

Leucanthemum x superbum - shasta daisies, formerly Chrysanthemum x superbum crosses

Nipponanthemum nipponicum - Nippon daisy, formerly Chrysanthemum nipponicum

Tanacetum coccineum - painted daisies, formerly Chrysanthemum coccineum

Tanacetum parthenium - feverfew or matricaria, formerly Chrysanthemum parthenium

Dendranthema _morifolium_
'Dakota Sunburst'
Hardy Mum   18"
Perennial ○ ◉   NEW for us in
Yellow, semi double   In our GARDEN
Very hardy form of Dendranthema that used to be called Chrysanthemum.
These mums are probably some kind of an adaptation of cushion mum.
Cushion mums can be fickle in our climate, so we are trying to find locally
available, hardier types.

Dendranthema _weyrichii_
'Pink Bomb'
Hardy Mum   Isu-fall   6-9"
Perennial ○ ◉   NEW for us in 98
Pink   In our GARDEN
Dark-green, glossy foliage is a summer-long staple while waiting for its
latest-of-flowers. Petals show in very late fall through frosts and snow. Plant
side by side to blend with C. 'White Bomb'. A very hardy plant, this is good in
rock gardens and have seen it combined with grass in sparse lawns for
effective late season display.

Dendranthema _weyrichii_
'White Bomb'
Hardy Mum   Isu-fall   9-12"
Perennial ○ ◉   NEW for us in 92
Clean white, gold center   In our GARDEN
Thick, dark-green, glossy foliage is covered with clean, white, single, daisy-like
flowers very late in season. Use in rock gardens or at the front of perennial
borders. Truly hardy.

Dendranthema _zawadskii (C. x rubellum)_
'Clara Curtis'
Hardy Mum   Isu-fall   24-36"
Perennial ○ ◉   NEW for us in 95
Deep pink with yellow center   In our GARDEN
Hundreds of single, daisy-like, pink blooms on tall bushy plants are a
free-flower-for-all in late season. Native to rugged, stony slopes of Russia and
eastern Europe, this and all D. zawadskii cultivars are valuable South Dakota
garden plants--fine, hardy mums.

Dendranthema _zawadskii (C. x rubellum)_
'Hillside Pink Sheffield'
Hardy Mum   Isu-fall   18-24"
Perennial ○ ◉   NEW for us in 98
Soft peach   In our GARDEN 98
Single peach colored flowers are held on strong clumps of disease-free,
drought-tolerant, dark-green foliage that never appear weedy. Use this for a
supply of lovely cut flowers. Hardy for sure.

 122

Dendranthema zawadskii (C. x rubellum)
'Mary Stoker'

Hardy Mum

lsu-fall   24-36"

Perennial ○ ◐

NEW for us in 95

Straw yellow turning tangerine

In our GARDEN

Hundreds of delicate and frilly, 2-3", straw-yellow flowers bloom in late season on tall bushy plants. Another of the truly hardy and exciting mum-like plants for our northern parts. Try all D. zawadskii plants; you won't be sorry.

Leucanthemum serotina, uliginosum

Hungarian Daisy

esu-msu   48-72"

Perennial ○ ◐

NEW for us in 98

White daisies

In our GARDEN

Flowers on tall and vigorous, drought tolerant plants, open toward the sun. Provide protection in zone 4 until we are sure if it can adapt to our climate.

Leucanthemum vulgare

Oxeye or Meadow Daisy

esu   12-24"

Perennial ○ ◐

NEW for us in 90

White, yellow center

In our GARDEN

Lively, sweet meadow daisy produces single flowers in early summer and naturalizes in sun or partial shade by abundant self-sowing. Drought-tolerant once established, it blooms second, sometimes first, year from seed. Cut them all for vase flowers and let only a few go to seed. This is the common, old fashioned daisy that people notice in early summer. As beginning gardeners, we've all shared this with one another and later, after it became a weedy problem, cursed it--a love-hate relationship.

Leucanthemum vulgare
'May Queen'

Oxeye Daisy

esu-msu LB   24"

Perennial ○ ◐

NEW for us in 98

White, yellow center

In our GARDEN

Now here is a solution to the problem with non-sterile L. vulagare. This sterile variety of the common field daisy will continue to bloom after others have stopped, and will not self-sow.

Leucanthemum x superbum
'Aglaya', 'Aglaia'

Shasta Daisy

esu   24"

Perennial ○ ◐

NEW for us in 98

White glow

In our GARDEN

Strongly lanced petals give frilly, powder-puff effect. Some report this is one of the best shasta; others give it thumbs down. We've tried to stock it for the past few years, and haven't yet grown it ourselves.

Leucanthemum x superbum
'Alaska'

Shasta Daisy   24"
Perennial   ○ ●   NEW for us in
Cheery white   In our GARDEN

This cultivar has been available for many years, standing the test of time. Favorable scrutiny from gardeners reflects its goodness, but we've moved our loyalty to some of the newer ones.

Leucanthemum x superbum
'Becky'

Shasta Daisy   esu-msu LB   36-42"
Perennial   ○ ●   NEW for us in   96
White single, yellow center   In our GARDEN   96

One of best shastas with up to 4", single, long-lasting flowers. Differs from the older cultivars with later and longer bloom period, bushy glossy foliage, and heat/humidity tolerance. After first flowering, trim back to encourage rebloom. Excellent cut flower. Drought-tolerant, tough and reliable in our garden since '96. We've hitched our shasta wagon to this and L. 'Switzerland'.

Leucanthemum x superbum
'Little Princess'

Shasta Daisy   esu-msu   12"
Perennial   ○ ●   NEW for us in   95
Single white, yellow center   In our GARDEN

The dwarf shasta favored by many over 'Snow Lady'. Drought tolerant, compact plant has large, single flowers that are excellent for cutting.

Leucanthemum x superbum
'Silver Princess'

Shasta Daisy   esu-msu LB   12"
Perennial   ○ ●   NEW for us in   99
White, yellow center   In our GARDEN

Another compact shasta daisy that maintains tidy, upright appearance, long flowering and drought tolerant. Comes true from seed and can be used as a bedding plant because it blooms for a long period of time.

Leucanthemum x superbum
'Snow Lady'

Shasta Daisy   esu-msu LB   12"
Perennial   ○ ●   NEW for us in   95
White, yellow centers   In our GARDEN

Compact daisy with large, 2.5", white flowers. Early season blooming and three months thereafter if deadheaded. Compare to L.'Little Princess'. Honors: 1988 All American Selection.

Leucanthemum   x superbum
'Snowcap'
Daisy, Shasta — esu-msu LB — 18"
Perennial ○ ● — NEW for us in 00
White, yellow centers — In our GARDEN

Pure white flowers last for long periods. New and outstanding from Blooms Nursery in England. Drought tolerant. Honors: Penn State Top 20 Perennial Performers.

Leucanthemum   x superbum
'Summer Snowball'
Shasta Daisy — esu-msu — 30"
Perennial ○ ● — NEW for us in 96
3-4", white, double — In our GARDEN 96

Unusual double shasta flower with near tennis ball size for excellent garden and cut flowers. A Blooms of Bressingham Nursery introduction from England.

Leucanthemum   x superbum
'Switzerland'
Shasta Daisy — esu-msu LB — 30"
Perennial ○ ● — NEW for us in 96
Large, single white — In our GARDEN 96

One of best shasta for hardiness and heat tolerance. Excellent cut flowers are large, single, self cleaning, and long blooming, beginning in June. Another Blooms of Bressingham introduction from England. This plant and C. 'Becky' are currently the two full sized shastas we recommend.

Tanacetum   coccineum
'Duro'
Painted Daisy, Pyrethrum — esu — 24-36"
Perennial ○ ● — NEW for us in 97
Bright purple red — In our GARDEN

Early summer flowers, painted daisies are perfect for cutting.

Tanacetum   coccineum
'James Kelway', 'Robinson's Red'
Painted Daisy, Pyrethrum — esu — 30"
Perennial ○ ● — NEW for us in 96
Rich scarlet — In our GARDEN

Single colored, early daisies for those of you who do not like the colors mixed, have ferny foliage and good cut flowers. Deadhead to prolong blooming.

Tanacetum   coccineum
'Robinson's Crimson'
Painted Daisy, Pyrethrum — esu — 36"
Perennial ○ ● — NEW for us in 96
Large, dark red — In our GARDEN

Excellent cut flowers are larger than those of other cultivars.

Tanacetum   <u>corymbosum</u>

Daisy   esu   24"
Perennial   ○ ◑   NEW for us in   97
Snow white, yellow centers   In our GARDEN   97

Ferny foliage and large clusters of small, yellow centered daisies combine cheerfully with the white margined, upright reed grass, Calamagrostis 'Overdam'. They both emerge and mature in early season and look good together for weeks.

Tanacetum   <u>parthenium</u>

Feverfew, Matricaria   esu-msu LB   18"
Perennial   ○ ◑ ●   NEW for us in   90
White   In our GARDEN

A mainstay in my garden for years that self-sows around and is easily shared or weeded from the areas where it is not wanted. Often it flowers the first year from seeding. Small and puffy, double white clusters are perfect as fillers in bouquets. When foliage is brushed, fragrance exudes. In traditional medicine, used for headaches and insect repellent.

Tanacetum   <u>parthenium</u>
<u>Gold</u> <u>Button, Dwarf</u>

Feverfew, Matricaria   esu-lsu LB   18-24"
Herb, Perennial   ○ ◑ ●   NEW for us in   96
Double yellow buttons   In our GARDEN

Sweet gold flowered feverfew that is not as hardy as the white one. Grow it as a short-lived perennial or seasonal annual. Blooms for a long time.

Tanacetum   <u>parthenium</u>
'Snow <u>Ball</u>'

Feverfew, Matricaria   esu-msu   12-24"
Perennial   ○ ◑ ●   NEW for us in   01
White double   In our GARDEN

Double button flowers on fragrant, cut leaf foliage used as headache remedy and insect repellent and for long-lasting cut flowers. Allow self-sown seedings to develop into next year's flowers in case the mother and father plants don't live. Creates sparkle in early summer garden and once you have it established, you'll love the way it pops up in unexpected places. (This may be the same as the species listed above.)

CHRYSOTHAMUS

<u>nauseosus</u>

Rabbit Bush   lsu-fall   12-48"
Shrub, Prairie Perennial, Containers   ○   NEW for us in
Yellow clouds   In our GARDEN

Native shrub to alkaline Northern Plains has billowing clouds of yellow tiny flowers on showy white stems and thin bluish leaves that give a willow-like appearance. Clip as drought tolerant hedge. Wood and bark yield rubber-like substance used by native tribes for chewing gum. Research has been done to determine if this plant could be a viable source of rubber.

 126

CIMICIFUGA

Undoubtedly one of my all-time favorite groups of plants, the Cimicifuga members will never leave my list of top perennials. They are aristocrats in the world of native plants.

One common name, fairy candles, well describes the graceful, wiry and airy, candle-like spires that light up the garden in sun (provide extra moisture in sun) or shade for nearly four weeks. White, plump flower buds line strong, tall, up to 6' stalks and make them appear as if they have been dipped into vats of pearls. Later, tiny petals surround bunches of obvious, fluffy stamens.

Pretty foliage is made up of segmented leaves, creating an Astilbe-like mound to knee height.

Another common name is bugbane, which is translated "cimex" = "bug" and "fugo" = "to drive away," and they do just that. A gardening friend has planted several near her woodland garden because the deer avoid them as well.

Difficult to propagate, some species and cultivars are hard to locate. But once begun, they are easy to grow, carefree, asking for little in return for all the pleasure they give.

The highlight of our fall garden is the well established, intensely fragrant, butterfly magnet, C. atropurpurea, planted near our office door. To die for!

'Hillside Black Beauty'

Fairy Candles, Bugbane	msu-lsu	48-80"
Perennial ○ ●	NEW for us in	98
White pearls upon a stalk	In our GARDEN	98

Fabulous! One of best fall plants in our garden. Pearly buds emerge into bottlebrush stalks. A new and rare, excellent introduction with smoky purple foliage.

acerina

Fairy Candles, Wandflower, Bugbane	lsu-fall	36-48"
Perennial ○ ○ ●	NEW for us in	84
Milky-white pearls	In our GARDEN	84

On this outstanding species from Japan, one of the very last to flower in fall, purple stems grow maple-like leaves that can reach 12" across. Pearly fluffy flowers are borne on branched stalks.

dahurica

Fairy Candles, Wandflower, Bugbane	lsu-fall	36"
Perennial ○ ○ ●	NEW for us in	84
Spikes of milky white pearls	In our GARDEN	84

Wide growing clumps and branched, late flowering stems, this is not a bit less elegant than all the other wonderful species of Cimicifuga. Can you tell I love this genus?

racemosa
Fairy Candles, Snakeroot, Black Cohosh
Perennial ○ ◑ ●
Spikes of milky white pearls

msu   72-90"
NEW for us in 85
In our GARDEN 85

This is the most elegant plant in my home garden where it has grown in both shade and sun--in sun it needs extra moisture. On a 15 year old plant, the divided foliage spreads 3-4' wide at knee height, then shoots up stalks of pearls sometimes over 8' tall. When I first purchased this plant, there was some confusion about its species. Is it C. racemosa or C. ramosa? There is a difference between the two and I'm not sure which one my plant is.

ramosa, simplex
'Atropurpurea'
Fairy Candles, Bugbane
Perennial ○ ◑ ●
Milky white pearls

msu-lsu   72-90"
NEW for us in 94
In our GARDEN 94

With this elegant aristocrat, leaves emerge green, then add purple hues. It is a highlight of our fall season. Sooo fragrant, no wonder butterflies are all over it.

ramosa, simplex
'Brunette'
Fairy Candles, Snakeroot, Black Cohosh
Perennial ○ ◑ ●
Pale rose flowers fade white

lsu   36-48"
NEW for us in 94
In our GARDEN 94

Awesome! I've tried to avoid this word, but it fits perfectly to describe this plant. Very dark purplish stems and foliage remain all season. White pearly flowers have purple origins.

simplex
'White Pearl'
Fairy Candles, Wandflower, Bugbane
Perennial ○ ◑ ●
Spikes of milky white pearls

lsu-fall   36-48"
NEW for us in 95
In our GARDEN

Another late blooming Cimi with 2' long, dense, white spikes.

CLEOME

serrulata
Annual, Self Sowing

3-4'
NEW for us in
In our GARDEN 95

This subtle bee plant has been self sowing in our garden since 1995. It was once weeded away accidentally; I'm glad it was persistant. Visitors are attracted to the long stamens that protrude conspicuously from the platform of small flowered clusters. I've read that this is a good dye plant, and it blooms all summer once begun.

 128

CONSOLIDA

Larkspur   20"
Annual, Self Sowing, Containers ◯   NEW for us in 96
Bright blue spikes   In our GARDEN 96

Self-sowing annual in our garden provide pretty cut flowers. Here's our great tip of the day: Gravel areas provided adjacent to self-sowing plants will warm up earlier and allow quicker germination of fallen seed.

CONVALLARIA

majalis

Lily of the Valley   spr-esu 9"
Perennial, Groundcover ◐ ●   NEW for us in 95
Fragrant white bells on stalk   In our GARDEN

Pretty stems of very fragrant, small white, bell-shaped flowers on short stalks and glossy leaves make an excellent groundcover in shade. Plant pips or rhizomes horizontally, 1" deep in spring. Slow to establish but eventually becomes invasive; separate from tamer plants. About the toxicity of berries and root stock--some say, "Yes," some say, "No."

COREOPSIS

From nature alone we had many garden-worthy, carefree, native tickseeds--bright, cheery and brazen. Now, we can add many cultivars that have been developed here and abroad by humans. Together, over 100 popular species are out there somewhere, easy to grow and long flowering, up to two months if dead-headed. (No, I'm not referring to and do not van around the country following the infamous rock group by the same name.) The genus name Coreopsis means "like a bug" a direct hint as to the shape and color of the seeds.

Two main divisions exist, easily identified by their foliage: the lance-leaf group and the thread-leaf group. Excellent for cutting, most flowers have warm, yellow color values; composite, daisy-like shapes; many height variances; and an affinity for butterflies. Some very nice annuals, genus Calliopsis, exist.

Preferring well-drained soil for both winter and summer and full sun when growing, all are drought tolerant once established.

'Tequila Sunrise'

Variegated Coreopsis   esu-lsu LB 14-16"
Perennial ◯   NEW for us in 00
Golden orange   In our GARDEN

A recent Coreopsis introduction with variegated foliage! Leaves are dark-green with creamy yellow edges and center markings. In spring and fall foliage there are pink highlights. May not be fully hardy for us; treat as a short-lived perennial or annual, and mulch for winter protection until we know for sure. Honors: Penn State Impressive Performance.

grandiflora
'Baby Sun'
Tickseed, Lanceleaf Coreopsis
Perennial ○
Yellow single

msu-fall LB   18-20"
NEW for us in 95
In our GARDEN

Most cultivars of C. grandiflora have been bred from Native American wildflowers. They are long blooming if faded flowers are removed.

grandiflora
'Domino'
Tickseed, Lanceleaf Coreopsis
Perennial ○
Gold with black center

msu-fall LB   15"
NEW for us in 96
In our GARDEN 97

A recently introduced dwarf form is compact and a cheery long bloomer.

grandiflora
'Double Sunburst'
Tickseed, Lanceleaf Coreopsis
Perennial ○
Golden yellow

msu-lsu LB   18-36"
NEW for us in 97
In our GARDEN

Fully double flowers on tall plants are always a perk-me-up!

grandiflora
'Flying Saucers', 'Walcoreop'
Tickseed, Lanceleaf Coreopsis
Perennial ○
Golden yellow

esu-lsu LB   18-24"
NEW for us in 97
In our GARDEN

A superior plant provides large, non-stop, 3" flowers of upright petals, held above dark green, neat, compact mounds throughout summer. Sterile plant produces no seed so plant is tricked into continual blooming while trying to recreate itself. Alas, it must rely on humans to grow it from cuttings. Little to no deadheading is required of us, and we get longer-lasting flowers, excellent in pots or landscape. New and patented from England and so far recommended for zones 5 and warmer. We've not grown it long enough to dispel this zoning supposition, but we are optimistic; many Coreopsis will adapt here.

lancelolata
'Sterntaler'
Tickseed, Lanceleaf Coreopsis
Perennial ○
Gold with brown centers

esu-lsu LB   12-18"
NEW for us in 00
In our GARDEN

Strong, drought tolerant perfomer that will bloom over long periods in summer.

 130

lanceolata
'Sunray'

Tickseed, Lanceleaf Coreopsis   esu-lsu LB   12-18"
Perennial   ○   NEW for us in 94
Golden yellow   In our GARDEN

An especially compact, double yellow form with compact clumps of rich green leaves and excellent for cutting. Deadheading is recommended to keep it in peak bloom. Honors: European Fleuroselect Award.

lanceolata, grandiflora
'Early Sunrise'

                                    msu-fall LB   18-20"
Perennial   ○   NEW for us in 95
Golden yellow   In our GARDEN

This 1989 All American Selection blooms summer-long. Compact plant, with bright yellow, double flowers for cutting.

tripteris

Tickseed   msu-lsu   72-90"
Prairie Perennial   ○   NEW for us in 96
Butter yellow   In our GARDEN 96

A giant of a native plant loved by butterflies and birds with two inch daisy-like flowers from mid to late summer. Self-sows and naturalizes in prairie setting with habit similar to sunflowers. Stands erect and sturdy when dry and flops and needs staking if over-watered, not an uncommon trait for plants that prefer dry soil. This plant is a visual anchor of the south, dry end of our Perennial Passion garden.

verticillata
'Moonbeam'

Tickseed, Threadleaf Coreopsis   msu-fall LB   18-24"
Perennial   ○   NEW for us in 92
Lunar yellow   In our GARDEN 93

No garden complete without this perky plant that blooms from late June to killing frost. Lovely lunar-yellow flowers blend well with every other flower color. Soil must be well-drained in both winter and summer. Very simply put--it will croak (and I'm not talking frogs here) if allowed to stand in winter wet. Even slightest elevation will help. Honors: 1992 Perennial Plant of the Year, Penn State Top 20 Perennial Performers, 20 Top Selling Perennials of '95.

verticillata
'Zagreb'

Tickseed, Threadleaf Coreopsis   msu-fall LB   24"
Perennial   ○   NEW for us in 95
Golden yellow   In our GARDEN

Similar to C. 'Moonbeam' but taller and more of a golden color, this drought tolerant plant is effective in warm color schemes. A long and profuse bloomer, it needs well-drained soils in summer and winter.

131

verticillata, rosea
'Rosea', 'American Dream'
Tickseed, Threadleaf Coreopsis

msu-fall LB   24"

Perennial   ○

NEW for us in   94

Rosy pink

In our GARDEN

Delightful and airy, pink daisy-like flowers on a thread-leaf plant that has a different habit than other Coreopsis relatives. It runs quickly by underground roots and doesn't bloom quite as long as C. 'Moonbeam', for example. Site with care; it can become invasive in good soil, but then set back by our tougher winters. Well-drained soils in summer and winter are necessary. This selection is a darker pink than earlier Dutch supplies. Honors: 1993 Netherlands Plant of the Year.

CORONILLA

varia
'Penngift'
Crownvetch

msu   12-15"

Perennial   ○ ●

NEW for us in   99

Pink

In our GARDEN

This close relative to common alfalfa makes an excellent erosion control for banks or any difficult sites in sun to part shade. As a nitrogen-fixing plant, requires no fertilizer. Soft pink, pea-like flowers billow on fluffy plants. When seeding, use drilling technique to get the seed into the soil. We've long admired this plant put to good use on the steep river bluffs between Mankato and Minneapolis, MN.

CORYDALIS, PSEUDOFUMARIA

Corydalis is a relative of Dicentra, the bleeding hearts, and attractive, ferny foliage is similar but much daintier. Small, delicate flowers with tiny spurs are sprinkled generously throughout the plants, and they seem to be in bloom throughout the season once they begin in early summer. Yellow-flowering C. lutea is the most common; others are slowly appearing in the marketplace. One reads about varying selections of blue-flowering Corydalis advertised in catalogs, and of the few we've tried, one has reliably and abundantly returned.

They prefer cool, semi-shady, woodland conditions with excellent drainage. They perform poorly in nursery containers.

If you provide their needs, they automatically colonize by self-sowing. It is difficult to determine if the original plants return or if it is the volunteer seedlings that are maintaining the colony. I love this gentle, unassuming plant and have had lovely, naturalized stands in shady areas for many years.

x dufu Temple China

False Bleeding Heart	esu-lsu LB	6"
Perennial ○ ●	NEW for us in	97
Mostly sky blue	In our GARDEN	97

The very desirable blue Corydalis that I've mentioned before, blooms like the others for most of the summer, and self-sows from exploding seed bundles. Supposedly it is more cold hardy because of semi tuberous roots, but returns from seed, too. Germination is aided by the fact that we have the plants growing near rocks in the shade where the soil warms up more quickly in the spring. In either case, we've enjoyed it without interruption (except for winter, of course) since '97, when I was first convinced it was worth a try.

lutea

False Bleeding Heart	esu-lsu LB	15"
Perennial ○ ●	NEW for us in	94
Yellow	In our GARDEN	94

Neat, dainty foliage blooms with numerous .75" flowers for most of summer months. Seen naturalized in stone walls and among paving stones in moist shade if soil is well-drained. I was personally amazed to see this plant growing out of north facing castle walls in Scotland. I'm more familiar with it as a common companion to the variegated Solomon seal in my shaded backyard garden, where it has been self-sowing for nearly twenty years.

ochroleuca

False Bleeding Heart	esu-lsu LB	12"
Perennial ○ ●	NEW for us in	94
Creamy white	In our GARDEN	94

We've grown this near the office entrance at Perennial Passion for a few years. It doesn't appear as if the original plants return, because we wait until well into late spring or early summer to see new seedlings emerge from the seed of the former season. I've read that it tolerates slightly more sun than C. lutea. If you like to experiment with shady plants, this and C. lutea are a must.

 133

CRAMBE

Giant, hairy, cabbage-like, two-foot leaves together form large basal mounds from which emerge clouds of small delicate flowers. This plant provides large and dramatic architectural weight and has been described as a blend between baby's breath and rhubarb! Allow it plenty of room to grow.

Full sun and reliably moist, alkaline soils are preferred. Good drainage is also recommended.

cordifolia

Giant Heartleaf Sea Kale	esu-msu	48-72"
Perennial ○	NEW for us in	96
White clouds	In our GARDEN	96

Clouds of tiny, star-shaped, fragrant flowers, excellent for cuts, are held high above 4-6' wide mounds of thick, blue-green, heart-shaped, gigantic leaves, a magnificent early performer in our garden. No staking is required. Winter protection has been recommended but as lazy gardeners we haven't done so.

maritima

Sea Kale	msu-lsu LB	24"
Perennial ○	NEW for us in	96
Clouds of white	In our GARDEN	99

The leathery, silver-blue cabbage-like leaves with purple tints are unforgettably beautiful. Large heads of tiny white flowers provide an effect similar to baby's breath.

CYMBALARIA

muralis

		3-4"
Annual, Self Sowing	NEW for us in	99
White, purple	In our GARDEN	99

Hardy annual, may be a perennial, but usually reseeds. Good modest groundcover in shade to part sun. White and purple flowers resemble snapdragon flowers. Sweet little leaves are rounded and lobed. They grow in low mounds and hummocks and and cover over low surfaces such as risers and stones. Thanks to Tom Rickers for sharing this plant.

 134

DELPHINIUM

Who has ever admired the grand beauty of well-grown Delphinium cultivars and not longed to grow them? Tall, elegant spikes support crowds of flowers, lovely blue, pink or white. Each flower has numerous petals, most of which make up the smaller, center, blade-petals aptly named a "bee." This dark, visually prominent center is packed with stamens and pistils. From behind, thrust spurred sepals. Combine flower parts and shape with a strong vertical, reach-to-the-sky statement and wow--visual ecstasy!

It's easy to comprehend why they are irresistible to gardeners despite problems of mildew, slugs, leaf blights, crown rot when planted too deep, and in general, short lives (about three years in the Northern Plains). It helps that cultivars are easily and inexpensively replaced from fresh seed or vegetative cuttings.

To help offset problems, provide them full sun with well-drained soil, adding lots of food (well-rotted manure or compost), fertilizer and some lime. By the way, you'll need stakes for many. Stems are hollow and will be ruined by wind and rain without some means of support.

There are two prominent groups. The elatum hybrids, 4-8' tall stems of above-described, numerous flowers include familiar Pacific, Mid-Century and Giant Imperial hybrids. The Belladonna hybrids are shorter with more side branches around a central stem of simpler, single, usually-sterile flowers. Staking is seldom necessary for these. Connecticut Yankee Series and the Scotland McGlashan hybrids are examples of many other independent crosses. The 'Compactum' selection is good in rock gardens. All provide beautiful cut flowers. Remove spent flowers for moderate repeat blooming later in season.

Annual larkspur is now placed in the genus, Consolida. It is a faithful self-sower and returns year after year in our garden at Perennial Passion.

Connecticut Yankee Mix

Larkspur, Connecticut Yankee
Perennial ○ ●
Mixed white, blue, purple

msu-lsu LB
NEW for us in 96
In our GARDEN

Smaller, freely branching bushy types. Flowers are borne singly in shades of white, blue, or purple. Charming and long blooming.

Magic Fountains, Dark Blue

Perennial Larkspur
Perennial ○
Dark blue

msu 36"
NEW for us in 98
In our GARDEN

Magic Fountains, Dark Blue, Dark Bee

Perennial Larkspur
Perennial ○
Dark blue, dark bee

msu 36"
NEW for us in 98
In our GARDEN

Fountain strain is genetically smaller than others. Shorter, yes, but stronger stems and bushier clumps require less staking. Heavy feeders and short-lived perennials.

belladonna x (cheilanthum, formosum)
'Bellamosum'

Belladonna Larkspur
Perennial ○
Dark blue

msu 36-48"
NEW for us in 96
In our GARDEN

Dark blue, finer foliage, shrubby type. Rarely need staking.

belladonna x (cheilanthum, formosum)
'Volkerfrieden', 'World Peace'

Belladonna Larkspur
Perennial ○ ●
Light gentian blue

msu 36-48"
NEW for us in 96
In our GARDEN

Light blue, single flowers on well-branched, prolific, strong plant. One of best for cutting.

elatum x cultorum
'Astolat'

Pacific Giant Larkspur
Perennial ○ ●
Lilac raspberry, dark bee

esu-msu 48"
NEW for us in 95
In our GARDEN

Magnificent spires for magnificent cut flowers. May offer more cut flowers in fall if pruned after first flowering is complete. Short-lived Delphinium begin decline after three year or less. Give rich, moist, well-drained soil.

elatum x cultorum
'Black Knight'

Pacific Giant Larkspur
Perennial ○
Deep velvety blue, black bee
Elegant.

msu 36-60"
NEW for us in 94
In our GARDEN

 136

elatum x cultorum
'Blue Jay'
Pacific Giant Larkspur

Perennial ○

Bright blue

msu 36-60"
NEW for us in 98
In our GARDEN

elatum x cultorum
'Guinevere'
Pacific Giant Larkspur

Perennial ○

Pink

msu 36-60"
NEW for us in 97
In our GARDEN

elatum x cultorum
'King Arthur'
Pacific Giant Larkspur

Perennial ○

Dark violet blue, white bee

msu 36-60"
NEW for us in 95
In our GARDEN

grandiflorum
'Blue Mirror'
Perennial Larkspur

Perennial ○ ●

Glowing dark blue

msu 16-24"
NEW for us in 97
In our GARDEN

Remove spent flowers and this will bloom forever. Relaxed habit and longer flowering, yes, but not the majestic spires of the elatum hybrids. This and 'Butterfly Blue Compactum' reliably self-sow if provided some quick warming grit near the plants where the seed can fall and germinate quickly in spring.

grandiflorum
'Butterfly Blue Compactum'
Perennial Larkspur

Perennial ○

Ultramarine blue

esu-lsu LB 9-12"
NEW for us in 95
In our GARDEN 96

The bushy dwarf in the Delphinium world. Blooms over very long period in full sun; a good rock garden plant. Deeply cut, glossy, branched foliage. Heavy feeders. Its self-sowing habit in well-drained soil makes us happy.

New Century or Millenium F2 Series
'Dreaming Spires'
Perennial Larkspur

Perennial ○ ●

Mixed, wide range

msu 48"
NEW for us in 98
In our GARDEN 99

Strong central stems for great cut spikes come from the New Century series. Large flat flowers and resistance to mildew distinguishes these from other hybrids.

DIANTHUS

The perennial, garden-variety Dianthus genus includes many species. Though they demonstrate many differences, they resemble one another in their adaptability to rock or wall gardens or use as edgings in front of taller plants. They grow in flattened mounds, creeping along by underground stems. With many, the tufted foliage has a distinct blue cast that provides desirable foliage contrasts.

Fragrant flowers, often with frilled, fringed petals, are upright on lax stems. Colors include white, pink and red shades with contrasting center eyes. These, like their carnation cousins sold in flower shops, provide a good source for cut flowers.

Necessary for vigor are average to dry, well-drained, neutral to alkaline and loamy soil. They are often drought tolerant. In the north full sun is enjoyed but provide a little shade in hotter climates. Since they are often short-lived, sometimes only three years, divide to reestablish vigor. Some of the non-hardy species sold as annuals will stage curtain calls the following year if winter has been cooperative or they have benefitted from cultural kindness.

The "higher ups" in charge of naming and sorting the plants of this world have not been able to fully organize or control this scandalous genus. As a group they have the ultimate "wandering eye" and continually cross pollinate with one another.

They are easy to grow from seed, but one must propagate the cultivars by division or cuttings.

'Cheyenne'

Pink	spr-esu LB	9-12"
Perennial ○	NEW for us in	96
Double gleaming pink	In our GARDEN	96

Exceptional, large and showy, long-lasting, fragrant flowers reach to 1'. New hardy cowpoke developed at Cheyenne, Wyoming, research station. Blooms late spring and continues intermittently throughout the summer.

'Desmond'

Pink	esu-msu	12"
Perennial ○	NEW for us in	00
Double red	In our GARDEN	

Prolific producer of large rich colored flowers. Silvery evergreen foliage displays them well.

'Hoffman's Red'

Pink	spr-esu LB	12"
Perennial ○	NEW for us in	97
Shocking scarlet red	In our GARDEN	97

A May and June showstopper, brightest red Dianthus. Wonderful lustrous, dark green foliage. Blooms again in fall.

 138

'Mountain Mist'

Cottage Pink
Perennial   ○
Pink

esu-msu   10"
NEW for us in 00
In our GARDEN

Armitage calls this "the great next dianthus". Misty blue-green foliage is excellent but scarcely visible in spring for the flowers that cover it.

'Peppermint Patty'

Pink
Perennial   ○
Luminescent pink

esu, rpts   10"
NEW for us in 99
In our GARDEN

Very blue foliage sporting fragrant, semi double flowers.

'Prairie Pink'

Maiden Rock Pink
Perennial   ○
Bright fushia pink

esu-lsu LB   18"
NEW for us in 95
In our GARDEN 96

A fine tall selection with large, double, long blooming, fragrant flowers. A U of Nebraska introduction.

'Shadow Valley'

Maiden Rock Pink
Perennial   ○
Double red

esu-lsu LB   12"
NEW for us in 96
In our GARDEN 96

Long-lasting flowers and green, rather than usual blue, foliage.

'Telstar Picotee'

Border or Cheddar Pink
Perennial   ○
Red, white edges

esu, rpts LB   12-15"
NEW for us in 99
In our GARDEN

Short-lived plant with frilled and pinked petal edges. Honors: 1989 All American Winner.

allwoodii x
'Frosty Fire'

Allwood or Modern Pink
Perennial   ○
Double, fiery red

spr-esu LB   6"
NEW for us in 96
In our GARDEN

Persistent, fringed, double, fragrant flowers on compact plants and one of most adaptable. Evergreen silvery-blue foliage. Honors: Canadian Ornamental Plant Foundation introduction (COPF).

allwoodii x
'Sweet Wivelsfield'

Allwood or Modern Pink
Perennial   ○
Pastel shades

esu-lsu LB   12"
NEW for us in 94
In our GARDEN 94

Long blooming hybrid with double and single flowers like a perennial sweet william. Shear as initial flowers fade and side branches will come forth.

amurensis

Pink
Perennial ○
Dark and light purple range

esu-lsu LB 12"
NEW for us in 00
In our GARDEN

Recently brought to Nebraska from Mongolia. Foliage is powder blue and supports flowers all summer.

chinensis
'Snowfire'

Maiden Rock Pink
Perennial ○
White fringed, red centers

esu-lsu LB 12-18"
NEW for us in 94
In our GARDEN

Long popular hybrid. Honors: All American Selection.

deltoides
'Arctic Fire'

Maiden Rock Pink
Perennial ○ ●
White with glowing red eye

spr-esu LB 6"
NEW for us in 97
In our GARDEN

Bright and cheery flowers first year from seed.

deltoides
'Brilliant'

Maiden Rock Pink
Perennial ○ ●
Bright crimson pinkn

spr-esu LB 6-9"
NEW for us in 94
In our GARDEN 99

Long-lasting flowers completely cover foliage in spring. Shear after first flowering for second bloom. Excellent groundcover in sun or partial shade.

deltoides
'Zing Rose'

Maiden Rock Pink
Perennial ○ ●
Cerise scarlet

spr-esu LB 6-9"
NEW for us in 94
In our GARDEN

A 6" creeper, outstanding in bloom, reaches over and grabs your attention!

deltoides
'Zing Salmon'

Maiden Rock Pink
Perennial ○ ●
Rich salmon

spr-esu LB 6-9"
NEW for us in 98
In our GARDEN

Compelling color.

gratianopolitanus
'Bath's Pink'

Cheddar Pink
Perennial, Containers ○
Finest soft pink

spr-esu LB 9-12"
NEW for us in 96
In our GARDEN

Fringed, 1", heavy blooming, fragrant, dependable and fine! Silvery, blue-green foliage maintains its attractiveness during high humidity. Rock gardens or front of border. Honors: Kentucky Theodore Klein 1999 Award, Georgia Gold Medal.

 140

gratianopolitanus
'Pretty Dottie'

Cheddar Pink   esu-lsu LB   6"
Perennial   ○   NEW for us in   94
White with maroon highlights   In our GARDEN   94

Long blooming fringed flowers over bluish, grassy foliage. An offspring of D. 'Spotty'. Scented and popular for rock gardens, edgings and over walls. Fleming introductions from Lincoln, Nebraska.

gratianopolitanus
'Tiny Rubies'

Cheddar Pink   spr-esu LB   6"
Perennial   ○   NEW for us in   96
Deep, ruby pink, semi-double   In our GARDEN

Small plants that bear so abundantly it's hard to believe. Covered in semi double blooms in for long periods. Beautiful steel blue foliage. Honors: Best seller in '97.

grationopolitanus
'Fire Witch', 'Feuerhexe'

Cheddar Pink   spr-esu LB   8"
Perennial   ○   NEW for us in   97
Glowing magenta   In our GARDEN

Summer-long flowers in repeat waves, heat tolerant. Mounded habit, with bluish foliage, can be used as groundcover. Can be sheared for neater regeneration of foliage and flower. One of the best of the genus.

grationopolitanus
'Spotti'

Cheddar Pink   esu-lsu LB   6-9"
Perennial, Containers   ○   NEW for us in   94
Glowing rose red, silvery white spots   In our GARDEN

Great little rock garden plant with sweet appeal. Vivid flowers keep coming all summer when spent flowers are removed. Same tufted, blue-green foliage. Fleming brothers introduction from Nebraska.

DICENTRA

The bleeding hearts provide enjoyment with three main species. Flowers are primarily pink or white, but sometimes yellow can be found.

The popular, old-fashioned or common bleeding heart, D. spectabilis, has plump, heart-shaped flowers dangling from graceful arching stems. Inner petals descend from the lower part of the heart's outer petals, hence the notion that it is "bleeding." The name together with the flower has sprung many an emotion. About midsummer, deeply cut and lobed leaves will turn yellow as the plant begins its retreat into dormancy. Unknown to most of us, by keeping this plant well watered with the spent flowers cut off, it will continue to bloom.

The fringed bleeding heart, D. eximia, with several cultivars, is becoming better known and appreciated and offers new attributes. Flowering lasts over a longer period than does D. spectabilis, blooming throughout most of the summer. The flower-form is slightly different from old-fashioned species. Lovely, blue green, lobed and dissected foliage does not go dormant.

D. formosa, Pacific bleeding heart, though more drought tolerant, is anatomically hard to distinguish from D. eximia. Much confusion about parentage surrounds cultivars of D. eximia and formosa.

Cultural requirements for all are simple--well-drained, amended soil that can dry out once in a while, and some shade in hot climates. Once fully emerged and in full growth, the eximia cultivars will tolerate more sun if kept moist, but will rot if allowed to languish dormant in wet soil.

eximia
'Bountiful', 'Zestful'

Fern Leaf or Fringed Bleeding Heart	esu-lsu LB 15"
Perennial ○ ◐ ●	NEW for us in 94
Dark pink	In our GARDEN

Blue-green foliage on summer-long blooming plant.

eximia
'Luxuriant'

Fern Leaf or Fringed Bleeding Heart	esu-lsu LB 12-18"
Perennial ○ ◐ ●	NEW for us in 94
Carmine red	In our GARDEN

Long blooming flowers appear over mounds of finely dissected, blue-green, basal foliage. Blooms heavily in spring and intermittently thereafter.

eximia
'Snowdrift'
Fern Leaf or Fringed Bleeding Heart   12-15"
Perennial   ○ ◑ ●   NEW for us in
Pure white   In our GARDEN
White flowers all summer.

eximia, formosa
'Alba Aurora'
Fern Leaf or Fringed Bleeding Heart   esu-lsu LB   12"
Perennial   ○ ◑ ●   NEW for us in   99
White   In our GARDEN   00
Grey-green foliage is beautiful with pure white flowers all summer.

formosa
'Adrian Bloom'
Pacific Bleeding Heart   esu-lsu LB   18-24"
Perennial   ○ ◑ ●   NEW for us in   94
Ruby pink   In our GARDEN
Long blooming fern leaf type, blue-green foliage.

formosa
'Bacchanal'
Pacific Bleeding Heart   esu-lsu LB   12-18"
Perennial   ○ ◑ ●   NEW for us in   94
Rose red   In our GARDEN
Good for naturalizing, blue-green foliage, ever blooming. Darkest flowers.

formosa
'Boothman's, Stuart Variety'
Pacific Bleeding Heart   esu-lsu LB   15"
Perennial   ○ ◑ ●   NEW for us in
          In our GARDEN
American bleeding heart blooms intermittently throughout the season. Very pretty blue hued leaves repeat the color of Allium senescens 'Glauca'.

formosa
'Langtrees'
Pacific Bleeding Heart   esu-lsu LB   12-18"
Perennial   ○ ◑ ●   NEW for us in   96
Dangling, white pantaloons   In our GARDEN
Arching wands of dangling flowers. Long blooming. Pretty divided and lobed, blue-green foliage.

spectabilis
'Alba'
Old Fashioned Bleeding Heart   spr-esu   24-36"
Perennial   ○ ◑ ●   NEW for us in   94
Lovely white   In our GARDEN
Impressive white form of the old-fashioned pink one that is so well-loved. Foliage is slightly lighter in color.

 143

spectabilis
'Gold Heart'
Old Fashioned Bleeding Heart   spr-esu   18-24"
Perennial   ○ ◐ ●   NEW for us in   00
Deep pink   In our GARDEN

Gold foliaged form of old fashioned bleeding heart matures to lime green by summer.

spectabilis
pink
Old Fashioned Bleeding Heart   spr-esu   24-36"
Perennial   ○ ◐ ●   NEW for us in   95
Rosy pink   In our GARDEN   96

The old-fashioned strings of hearts that we all remember and love! Excellent cut flowers. Foliage fades into dormancy by middle to late summer when spent flowers are not removed and plant allowed to dry. Plan another plant replacement to grow into the vacated area.

DICTAMNUS

Handsome plants, exquisite in many ways, make up the gasplant group. White or pink, 1" blossoms, with long stamens prominently hanging out, bottom petal drooping, occur in marvelous, old-fashioned displays on vertical stalks in early summer. They coincide with late peonies and iris when there may be few other flowers performing. Blooming period is about two weeks, followed by a bonus--interesting starry, but poisonous seedpods.

Foliage is rich, dark-green, and glossy and has season-long appeal. Rub leaves here and there for lemony perfume. Clumps may reach 4', but because of woody stems, support is not usually required. Because they are slow to establish, it is difficult to find mature plants to purchase.

They are undemanding and long lived once established and of easy care. Give them well-drained soil in a sunny or lightly shaded location with average moisture. They prefer cool nights. In fertile soils, dryness may be tolerated.

But don't try to move them; they may carry a grudge to the point of never returning. I know of no one who has tried this, but on a warm evening one may be able to ignite the oils that are produced by the flowers. From thence cometh the name, gasplant.

albus
'Albiflorus'
White Gas Plant   esu-msu   36-48"
Perennial   ○ ◐ ●   NEW for us in   95
Glistening white   In our GARDEN   97

The main, outstanding species. Permanent and long lived when established. After enjoying the beautiful flowers, relish the ornamental seed heads too.

 144

<u>albus</u>
'Rubra' (purpureus) <u>Fraxinella</u>

Pink Gas Plant   esu-msu   36"
Perennial   ○ ◐ ●   NEW for us in 95
Deep rose pink, darker veins   In our GARDEN

Hard-to-find pink form. Same excellent foliage and seed heads. Exquisite but slow to establish but worth the wait.

DIGITALIS

I've valued and respected the foxgloves ever since our son, when an infant, was medicated with the heart regulator, digitalis. And over the years we've tried several of the large, showy types that many gardeners admire and desire, cultivars of D. purpurea, biennials or short-lived perennials. Unfortunately, most of these are difficult to sustain in South Dakota. Lucky for us, there are several other fine, maybe not-quite-as-showy species that are perennials here. We recognize them as worthy and rare garden plants. These still provide upright, visual thrusts that always create movement and excitement, a quick contrast to lateral growing plants and an easy design solution.

Digitalis is interpreted as "finger" in reference to the thimble-like flowers that grow on vertical spikes. Flowers have lobed and hairy petals and lips; the pouting bottom lip hangs lower. Petals are shades of pink and yellow, often effectively and noticeably spotted. Leaves, many hairy or woolly, are easy to identify in large, basal rosettes and also spaced up and down the stalks.

They will put forth their best show in enriched, well-aerated, yet consistently moist soil. Provide some shade in hot climes. Mulch cultivars of D. purpurea and other non-hardies in winter with well-aerated organic material, such as oak leaves. I've noted which species are hardy. Do not eat any parts of these plants for they are poisonous. Deer must know this too, because it is written that they will avoid this plant.

ferruginea gigantea
'Yellow Herald', 'Gerber Herold'

Rusty Foxglove   48-60"
Perennial   ○ ◐ ●   NEW for us in 00
Rusty red tinged gold   In our GARDEN 00

Attractive, sturdy, towering European native, German selected cultivar that is taller than the species. One shouldn't compare the smaller, delicate flowers of the perennial foxgloves to the large showy biennial ones. Bigger is not always better and for us in S.D. the perennial ones are much more reliable and a better investment.

145

grandiflora (ambigua)

Fairy or Finger Foxglove   esu-msu LB   18-24"
Perennial   ○ ◐ ●   NEW for us in   95
Yellow with brown markings   In our GARDEN   96

True perennial foxglove, hairy, 2" thimble flowers hang pendant on spikes. Shiny, 8-10", leaves, obvious veins. Easy, desirable and among most reliable of the genus. Reblooms later in summer in our garden if deadheaded after first flowering in June. Shrubby form rather than upright thrust.

lutea

Fairy or Finger Foxglove   esu-msu   24"
Perennial   ○ ◐ ●   NEW for us in   94
Creamy yellow   In our GARDEN

Charming, old-fashioned smaller perennial. Spikes of pale yellow, nodding, tubular bells, smaller than D. grandiflora. Prefers moist sun and tolerates shade.

mertonensis x

Strawberry Foxglove   msu   24-36"
Perennial   ○ ◐ ●   NEW for us in   94
Raspberry red   In our GARDEN   X

Leaves and spiked stems with large finger flowers appear beefed-up like someone trained on weights. Tetraploid plant has twice the chromosomes as parents. One of most popular perennial foxglove, it is considered hardy but is short-lived, probably because of one biennial parent. Divide every two years. Dirk Diggler eat your heart out! Honors: 1987 U of Georgia Gold Medal Award.

obscura

Willow Foxglove   12-18"
Perennial   ○ ◐ ●   NEW for us in   99
Beige orange, red veins   In our GARDEN   99

Semi shrubby, smooth narrow, willow-like leaves, short spikes, 15". From Spain and northern Africa.

purpurea

Foxglove, Fairy or Finger Flower   esu-msu   24-36"
Perennial, Biennial   ○ ◐ ●   NEW for us in   96
Coppery pink   In our GARDEN   X

Mixed biennial cultivars. Very showy in bloom and everyone wants it. Hard to sustain in S.D. gardens. Give optimal conditions, it will need all the help it can get.

thapsi
'Spanish Peaks'

Foxglove   esu   12"
Perennial   ○ ◐ ●   NEW for us in   99
Raspberry rose   In our GARDEN   99

Another rarely found, true perennial foxglove. Compact and lovely, small, thimble-like flowers held on stalks above furry leaves. Honors: 1999 Rocky Mountain Plant Select.

 146

DIPSACUS

sativus
Fuller's Teasel   30"
Biennial   ○ ◐   NEW for us in 95
Greenish white spine covered heads   In our GARDEN 95

In '95 I wrote about teasel: "Planted under west arbor; awaiting its second season in '96. Keeping our fingers crossed." In spring '98 I wrote: "These teasels have self-sown worse than dandelions. True, their second year they reliably returned and produced showy spiny seed heads, excellent for drying. But don't ever let them go to seed again! We weeded them, it seemed, for hours, and they continued to crop up all summer!" Another successful plant experiment!?

DODECATHEON

meadia
Shooting Star   spr-esu   10-12"
Perennial   ○ ●   NEW for us in 94
White   In our GARDEN

A charming woodland wildflower. Little downward pointed stars on short stalks bloom for a long time in spring while weather remains cool. Plant will eventually fade to dormancy. Don't forget where you've planted them! I grew these successfully many years ago, then neglected them by allowing vinca to overtake them.

meadia
pink
Shooting Star   spr-esu   10-12"
Perennial   ○ ●   NEW for us in
Pink   In our GARDEN

See the description for white shooting star, Dodecatheon meadia.

DUCHESNEA

indica
False Strawberry, Aztec Indian Berry   esu-msu   8"
Perennial   ○   NEW for us in 97
White, red fruit   In our GARDEN

Strawberry leaves with little bright red fruit spread quickly to form a groundcover. Lovely foliage as edger in well-drained soil and rock garden conditions but can be aggressive. Drought tolerant.

 147

ECHINACEAE

Butterflies will flock, swarm or mob your garden when you provide them with any species of coneflower. One of the finest, easy care, showy perennials, they belong in every garden. Easy to love and nurture, all they ask for is heat and sunshine in average to poor soils. Like most upland natives, they adapt to drought, so use them when xeriscaping. As a garden plant they are hard to improve upon. Of course, when a will is determined, a way will be made, and breeders have introduced several cultivars to tempt us more.

Flowers have a composite, daisy-like form. A strong, prominent cone holds stiff, stubble-like, orange bracts, around which attach lax, mahogany-pink or white disk-flowers. The total package can sometimes stretch to six inches in diameter. The angle of rays or petals, as related to the central cone, may be rigidly horizontal or even slightly upturned on some of the recently cultivated selections. Flowers are long-lasting, whether left a-bloomin' in the garden from midsummer to frost or cut and arranged in a vase. The hard central cone dries well for arrangements or potpourri. Foliage is coarse, but acceptable. Fertilizer is not necessary for them to perform well; they may become lanky in rich, wet soils. They increase steadily and self-sow, but never obtrusively.

Plants may grow 3-4' tall in full sun but also do fairly well in partial shade. At home, I was surprised when seeds ventured to cheer up some shady pockets around the yard where they managed quite nicely.

The native species, E. purpurea, has been known for centuries among Native American and other ancient cultures as a valuable therapeutic plant. Used to boost immunity before the advent of sulfur drugs, it has recently made a strong comeback. There are growers in S.D. and elsewhere who cultivate acres of Echinaceae as a root crop for natural medicine demands.

'Kim's Knee High'

Dwarf Purple Coneflower   msu-lsu   18-24"
Perennial   ○ ◐ ●   NEW for us in   00
Bright pink, copper center   In our GARDEN

Bright clear pink flowers have relaxed petals. This patented plant is a dwarf version, only to 24", of the well known taller coneflowers. All of the others are nearly two or more times taller. There have been reports that seed-grown plants of this cultivar vary in height, and some are taller than purported.

pallida, angustifolia

Pale Purple Coneflower   msu-lsu LB   36-60"
Prairie Perennial   ○ ◐   NEW for us in   96
Pale lavender pink   In our GARDEN   97

Dark central cone with extremely long, pale, lax and wispy petals. These attached to long, supple stems remind me of a beautiful sea anemone rising and floating in the prairie air. Long stems provide good cut flowers. This native differs in appearance from most garden coneflowers.

purpurea
'Bravado'

Purple Coneflower   msu-lsu LB   30-36"
Prairie Perennial   ○ ◐   NEW for us in   98
Rosy pink, copper center cone   In our GARDEN

Extra large, wide, 4-5" blossoms. Their ray flowers (most of us still call them petals) are supposed to have strong horizontal position, not the typical relaxed, pendant habit.

purpurea
'Bright Star', 'Leuchstern'

Purple Coneflower   msu-lsu LB   30-36"
Prairie Perennial   ○ ◐   NEW for us in   94
Rosy red with a maroon center   In our GARDEN   97

Intensely colored, free-flowering coneflower. Excellent for cutting, butterflies, long blooming, dried flowers and to treat some of your ills. Variability among individuals because of their origin as seed-grown plants.

purpurea
'Magnus'

Purple Coneflower   msu-lsu LB   30-36"
Prairie Perennial   ○ ◐   NEW for us in   94
Deep rose, copper center   In our GARDEN   98

Petal-like ray flowers grow horizontal and do not droop as much as others. All the wonderful attributes of coneflowers. Stunning massed or when grouped with almost any other summer blooming perennial. Coneflowers never disappoint, and oh, so reliable for South Dakota gardeners! Honors:1998 Perennial Plant of the Year, 1999 Arkansas Select Plant, Penn State Top 20 Perennial Performers, 2002 Oklahoma Proven Plant.

   149

purpurea
'Springbrook Crimson'

Purple Coneflower

Prairie Perennial ○ ●

Bright magenta, copper cone

msu-lsu LB 24"

NEW for us in 99

In our GARDEN 99

Same high centered flower but smaller diameter at 1.5". Rich saturated flower color is nonfading and sets this one apart.

purpurea
'White Swan', 'Cygnet White'

White Coneflower

Prairie Perennial ○ ●

Pure white petals, coppery cone

msu-lsu LB 24"

NEW for us in 94

In our GARDEN 97

We love the green-tinged white coneflowers. Their copper centers glow in contrast. In our experience, the whites are not as long-lived as the purple flowered ones. They may not perpetuate themselves as well by self-sowing. Try winter mulching. Contrast with yellow Asiatic lilies for a great combination.

tennesseensis

Coneflower

Prairie Perennial ○ ●

Rosy pink

esu-fall LB 18-30"

NEW for us in 98

In our GARDEN 98

This time attractive, uplifted petals are a cheerful face. Bloom early 'til frost; some flowers last for six weeks. Best coneflower foliage, clean, neat with slight sheen. On rare and endangered species list, ours are greenhouse grown. First recommended to us as hardy by Nebraska plantsman. We've witnessed survival through two winters and are optimistic, as usual, about future seasons!

lobata

Cucumber Vine

Prairie Plant, Self Sowing Annual Vine ○ ●

Foamy white clusters

msu-lsu 12+'

NEW for us in 96

In our GARDEN 96

Trailing and climbing annual naturalizes by self-sowing. Showy, foamy white flowers have separate sexes; male and female parts are on different flowers, but both sexes will occur on the same vine. The female flowers tend to develop conveniently below clusters of male flowers. The inedible 2" seed pod is a spiny contraption in which develop four large seeds. As the pods dry, the bottom splits open, and out drop the seeds. These must have cold stratification, or they will not germinate. If you gather them from the wild or from our garden (the nearly wild), plant them outdoors in small hills, late in the fall. Water them in, and then, come spring, stand back! For years hence they will continue to self-sow.

ECHINOPS

The common name, globe thistle, well-describes the flowers produced by this plant. Upon first glance the flowers appear to be perfect, 2" spheres. Examining closely (watch out for bees; they love these flowers), an excellent opportunity to use a magnifying glass, one observes hundreds of tiny florets, crowded onto the surface area of the sphere. Most species produce sought-after steely blue flowers, excellent for cutting and drying. To dry, cut when blue has developed but before petals have opened and hang upside down in a warm, dry, dark area.

Leaves are large and elongated, deeply cut, toothed with wavy edges, and, yes, have thistle-like prickles. They are often misidentified as a noxious thistle by the uninformed. Many side-ways glances have been aimed their way. The undersides of the leaves are hairy and light, silvery gray. Plant heights range between 3-6' and can grow nearly as wide, no demure things. Allow plenty of room at the back of the garden.

Echinops are carefree plants. Give them sun, very little moisture (drought-tolerant once established), well-drained soil and leave them alone. They rarely need dividing or staking. Confusion exists regarding identification of differing species.

bannaticus
'Taplow Blue'
Globe Thistle   LB   24-48"
Perennial   ○   NEW for us in   95
Steel blue   In our GARDEN
One of the popular cultivars.

ritro
Globe Thistle   msu   36-48"
Perennial   ○   NEW for us in   95
Steely blue   In our GARDEN   96
One of the best of blue flowers. The foliage is large and prickly. Honors: 2000 Dried Cut Flower of the Year.

ritro
'Veitch's Blue'
Globe Thistle   LB   24-48"
Perennial   ○   NEW for us in
Darker steel blue   In our GARDEN
Richer blue, European favorite.

sphaerocephalus
'Arctic Glow'

Globe Thistle

Perennial ○

Silvery white

msu   30"

NEW for us in

In our GARDEN

Stronger grower and larger flowers than other globe thistles. This time, white flowers contrast well with silvery foliage and dark stems. Compact and upright, no staking required.

EPIMEDIUM

The common name, barrenwort, belies the aristocratic quality of the Epimedium. Though grown mainly as shrubby groundcovers with emphasis on handsome foliage, the flowers are intriguing. They dangle delicately from wiry stems, sometimes camouflaged by the pretty leaves. Resembling little bishops' hats, some have backward thrusting spurs.

Leaf color may emerge in spring with pink and red tinges; in fall they turn yellow or, again, red. Though lovely clumps are slow to develop, they do eventually thicken. To hasten their proliferation, provide them ideal conditions--partial shade and rich amended soil that is consistently moist. Sun is tolerated, provided there is top-notch soil conditions. Once established, they live for many years.

Success with these plants in South Dakota varies from gardener to gardener and species to species. All are adaptable to either zone 5 or 4. Select those with best chances of success. Try E. alpinum 'Rubrum', grandiflorum, pinnatum, x rubrum, and x youngianum. Protect young plants from rabbits.

alpinum
'Rubrum'

Alpine Barrenwort

Perennial, Groundcover ◐ ●

Rich, ruby red, white spurs

spr-esu   15-18"

NEW for us in 94

In our GARDEN

One of most elegant groundcovers when successfully grown. Fickle about its placement. This species is one to try in Northern Plains. Foliage starts out bronze then turns green.

cantabrigiense x

Barrenwort

Perennial, Groundcover ◐ ●

Red orange

15-18"

NEW for us in

In our GARDEN

Another to try in Northern Plains. Beautiful leaves are bronze in spring, later to green and again red in fall. Provides a nice aristocratic shady gound cover under rhododendrons or other shade-tolerant shrubbery where soil conditions are adequate.

 152

EQUISETUM

hyemale

Horsetail, Scouring Rush   36"
Prairie Perennial, Water   **O**   NEW for us in 96
Foliage effect   In our GARDEN

Native, ancient plant with long, hollow serpentine tubes, no leaves, that adds curious elegance to dried arrangements. Plant only in isolated or native sites, or shallow contained water garden. Works well as erosion control. ACHTUNG! You'll want to tear this and your hair out if this ever gets into your garden.

scirpoides

Horsetail, Dwarf Scouring Rush   48-72"
Perennial, Water   O **O**   NEW for us in 95
Foliage effect   In our GARDEN

Very hardy North American native. Keep moist and plant in an area isolated from other plants or you'll be sorry. Shorter and narrower tubes than E. hyemale. Shallow water gardens.

ERIGERON

Some groups of the carefree, lovely daisy fleabane can be well grown in South Dakota. Easily mistaken as a colorful daisy or even an aster, it is a distinct genus, with wild origins, from which several cultivars have been selected. They make carefree garden plants, a comforting thought, preferring infertile, well-drained soil in full sun.

Flowers have two rows of very thin, fringe-like petals, tightly wrapped around the yellow center disk. They reflect many colors, usually warm pink, red and blue-purple, also yellow, orange and white and are excellent for cutting. Bloom periods vary within species, from early summer to fall. Effective in our garden combined with silvery lamb's ears, Salvia nemorosa 'Plumosa' and rosy pink hardy shrub roses bringing up the rear.

Grows just fine in poor soils with good drainage and is drought tolerant when established.

speciosus x
'Azure Fairy', 'Azure Beauty'

Daisy Fleabane   esu-msu   30"
Perennial   O **O**   NEW for us in 94
Lavender blue, yellow centers   In our GARDEN 97

speciosus x
'Prosperity'

Daisy Fleabane   esu-lsu LB   18"
Perennial   O **O**   NEW for us in 99
Lavender blue   In our GARDEN

Large, near double flowers for cutting. Repeat flowers when deadheaded. From England's Blooms of Bressingham.

 153

ERYNGIUM

Sea holly is one of the plants I've been hooked on since my early gardening days; I've wanted to try every species and cultivar I could gather, no easy task. Too bad they've been long neglected by gardeners; they are such great plants for South Dakota soils and climate.

I particularly love their unusual, spiny, oval flower heads. Many appear larger than they actually are because of wide collars of prickly bracts. Bracts and flowers may be shimmering blue, silvery white or a combination thereof. Without a doubt, they are absolutely fabulous in fresh or permanent flower arrangements, drying perfectly, lasting for years.

Stiff, leathery leaves are silvery-blue-green, with spiny edges. Some are entire, lance-like, others deeply lobed and cut. Heights are species-specific and range from a couple of feet up to six feet.

Easy-care perennials, they tolerate poor, dry soils and high salt levels. Cool temperatures and full sun bring out their best colors. In rich, moist soils they may get floppy and need staking. Good drainage is essential, especially during winter. Sprinkle generous amounts of gravel around the bases of these plants to enable their crowns to stay dry. Once established, they are long lived and prefer not to be disturbed. Eventually you will find self-sown seedlings near the parent plants.

alpinum
'Blue Star'

Alpine Sea Holly   esu-msu   12-24"
Perennial   ○ ●   NEW for us in 98
Dark metallic blue   In our GARDEN
The classic one, fringed, large, very blue.

alpinum
'Donardt'

Alpine Sea Holly   msu   30"
Perennial   ○ ●   NEW for us in 95
Blue head, feathered collar   In our GARDEN

The E. alpinum cultivars provide some of the most beautiful blue flowers. They are still hard to locate in U.S. Heart-shaped, basal leaves, exploding petals and bracts. Tolerates heavy soils and slight shade.

bourgatii

Sea Holly
Perennial ○ ●
Silver blue

msu   12-24"
NEW for us in 96
In our GARDEN   X

Exquisite blue-gray, white veined, succulent foliage. Large bracts surround .75", silvery blue flowers on wiry stems. Slow to establish and probably for the experienced gardener but don't follow my example. Though suggested zone 5, I grew this for four years from a small mail order plant. Just when it was getting some girth, I made the mistake of moving it. Need I say more? Where can I find another?

giganteum
'Miss Wilmott's Ghost'

Giant Sea Holly
Biennial ○ ●
White spiny heads

msu   24"
NEW for us in 96
In our GARDEN   X

A pass-along story tells of an English gardener, Miss Wilmott, who anonymously shared the seed (by sowing it from her pocketbook) of this biennial plant as she visited the gardens of others. A rosette of spineless leaves grew at first and the second year taller, ghost-silver foliage with superb, 3-4", white, spiny flower heads appeared. I had looked for this plant for a long time. It completed its second, flowering year in '97. Alas, no new seedlings were noticed in '98 or '99.

planum
'Blaukappe', 'Blue Cap'

Sea Holly
Perennial ○ ●
Rich deep blue

msu-fall LB   24-30"
NEW for us in 00
In our GARDEN

Attractive through all stages and when flowering for most of the summer, bee covered. It's amazing to see spiny foliage and stems with silvery blue hues. Rated high in field trials and we heard predictions that this is a good candidate for a future Perennial Plant of the Year. Honors: Penn State Top 20 Perennial Performers.

yuccifolium

Rattlesnake Master
Perennial ○ ●
Silvery white

msu-lsu   24-60"
NEW for us in 94
In our GARDEN 95

Exciting eastern U.S. native. Sword-like, spined leaves and 1" button-like flowers in abundance like dried knobs at ends of branched stems. Unusual cut and dried flower. Roots highly valued among Native American people.

 155

EUONYMUS

fortunei
'Kewensis'

Dwarf Wintercreeper   1-6"
Perennial, Groundcover, Dwarf Vine   ○ ●   NEW for us in 85
Foliage effect   In our GARDEN 85

Delicate, small scale, evergreen groundcover. Tuck into small spaces that get winter shade such as north facing rocks or garden steps. Eventually woody stems will push up and cover stair risers, a great effect. If you cannot provide winter shade, mulch with oak leaves or other loose material.

EUPATORIUM

Stunning architectural plants, boneset is also enjoyed for late summer, cotton-candy-fluffy, fall bloom. Flowers are small and by themselves make no grand statement; but the way they grow on this plant, massed upon the top of broad, large stages or corymbs, is impressive. Butterflies share the limelight. Red dye can be made from flowers, which are also good for cut flowers.

Leaves are whorled around tall stems that may reach six feet on some species. Many would be unmanageable in our small gardens and are best for large gardens or wild or naturalized areas. A few species can be adapted to a controlled environment.

They grow in fertile, moist soils, full sun or partial shade. Some tolerate standing water.

The U.S. native plant, stunning Joe-Pye weed, has been a mainstay of English gardens, but rarely seen in American gardens. I guess "The grass is always greener. . .," or rather, "The flowers are always grander on the other side of the ocean."

maculatum
'Gateway'

Joe Pye Weed, Boneset   msu-fall LB   60-72"
Perennial   ○ ○ ●   NEW for us in 96
Rosy red   In our GARDEN

One of most dramatic, fall-blooming plants. Towering and loaded with heavy, large, reddish, flat topped clusters, loved by butterflies. Stems and stalks are purple. A European hybrid of our native. Abundant cuts and long-lasting as cut flowers. Heat and drought tolerance. Honors: Cut Flower Association special designation, Kentucky Theodore Klein Plant Award.

maculatum, purpureum
'Atropurpureum'

Joe Pye Weed, Ageratum, Smokeweed   lsu-fall LB   70-90"
Perennial   ○ ○ ●   NEW for us in 95
Smoky rosy lavender   In our GARDEN

Same attributes of all others in this genus. Many are referred to by common name, Joe Pye weed. Joe Pye was a well known Native American healer.

 156

<u>rugosum</u>
'Chocolate'
Joe Pye Weed, Boneset;,Snakeroot
Perennial   ○ ◐ ●
Glowing white

lsu-fall   48"
NEW for us in 98
In our GARDEN 99

We're always attracted to white fall flowers. Here, they contrast beautifully
with shiny purple stems and chocolate colored leaves. Excellent as cut flowers.
Plant parts are toxic to animals.

EUPHORBIA

A diverse genus, the spurges contain hundres of species of
perennials, annuals and biennials. Many are not hardy, but a few
very important ones can be easily grown in South Dakota.

What appear to be warm yellow, red or green petals are really
long-lasting, colorful bracts, attracting insects to the less obtrusive
cyathium, a stamen and ovary fused together. (Tricky!) This is all
revealed in spring or early summer.

Foliage is lovely and varied among species; some have dense basal
rosettes or blue-green leaves. Most are quite pictorial, contrasting
well with colorful bracts and still attractive when tiny flowers are
not present. Some of the short ones remind me of succulent-like
sedums.

Ingratiating you with their care-free offer, you will provide them
well-drained, not-too-rich soils. Most tolerate a range of soil
moisture, but they are predominantly drought tolerant. It's best to
plant them as young plants so that transplanting the long tap roots is
less complicated or stressful to the plants. Once established, they
live a long time, having few pests and diseases. Some are quite
invasive--watch out! One species of immigrated Euphorbia has been
designated as a noxious weed in South Dakota.

A milky sap is produced by all, poisonous in some. Some people are
allergic to this liquid and will wear gloves to avoid potential
reactions or contact with open wounds.

<u>corollata</u>
Flowering Spurge
Prairie Perennial   ○ ◐
White clusters

msu-lsu LB   36"
NEW for us in 96
In our GARDEN 97

Delicate, vivid white, starry bracts on a shrubby form give effect of airy baby's
breath in middle to late summer. Blue-green foliage turns red in fall. Tolerates
range of soils from moist to dry. Native to Nebraska.

   157

cyparissias
Cypress Spurge

Perennial ○ ●

Yellow bracts to purplish orange

esu-lsu   6-12"

NEW for us in 95

In our GARDEN

Mounds of blue foliage spread by underground stolons and can be invasive. Forms large patches when naturalized on dry, sandy sites. Foliage may turn orange when dry.

dulcis
'Chameleon'
Spurge

Perennial, Containers ○ ●

Chocolate orange

spr-esu   18"

NEW for us in 98

In our GARDEN

Grey-purple foliage in early summer gradually intensifies to reddish-purple embers. Relaxed, orange flower clusters contrast well with foliage in early season. Contrasts well with silver and chartreuse foliages. Will eventually colonize by self-sowing. This is a keeper; fame is just around the corner. Still "for trial" for us but winters easily in containers. All systems say, "Go."

myrsinites
Donkey Spurge

Perennial, Containers ○ ●

Yellow bracts

esu   8-10"

NEW for us in 94

In our GARDEN

Succulent, silvery, showy. Effective foliage trails and blooms in spring. Try in rock gardens and containers for foliage effects. Honors: U of Georgia Athens Better Performers selection.

polychroma, epithymoides
Flowering Spurge

Perennial, Containers ○ ●

Yellowish flowers, large bracts

esu   15"

NEW for us in 94

In our GARDEN

Early flowers that are really bracts. Red seed head and red fall color are better revealed in sun though the plant likes partial shade, dryness and alkaline soil. The well know, long popular species for this area.

FILIPENDULA

Meadowsweet plants are magnificent when blooming for a couple of weeks in early summer. Enjoy these fluffy panicles of white or pink flowers while you can. Stems are strong and make excellent cuts. Fern-textured or palmate leaves distinguish most of these plants.

They are carefree provided they have slightly alkaline soil, full sun to partial shade, and consistent moisture. Woody roots lie just under the soil surface. They would appreciate a little winter mulch in case of open, snowless winters. Consider this important fact when siting these in your garden. All species of meadowsweet (except F. vulgaris) grow naturally in areas of reliable moisture.

rubra
'Venusta', 'Magnifica'

Meadowsweet, Queen of the Meadow	esu-msu 48"
Prairie Perennial, Water ○ ●	NEW for us in 94
Rose pink plumes	In our GARDEN

One of showiest for moist non drained sites, boggy conditions where they may remain undisturbed for years. Vigorous plant has palmate, dark-green leaves and fragrant plumes of many tiny flowers. Cut back after bloom; will regrow fresh mounds of foliage.

ulmaria
'Variegata'

Variegated European Meadowsweet	esu-msu 18"
Perennial ○ ●	NEW for us in 97,
White, feathery	In our GARDEN 00

Fern-like dark-green leaves have a yellow center blotch when first emerging. Later a disappointment, because purported variegation just isn't there. Supposedly it is more evident when grown in shade. Average to moist soils are suggested, but it is pretty with compact mounds and white feathery clusters of many tiny flowers in our mostly dry garden

vulgaris, hexapetala
'Flore Plena'

Double Meadowsweet	esu-msu 18-30"
Perennial ○ ●	NEW for us in 96
Pure white	In our GARDEN

Showy, double, long-lasting flowers, this meadowsweet likes it drier than most of its cousins. Ferny carrot leaves grow into low rosettes and provide a good plant for the perennial border.

<u>vulgaris, hexapetala</u>
'Kokome'
Double Meadowsweet — msu-lsu 8-12"
Perennial ○ ◐ — NEW for us in 99
Light rosy pink — In our GARDEN

New and nice miniature form of F. 'Flore Plena' with foamy clusters of flowers in mid and late summer.

FRAGARIA

Strawberries, I learned when young, wouldn't flourish in the heavy clay soil I was stuffing them into. When visiting friends in Omaha that summer, I saw for the first time, the very simple raised, sand-amended bed they had built just for their strawberries. Gardening Grandpa didn't have raised beds in his homestead garden, but his soil was so heavily amended it turned over like chocolate cake. What a treat to find the berries there--chocolate covered strawberries! Now the treats are my memories of him.

Many ornamental strawberries have been introduced, known for flowers and uses in hanging baskets or other containers. Some, not all, have decent fruit production and taste.

Provide all strawberries with well-drained, rock garden conditions, non-acid soil and consistent moisture, and they will thrive. Since you aren't growing the ornamental selections for crop production, consider them as drought tolerant.

'Lipstick'
Alpine Strawberry — esu-fall LB .5'
Perennial, Containers ○ — NEW for us in 00
Dark rose pink — In our GARDEN

Keeps blooming when happy, darker pink than 'Pink Panda'. Sandy, rock garden conditions and it grows into healthy groundcover. Just a few berries produced. Use to edge, blanket or to trail out of containers.

'Pink Panda'
Strawberry — esu-lsu LB 3-6"
Perennial, Containers ○ ◐ — NEW for us in 97
Pink strawberry flowers, red fruit — In our GARDEN

Strawberry and Potentilla hybrid has large pink flowers that appear in abundance in early summer and intermittently throughout the season. Bright-red, tasty fruit grow from aggressive and quickly spreading runners that grow several feet in one season. Runners dangle from containers or spread far out in the garden. Provide strawberry culture = sandy, well-drained, non-acid soil. Partial shade works too. Blooms of Bressingham introduction. Honors: Exceptional field rating of 1997 Michigan trials.

 160

'Variegata'

Variegated Strawberry

Perennial, Containers   ○

White, red fruit

esu-lsu LB   36-48"

NEW for us in 95

In our GARDEN 96

Lovely and unusual, green and white variegated foliage later contrasts with red fruit. Very effective in annual baskets, but also hardy in rock gardens. A little afternoon shade keeps light foliage from burning. Rogue out any plants that revert to all green foliage.

vesca

'Improved Rugen'

Strawberry

Perennial, Containers   ○

White, sweet red fruit

esu-lsu LB   6"

NEW for us in 96

In our GARDEN

Typical strawberry leaves and small, pointed, sweet strawberry fruit come all summer, with heaviest production at the end of season. Use as a tidy, low and mounding rock garden, container or edging plant. Produces no runners. Likes rock garden conditions, soil that is heavy on grit and well-drained. If I could choose only one ornamental strawberry I would choose this one, a classic European strain.

GAILLARDIA

Many, many requests are made each year for the ever-popular blanket flowers. It's easy to understand why. They are tolerant of heat, drought and poor soils and bloom for long periods in spite of neglect. Only a couple are truly perennial. Some of the easy-to-grow hybrid tetraploids (crosses between perennial and annual Gaillardia) are shorter lived than the perennial species and will eventually drift away (disappear, fail to return, die, however you want to say it). Their demise happens sooner in heavy, winter-wet soils. Usually, however, they leave seed behind and pop up in subsequent years in other places nearby.

In spite of their short lives, their value is great due to extremely long-flowering periods. Flowers are held singly with dark, fuzzy center disks and toothed, colorful petals or rays in shades of copper, wine-red, gold, yellow, burgundy and various combinations thereof. Butterflies like these, too.

Foliage is hairy and toothed. When flowers begin to wane in late summer, cut them back for renewed fall bloom. Cultivars vary in height from six inches to three feet.

<u>aristata</u>
'Golden Goblin', 'Goldkobold'

Blanket Flower	esu-lsu LB 9-12"
Perennial ○	NEW for us in 94
Bright yellow gold	In our GARDEN

Strong, compact shrublet form of dependable Gaillardia.

<u>aristata</u>
'Golden Goblin', 'Goldkobold'

Blanket Flower	esu-lsu LB 9-12"
Perennial ○	NEW for us in 94
Bright yellow gold	In our GARDEN

Strong, compact shrublet form of dependable Gaillardia.

aristata
'Monarch'

Blanket Flower	esu-lsu LB	24"
Perennial ○	NEW for us in	96
Shades of yellow, orange, red	In our GARDEN	

Bright range of colors on robust, 2' plants that bloom all summer. Superb for cuts. Seed-grown plants will vary in size and flower color.

grandiflora x
'Burgundy'

Blanket Flower	esu-lsu LB	24-36"
Perennial ○	NEW for us in	94
Wine red	In our GARDEN	

Popular garden flower, easy culture, heat tolerant. A tetraploid cross of G. grandiflora. Inherently short-lived, but worth replanting.

grandiflora x
'Goblin', 'Kobold'

Blanket Flower	esu-msu LB	12"
Perennial ○	NEW for us in	94
Red petals bordered in yellow	In our GARDEN	

Another popular tetraploid. One of the most dwarf crosses, but holds the large flowers you'd expect from larger plants. Time tested, one of the best.

GALIUM (ASPERULA)

The name "sweet woodruff" conjures up delights, so this plant must have something wonderful to share. Only one species really deserves this description. - It is the lovely groundcover of lax, trailing, square stems (an instant reminder that this plant is in the greater mint family), and fully whorled around the stem, slightly glossy, bright-green leaves. Foliage is sweet scented and was/is used to flavor May wine. In spring a mass of low, foamy white flowers, resembling newly fallen snow, endears and compels.

One of the most memorable springtime scenes is a mass of this plant blooming in Mary's white shade garden. Mary blooms there, too. Combined with newly unfurled blue hosta leaves, the impression is rich, subtle and charming. One of the best examples of planning-first-in-green I can think of. To sustain this picture year after year, plants need reliably moist, slightly acid conditions, humus-rich soil and shade to part shade.

There are other worthy plants in this genus, but they are hard to locate.

odoratum

Sweet Woodruff, Bedstraw	spr-esu	6"
Perennial, Groundcover, Herb ○ ●	NEW for us in	85
White whorls	In our GARDEN	85

Acid-loving groundcover for shade. Soil conditions are imperative to success of this plant.

triandrum

Tall Woodruff	esu	18"
Perennial, Herb ○	NEW for us in	85
White small and fluffy	In our GARDEN	96

I believe this is the correct species of an antique plant, one of several lovely and unusual plants shared with me by experienced gardener, Stella Mortenson. She liked it better than baby's breath.

GAURA

lindheimeri
'Siskiyou Pink'

Gaura	esu-lsu LB	18-30"
Perennial, Tender ○	NEW for us in	00
	In our GARDEN	

Red tints in leaves connect well with wine-red flower buds and pink flowers. Full sun best and drought tolerant. May be tender here, but worth growing as an annual for summer long bloom. Honors: Penn State Impressive Performance, 2001 Oklahoma Proven Plant.

 164

GENISTA

multibracteata (tinctoria)

Woadwaxen   msu   24-36"
Perennial, Sub-shrub   ○   NEW for us in 96
Yellow   In our GARDEN

Actually a woody, dark-green sub-shrub, selected from Grand Rapids, Minnesota. Leguminous, nitrogen-fixing, dye plant.

tinctoria
'Royal Gold'

Woadwaxen   2-3'
Perennial, Sub-shrub   ○   NEW for us in 00
Yellow   In our GARDEN

Pea flowers on small die-back shrub that we call a sub-shrub. Tolerates poor soils, and loves the heat.

GENTIANA

Gentians are plants to lust over for their beautiful, near-perfect-blue flowers in cool spring or fall seasons in the temperate and alpine climates of the world. Yellow, white and some red and gold colors are also found.

Technically, many are hardy in zone 3 or 4, but in the U.S., most are native from the Rocky Mountains and west. Some are native to the Northern Great Plains and S.D. Aren't we lucky? It is impossible to lump them into one description because of varying soil needs, habit and size. Growing non-native types is tricky because so many require strict alpine conditions of sun, lots of water, perfect drainage and cool nights.

Gentians are often hard to propagate from seed or cuttings, hence seldom seen listed in catalogs. For us here in the Northern Plains start with G. acaulis, andrewsii and puberulenta. Taller G. andrewsii could be suitable for borders and landscape. G. aucaulis is best for rock gardens.

andrewsii

Bottle Gentian   18"
Prairie Perennial   ○ ●   NEW for us in 98
Azure blue   In our GARDEN

S.D. native has tubular flowers that never open. One of easiest to grow because strict alpine conditions do not have to be applied, but still needs cool nights and good drainage.

dahurica

Gentian   msu-lsu   6-12"
Prairie Perennial   ○ ●   NEW for us in 98
Intense blue   In our GARDEN

One of the easiest to grow with long, narrow, basal leaves and 1" spotted flowers.

paradoxa x septemfida
'Blauer Herold'

Gentian	15"
Perennial ○ ●	NEW for us in 98
Bright blue	In our GARDEN

Excellent large flowered gentian. Hard to take one's eye away from the flowers; a beautiful row of hairy, fringed petals lines the inside of the main large cup.

puberalenta

Gentian	spr-esu
Perennial ○	NEW for us in
Gentian blue	In our GARDEN

Spring blooming SD native.

septemfida
var. lagodechiana

Autumn or Everyman's Gentian	lsu-fall 6"
Prairie Perennial ○ ●	NEW for us in 98
Deep blue	In our GARDEN

A favorite in U.K. and Europe with fall occurring, brilliant blue flowers, deeper in color than the species. One of easier, showy, fall blooming selections. Compact grower looks in place in rock gardens. Moist, acid, well-drained situations. Resents transplanting.

GERANIUM

Move over Pelargonium, the real Geranium has arrived! Now that these capital-G--Geranium plants are rapidly gaining in popularity, we'll be forced to take a position, bravely change our course, buck the crowd and call those large, bright red, bold flowers we treat as annuals by their proper, capital-P name--Pelargonium! What will marketing do?

With increased travel by Americans to Europe, the gross diversity and beauty of hundreds of underused cultivars of true Geraniums are being taken home. . .literally. Many can be acclimated to zone 4 or lower, but many are tender, for higher (in number) zones only. For now, we are most at ease with cultivars from the species G. endressii, oxonianum, himalayense, macrorrhizum, magnificum, phaeum, platypetalum, renardii, sanguineum. With so many available and fitting so many different applications, at least one or several niches can be found for them in all gardens, where they might continue to hybridize on their own.

Of easy culture, most prefer moist, well-drained soils in sun or partial shade, some tolerate full shade, but all will flower better with some sun. Diseases and pests are rare.

Flowers, born in pairs or clusters, have only five petals. Some are long flowering; dead-heading helps. Colors are cool and bright pink, magenta, lavender, or white shades with prominent veining. Invisible to the human eye are nectar guides, distinct maps that the flowers make clearly visible to bees, who can utilize light waves that are unavailable to us. With an ultraviolet light source we could make out these designs that direct them to their food source at the center of the flower. The mysterious adaptations that insects and flowers have made to help one another never ceases to amaze me!

Pretty leaves are lobed in various configurations and tints and are fragrant on some species. Red and other fall color is spectacular for many. They form soft, sturdy or sprawling mounds from six inch rock garden types to three foot shrubby types. Sometimes they are called cranesbill because of their beak-like fruit.

'Brookside'

Cranesbill Geranium
Perennial ○ ◐ ●
Rich sapphire blue

esu-msu LB   24-30"
NEW for us in 00
In our GARDEN

What has been knighted as "the improved G. 'Johnson's Blue'." Those of you who have gardened for a while probably have grown the old J.B. plant, and recognize what a stalwart of early summer it is. Now you have this choice that will form wide clumps of attractive foliage and hundreds of flowers in one season.

'Patricia'

Cranesbill Geranium
Perennial ○ ◐ ●
Magenta, black blotch

esu-fall LB   24"
NEW for us in 98
In our GARDEN

Stunning tall, shrubby cultivar. Magenta pink of G. psilostemon with black, center blotch that forms a star. Large flower, long bloomer and vigorous, neat grower. Bold dark-green foliage. G. psilostemon and endressii cross.

cantabrigiense x
'Biokovo Karmina'

Cranesbill Geranium
Perennial ○ ◐ ●
Deep pink

esu-msu   10-12"
NEW for us in 96
In our GARDEN

Deeper pink form of G. 'Biokova'. Tidy form and habit.

cinereum
'Ballerina'

Cranesbill Geranium
Perennial ○ ◐ ●
Pink, purple lilac center

esu-msu   6"
NEW for us in 94
In our GARDEN

Excellent dwarf cultivar. Plant in shade garden and allow natural leaf cover for winter protection.

cinereum
'Lawrence Flatman'

Cranesbill Geranium
Perennial ○ ◐ ●
Magenta, dark blotch

6"
NEW for us in 00
In our GARDEN

Small mounds of intense magenta flowers with distinct veins. Compact habit similar to G. 'Ballerina'. Dark foliage has darker blotches. Blooms of Bressingham introduction. Honors: Exceptional field rating of 1997 Michigan trials.

cinereum
var. subcaulescens

Cranesbill Geranium
Perennial ○ ◐ ●
Bright pink

esu-msu   18"
NEW for us in 98
In our GARDEN

Striking pink blossoms are fabulous in late spring and early summer. Mounding habit rather than spreading.

 168

endressii
'Wargrave Pink'
Endress Cranesbill
Perennial ○ ◐ ●
Warm, salmon pink

esu, rpts   12"
NEW for us in 96
In our GARDEN

Vigorous in flower, strong growing, mounding, border species. Shiny, evergreen leaves with showy flowers. Clip hard to rejuvenate if lanky in midsummer. The most popular Endress cultivar. Provide drainage.

macrorrhizum
'Bevan's Variety'
Bigroot Cranesbill
Perennial ○ ◐ ●
Magenta and red

esu-msu LB   12-18"
NEW for us in 98
In our GARDEN

Showy, 1" flowers held high above lemon-fragrant and fuzzy foliage. Distinct from others; one of best flowering. Evergreen with good winter cover, and tolerates some drought in shade. Use as groundcover, border or specimen.

macrorrhizum
'Ingwersen Variety'
Cranesbill Geranium
Perennial ○ ◐ ●
Soft pink

esu   12-24"
NEW for us in 99
In our GARDEN 99

A fine, fine form, 2' of glossy, lobed and toothed leaves from Europe. Good groundcover in dry shade.

macrorrhizum x
'Johnson's Blue'
Cranesbill Geranium
Perennial ○ ◐ ●
Brilliant, blue lavender

esu-msu LB   18"
NEW for us in 95
In our GARDEN 96

A popular Geranium noted for long-blooming, brilliant, blue-lavender flowers. Sets few seeds, a trick to keep the plant in flower. Vigorous, deeply divided, rambling foliage. Purported to bloom summer long, but doesn't.

oxonianum (endressii) x
'Claridge Druce'
Cranesbill Geranium
Perennial ○ ◐ ●
Rose pink, dark veins

esu-lsu LB   18"
NEW for us in 94
In our GARDEN

One of excellent, vigorous, weed-proof and free-flowering selections. Broad stout mounds of glossy, grey-green leaves, even in shade, that turn red in fall. Trim foliage back if it declines in summer heat. A cross of G. endressii and versicolor.

phaeum
var. 'Purpureum'
Morning Widow, Cranesbill Geranium
Perennial   ○ ◒ ●
Dark maroon

esu-lsu rpts   18-24"
NEW for us in   96
In our GARDEN   96

Charming novelty with back-swept petals, immodestly exposing parts. Blossoms held high above toothed, basal leaves. Moist, shady areas. Reliable here since '96.

psilostemon x procurrens
'Ann Folkard'
Trailing Geranium
Perennial   ○ ◒ ●
Rich magenta, black center

esu-msu   12-24"
NEW for us in   96
In our GARDEN   97

Vigorous cultivar with foliage that begins as chartreuse and mellows to light green. Used effectively rambling and relaxing through shrubbery and other supporting perennials that also shade their roots. Their luscious bright magenta flowers with black throats are distinct and long-lasting. Popular and high demand in markets outside of S.D. This has returned for us since '96.

renardii
'Tscheida Blue'
Cranesbill Geranium
Perennial   ○ ◒ ●
Pale blue flowers

12"
NEW for us in   97
In our GARDEN   97

New in '97, planted west of office window. Soft pebble-like bumps on the leaves create interesting foliage effect.

renardii
white
Cranesbill Geranium
Perennial   ○ ◒ ●
Blush white

9-12"
NEW for us in   94
In our GARDEN   94

Unusual foliage is better than the reticent flowers. Krinkled and quilted, sage-colored leaves grow into modest mounds.

sanguineum
carmine red
Bloody Cranesbill
Perennial   ○ ◒ ●
Bright magenta

esu-msu LB   9-12"
NEW for us in   98
In our GARDEN

Many 1.5" flowers continue periodically all summer, ending the season with mounds of fragrant foliage that turn red in fall. Very hardy, pest and trouble-free, heat and cold tolerant. Sun or shade, but bloom best in sun. One of most common species in U.S.

 170

sanguineum
'John Elsley'

Creeping Bloody Cranesbill
Perennial ○ ◐ ●
Bright pink

esu-lsu LB   6-12"
NEW for us in   00
In our GARDEN

Low and trailing habit of this creeping species, again in this newly introduced cultivar. Large, showy flowers and fragrant foliage, a Blooms of Bressingham introduction.

sanguineum
'New Hampshire Purple'

Bloody Cranesbill
Perennial ○ ◐ ●
Deep red purple

esu-msu LB   9-12"
NEW for us in   98
In our GARDEN

Prostrate grower with bright flowers of heavy texture and fragrant foliage. Very long blooming, from July to frost. Use as groundcover in partial sun settings.

sanguineum
var. striatum (var. lancastriense, prostratum)

Cranesbill Geranium
Perennial ○ ◐ ●
Light pink, red veins

esu   6-9"
NEW for us in   96
In our GARDEN

Popular cultivar, maybe the best form of G. sanguineum. Abundant flowers in spring and intermittently the rest of summer. Tolerates heat, cold and moisture fluctuation better than any others. Grows into tight prostrate cushions of fragrant foliage,

sanguineum x cantabrigiense
'Shepherd's Warning'

Bloody Cranesbill
Perennial ○ ◐ ●
Bright rose pink

12"
NEW for us in   00
In our GARDEN

One of best sanguineum cultivars from Scotland. Fragrant foliage takes on a beautiful red color in fall. Good for rock gardens or walls.

wlassovianum

Cranesbill Geranium
Perennial ○ ◐ ●
Bright reddish purple

esu-lsu LB   24-30"
NEW for us in   99
In our GARDEN

Native to China, a rounded mound grows rapidly and creates one of largest specimens. Purple centers in dark green leaves turn bright red in autumn. Prolific 1" flowers are borne all summer. Reported hardy to -35 F and heat tolerant in the southern climes.

GEUM

triflorum

Prairie Smoke	esu 9-12"
Prairie Perennial ○ ●	NEW for us in 98
Distinct red purple, feathery seeds	In our GARDEN

High Plains native, cup or bell-like, nodding, purplish flowers, three flowers per stem in very early season. More showy than the flowers is the fine feathery seed capsules that remain for six weeks. From the rose family, the bipinnate leaf pattern is distinct for the genus--30 little leaflets for each 6" leaf.

GYMNASTER, ASTER

savatieri, savatori

'Variegata'

Aster	lsu-fall 30-36"
Perennial ○ ●	NEW for us in 98
Blue violet	In our GARDEN 99

Showy variegated leaves grow into aggresive strong clumps. Related to Aster and Boltonia.

GYPSOPHILA

Baby's breath includes several species and cultivars, including creeping, rock garden plants and annuals. It is mostly known for the large bushy clumps that in midsummer are covered with clouds of as many as one thousand tiny flowers. Some grow so tall and full that they become top heavy and need staking. It is a valuable commercial flower used as filler and foil, both fresh and dried, by every florist in the country. Most are white; a few pale-pink forms are available.

Of all potential trials that plants endure, there are three main situations that this plant abhors: transplanting its large, fleshy roots; wet feet in summer or winter; and acid soil. "Gypso" is from "gypsum" and "philos" means "friendship"--friendly to alkaline or high pH soils. Many cultivars of large baby's breath have probably been grafted, and the graft union should be planted below the soil surface to enable the stem to grow roots.

As blossoms mature and begin to fade, cut the entire plant back and it may rebloom in fall. Continue cutting for continued bloom.

Creeping baby's breath, an underused, dependable, drought-tolerant plant that can tolerate some acidity, is excellent trailing over rocks. After heavy spring bloom they continue with light flowering throughout the summer.

paniculata
'Compacta Plena'

Baby's Breath	esu-msu	18"
Perennial ○	NEW for us in	98
Double white	In our GARDEN	

Resembles G. 'Bristol Fairy', but one-half the stature of the large baby's breath allows more versatile use. Slightly less double form and fewer flowers.

paniculata
'Perfecta', 'Fairy Perfect'

Double Baby's Breath	msu LB	24-36"
Perennial ○	NEW for us in	95
White	In our GARDEN	

Long known as a cut and dried flower, these double blossoms are twice the size of others. Drought tolerant. One of best.

paniculata
'Pink Fairy'

Baby's Breath	msu LB	18-24"
Perennial ○	NEW for us in	95
Pink, double	In our GARDEN	96

Clouds of double pinks reoccur all summer long. More compact and versatile than larger forms such as G. 'Perfecta'. Drought tolerant.

paniculata
'Pink Festival'

Baby's Breath

Perennial ○

Pink

msu LB   36-48"

NEW for us in 96

In our GARDEN

Prolific double, free-flowering baby's breath for the large garden. New patented plant. Drought tolerant.

repens
'Alba'

Creeping Baby's Breath

Perennial ○

Pure white

esu-msu LB   24-36"

NEW for us in 94

In our GARDEN

Very unlike its large billowy paniculata cousins, this is a groundcover. Blooms heavily early in summer, then intermittently the rest of the season. Forms a dense mat in sun in well-drained rock gardens. Drought tolerant.

repens
'Dorothy Teacher'

Creeping Baby's Breath

Perennial ○

Pure clear pink

esu-lsu LB   2"

NEW for us in 98

In our GARDEN

Extremely compact, tiniest, blue-green leaved English import, a substitute for G. repens 'Rosea'. Heaviest in flower in early summer, but continues moderate reflowering throughout the season. Best in rock gardens or at extreme front of borders.

 174

HELENIUM

Many years ago I planted our first sneezeweed and was delighted by the lovely, reflexed, ballerina flowers in late summer. As huge gatherings of cut flowers in the arms of our three little girls, they made unforgettable fall snapshots.

These plants grow large and bushy and are best planted at the back of the garden. One could prune stems in late spring to decrease later height, but this will also delay flowering. Flowers don't begin until late summer, but then last for many weeks, sometimes until frost. There are many cultivars available, mostly in warm-yellow to orange colors with yellow centers.

They adapt well to cold climes and a wide range of soils, needing full sun to partial shade and reliable moisture. Occasional division would be enjoyed. Butterflies would like that, too.

'Bruno'

Sneezeweed, Helen's Flower   msu-lsu   48"
Perennial   ○ ●   NEW for us in   98
Rusted red   In our GARDEN

Fall blooming, velvety-petaled flowers remind me of ballerina skirts. Blooms of Bressingham introduction.

autumnale x
'Butterpat'

Sneezeweed, Helen's Flower   lsu-fall LB   36"
Perennial   ○ ●   NEW for us in   97
Pure yellow   In our GARDEN   97

One of best classic yellow cultivars. Extra large flowers last for weeks in late summer on tall upright plant. Beautiful in arrangements.

bigelovii
'The Bishop'

Sneezeweed, Helen's Flower   msu-lsu   24-30"
Perennial   ○ ●   NEW for us in   99
Deep gold   In our GARDEN

New, more compact cultivar, forms nice clump. Long-lasting flowers.

HELIANTHUS

Blessed are we who have gazed over fields of sunflowers, as if lucky old sun had reproduced by the millions, and all these sunny faces have directed back to her, all at once, her own life-giving glow! True, it is as if sunflowers do have a bit of the old sun in each of them. Robust and energetic (interpret as invasive for some), large, spreading--give them room!

Ornamental garden varieties, as well as species that are grown worldwide by the field-fulls for important nutritious food and oil crops, are included in this genus. The most prolific flower production results from adequate fertilizer (but not too much as to over-nurture foliage) and a reliable, frequent water source. They tolerate a wide range of soils. In the book "Buffalo Bird Woman's Garden" the early cultivation of sunflowers really comes to life!

Flowers top off long stalks at three to ten feet, depending on plant and culture, and may be borne singly or in open clusters. In ornamental cultivars, flowers range from two to five inches across. Long, vibrant petals in a single row surround a large, dark, disk center. Sunflowers have been "in," in (two ins?) the fresh and preserved flower market for several years. It also has an "in" with butterflies.

maximillianii

Maximillian's Sunflower
Prairie Perennial ○ ●
Gold, dark center

msu-lsu 24-100"
NEW for us in 98
In our GARDEN

Daisy-like flowers closely packed together on many tall spikes form large clumps. Use as backdrop or hedges. Support it early in summer to avoid later flopping. With abundant water it will get very tall and roots can get aggressive. Tuberous roots, like those of H. tuberosum, Jerusalem artichoke, can be eaten.

microcephalus, strumosa

Sunflower
Perennial ○ ● ●
Bright yellow

msu-lsu LB 60-72"
NEW for us in 98
In our GARDEN

One of best of the species. Delicate textured plant, smaller, elongated leaves. Flowers are abundant from 1-1.25". Average moisture to drought tolerant. Dry shade works too.

 176

HELIOPSIS

"Now, this is a real flower!" we overhear some visitors exclaim. And what reliable, bright flowers they are! Long, sturdy stems support large, three to four inch, daisy-like heads. They truly are "sun-like," which is the literal translation of their Latin name, heliopsis. Long ray-flowers or petals are a deep orange-yellow with large brown or greenish disk-flower centers. They come in singles, semi-doubles or doubles and bloom over a long period, from midsummer to fall. Dead-head faithfully to extend blooming period.

One of the easiest perennials you can grow, false sunflowers perform adequately in poor soils and drought and respond even better with some fertility and moisture. They have no pests or sicknesses of any significance and, even more, require no staking for their three to five foot heights. How much easier can it get?

Many species are very wild-looking and probably too rangy for anything but a prairie or naturalized setting. But the cultivars of H. scabra or helianthoides offer some worthy plants. (How cavalier of me to designate a plant as worthy, as if assuming there is any such thing as an unworthy plant; shame on me. Pardon the ancient, mid-century expression!)

Leaves have a rough finish, but otherwise the plant is attractive. Divide every three years to keep them vigorous and perennial. Butterflies like these blooms, too.

Lorainne's Sunshine'

False Sunflower		msu-lsu LB	24-36"
Perennial	○ ●		NEW for us in 00
Golden yellow			In our GARDEN

Variegated foliage has white leaves with green veining and long-blooming daisy flowers that are produced from midsummer to fall. Discovered in Wisconsin. Variegation diminishes in late summer. Excellent cut flower. Honors: Canadian Ornamental Plant Introduction.

helianthoides
'Ballerina', 'Spitzentanzerin'

False Sunflower		msu-fall LB	24-48"
Perennial	○ ●		NEW for us in 97
Golden yellow, darker center			In our GARDEN

New, more compact, sturdy stemmed plant from Germany. Shiny, dark-green foliage. Blooms all summer with large, semi double flowers.

helianthoides
'Summer Sun'
False Sunflower

Perennial ○ ●

Bright yellow, darker center

msu-lsu LB   30-48"

NEW for us in   96

In our GARDEN   96

Longest bloomer, ten weeks, within this tall, daisy-like group. Semi double, 4" blossoms.

HELLEBORUS

Only a few short years ago most of us gardeners probably hadn't yet heard of the Lenten or Christmas rose, let alone believe that they could actually prosper in South Dakota. It'd take many moons to convince a Dakotan that such a plant will bloom <u>outside</u> in the wintertime. She'd think you were pulling her suspenders.

It tricked me. I'd keep reading in those southern catalogs (from S.C. or South Carolina for example), "Get Your Hellebores While They Last; They Bloom in December, January or February." Living up to my reputation as a slow learner, I'd think, "Plants that bloom in the winter? In South Dakota? Get real."

Now, don't think it's easy to confuse S.D. with S.C. But then my brain finally ignited, and I sheepishly thought, "Ohhh, how silly of me. When a S.C. garden catalog describes late winter as January, it refers to the south of the country, not the south of Dakota! Duh. April...April is our late winter." Now I get it. Lots of things pop up from the earth and bloom in April or soon after old Frostie emits a last steamy breath and makes his final escape.

I have not grown hellebores, but this is the season I'll eliminate the negative. I'm convinced they are worth a good effort. And besides, far more progressive Dakota gardeners than I have been asking for them.

Of two reliable perennial references, one rates three out of four species as adaptable to zone 3-9; the other selects two out of five for zone 4 and colder. I'll supply only plants suggested by these experts. As a beginner I'll start with H. orientalis, which maintains dormant underground buds. A description: Charming, nodding, one to four inch, cup-like blossoms, in shades of green, pink or purple, that emerge you-know-when. Blossoms last for weeks because of the cool weather. Foliage is handsome, sometimes evergreen. Give it reliably moist soils in shade with alkaline or neutral soil. They are long lived but may establish slowly and with difficulty. Do not disturb them. Later, some may self-sow.

'Winter Joy Bouquet'

Lenten Rose, Hellebore   spr   18"
Perennial   ○ ●   NEW for us in
Mixed colors   In our GARDEN

Lovely apricot, pink, rose and yellow pastels grow above leathery leaves. Provide non acid soil that is consistently moist for success for Hellebores and protect in winter.

179

foetidus

Stinking Lenten Rose, Hellebore spr LB 18-24"
Perennial ○ ● NEW for us in 94
Pale-green, rimmed purple In our GARDEN

Toothed stem leaves with leaflets arranged like a fan. Flowers are lovely to look at but are "fetid," from the species name. Don't inhale too deeply. Suggested for zone 3 by one source and zone 5 by another. Freely self-sows. Tolerant of broad growing conditions. Provide humus-rich soil and partial shade.

orientalis

Lenten Rose, Hellebore spr 12-15"
Perennial ○ ● NEW for us in 97
Spotted white, pale green, pink, plum In our GARDEN 99

Spotted, 3-4", nodding flowers in mixed cool shades bloom for up to ten weeks during the coolness of early spring. Clumps build up quickly and will eventually sprinkle new plants from seed.

 180

HEMEROCALLIS

Chronicling the hybridization of Hemerocallis would create a fascinating memoir. For the last 100 years, hundreds of professionals and amateurs, many of them back-yard gardeners like ourselves, began to cross-pollinate naturally occurring, daylily species. If progeny or offspring from these crosses exemplified desirable characteristics, they would be selected, saved, propagated, and used in subsequent crosses. This scene was repeated over and over again, ad infinitum. Now a century later, we enjoy the fruits of these efforts: daylily cultivars by the thousands. Hundreds more are introduced each year. I've heard more than one daylily breeder speculate about his or her search for the proverbial blue daylily and the millions that will follow, millions of dollars and millions of daylilies!

Translating the word, "hemerocallis" gives us "beauty for a day." Though each blossom only lasts one day, a well-selected cultivar can produce a dozen scapes (bloom stalks), which continue to flower for several weeks by building new buds. The original species are still charming and worthy though now passed over because of the new kids on the block; in fact, it's sometimes hard to find some of the original species daylilies. Thanks in part to daylilies, color has finally escaped from the garden and into the landscape where their popularity has mushroomed. (Whether because of customer demand or their own creativity, landscape designers have finally added perennials to their palettes, which before had been limited to trees, shrubs, and turf grass.

To avoid disappointing colors, select plants while they are blooming. Many times gardening friends and I have ordered daylilies identified as "pink" that have invariably turned out to be peach or salmon. Consider yourself warned! Because of the warm yellow and orange hues of the original species breeding stock, it's difficult to get a "pink" daylily that doesn't lean toward warmer shades of peach or yellow. Some that have lavender or purple hues in their genetic makeup may tend toward a cooler pink. If choosing among cultivars, always buy named plants. Generic plants termed "yellow" or "red" will often cost the same as many excellent cultivars. Buy award winners if available. For our climate, dormant

and sometimes semi-evergreen types are best.

Carefree daylilies demand little more than well-drained soil, sun, or part shade, but will bloom and increase more rapidly with amended soil and extra moisture. The repeat-blooming cultivars, such as 'Stella de Oro' or 'Happy Returns', will perform as advertised, if divided every two or three years along with supplemental fertilizer.

To maintain some order in this vast genus they are classified by the following six categories:

1. Winter state: D - dormant, SE - semi evergreen, E - evergreen; **2.** Season of bloom: E - early, M - midseason, L - late season, rpts - repeat blooming, ext - extended bloom; **3.** Chromosome count: DIP - diploid, the natural number of chromosomes, and TET - tetraploid, double the number. (A tetraploid is not necessarily more desirable than a diploid.); **4.** Height of flower in bloom: From 12" miniatures or dwarfs up to 6' giants; **5.** Color of the funnel-shaped flower: All colors and blends except pure white and true blue; **6.** Blossom size, shape: Miniature, 2" to wide, flaring 8". They also come ruffled, scented, overlayed, and more.

'Anzac' dip   Dormant   msu-lsu LB   28-32"

Flower Description: NEW IN 98
Red, light green throat large, 7"   GARDEN

Honors: 1971 Honorable Mention.

'Black Eyed Stella' dip   Dormant   esu-lsu LB   12-15"

Flower Description: NEW IN 96
Yellow, red eye small, 3"   GARDEN

Introduced in 1989.

'Charles Johnston' tet   Semi evergreen   msu   24"

Flower Description: NEW IN 00
Brilliant red self 6", fragrant, ruffled   GARDEN

Blooms on short stems. Honors: '88 Award of Merit, '85 Honorable Mention.

'Chicago Apache' tet   Dormant   msu-lsu   30"

Flower Description: NEW IN 95
Choice, velvety, blood red 5", crimped   GARDEN 97

Sun-fast color, ruffled edges are darker. Resistant to thrips compared to other reds. Very good, vigorous grower. Wind-resistant, healthy looking foliage.

'Chicago Royal Robe' tet   Semi evergreen   esu-msu 30-36"

Flower Description: NEW IN 97
Plum purple, green throat 5.5"   GARDEN

Honors: 1989 Honorable Mention.

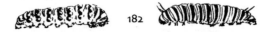

Dreamsicle dip   Evergreen

Flower Description:
Orange blend 3"

Isu-tall   36"

NEW IN 90
GARDEN 94

Our own coined name because of luscious melt-in-your-eyes orange. Very late blooming in our garden, just when a new lift is expected. Combines well with tall Salvia farinaceae 'Indigo Spires' or shorter 'Victoria Blue' or 'Rhea' or self-sowing annual Verbena boniarensis. A gift from Kay Coddington's original garden.

'Eenie Fanfare'   Dormant

Flower Description:
Bright red, white edges 2"

msu   12-15"

NEW IN 98
GARDEN

Bright, perky miniature.

'Elaine Strutt' tet   Dormant

Flower Description:
Glowing coral self 4", fragrant

msu   38"

NEW IN 98
GARDEN

'Fairy Tale Pink' dip   Semi evergreen

Flower Description:
Light pink, green-gold throat 5.5", ruffled

msu, rpts   24"

NEW IN 00
GARDEN

Honors: '90 Silver Medal, '87 Award of Merit, '90 Stout Silver Medal, #1 Popularity Poll for several years.

'Gentle Shepherd' dip   Semi evergreen

Flower Description:
Sparkling near white, green throat ruffled, creped 5"

esu-msu   30"

NEW IN 96
GARDEN 99

One more of the few near-white selections. Upward facing flowers, flat, oval, ruffled and overlapping petals. All segments flare and are creped. Excellent substance. Honors: 1981 Junior Citation, 1984 Honorable Mention, 1987 Award of Merit.

'Happy Returns' miniature   Dormant

Flower Description:
Canary yellow, ever bloomer 3.25", fragrant

esu-fall LB   18"

NEW IN 96
GARDEN 96

A heat-resistant daughter of 'Stella de Oro' but a truer, brighter yellow color. Still has marathon blooming habits, 21 weeks of bloom! Honors: 1992 Honorable Mention Award, 2001 Mich. Grower's Choice Award.

'Indian Love Call'

Flower Description:
Red self 4"

msu   26"

NEW IN 99
GARDEN

'James Marsh' tet

Flower Description:
Fire engine red 6.5", choice

msu   28"

NEW IN 00
GARDEN

Stalwart and showy.

'Lemon Lollipop'

Flower Description:
Lemon yellow 3", ruffled, creped,

esu rpts LB   18"
NEW IN 00
GARDEN

Grower claims this reblooms as well as 'Stella', only this one is very fragrant.
Honors: 1990 Honorable Mention, 1994 Ernest Plouf Fragrance Award.

'Little Grapette' dip   Semi evergreen

Flower Description:
Grape, green center 2"

esu, rpts   12-18"
NEW IN 90
GARDEN

Many awards during 1970's. Miniature plant. Honors: 1974 Honorable Mention,
1977 Award of Merit, 1975 Don Fischer Award.

'Little Winecup' dip

Flower Description:
Cherry wine, green throat 2"

esu rpts   20"
NEW IN 00
GARDEN

A cheery little face.

'Lullaby Baby' dip   Semi evergreen

Flower Description:
Pastel peachy white, green throat 3", ruffled, rounded

esu   20"
NEW IN 98
GARDEN

Tested to be superior long bloomers. Extended blooms develop at varying
heights. Ruffled petals and rounded flowers. Honors: 1998 All American Daylily.

'Luxury Lace' dip   Dormant

Flower Description:
Mauve pink, green throat ruffled

msu, re 24-30"
NEW IN
GARDEN

Honors: 1959 Honorable Mention, 1962 Award of Merit, 1965 Annie Giles Award,
1970 Lenington All American, 1965 Stout Medal.

'Mary Todd' tet   Semi evergreen

Flower Description:
Large, ruffled, golden yellow 6", heavy, ruffled

esu-msu 24-20"
NEW IN 94
GARDEN

Wide petals, heavy ruffling, extremely heavy texture. Honors: 1970 Honorable
Mention, 1972 President's Cup, 1973 Award of Merit, 1978 Stout Medal (highest
medal awarded), 1974 RC Peck Medal.

'Mini Stella' dip   Dormant

Flower Description:
Yellow, everblooming, fragrant 2"

esu-fall LB   10"
NEW IN 96
GARDEN

This was the outcome when, now-common, H. 'Stella de Oro' was crossed with
another daylily. It is more yellow than the original gold Stella. Flowers are quite
small, 2", and fragrant. Like its parent, it is an excellent long bloomer, beginning
in early summer, but requires regular dividing and feeding to keep it up.

'Olive Bailey Langdon' tet   Semi evergreen   msu, rpts   28"
Flower Description: NEW IN 00
Purple 5"   GARDEN

Honors: 1977 Honorable Mention, 1980 Award of Merit, 1985 Lenington All American.

'Orange Vols' tet   Dormant   msu   28-36"
Flower Description: NEW IN 00
Fire orange bitone large, 6.5"   GARDEN

Grower describes as an improved 'Rocket City'.

'Pink Damask' dip   Dormant   msu, re   30"
Flower Description: NEW IN 95
Rose pink self 4.5"   GARDEN

Honors: 1954 Honorable Mention, 1957 Award of Merit.

'Prairie Blue Eyes' dip   Dormant   msu   32"
Flower Description: NEW IN 97
Lavender blue, yellow green throat 5.25"   GARDEN

Honors: 1973 Honorable Mention, 1976 Award of Merit.

'Red Ribbons'   msu   36-48"
Flower Description: NEW IN 00
Bright red Huge 8" spider   GARDEN

Ribbon-like petals on spider form flower.

'Red Volunteer' tet   Dormant   msu   30"
Flower Description: NEW IN 96
Large, rich red Huge 7"   GARDEN 96

Honors: 1989 Honorable Mention, 1994 Award of Merit. Huge flowers grow 7" across.

'Ruffled Apricot' tet   Dormant   esu-msu   30"
Flower Description: NEW IN 96
Apricot, lavender pink ribs, golden throat 7", ruffled   GARDEN

Beautiful, large tetraploid flower. Honors: 1976 Honorable Mention, 1976 President's Cup, 1976 RC Peck Award, 1977 Award of Merit, 1982 Stout Medal (highest award).

'Siloam Show Girl'   msu   18"
Flower Description: NEW IN 00
Red, dark red zone 4.5"   GARDEN

Honors: 1953 Honorable Mention, 1956 Award of Merit.

   185

'Siloam Virginia Henson' dip   Dormant   esu-msu   18"

Flower Description:
Pink, red eye 4"

NEW IN 97
GARDEN

Honors: 1983 Honorable Mention, 1986 Award of Merit, 1985 Annie Giles Award, 1989 Don Fisher Award.

'So Lovely'   Semi evergreen   msu   30"

Flower Description:
Near white, green throat 5.5"

NEW IN 95
GARDEN 95

Hard-to-find, near-white cultivar.

'Stella de Oro' dip   Dormant   esu-lsu LB   12-18"

Flower Description:
Golden yellow, fragrant 2"

NEW IN 90
GARDEN 96

Dependable rebloomer and currently very popular. Overused in landscape; so many other excellent cultivars from which to choose. Introduced in 1975. Honors: 1979 Don Fischer Memorial, 1979 Honorable Mention, 1982 Award of Merit, 1985 Stout Medal (highest award).

'Suzie Wong' dip   Dormant   esu-msu   24"

Flower Description:
Bright, cheery yellow, ruffled 3" ruffled

NEW IN 95
GARDEN

Shorter variety with ruffled flowers. Honors:1964 Honorable Mention, 1967 Award of Merit, 1971 Annie T. Giles Award.

'Yellow Lollipop' dip   Dormant   esu-lsu   16-20"

Flower Description:
Golden yellow, green throat 3"

NEW IN 97
GARDEN

Honors: 182 Honorable Mention, 1985 Award of Merit, 1986 Lenington All American.

hyperion

'Hyperion' dip   Dormant   esu-msu, re   42"

Flower Description:
Buttery, flaring, large yellow, fragrant 7-8" flaring

NEW IN 94
GARDEN

One of the first flowers that comes to mind when searching for fragrant flowers. Since 1924. Tall and rigid stems. Excellent naturalized. Very large, flaring blossom.

lilioasphodelus (flava)
'Flava' (Lemon Lily)   Dormant   esu   36"

Flower Description: NEW IN 98
Yellow, sweetly fragrant 4.5", lily form   GARDEN

A must for your garden if you are focusing on fragrance. One of early species of
daylilies, a sturdy plant that spreads quickly. Once very popular, was commonly
called "lemon lily", but lost in the dust of thousands of new cultivars. A famous
aphrodisiac, gum-jum, was made from dried buds of this plant and imported from
the Orient. Shade tolerant.

HEPATICA

Americana

Liverleaf

Perennial

White

spr 6"

NEW for us in 85

In our GARDEN

True woodland wildflower. Three lobed, dark-green leaves are heart-shaped and fade and recede into dormancy by midsummer. Small scale plant best for tucking into small spaces.

HERNIARIA

glabra

Burstwort

Perennial

Tiny white

1"

NEW for us in

In our GARDEN

Flat growing with tiniest of leaves. Provide good drainage and sun or part shade. Original groundcover throughout the Minnesota Arboretum Japanese Garden. It took a few years to get it right because of major weed problems intertwined throughout the original planting.

HESPERIS

Dame's rocket is a charismatic, old-fashioned plant that has been popular in gardens for centuries. Though not native, it has been around S.D. since the early homesteaders brought it along with them. And for the past many springs and early summers, their white, purple and lavender shades have effortlessly brightened the shady dry nooks and periphery of our yard where they have naturalized. Graceful foliage quickly grows to two to three feet, and hundreds of half-inch, sparkling flowers assemble at the top in loose, open clusters. Evenings tell of their fragrance.

I have always thought that the acclimatization of Hesperis is an example of a good non-native, a foreigner that moves in and assimilates with its surroundings without competing with or choking out the natives in the way Lythrum and other noxious weeds have done. But this winter, there have been messages from states to our west, that this plant might be banned.

As biennials, plants die after flowering, prolifically leaving seed behind to germinate and bloom in two years, repeating the cycle. If you remove some of the old flowers before they set seed, you might anticipate a second production of flowers later in the season.

They are easy to grow in well-drained, alkaline soil that is reliably moist during the germination period. Otherwise, from my experience, they are very drought tolerant. They are valuable as garden plants or for informal, naturalized areas in shade or part sun. Once established, they will continue to return as long as these conditions are met. There is a double form out there, somewhere, hard to propagate and rare; if you find it, please tell me where!

matronalis
Dame's Rocket Mix

Dame's Rocket, Sweet Rocket, Dame's Violet   esu-msu   24-30"
Biennial, Non-native Prairie   ○ ●   NEW for us in 96
Purple, lilac, white   In our GARDEN

Admired a few years ago for natural beauty when used to reclaim ditches along Sioux Falls' interstates; and then, just as they were blooming, the order came, and the ditches were mowed!

HEUCHERA

Coral bells are long-lived, North American native perennials from which hundreds of cultivars have been hybridized. Foliage and flower provide a lovely contrast. Dainty, wiry stems of many tiny flowers rise high above thick, evergreen, kidney-shaped, basal foliage. Durable, long-lived and easy, they bloom steadfastly in June or longer and provide excellent cut flowers for arrangements.

The H. americana hybrids are tough and reliable and the species from which many unusual cultivars have been bred. These hybrids have striking foliage effects, unusually mottled, variegated or colored, and oodles of different named cultivars and descriptions are out there to confuse us. Often, those with the most outstanding foliage have flowers of little significance. Occasionally you may find one that has both glorious foliage and flowers. With so, so many Heuchera being introduced (there are over eighty and still counting on my "to try" list), how does one choose?

Part shade or substantial sun will agree with them; soil should be rich, well-drained and moist, according to most books. Rich and well-drained I can vouch for; but at the nursery, when other potted plants begin to languish and are ready for their daily dose of water, the coral bells are the last group to show effects of dryness.

Technically Heuchera are evergreen plants, maintaining leathery clumps of leaves that never go completely dormant. In South Dakota or similar climates, clumps may be heaved out of the ground in spring freeze-thaw cycles. For this reason you may want to provide winter mulch. Divide in spring if flower stalks begin to decrease and crowns become woody, usually after four or more years.

'Cascade Dawn'
Coral Bells, Alum Root   esu-msu   24-30"
Perennial, Groundcover, Containers   ○ ◐ ●   NEW for us in 00
Tiny white bells on stalks   In our GARDEN
Purple and burgundy and silver foliage, dark veins.

'Chocolate Ruffles'
Coral Bells, Alum Root   esu   24"
Perennial, Groundcover, Containers   ○ ◐ ●   NEW for us in 97
Small white bells   In our GARDEN
Foliage up to 1' is deep, chocolate-brown with purple undersides. Hundreds of small white flowers are born on 2.5', purple stalks. Leaves deeply cut and very ruffled. One of the scores of newly patented hybrids.

 190

'Montrose Ruby'
Coral Bells, Alum Root
Perennial, Groundcover, Containers   ○ ◑ ●
Small white bells

18'

NEW for us in
In our GARDEN

New unusual and unique, silver marbling upon dark-purple ruffled leaf. So-sc
flowers. A cross between 'Palace Purple' and 'Dale's Strain'. Won't fade in hot
weather.

'Northern Fire'
Coral Bells, Alum Root
Perennial, Groundcover, Containers   ○ ◑ ●
Vivid red

esu-msu   24-30'
NEW for us in 0(
In our GARDEN

Th is Canadian introduced coral bell is grown for flowers, but bright shiny green
basal leaves need not apologize to all the new purple foliaged coral bells
coming into the marketplace. Honors: COPF Introduction; Morden Research
Station.

'Plum Pudding'
Coral Bells, Alum Root
Perennial, Groundcover, Containers   ○ ◑ ●
Tiny white bells on stalks

esu-msu   24'
NEW for us in 01
In our GARDEN

Dark burgundy basal leaves and stems, compact plants.

'Purple Petticoats'
Coral Bells, Alum Root
Perennial, Groundcover, Containers   ○ ◑ ●
Tiny white bells on stalks

esu-msu   24-30"
NEW for us in
In our GARDEN

Low growing mounds of ruffled foliage that is purple on the top and burgundy
underneath. Plants grow tight and compact.

'Raspberry Regal'
Coral Bells, Alum Root
Perennial, Groundcover, Containers   ○ ◑ ●
Double, raspberry red

esu-lsu LB   30-36"
NEW for us in 96
In our GARDEN 99

Very long blooming and showy, double-red flowers on long strong stalks,
marbled foliage with silver highlights. One of finest coral bells; rare and
underused. Excellent cut flowers.

'Regal Robe'
Coral Bells, Alum Root
Perennial, Groundcover, Containers   ○ ◑ ●
Tiny chartreuse bells on stalks

esu-msu   24-30"
NEW for us in
In our GARDEN

Large marbled leaves, up to 8", with metallic lavender glow that changes with
season. Chartreuse bells on tall stalk. Shade tolerant and evergreen.
Introduced in '98.

'Regina'
Coral Bells, Alum Root
Perennial, Groundcover, Containers   ○ ◑ ●
Pink flowers on stalks

esu-msu   24-30"
NEW for us in
In our GARDEN

One of few coral bells that has burgundy foliage and colorful flowers. Here
they coordinate on one outfit.

 191

'Torch', 'Fackel'

Coral Bells, Alum Root   esu-msu   24-30"
Perennial, Groundcover, Containers   ○ ◐ ●   NEW for us in   95
Glowing red bells   In our GARDEN   95

Taller than most, excellent, showy cut flowers for florist market. Resembles H. 'Raspberry Regal'.

americana
'Constance'

Coral Bells, Alum Root   esu-msu   8"
Perennial, Groundcover, Containers   ○ ◐ ●   NEW for us in   95
Pink, white bicolor   In our GARDEN

Handsome miniature plant and one of few with bicolor flowers. Short in stature.

americana
'Dale's Strain'

Coral Bells, Alum Root   esu   15"
Perennial, Groundcover, Containers   ○ ◐ ●   NEW for us in   96
Subtle white bells on stalk   In our GARDEN   99

Variable, silver-blue foliage, heavily marbled with white, red and silver veins. Use as drought tolerant groundcover in mostly shade.

brizoides x
'Mt. St. Helens'

Coral Bells, Alum Root   esu-msu LB   12-18"
Perennial, Groundcover, Containers   ○ ◐ ●   NEW for us in   96
Brick red   In our GARDEN   96

Standing ovations for great performances. Erect stems of vivid, bell-shaped flowers for a long period. Thick, ruffled foliage. All Heuchera excellent for June flowers and beyond while waiting for the rest of perennials to catch-up.

brizoides x
'Pluie de Feu', 'Rain or Ring of Fire'

Coral Bells, Alum Root   msu-lsu LB   12-24"
Perennial, Groundcover, Containers   ○ ◐ ●   NEW for us in   98
Cherry red   In our GARDEN   99

Silver mottled leaves, purple veins. Outstanding bright flower color and excellent foliage. Seedling of H. 'Eco Magnifica'. We cut flowers of these plants back as they are fading and they rebloom later in the summer.

brizoides x
'Snow Angel'

Coral Bells, Alum Root   esu-msu   12-24"
Perennial, Groundcover, Containers   ○ ◐ ●   NEW for us in   94
Pink bells on a stalk   In our GARDEN   99

Obviously variegated. Creamy blotches dot green mounds that brighten shady gardens. Handsome, evergreen foliage contrasts beautifully with bright pink, bell-shaped flowers. Great cut flowers.

 192

micrantha
'Palace Purple'

Coral Bells, Alum Root
Perennial, Groundcover, Containers ○ ◐ ●
Blush white

esu-msu   18-24"
NEW for us in   95
In our GARDEN   95

Fine, red-purple, ivy-shaped foliage in mounds up to 1.5'. Fragile-looking white flowers on abundant stalks. Because of demand, seed-grown plants have been used and all do not have the foliage hues of the original cultivar. Carefully choose the most colorful plants or demand vegetatively produced plants. Honors: 1991 Perennial Plant of the Year.

micrantha
'Pewter Moon'

Coral Bells, Alum Root
Perennial, Groundcover, Containers ○ ◐ ●
Light pink

esu-msu   12"
NEW for us in   00
In our GARDEN   00

Silvery pink flowers and outstanding foliage. Foliage is a silvery-pewter with similar netting pattern on rounded, flat, clumping leaves. Leaves are red beneath. This hybrid originates in Europe. Vigorous and wonderful little plant that maintains compactness. Honors: Penn State Top 20 Perennial Performers.

micrantha x
'Carousel'

Coral Bells, Alum Root
Perennial, Groundcover, Containers ○ ◐ ●
Hot pink

esu-msu   24"
NEW for us in   96
In our GARDEN   96

Rounded basal leaves, typical of coral bells. This time they're rounded, glossy and heavily silvered. Blossom is extremely heavy with intense pink flowers. Showy and charming for the June month.

sanguinea
'Brandon Pink'

Coral Bells, Alum Root
Perennial, Groundcover, Containers ○ ◐ ●
Large showy pink stalks

esu-msu   24-30"
NEW for us in   00
In our GARDEN   00

Spikes of showy flowers have not been sacrificed. Heavy dark green basal foliage. A recent non seed propagated cultivar. Honors: Canadian Morden Introduction.

sanguinea
'Fire Fly', 'Leuchtkafer'

Coral Bells, Alum Root
Perennial, Groundcover, Containers ○ ◐ ●
Vermillion red

esu-msu   24"
NEW for us in   95
In our GARDEN

Fragrant, showy vermillion-red flowers on a stalk.

 193

villosa

purpurea

Coral Bells, Alum Root   esu   18"

Perennial, Groundcover, Containers   ○ ◐ ●   NEW for us in   95

Small white bells on stalks   In our GARDEN   94

Better than H. 'Palace Purple'? Crinkled and fuzzy purple leaves that are like chartreuse H. 'Autumn Bride' in quality. Plant them side by side for great foliage contrasts. Dry shade tolerant.

villosa x

'Autumn Bride'

Coral Bells, Alum Root   lsu-fall   24"

Perennial, Groundcover, Containers   ○ ◐ ●   NEW for us in   98

Pure white stalks   In our GARDEN   98

Unusual late flowering coral bell explodes in late summer with white-flowering stalks and we love white flowers in the fall. Foliage is wonderful with heavy velvety texture and chartreuse color that provides needed foliage contrasts. This plant is unique among the myriad of coral bell cultivars offered today. Tolerates dry shade.

 194

HEUCHERELLA

Back in 1912, it probably didn't take too much head-scratching to christen a new genus as "Heucherella" and give its common name as "foamy bells." These monikers were befitting to this new plant and combined the genera names and common names of the two parents: Heuchera, coral bells, and Tiarella, foam flower.

Heucherella is the result of intergeneric (between two separate genera) xenogamy (cross pollination), an unusual occurrence of cross pollination between two separate genera. In addition to a blend of two names and physical and physiological characteristics, it adds two new words to my vocabulary.

The offspring have the three to four inch, heart-shaped leaves of Tiarella and the taller stalks and larger flowers of Heuchera. Flowers may last for up to eight weeks while on the plant during cool spring and early summer days and last a long time as cut flowers, too. They are delightful as patches of ground cover in shade to part sun. You will have to encourage their increase by dividing them because they are sterile and will not make seed. Provide to them growing conditions similar to that of both genera--well-drained, amended, humus-rich soil that is reliably moist.

alba
'Bridget Bloom'

Foamy Bells	esu-lsu LB	18"
Perennial, Groundcover ○ ●	NEW for us in	94
Clear, shell pink	In our GARDEN	99

Tiny bell-flowers, lasting at least eight weeks, grow up and down many wiry stems that are held far above basal foliage mounds. This genus is not quite as easy to establish as Heuchera or Tiarella, and will take a couple of years to grow into substantial clumps. Blooms of Bressingham introduction.

alba
'Crimson Clouds'

Foamy Bells	esu-lsu LB	18"
Perennial, Groundcover ○ ●	NEW for us in	
Dark pink	In our GARDEN	

Dark green to purple leaves.

HIBISCUS

As a very young gardener I grew several plants of this Hibiscus species, rose of Sharon, from seed and lined them out in the vegetable garden. They have captivated me since 'cause, like an old friend, we have "history."

These herbaceous-acting Hibiscus are very definitely woody plants. We add them to our perennial melting pot because top growth dies back with autumn frosts and reemerges in spring (very late I might add, not until mid-June in '97), after which it grows like crazy into large-leaved, tall, woody shrubs.

Then, by late summer, from all this new growth, the fireworks begin! Long, fat, tightly-furled buds spiral open to flowers that are unforgettable for their immense, six to ten inch diameters and for their resemblance in form and longevity to those of normally tropical Hibiscus, each flower lasting for only one day. Butterflies are seduced and provided with ample petal-platforms for their touch downs.

Culture is full sun, good ventilation and plenty of non-marshy moisture (try to repeat this three times in rapid succession), and providing these requirements will induce more flowers. Pick off spent flowers to avoid seed-set and extend blooming period.

We've experienced these as hardy but not live-forevers. Whether this is due to culture, disease or just irrational winters, we're not sure. Winter mulch will make a difference.

moscheutos
'Blue River II'

Rose Mallow, Rose of Sharon — lsu-fall LB   48"
Perennial, Sub-shrub   ○ ● — NEW for us in   98
Pure white — In our GARDEN   99
One of best for long flowering. 10" flowers. Foliage has blue hints.

moscheutos
'Disco Bell' Mix

Rose Mallow, Rose of Sharon — msu-fall   30"
Perennial, Sub-shrub   ○ ● — NEW for us in   96
Mixed white, red, pink — In our GARDEN
More compact plant; same huge flowers.

moscheutos
'Disco Bell Pink'

Rose Mallow, Rose of Sharon — lsu-fall   30"
Perennial, Sub-shrub   ○ ● — NEW for us in   96
Rose pink — In our GARDEN   97
Compact shrub but same large flowers.

 196

moscheutos
'Lady Baltimore'
Rose Mallow, Rose of Sharon
Perennial, Sub-shrub ○ ●
Deep pink, red center
Well-known hybrid, 6-9" ruffled flowers.

lsu-fall   48-72"
NEW for us in 01
In our GARDEN

moscheutos
'Lord Baltimore'
Rose Mallow, Rose of Sharon
Perennial, Sub-shrub ○ ●
Brilliant crimson red, ruffled
Heavy bloomer, ruffled flowers and lobed leaves.

msu-fall   60-100"
NEW for us in 96
In our GARDEN

moscheutos x
'Sweet Caroline'
Rose Mallow, Rose of Sharon
Perennial, Sub-shrub ○ ●
Two-toned bright pink

lsu-fall LB   48-72"
NEW for us in 94
In our GARDEN

Ruffled, reflexed petals of 6-8" flowers on large, patented plants. Dark veins and eye zone distinguish this from the rest.

moscheutos x coccineus
'Old Yella'
Rose Mallow, Rose of Sharon
Perennial, Sub-shrub ○ ●
Light yellow, red throat

msu-fall   48"
NEW for us in 00
In our GARDEN

Ten inch diameter, thick, creamy yellow flowers. Plant form is more upright than spreading. In '99, one of latest Nebraska Fleming introductions. Their Hibiscus introductions are more compact with denser foliage and thicker stems. Flowers are thicker too, with overlapping petals. Knowing this is from a stone's throw down under gives me confidence in growing these, not to mention a sense of pride in regionally developed plants.

HIERACIUM

aurantiacum
Orange Hawkweed
Perennial or Biennial ○ ●
Glowing red orange

esu   12-18"
NEW for us in 95
In our GARDEN 95

A '95 experiment from seed resulted in a silky haired plant that has naturalized itself in and around the nooks and crannies of field stone in our garden. Showy orange flowers have many radiating petals and top off long 12" stems. So far not obtrusive, but welcomed wherever they choose to self-sow and put down roots. Well, ok, we've had to pull a few. It's easy to do.

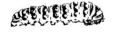 197

HOSTA

Recipe for Hosta. Stir together the following ingredients:

<u>A</u>. Large volumes of dark-green, light-green, lime-green, blue, chartreuse, gold, yellow, cream and white pigments.

<u>B</u>. The same of puckered, twisted, thick, thin, tiny, large, broad, narrow, pointed, rounded, shiny and dull leaves.

<u>C</u>. Measures of all lengths from four inches to four feet.

<u>D</u>. Strength, durability, hardiness and reliability.

Blend well; divide into 2000 cultivars. Add adequate, well-drained soil, moisture, copious amounts of shade, and several rays of sun. Observe, nurture, cherish, and be stilled by the strength of their forms.

Hosta are unbeatable plants that provide focal points and necessary weight in a well-designed garden. Most require a shady site, but several are sun tolerant. They are grown primarily for their foliage, and many display outstanding stalks of flowers. Over the past couple of decades, gardeners have renewed their love affair with Funkia lilies, though they've been grown in the United States for 150 years, having been brought to other countries from Japanese and Chinese woodlands. Prices range widely, and the numbers are dependent on demand, ease of propagation, and newness on the market of a particular cultivar. Generally, Hosta with heavily textured, high-quality leaves are slower to increase, resulting in higher prices.

Many take a few years to turn into the elegant, mature and established clumps that colorful catalogs market to you. Though good growing conditions are recommended, I have witnessed many Hosta thriving in less-than-ideal conditions and even tolerating drought if in complete shade.

If you are a grower of Hosta, you shudder at the sound of a simple four-letter word, "s-l-u-g." These little, slimy, shell-less snails love the same environment as do these plants, and they savor their leaves. Unsightly holes remain after their nighttime forages. Thick, heavy-leaved cultivars and mature plants show less effects of damage. There are a number of controls recommended. Beer traps and handpicking seem futile. But gritty substances such as ashes or

quartzite crusher dust (our indiginous stone) placed around the entire circumference of the clumps discourage slimy bellies. An encircling copper band apparently provides enough of a charge to keep them from oozing near the plant. There are chemical methods of pellets or gels containing metaldehyde, which we try to avoid because of potential harm to birds and other animals.

My garden-guru friends and I have had years of experience with some of the best new cultivars and the old original species brought from Japan that our lucky grandparents may have grown. Over the years we have taken Hosta hiatus to the national Hosta display garden at the Minnesota Landscape Arboretum in Chanhassen, Minnesota, and visited friendly, encouraging grower-mentors like dear Mr. Savory.

We prioritize selections from growers who provide field-grown rather than tissue-cultured plants. Though tissue culture is the great new wave in plant propagation, I've witnessed many plants increased in this way that bypass some of the main characteristics that a particular cultivar is to display. A plant may show all the identifying characteristics when young, and then as it matures, it begins to change and revert to something else that no one recognizes.

'Abiqua Moonbeam', 'Mayan Moon'

Blue-green center color with gold edge
SUN-tolerant foliage
Near white, lavender flowers   msu   Medium
Sport of H. 'August Moon'.

'Antioch'

Light-green center, wide cream edge
Lavender flowers   msu   Large
Honors: Favorite Hosta List.

'August Moon'

Gold color
Cupped, seersucker leaf, SLUG-resistant foliage
White flowers   msu   Large
One of the best gold-leaved cultivars is at its loveliest in 100% shade. Leaf is a heavily corrugated, seersucker type that is slug-resistant.

'Baby Bunting'

Very small, blue-green leaves
Dense, compact mound
Pale lavender   msu   Dwarf, 6"
Of all dwarf hosta, this stands out. Honors: Award winner.

'Big Daddy'

Deep blue-green color

Heavy substance, large, puckered and cupped foliage

White flowers   msu   Large 24"

One of finest quality substance in a Hosta cultivar. Cupping and puckering is unique and outstanding.

'Black Hills'

Very dark-green color

Thick, heavily puckered, sparkling, SLUG-resistant foliage

Lavender flowers   esu   Large

Dark-green rounded leaves are heavily puckered. Introduced by Mr. Savory from Minneapolis, our garden group's original Hosta mentor. Honors: 1990 Eunice Fisher Award.

'Blue Angel'

Very blue color

Heavy texture, huge cordate leaf, SLUG-resistant foliage

White flowers   msu, LB   Large 48"

Extremely heavy-textured, huge blue leaves and huge plant create a tropical feeling--spectacular! Produces many white, long blooming, hyacinth-like flowers that can be used for cutting. Honors: PAL award, Favorite Hosta List.

'Blue Arrow'

Blue-green color

Erect, lance-shaped, glossy foliage

White, bell-shaped flowers   Medium

Very thick substanced leaves on a semi erect form.

'Blue Cadet'

Blue-green color

Rounded leaves, fast growing, SLUG-resistant foliage

Lavender flowers   lsu   Small 12"

One of the most popular small cultivars for blue leaf color. The leaf is small, rounded with heavy texture. Flowers are lavender. Heavy textured leaves are very desirable. Use them for built-in slug resistance.

'Blue Mammoth'

Very blue, powdered color

Heavy texture, huge, quick growing foliage

White, bell-shaped flowers   Large

Grows quickly into a large clump. Powder-blue, giant leaves are heavily corrugated. Flowers are white and bell-shaped.

'Blue Seer'

Intense blue color doesn't fade to green

Thick, puckering, SLUG-resistant foliage

Abundant lush white flowers   Medium

Heavy puckering on one-of-best blue leaves. Abundant flowers and slug-resistant.

 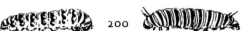

'Blue Umbrellas'

Blue-green color in spring, later green
Heavy, waxy, SLUG-resistant, SUN-tolerant foliage
Lavender, edged white, numerous flowers   msu   Large 24-36"
A rapid grower considering the heavy textured, puckering leaves. Very floriferous with unique off-white to lavender flowers with white edges. Eventually makes a giant mound of large, puckered, rounded leaves.

'Brave Amherst'

Blue-green centers, half-inch gold margin
Rounded leaves, thick substance, rounded mound form
White flowers   esu
Forms very broad and comparatively low, 4-5' wide mounds. Honors: Best New Hosta of 1997.

'Daybreak'

One of deepest gold colors
Heavy veins, SUN-tolerant and SLUg-resistant foliage
Lavender flowers   Medium
Deep gold leaved variety. Texture is very heavy with prominent veins, lavender flowers. Honors: PAL Award, "Popular Unpopluar Hosta" list.

'Fragrant Bouquet'

Apple-green leaf center, wide yellow margin
Wavy, heart-shaped leaves, heavy mound, rapid grower
White, fragrant, numerous flowers   esu   Medium
Leaves emerge as golden, turning to apple green while retaining creamy yellow margins. Flowers are exceptional, 3" long, wide open and fragrant, attached to 3' scapes. Establishes and increases quickly. Honors: 1998 Hosta of the year, "Popular Unpopluar Hosta" list.

'Frosted Jade'

Frost-green leaf center enjoys definite white edge
Flat, heart-shaped leaves
White flowers   Large
Honors: Many awards, "Popular Unpopluar Hosta" list.

'Gold Drop'

Golden color
Small heart-shaped leaves, SUN-tolerant foliage
Lavender flowers   msu   Small 8-12"
Nice small clumps make good edging in shade.

'Gold Edger'

Golden color
Heart-shaped, SLUG-resistant, SUN-tolerant foliage
Lavender flowers   msu   ?
A beautiful, small, front-of-the-shade-garden plant. The gold colored leaf creates subtle contrasts with blue forms. Quick-growing, substantial clumps are heavy with bloom. Very nice planted with H. 'Halcyon'.

 201

'Gold Standard'

Chartreuse and green variegated

Quick growing leaves and mounded foliage

Pale lavender flowers   msu   Medium 24"

Quick to increase and form a clump. Variegated chartreuse and green foliage is subtle and blends better in the garden than most green and white variegated leaves. Beautiful when mature, which it does quickly. Coloration varies depending on amount of sun exposure. Honors: Favorite Hosta List.

'Golden Prayers'

Yellow and gold color

Pale lavender flowers   Small 12"

Yellow and gold leaves keep intense contrasts even in shade. Great in containers if you have no more room in your garden.

'Golden Scepter'

Bright gold color

Heart-shaped foliage

Lavender numerous flowers   msu   Small to medium

Use as an edging plant in shade garden. Recognized for leaf quality and number of flower scapes.

'Golden Tiara'

Light-green centers, yellow margins

Heart-shaped, rapid clumping, SUN-tolerant foliage

Purple striped flowers   msu   Medium small

Small to medium size cultivar by Mr. Savory of Minneapolis, whom we would always visit during Hosta hiatus. Heart-shaped, green leaves with gold borders hold their coloration all season. Very quick to increase. Heavy bloomer, covered with purple spikes; tolerant of extra sun. Honors: Small Hosta Award, Favorite Hosta List.

'Great Expectations'

Cream center, wide blue-green margins

Round, puckered, wide, SUN-tolerant foliage

Large white masses of flowers   esu   Large 24"

Blue leaves with gold center in spring and white center in summer. Shade to 3/4 sun. Best natural sport of H. sieboldiana 'Elegans'. Many saw this in '97 "Better Homes and Gardens" and came looking. Honors: Favorite Hosta List.

'Halcyon'

Chalky blue color

Heavy substance, spear-shaped, SLUG resistant, slight SUN-tolerant foliage

Near-white numerous flowers   msu-lsu   Medium small

A very blue cultivar that always looks good. Combines well with H. 'Gold Edger' as a border-edger. Heavy flowering. Honors: Favorite Hosta List.

 202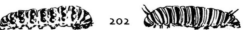

'Invincible'

Bright green color

Thick and tough, glossy, SUN-tolerant, rapid growing foliage

Pale lavender blue, fragrant flowers   msu   Small 12"

Bright and very shiny, very thick, blade-like leaves, fast grower, fragrant flowers. Honors: Best blooming Hosta list.

'Knock Out'

Yellow, green margin

Oval leaves

                                                   36"

'Krossa Regal'

Blue-gray color

Vase form, pointed wide leaves, SLUG-resistant foliage

Lavender flowers   lsu   Large 36"

Large, heavy, leathery and pointed leaves with vase-like form. Leaf tips do not brush the ground. Our favorite for pivotal plant or striking focal point. If you are Hosta collector, you should have this one. Honors: Favorite Hosta List.

'Lemon Lime'

gold

Narrow, lance-shaped, wavy edged foliage

Lavender, purple stripes, numerous flowers   msu   Small

Solid chartreuse color survives throughout growing season. Small, narrow, wavy leaves prefer some sun to hold chartreuse color. Many lavender flowers appear and later, reappear. A fast grower, quickly establishes a clump. Savory introduction.

'Louisa'

Dark-green centers, narrow white margin

Lance-shaped leaves, neat rounded form

White flowers   msu   Small

Small white-margined cultivar forms small low clumps of foliage.

'Lucy Vitols'

Yellow green center color, narrow green margin

Heavy texture and puckering foliage

Light lavender flowers   Medium

Honors: "Popular Unpopluar Hosta" list.

'Patriot'

Bright-green center, broad white margin

Slight SUN-tolerant foliage

Pretty lilac flowers   esu   Medium

Sound, outstanding new cultivar that will withstand the test of time. Dark-green leaves with showy, crisp, 1" white margin, wider than that of H 'Francee'. Sport of H. 'Francee'. Honors: 1991 American Hosta Awards, 1997 Hosta of the Year, "Popular Unpopluar Hosta" list.

'Pearl Lake'

Blue-green color

Heart-shaped foliage, dense mounded form

Numerous lavender flowers   msu   Medium

A good increaser, blue-green, heart-shaped, puckered leaves provide a great profusion of lavender flowers on tall scapes in July. Excellent for cutting and overall, massed effect. Honors: Best All Around Hosta.

'Piedmont Gold'

Yellow-gold color

Long leaves curve and twist, rapid grower, SUN-tolerant foliage

Many white flowers   msu   Medium

Tall clump parented by H. plantaginea. Honors: Favorite Hosta List, Large Hosta Award.

'Platinum Tiara'

White-edged 'Golden Tiara'

Rapid, strong-growing foliage

Dark lavender flowers streaked white   Medium 24"

Sport of 'Golden Tiara' with white ribbon border. Rapid, strong grower and quick to form clumps. Another introduction by Mr. Savory of Minneapolis.

'Purple Dwarf'

Green color

Tight little miniature form, puckered foliage

Numerous purple flowers   Small

Tidy, compact and effective dwarf best used in multiples. Flowers heavily for such a little guy.

'Regal Splendor'

Blue-green center, cream border

Vase shape, heavy, thick foliage

Orchid flowers   esu   Large

Superb light margined sport of the long popular 'Krossa Regal'.

'Shade Fanfare'

Light-green or gold center, broad cream edge

Rapid growing, SLUG-resistant, SUN-tolerant foliage

Numerous lavender flowers   msu   Medium

A distinguished plant that gathers much attention. Medium sized leaves have wide creamy margins, are puckered with good texture, have lavender flowers produced on abundant scapes, and grow rapidly. Honors: Favorite Hosta List.

'Snow Cap'

Powder-blue leaf centers, cream margins

Heavy substance, mounded form, SLUG-resistant foliage

White flowers   msu   Medium

Powder-blue leaf centers. Very nice, slow increaser.

'Snowflakes'

Bright-green color
Narrow, elongated foliage
Large, pure white flowers   lsu   Small
Miniature green with big white flowers. Showy small Hosta.

'So Sweet'

Green center color, white and gold margins at same time.
Glossy, SUN-tolerant foliage
Numerous, very fragrant, white flowers   msu   Medium Small
One of finest, fragrant Hosta flowers. Honors: Hosta of the Year '95, Best Blooming Hosta,1995 Hosta Plant of the Year.

'Spritzer'

Yellow and white center, green margins
Morning SUN-tolerant, narrow, pointed foliage
Lovely flower buds turn to light blue flowers   msu   Medium-small
Honors: "Popular Unpopluar Hosta" list.

'Striptease'

Unique and attractive, very popular all over eastern seaboard. We've seen prices on this plant at over $75. So far all the ones we've ordered have not come true to color. They've had a streaky, messy look to the leaf color patterns, as if someone stirred the pigment either too much or too little. Tissue cultured Hosta do not always resemble the parent plant exactly. Non-true starter plants should be rouged out, but sometimes are not.

'Sum and Substance'

Chartreuse, golden color in sun
Glossy, rounded, textured, SLUG-resistant, SUN-tolerant foliage
Lavender flowers   lsu   Large 36"
Stunning, extra large cultivar effective as a single specimen or focal point. Heavy texture helps minimize slug damage. Honors: 1984 Midwest Gold Award, 1987 President's Exhib, 1992, '93, '94 Most Popular Hosta Award, Favorite Hosta List.

'Sun Power'

Gold color
Large, twisted leaves, wavy edges, SUN-tolerant foliage
Numerous lavender flowers   lsu   Large
Many light-orchid flowers on abundant scapes. Grows rapidly into a nice golden clump. Sun-tolerant without burning. Honors: 1986 Midwest Gold, Favorite Hosta List.

'Whirlwind'

White and chartreuse center color, deep green edges, unusual leaf
Twisted, different foliage
Lavender flowers   msu   Medium
Unusual habit and form provides interesting contrast to ordinary rounded clump forms. Honors: "Popular Unpopluar Hosta" list.

 205

'Wide Brim'

Blue-green center, wide cream and gold margin
SUN-tolerant foliage
Numerous pale-lavender flowers   msu   Large
Flower buds are attractive, later giving heavy bloom. Increases rapidly. Wide irregular, cream margins have gold tints when mature. Honors: PAL Award.

'Yellow Splash Brim'

Dark-green leaf centers, cream margins
Undulating, elongated foliage
Lavender flowers   esu   Small-medium

'Zounds'

Yellow-gold metallic color
Glossy, metallic, twisting, rounded form, SUN-tolerant foliage
Light lavender, near-white flowers   msu   Medium 18-24"
Brighten up a shady area with metallic, golden glossy leaves that seem to glow and hold color until frost. Unique color, heavy bloomer, rapid grower, sun-tolerant.

clausa

var. clausa

Green
Upright, stoloniferous, groundcover foliage
Purple flower buds do not open   msu-lsu   Medium 1.25'
Spreads by creeping, underground roots called stolons to make an excellent shady groundcover as it slowly moves in and makes itself comfortable. Late-season, purple buds, that do not open, are effective massed together and used for cut flowers.

fluctuans

'Variegated', 'Sagae'

Frosted green center, bright yellow wide margins
Twisted, heavy substance, vase-shaped, SUN-tolerant foliage
Pale orchid flowers   msu   Large
Striking specimen plant. Matures to very large size with huge elephant-ear-scale-leaves. Honors: 1987 Benedict Award, 1982 President's Exhibitor Trophy, Favorite Hosta List, 2000 Hosta of the Year.

fortunei

'Francee'

Dark forest-green centers, white edge
Neat heart-shaped leaves, rapid growing, SUN-tolerant foliage
Lavender flowers   lsu   Medium 18"
Rapid grower holds up well in extra sun all summer long. It is the best white-margined clone of H. fortunei. Honors: 1976 Eunice Fisher Award, Favorite Hosta List and, for your information, a favorite of Muhammad Ali.

fortunei
'Gloriosa'
variegated
Quick growing and clumping foliage
Lavender flowers   msu   Medium 1.5'
Crisp, narrow, white margin on dark-green leaf is subtle, does not dominate. Difficulty locating this one. One of my favorites within the green-white variegated group.

fortunei
'Gold Crown', 'Aureo Marginata'
Dark-green leaf centers with creamy edge
Rapid increaser, SUN-tolerant foliage
Lavender flowers   msu   Medium 24"
Rapid increaser. An old popular variety.

fortunei
'Paul's Glory'
Gold center color fades to white, blue-green margin
Classic form
Lavender flowers   Medium to large
Chartreuse center with dark green edge holds color throughout the summer. Fantastic specimen always stands out. Honors: 1999 Hosta of the year.

kikutii yakusimensis
'Kifukurin'
Dark-green center color, cream margin
Pointed, narrow foliage
Large lavender flowers   msu   Medium
Honors: "Popular Unpopluar Hosta" list.

lancifolia
lancifolia sp.
Bright-green color
Glossy, SUN-tolerant, lance-shaped foliage
Lavender flowers   lsu   Medium 18"
Will take full sun with extra moisture. Shiny-green leaves provide a plant good for landscape and massing. Lavender flowers bloom in late summer. Long known, old species formerly known as H. cathyana. Grown in my garden for 40 years.

longissima
(longissima)
Green color
Long, lance-shaped leaf, upright form
Numerous, dark lavender flowers   lsu   Small 9"
Narrow, long, arching leaves form this compact plant. Heavy in flower with dark-lavender blooms in late season. Native to bogs in Japan. Flood tolerant, use in shallow water gardens. Honors: "Popular Unpopluar Hosta" list.

 207

medio variegata, undulata
Medio variegata

Green edge, white center
Wavy foliage
Lavender flowers   msu   Medium
In existence for many years, recently gaining popularity with the new surge of interest in perennials.

montana
'Aureo Marginata'

Green centers, gold cream margins
Elongated, heart-shaped, very large, SUN-tolerant foliage
Lavender flowers   msu-lsu   Large 42"
Dense flowers on striking, large, distinctive cultivar. Always admired when seen as mature plants. Honors: 1985 Alex Summers Distinguished Merit Award, Favorite Hosta List.

montana
'Inniswood'

Bright-yellow leaf centers, dark-green margins
Lavender flowers   lsu   Medium
Of the montana lineage. Sport of H. 'Sun Glow'. Honors: 1986 Savory Shield Award.

montana
'On Stage'

Yellow, center, green, two-toned margins
SUN tolerant
Light, lavender blue   msu   14" Medium
Reverse of *H. montana 'Aureomarginata'*.

plantaginea
'Aphrodite'

Bright-green color
Glossy, SUN-tolerant foliage
Double white, fragrant flowers   Medium
One of last Hosta to emerge in spring. The plantaginea species is a bit tender, and we eventually lost the ones we had planted by our office. Best vigor with half day sun. Honors: Best blooming Hosta list.

plantaginea
var. grandiflora

Light-green color
Shiny, SUN-tolerant foliage
White flowers with heavenly fragrance   lsu   Large 30"

An old-fashioned, species plant. Large, very fragrant, pure-white blossoms occur in late summer. Large, shiny, bright green leaves. Actually performs and increases better if it is in sun. Provide extra water during drought. Native to China. Slow-growing; worth the wait. Last to emerge in spring and somewhat tender in our area.

plantaginea x
'Honeybells'

Light-green color
Thinly textured, shiny foliage
Very fragrant, pale lavender flowers   msu   Large 30-36"

Very quick to increase, very fragrant blossoms, an offspring of H. plantaginea. Light green leaves with light lavender blooms in late season. Much more vigorous and hardy than the species plantaginea.

plantaginea x
'Royal Standard'

Bright-green color
Large, SUN-tolerant, glossy foliage
Numerous white, fragrant flowers   lsu   Large 36"

A broad-functioned cultivar because it will tolerate sun. It is more prolific in sun and quick to make a large clump producing many stalks of white fragrant blossoms in August. An offspring of H. plantaginea and much hardier than that mother plant.

sieboldiana
'Elegans', 'Blue Giant'

Green, flushed blue color
Thick and crinkled, SLUG-resistant foliage
White flowers   msu   Large 30-36"

One of the old stalwarts of Hosta cultivars, since 1905. It becomes a giant of a plant with heavy substance, crinkled, slug-resistant leaf that has a blue cast. Honors: Favorite Hosta List, '86 Midwest Blue Winner.

sieboldiana
'Frances Williams'

Blue-green and chartreuse variegation
Huge, rounded, thick, puckered, SLUG-resistant foliage
Near white, pale lavender flowers   msu   Large 24-36"

Defies my limited ability to describe. Heavy seersucker and slug-resistant leaf, extra large and rounded shades of blue-green with wide, irregular chartreuse margins. Honors: 1984 Alex J. Summer's Distinguished Merit Award, Favorite Hosta List.

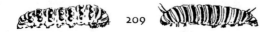

sieboldii

'Kabitan'

Yellow center color, green margins
Lance-shaped, wavy-edged, spreading foliage
Pale lavender flowers   msu   Dwarf

Bright yellow foliage when first emerging in spring. This plant tends to be rhizomatous and may send up off-shoots beyond root boundary. Bright chartreuse and green variegation offers bright focal points in the shade garden when used in groups or as a border. One of best dwarf selections.

tardiana

'Blue Moon'

Deep blue-green color
Flattened clump, heart-shaped, SLUG-resistant foliage
White, bell-shaped flowers   lsu   Dwarf 8"

Very thick and heavy, very blue leaves create a small flattened mound of heart-shaped, cupped foliage. A Hosta lover's delight for a groundcover or edging in shade.

tardiana

'June'

Bright gold center color, blue border
Heavy substance, SLUG-resistant foliage
                                                                                     Medium

A gold leaved, bordered blue, sport of H. 'Halcyon'. If you are looking for those scarce gold centered, darker margined types, here is one of the few.

tokudama

'Aureo-nebulosa

Irregular blue and green margins around shaded center
Cupped, heavily puckered leaves, SLUG-resistant foliage
Beautiful white flowers   Medium 12"

Fabulous, though slow-growing, choice. Honors: Favorite Hosta List.

tokudama

'Flavo circinalis'

Blue-green center color, gold margins
Slightly pointed leaves, SLUG-resistant foliage
Near white flowers   msu   Medium

A Tokudama Hosta. Lush, slug-resistant, and thick-textured, its blue-green and creamy-gold foliage looks as if freshly painted with water colors. Will grow very slowly so a mature plant is nearly as precious as gold! Honors: Favorite Hosta List.

tokudama

'Golden Medallion'

Golden color

Cupped, heart-shaped foliage

White flowers　　　　　　　　　　　　　msu　　　　　　Small

Fine gold miniature.

tokudama

'Love Pat'

Intense blue color

Upright, deeply cupped, quilted, SUN-tolerant foliage

Numerous pale lavender flowers　　　　　　lsu　　　Medium 18-24"

Of all blues this holds its color through most of summer. Honors: 1988 Midwest Blue Award, Favorite Hosta List.

undulata

'albo-marginata', 'Silver Edged'

Green center leaf, white variegated margin and splashes

SUN-tolerant foliage

Lavender flowers　　　　　　　　　　　　msu　　　　　Medium

Good all around species plant. Fast increaser, sun-tolerant. An old variety, it still is one of best variegated types for landscape use if you like the way the white margin commands all the attention. Remember, white/green Hosta can steal the show.

ventricosa

'Aureo marginata'

Green center color, yellow margin matures white

Heart-shaped, twisted foliage

Mauve flowers　　　　　　　　　　　　　msu　　　Medium 18-24"

Honors: Favorite Hosta List.

venusta

'Venusta'

Green color

Rapid increaser, dwarf mounded clumps of foliage

Numerous lavender flowers　　　　　　　msu　　　　Dwarf 6"

Rapidly increases, heavy in flower, great little groundcover that's worth the wait. Honors: "Popular Unpopluar Hosta" list.

cordata
'Chameleon'

Chameleon Plant

Perennial ○ ◑ ●

White on 2" stalks

esu 6-12"

NEW for us in 95

In our GARDEN X

Green, pink and white variegation on low spreading plants. Grown primarily for foliage. It didn't survive in our garden, but we only tried it once in '95.

IBERIS

Compact candytufts have been grown in gardens around here for decades. They are actually a little woody sub-shrub or semi-evergreen and withstand snowless winters better if mulched. Iberis serve well in the front of the border or as rock garden plants. Sun is preferred, but they blossom well in shade with just a few rays each day. Dark green, glossy foliage contrasts beautifully with shiny white flowers on short branches in spring; some rebloom in fall. Shear after spring blooming to promote new growth and cut back every two years. The species, I. sempervirens, is the most popular and one of the hardiest. There are some species that are grown as annuals and as cut flowers. These plants absolutely must have well-drained soil in winter and summer; lime is beneficial, but in S.D. it is most likely that the soil is already alkaline.

sempervirens
'Little Gem', 'Weisser Zwerg'

Candytuft
Perennial, Sub-shrub ○ ◐ ●
Small, bright white

spr-esu   6"
NEW for us in 94
In our GARDEN 99

Evergreen shrublets take on reddish foliage when temperatures cool in fall and winter. Still one of the best, most compact forms of candytuft.

sempervirens
'Purity'

Candytuft
Perennial, Sub-shrub ○ ◐ ●
Crystal white

spr-esu   9-12"
NEW for us in 96
In our GARDEN

Flowers are large and long-lasting over lush, dark-green, shrubby and compact foliage that does not sprawl too much.

sempervirens
'Snowflake'

Candytuft
Perennial, Sub-shrub ○ ◐ ●
Glowing white

spr-esu   9-12"
NEW for us in 00
In our GARDEN

Clusters of 2-3" flowers completely cover evergreen foliage in early spring. Plant beneath deciduous trees; more shade is tolerated after flowering is complete.

IPOMOEA

leptophylla

Bush Morning Glory, Old Man of the Prairie   msu   36"

Prairie Perennial   ○ ●   NEW for us in   00

Pink with dark center   In our GARDEN

Bushy mounds can reach 5' across supported by a large underground tuber. In summer, dark throats on 3" flowers open every morning and close by noon. This is a cold hardy, drought-tolerant, native to western Great Plains and Rocky Mountains that we are growing for the first time in 2000. Provide sandy or well-drained soil.

IPOMOPSIS, GILIA

rubra, aggregata

Scarlet Rocket, Scarlet Gilia, Standing Cypress   msu   48-72"

Biennial   ○   NEW for us in   94

Intense ruby red   In our GARDEN

Leaves and flowers are whorled around tall stems, and en masse, these look like a small forest of brightly colored bottle brushes. Scarlet blooming stalks grab your attention and are loved by hummingbirds. This true biennial must have poor, dry and gritty conditions, otherwise will rot, and not be able to return by self-sowing. For the past several years I have planted these and lost them. Only by locating them in nearly pure gravel, alongside the driveway, did one finally return last year and bloom for the first time. I'll be looking for seedlings come spring. Sweet little chamomile likes it there too, and follows a similar propagation pattern.

IRIS

I recently learned that according to legend, the plant genus Iris has as its namesake the Greek goddess who is messenger to earth from the gods in heaven. When Iris comes to earth walking to and fro, rainbow colors are left in her footprints. This reminded me of my mother. Starting with a few odd species of Iris given to her by my grandfather, who lived on the family homestead, Mom assisted nature by creating a ribbon of flags around the old Bailey rooming house in Mt. Vernon, that had been converted to our childhood home. The fans of leaves quickly covered the juncture where the old stone foundation gave way to sparse grass. From thereafter, every late May and June, we were rich in flowers. Purple and yellow flags became the background for every family photo or 8 mm moving picture. We could pick all we wanted to give to Mom. Later the strappy leaves, bent over in all directions, a few remaining upright, created the "line and contrast" of our landscape design. They also provided privacy for the stray mongrel we soon loved as Ikey (as in Dwight D.) and her new-born puppies under the front porch.

Generous Iris increase quickly from thick, fleshy rhizomes that lie very near or even upon the earth's surface. Long, dangling roots are eagerly embraced and held by nurturing soil. The old German Iris that my mother grew is just one of myriads of species and cultivars. There are thousands of others, nature's originals before humankind began to meddle, occurring world wide. They vary greatly in habit, color and culture. There could be several to suit your needs. Few flowers are lovelier; their beauty belies their hardiness and toughness. They remind me of exotic, large orchids.

Many of the Iris grown in the U.S. are from the bearded group; there are thousands of cultivars, so many that they have been sub-divided. Miniature Dwarf Bearded (MDB), called I. pumila, are the shortest plants, hold two- to three-inch flowers and are the first to bloom. About a week later, Standard Dwarf Bearded (SDB), also called lilliputs, begin to bloom. Also short, they have three- to four-inch flowers. Next come Intermediate Bearded (IB) growing over 1.5' without staking. Last is Tall Bearded (TB), the most popular. Many of the TB Iris are tetraploid, containing twice the usual chromosome number. Deer avoid them.

Also popular are the Siberian Iris, with pretty relaxed, flowing leaves, popular in Japanese gardens. To keep them blooming, keep vigorous with consistent moisture in well-drained soil and divide every three or four years. Don't forget about little Iris cristata as well as many other species and natives that one can try.

Though best to divide or transplant Iris every two or three years in

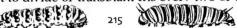

late July when they are dormant, Mom divided hers on one of the coldest days in April. They were undaunted. Some of their inherent maladies can be hard to manage, but they tend to be most troublesome in heavy, poorly drained soil. The iris borer is best controlled by removing old debris. Discard mushy rhizomes that are caused by soft rot. Leaf spots called scorch can result in death of plants if not kept under control. Keep them vigorous with lots of sun and well-drained soil.

cristata

Dwarf Crested Iris			6-8"
Perennial, Containers	○ ●	NEW for us in	95
Light blue		In our GARDEN	95

Little woodland species hug the ground and form mats with little spear leaves jutting out in all directions. Delicate blossoms huddle close to the foliage in spring. This growth habit provides a good groundcover in humus-rich soil and moist to dry shade.

laevigata

Fleur De Lis, Rabbit Ear Iris		esu	18"
Perennial, Water	○ ◐	NEW for us in	99
Cream, pink glaze		In our GARDEN	

Wide, flattened flowers are supported by roots that require alkaline soils and consistent moisture, and grow in shallow water gardens.

pallida
'Albo-variegata',' Argentea'

Sweet or Florentine Iris, Orris Root		esu-msu	24-48"
Perennial, Water	○ ◐	NEW for us in	96
Lavender blue		In our GARDEN	

Exceptional gray-green foliage with white striped variegation contrasts with sweetly fragrant, common bearded flowers. Grown for perfume and the powdered rhizome, orris root, which is an indispensable and expensive ingredient in potpourri. It absorbs and retains fragrance oils and releases them gradually over time. Save dollars and grow your own.

pseudacorus

Flag Iris		esu	36-48"
Perennial, Water Plant	○ ◐	NEW for us in	97
Bright yellow		In our GARDEN	97

Moisture loving species boldly punctuates the large rock garden at McCrory Gardens in Brookings or can grow in shallow water gardens. Very tall stalks support bright flowers.

 216

setosa
tricuspis
Bristly, Arctic or Alaska Iris
Perennial ○ ◐
Red violet

esu   18-30"
NEW for us in 00
In our GARDEN

Red violet flowers and taller plant from Canadian east coast. Very cold tolerant. So-called "bristly Iris" because the inner petals have a bristly texture. Provide a little extra moisture during dry periods.

sibirica
'Ann Dasch'
Siberian Iris
Perennial ○ ◐ ●
Blue and purple

esu   24-30"
NEW for us in 97
In our GARDEN

Blue on purple bicolor reminds one of stone-washed denim. Unusual alternative in Siberian Iris.

sibirica
'Butter and Sugar'
Siberian Iris
Perennial ○ ◐ ●
Bright yellow falls, white standards

esu   24-36"
NEW for us in 95
In our GARDEN

Delicate, beardless flowers have an aristocratic appearance. Strap-like foliage is long and flowing and requires consistent moisture throughout the season. A few years ago this was selling for over $20.00 a division. Honors: Iris Society 1981 and 1986 Morgan Award.

sibirica
'Tycoon'
Siberian Iris
Perennial ○ ◐ ●
Large, deep purple blue

esu   24-36"
NEW for us in 97
In our GARDEN

sibirica
'White Swirl'
Siberian Iris
Perennial ○ ◐ ●
Large white with some yellow

esu   36"
NEW for us in 99
In our GARDEN

Hardy, healthy, large white form of Siberian iris. Many successful offspring from this pollinating parent have been grown. Honors: Iris Society Morgan Award.

 217

spuria
Butterfly or Seashore Iris

Perennial ○ ●

msu   48"
NEW for us in 96
In our GARDEN 96

Tricky to meet exact growing requirements for spuria, but when done, nothing more beautiful than this Iris in bloom. Provide plenty of moisture until established; afterwards water well in spring and fall and allow to dry during hot summer months while flowering. Full tall clumps can be as wide as tall when mature. Hard to transplant when established, these are heavy feeders, so when planting, amend with manure, long-lasting soil amendments, or fertilizer.

KALIMERAS, ASTEROMOEA

This small group of orphanage plants from Asia is a little known genus, which is related to other plants in the Asteraceae family, such as Aster and Boltonia, that we've grown for some time. Except for daintier leaf and texture, it's actually hard to sort out the differences among these strangers and those we already know. Like our old acquaintances, they provide cut flower samples, and they are long blooming, part-shade tolerant, easy to grow and attractive to butterflies.

monjolica, pinnatafida
'Hortensis'

Orphanage Plant, Ghengis Khan Aster, Japanese Aster	msu-lsu LB	24-36"
Perennial, Containers ○ ◐ ●	NEW for us in	94
White, pale yellow centers	In our GARDEN	94

This plant provides dainty white flowers for many weeks and adapts well to containers. It is a pest and disease resistant Aster cousin for shady sites and a butterfly plant. In 2000 we found a variegated form to try. Honors: 1998 Georgia Gold Medal Winner.

 219

KIRENGESHOMA

Lovely perennial, the yellow waxbell requires special treatment for success. A plant for connoisseurs, the experienced gardener will site and nurture it with care. Give it rich, non-alkaline, well-drained soil that is constantly moist. Sun requirements are also important; provide shade in the heat of the day and keep from wind. In preparation for winter, cover with a thick mulch of oak leaves or other aerated organic material.

This plant grows three to four feet tall. Beautiful foliage is large and lobed, hairy and toothed. Yellow, nodding, bell-shaped flowers occur in late summer and fall in the upper parts of the foliage. They are not particularly showy but lovely none-the-less, weighting the branches slightly downward. The strange, horned fruits seem out of place on this graceful aristocrat.

palmata
Yellow Waxbells
Perennial   ○ ●
Waxy, nodding yellow bells

Isu-fall   24-48"
NEW for us in   95
In our GARDEN   99

Waxy, funnel-shaped flowers in sprays are held over 4", maple-shaped leaves and purple stems in late summer. Moist, rich, neutral to acid soil in semi shade are required.

KNAUTIA

We've been predicting that this new-kid-on-the-block Knautia, though short-lived, will become very popular. We planted it first in 1993, and many of you were lusting over it in our entrance garden in '94. It has wintered well for us at the nursery, both in the ground and in pots. It prefers full sun and non-acid, well-drained soil and is drought tolerant when established.

macedonica (rumelica)
Perennial Scabiosa
Perennial   ○ ◑
Shiny dark crimson

esu-fall LB   24"
NEW for us in   93
In our GARDEN   95

Hundreds of 1", pincushion flowers, similar to those of Scabiosa, begin to bloom in early summer. An uncommon, dark-wine-red color, they provide cut flowers for the rest of the summer on two foot sprawling plants and are attractive to butterflies. Combine this plant with silver foliage plants and ornamental grasses.

LAMIASTRUM

galeobdolan
'Florentinum', Variegatum

Yellow Archangel

Perennial, Groundcover, Containers ○ ◐ ●

Short yellow spikes

esu   12"

NEW for us in 95

In our GARDEN

Yellow flowers whorl around short spikes in late spring, contrasting well with green and white splashed, variegated leaves. A warning comes with words of praise. Archangel is not all that angelic. Isolate from others, or it can be sinfully invasive. Grow in shade or sun; mow if it gets too rangy. Those who tempt this plant into areas of other perennials and groundcovers should stand before a firing squad of pea-shooters. In response to pleas for mercy and forgiveness, use fresh, not dried, peas for ammunition!

galeobdolan
'Herman's Pride'

Yellow Archangel

Perennial, Groundcover, Containers ○ ◐ ●

Bright yellow

esu   9-12"

NEW for us in 96

In our GARDEN

Beautiful, small, silvery leaves, green leaf veins, serrated edges and neat, low mounded habit provide delicate appeal in shade. Flowers are whorled around the flower stem in evenly spaced increments. Grows naturally in shady woods and along banks, marshes and moist rocky areas. This plant is very different and well behaved compared to its relative, the other archangel, L. 'Florentinum'.

LAMIUM

The common name, spotted dead nettle, does not well-describe Lamium. First of all, anyone can tell it isn't dead. Secondly, it really isn't spotted but, in my opinion, splashed.

Most, though not all, cultivars of Lamium provide easy, variegated groundcovers in difficult dry-shade sites. For over ten years they have served me well as a trouble-free bank stabilizer in our shade garden. They are lovely and moderately showy in bloom in early season and continue in a more demure fashion for the rest of the season. Shear later in summer to encourage compactness and continued flowering. For another application of great foliage color contrasts, add combinations of Lamium to hanging baskets and containers planted with colorful annuals for partial shade.

Foliage can be green or chartreuse, splashed with silver or white. Some seem to be almost completely white, with very little green men, I mean, pigment, at all. Especially effective is the gold leaved forms contrasted in the same scheme with the silver leaved forms. Leaves mound and undulate, lapping near pink or white, two-lipped flowers that line upright, short, square stems. These short stems are a dead (pardon my pun) giveaway that they are in the mint family, which also hints of their vigor.

I far prefer the Lamium cultivars over the yellow archangel, Lamiastrum 'Florentinum'. Tomato justice (bombardment with ripe tomatoes) to anyone who advise aggressive groundcovers near vulnerable garden plants. Why saddle someone with that problem?

'Beedham's White'
Spotted Dead Nettle, Golden Lamium   esu-Isu LB   12"
Perennial, Groundcover, Containers   ○ ◐ ●   NEW for us in 99
Short spikes of bright white   In our GARDEN

Bright golden foliage with white flowers is excellent trailing from containers and provides wonderful foliage contrasts with, for example, blue leaved Hosta. This plant is not as vigorous as the cultivars with green and silver leaves, but they complement each other well.

maculatum

'Aureum'
Spotted Dead Nettle, Golden Lamium   esu-Isu LB   12"
Perennial, Groundcover, Containers   ○ ◐ ●   NEW for us in 99
Bright white short spikes   In our GARDEN

Golden foliage and white flowers combine very well with the silver and green leaved cultivars. Less vigorous than most other selections, and provides beautiful contrasts with so many annuals grown in containers.

maculatum
'Beacon Silver'
Spotted Dead Nettle

esu-lsu LB   6-9"

Perennial, Groundcover, Containers   ○ ◐ ●   NEW for us in   95

Rosy-pink   In our GARDEN

A popular shade-brightener. Silver leaves are edged in green. Try it in hanging baskets.

maculatum
'Checquers'
Spotted Dead Nettle

esu-lsu LB   9-12"

Perennial, Groundcover, Containers   ○ ◐ ●   NEW for us in   95

Deep mauve pink   In our GARDEN

Silver splashes brighten the center of each leaf. This plant is a quick-cover solution in shady locations.

maculatum
'Pink Pewter'
Spotted Dead Nettle

esu-lsu LB   6-9"

Perennial, Groundcover, Containers   ○ ◐ ●   NEW for us in   94

Clear pink   In our GARDEN

Silver and green leaves and clear pink flowers provide lovely contrast. Excellent in containers.

maculatum
'Red Nancy'
Spotted Dead Nettle

esu-msu   4-6"

Perennial   ○ ◐ ●   NEW for us in   00

Rose   In our GARDEN

Silvery foliage and rosy flowers (not red) are a nice contrast. Brand new in 2000, we are always glad to add another reliable Lamium to our repertoire.

maculatum
'Shell Pink'
Spotted Dead Nettle

esu-lsu LB   6-9"

Perennial, Groundcover, Containers   ○ ◐ ●   NEW for us in   94

Shell pink   In our GARDEN

New pink flowering form with white marbled leaves. Great contribution to containers.

maculatum
'White Nancy'
Spotted Dead Nettle

esu-lsu LB   6-9"

Perennial, Groundcover, Containers   ○ ◐ ●   NEW for us in   94

Sparkling white   In our GARDEN

A popular and desirable, lovely, white flowered form of 'Beacon Silver' with more vigor. Mostly silver leaves have narrow green edge. Not as drought tolerant as some, give extra moisture in sun. Contributes well to containers.

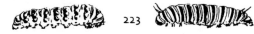

LATHYRUS

New hybrids of sweet peas, developed after 300 years of cross-pollinating and "upgrading" have not lost their charm and still entreat old-fashioned memories. They provide larger and more-colorful, long-lasting blooms on vigorous vines, excellent for cutting. But some, in the breeding process to make bigger and better flowers, have lost much of the fragrance and heat tolerance identified with the old-fashioned varieties.

Besides the annual and perennial climbing varieties, there are shrubby, some sprawling, non-climbers that have the same, attractive pea-like flowers and tendrils. They all may not be long-lived perennials, but are worth reestablishing when necessary. For the first time, I recently read that they should be planted like asparagus or Clematis. Plant roots deep, a six to eight inch hole isn't exaggerated, but only add a small amount of soil at first. As foliage twines upward, continue to add more soil, being careful to never cover the foliage. Once it has grown far enough to escape the confines of the hole, you can complete the filling in to ground level. Sweet peas prefer cool, moist weather with much sun. They may be drought-tolerant after establishment. Some foliages dry up and go into dormancy after flowering.

latifolius
'Pink Pearl'

Sweet Pea Vine
Perennial, Vine   ○ ●
Pink

esu-msu
NEW for us in   94
In our GARDEN

Long-lasting flowers on vigorous vines. Sweet peas are best grown from seed. Follow instructions under the genus, Lathyrus, heading.

 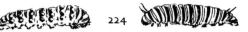

LAVANDULA

To "see a sea" of lavender is to imagine one has died and gone to heaven. The "olfac" penetration is to want for no other fragrance! In all ways this is truly one of nature's most beautiful herbs. It is soothing and therapeutic to all senses--sight, touch, smell, taste and sound. (Pardon the liberty taken. I'm trying to imagine the sound of woody stems brushing together.) Many sources record its health benefits when eaten.

When planning-first-in-green, the foliage of this woody shrublet is ideal. The soft, silvery- blue color provides excellent contrasts and calming effects. Small cool, blue-lavender flowers are whorled in 4" long sections at the top ends of woody stems.

Now that I've totally sold you on the attributes of this plant, you must be told that most, if not all, varieties show only borderline hardiness for South Dakota. Offering it ideal growing requirements will boost and enable its adaptation. Because it is such a desirable plant, gardeners may take these precautions to enable its winter survival: 1. Thriving on heat, it must have well-drained soil in full sun. Plant into 8-12" raised areas. 2. Allow plenty of room for air movement around individual plants. 3. Mulch root area with loose material for winter but DO NOT cover the crown. Aeration is important while mulched. 4. Prune to 5-6" in spring only, above fresh, new growth. Do not prune in fall. 5. Do not overwater. 6. And finally, replant when necessary.

Before flowers are open, but color is beginning to show, is the best time to gather flowers for drying. They last for years in arrangements. Crush leftover blossom and stem pieces for bowls scattered throughout your home. Natural potpourri! We have been advised that the scent of lavender is one fragrance highly attractive to the male sex. Isaac Walton is quoted, "Let us go to that house for the linen looks white and smells of lavender, and I long to be in a pair of sheets that smell so." The odor "...a simple purity...sweet fragrance...subtle strength...of the domestic virtues...the symbolic perfume of a quiet life."

'Lavender Lady'

Lavender   18"
Herb, Half-hardy Perennial, Containers   ○   NEW for us in 95
Medium lavender   In our GARDEN

Blooms first year from seed. Plant as an annual in pots or baskets in loose, well-drained soil. Thrives on heat and drought. Honors: 1994 All American Selection.

 225

angustifolia
'Munstead Strain'

Lavender

esu-msu   18"

Herb, Half-hardy Perennial, Containers   ○   NEW for us in   95

Blue   In our GARDEN

One of the hardier Lavender, though we expect die-back from most each year. Cover well with loose leaves or treat as annual. Irresistible combination of fragrance and appearance.

angustifolia (vera officinalis)

English Lavender

esu-msu   36"

Herb, Half-hardy Perennial, Containers   ○   NEW for us in   96

Pleasing blue   In our GARDEN

Of all lavenders, one of the most appealing to the nostril. Blue-grey ornamental foliage is beautiful in combination with lovely lavender-blue flowers on long spikes that dry perfectly and retain fragrance. Used in many cosmetics, perfumes, soaps, food, and for healing purposes.

angustifolia x latifolia
'Hidcote Blue'

Dwarf Lavender

esu-msu   12"

Herb, Half-hardy Perennial, Containers   ○   NEW for us in   95

Deep blue purple, fragrant   In our GARDEN

This cultivar is allowed darker flowers, more compactness, greater hardiness, and is an improvement of L. vera.

LEONTOPODIUM

alpinum

Edelweiss

esu   6"

Perennial   ○   NEW for us in   96

White and woolly   In our GARDEN

Lovely, small alpine plant of Swiss Alps origin, requires perfect drainage and must have rock garden conditions to put forth its silvery-grey foliage and white flower combination.

 226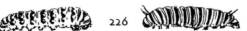

LESPEDEZA

From seed, back in '93, we grew a species from the genus Lespedeza, but it had escaped my memory and our garden confines. I think it died. Thank goodness for near-to-the-best-gardener-I-know, Sunni. She took a trial plant home that year and still reports on it annually. She led me to it last year and it made me happy to see what we started and what she had maintained. But frankly, I wasn't impressed by these pale-looking, pea-like flowers in late summer on new woody growth. The positive, redeeming factors were that the plant is a nitrogen fixer and will never take over your garden. We mused together, "This plant may work. Now, if we could just find some selections with more attractive flowers."

Now, several years after our first experiment, we notice an occasional offering of bushclover in some of the rare-plant, mail-order catalogs. They are marketed as "loose clusters of pea-like flowers on relaxed, arching stems." At first I couldn't make up my mind. Should I order them or would they just turn out like what Sunni has patiently nurtured in the out-of-the-way corner of her garden? Well now we both have new and different plants. I can't wait to see how they flower in 2000, the year of new beginnings for Lespedeza.

bicolor

Bush Clover	lsu-fall 48-120"
Sub-shrub, Perennial ○	NEW for us in 94
Bright, rosy purple	In our GARDEN

This must be the one we grew from seed back in the early 90's, because by other accounts it is described as "less showy, useful but not outstanding."

thumbergii
'Gibralter

Pink Bush Clover	lsu-fall 60-72"
Sub-shrub, Perennial ○	NEW for us in 99
Rich lavender purple	In our GARDEN

Pea flowers are a showy, glowing purple, appearing on new wood that develops into arching branches by late summer, and dies back to snow levels in winter. We succumbed and ordered this in '99; it sounded promising. I'll believe the promises, if I witness them. The color is ever bit as compelling as promised. Sad-making, they froze along with the annuals with first hard frost.

thumbergii (Sieboldii)

Bush Clover	lsu-fall 100"
Sub-shrub ○	NEW for us in
Rose-Purple	In our GARDEN

Called the treasure of the group and the one we should have grown. We'll try, try again. Purportedly stunning in flower and needs lots of room. Can be trimmed way, way back in early spring if it tries to colonize the area. A season-finale plant.

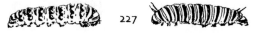

227

Liatris

Leave it to Holland to discover a native American wildflower to add to their fresh and dried, Dutch-cut-flower repertoire. South Dakota is one state where Liatris grows naturally. Plant corms four to six inches deep in fertile soil. Drainage is essential (as I continually harp), especially in winter. Most are drought tolerant because of the bulb-like corm, but it can't be completely dry all summer long.

On some, bright, rosy-purple or white flowers seem to glow for several inches at the top of stiffly upright, unbranched, terminal spikes. Others appear more as tufts and spurts at the tops of stalks. They provide intense color and form as fresh or dried cuts in arrangements as well as in the garden. The multitudes of fiber-like little flowers that cover these stalks are disk flowers only, producing no ray or petal flowers. They open from the top-down, unique in that most of nature's flower spikes open from the bottom-up. What environmental purpose does this serve, I wonder? Could it relate to the butterflies which are so attracted to them? Or does it enable pollination of the lower flowers from the earlier-maturing upper flowers?

Leaf structure and plant form provide excellent plan-first-in-green material. Long, narrow, lance-like, bright-green foliage is thick on the lower stalks; leaves thin out and become smaller as they ascend. Some of the species reseed mercilessly.

ligulistylis

Large Headed Gayfeather, Meadow Liatris	msu-lsu LB	42"
Prairie Perennial ○	NEW for us in	99
Showy purple pink	In our GARDEN	

A selection from an eastern S.D. ecosystem. Terminal flowers of long spikes, open from July to September, are the largest.

microcephela

Tiny Headed Gayfeather, Dense Gentian	msu-fall LB	24"
Perennial ○	NEW for us in	98
Glowing pink lavender	In our GARDEN	

Delicate flowers on airy open stalks and grassy leaves in late summer and fall, are much later than others, and very different from usual, stiff upright, 'Kobold'. Perfect stems for cutting and drying are produced on this drought tolerant native to southeastern U.S.

 228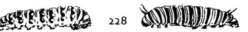

spicata
'Floristan White'
Gayfeather, Blazing Star

Perennial ○

Creamy white

msu   24-36"

NEW for us in   98

In our GARDEN

Many spikes produce excellent cut and dried flowers. The Liatris genus is mostly drought tolerant.

spicata
'Kobold'
Gayfeather, Blazing Star

Perennial ○

Bright lavender

msu   18-24"

NEW for us in   94

In our GARDEN   96

One of most outstanding, purple cultivars is more compact and rigidly upright than common, taller spicata species, which sometimes get gangly and flop. Combine with yarrow and other midsummer bloomers. Drought tolerant plant cannot tolerate winter wetness either.

LIGULARIA

Funny how one can remember the firsts, like the first kiss, first car...now, the first Ligularia. Along the banks of Betty Ann's Rice Creek Garden in Minnesota was the first time I observed a spectacular clump of this genus. There it had ideal conditions of rich, humus-rich woodland soil that was constantly moist and mostly shaded with filtered sun. If you can duplicate this scene, you can surely grow this stately plant. If you can't, keep the hose handy.

There is never a doubt why its common name is elephant ears, and the foliage alone is enough reason to grow this plant. Huge basal clumps are built of mounding leaves that are elephant-ear large, dark green or purple and leathery. The extra bonus is erect flower spikes holding many small, warm-yellow or orange flowers at top mast, up to six feet.

dentata
'Desdemona'
Bigleaf Ligularia, Groundsel, Elephant Ears

Perennial ○ ●

Golden yellow

msu   36-42"

NEW for us in   96

In our GARDEN

Dark, beet red leaves emerge early from fleshy clumps. Eventually the upper surface of the leaf greens-up while underside remains purple. Similar to L. 'Othello', it needs consistent moisture and wilts in direct sun even when soil is wet.

dentata
'Othello'
Bigleaf Ligularia, Groundsel, Elephant Ears
Perennial ○ ●
Bright yellow orange on stalk

msu 36-48"
NEW for us in 96
In our GARDEN 97

Grown mainly for large, kidney-shaped, dark-green to purple leaves that form huge basal mounds. Spikes of flowers tower over. Very closely matched to L. 'Desdemona', it wilts in direct sun; site in moist soil that never dries out.

przewalskii
Shavalski's Ligularia, Leopard Plant, Golden Ray
Perennial ○ ●
Yellow spikes

msu 48"
NEW for us in 94
In our GARDEN

Tall, deeply cut foliage has blackish red stems and tints in the leaves. This one tolerates fluctuating soil moisture better than others.

stenocephala, senecio
'The Rocket'
Narrow Spiked Ligularia
Perennial ○ ●
Dramatic yellow gold spikes

msu 48-60"
NEW for us in 96
In our GARDEN 97

Spikes of flowers tower over, but foliage is also interesting. Large, kidney-shaped, dark-green to purple leaves form huge basal mounds.

LILIUM

Few gardeners can resist planting more than just a few true lilies. They are an ideal garden plant and provide vast numbers of species and cultivars. Differences in planting depth, soil condition, bloom time, and hardiness separate many groups and varieties. They are native to many parts of the world; many are very hardy to the Northern Plains and live for a long time. Choose from Asiatic, Oriental, and L. tigrinum as some of the more common types. The recently available L. asiflorum, called LA hybrids, are crosses between asiatic and longiflorum lilies and boast larger and longer lasting flowers and heavier and stronger-growing foliage for better perennializing. Then there are the other species; the list seems to go on forever. How will we ever have time to try them all and where shall we begin our selection? Let the force be with us. . .and hand me a dart. . .Lilium martagon, auratum, parkmanii, bulbiferum, candidum (Madonna lily), formosanum, henryi, Aurelian hybrids, longiflorum, philadelphicum, regale, pumilum, speciosum, superbum and turk's caps.

All produce large and beautiful cut flowers in a variety of forms, often spotted, in nearly every color except blue. They bloom on upright stalks of glossy, dark-green leaves, at varying heights in early, mid or late season. Butterflies are attracted to them.

Culture of most is very easy. Some require full sun; others prefer part shade or full shade. A main requirement is well-drained soil.

Because plants are strongly vertical and have very little width, it is easy to find all sorts of niches in which to place them. Lily foliage grouped in masses can fulfill the same function as small shrubs. One of my favorite combinations is Lilium with fern. Under the shade of trees, lilies are sited in sunny pockets of at least two hours of direct sun; the fern are planted in full shade. Another partial shade grouping is masses of lilies growing through a ground cover of Canadian ginger.

Since both stem and leaves of lilies aid in food storage for next year's flowers, don't take extremely long stems when making cuts. If left uncut in the garden, be sure to remove flowers as they fade so that plants use no energy in making seed. Scaled bulbs increase readily, and there will eventually be an abundance to share or spread around in your own garden.

L.A. 'Parade'

Asiflorum Lily, L.A. Hybrid esu-msu 32"
Perennial, Scaled Bulb ○ ◉ NEW for us in 00
Showy large red In our GARDEN

Part of the L.A. group or Lilium asiflora, crosses that produce larger and longer-lasting flowers and vigorous foliage.

L.A. 'Yellow'

Asiflorum Lily, L.A. Hybrid esu-msu 36-40"
Perennial, Scaled Bulb ○ ◉ ● NEW for us in 98
Yellow In our GARDEN

Extra large Asiatic type flower challenges the Orientals in size. Asiflorum Lilies are crosses between longiflorum and asiatic lilies.

'Polyanna'

Asiatic Lily esu-msu 36"
Perennial, Scaled Bulb ○ ◉ ● NEW for us in 00
Bright, light yellow In our GARDEN

asiaticum
'Caressa'

Asiatic Lily msu 28"
Perennial, Scaled Bulb ○ ◉ ● NEW for us in 00
Rose petals, white center In our GARDEN

asiaticum
'Chianti'

Asiatic Lily msu 30'
Perennial, Scaled Bulb ○ ◉ ● NEW for us in 96
Pink In our GARDEN

Upward facing flowers for forcing, cutting, and gardening.

asiaticum
'Connecticut King'

Asiatic Lily msu 30"
Perennial, Scaled Bulb ○ ◉ ● NEW for us in 94
Butter yellow with gold, unspotted In our GARDEN 95

Excellent, upward facing garden performer.

asiaticum
'LaToya'

Asiatic Lily msu 38"
Perennial, Scaled Bulb ○ ◉ ● NEW for us in 94
Purple rose red blend, dark buds In our GARDEN

Fragrant lily with a dark color that is always in demand.

asiaticum
'Lennox'

Asiatic Lily msu 36"
Perennial, Scaled Bulb ○ ◉ ● NEW for us in 99
White In our GARDEN

 232

asiaticum
'Lollypop'
Asiatic Lily
Perennial, Scaled Bulb ○ ● ●
White, rose tips

msu 24-36"
NEW for us in 98
In our GARDEN

Wonderful color combination on upward facing flowers, unlike any other. Over one-half of the petal tip is bright rose-pink with contrasting crisp white centers. Easy and hardiest of lilies has a high bud count and grows well in pots.

asiaticum
'Marseille'
Asiatic Lily
Perennial, Scaled Bulb ○ ● ●
Pale pink, darker center, bicolor

msu 36"
NEW for us in 94
In our GARDEN

Strong bicolor, two colors on one flower.

asiaticum
'Menton'
Asiatic Lily
Perennial, Scaled Bulb ○ ● ●
Light salmon pink

msu 28-36"
NEW for us in 94
In our GARDEN

Nice soft color blends well with others.

asiaticum
'Monte Negro'
Asiatic Lily
Perennial, Scaled Bulb ○ ● ●
Dark red

msu 30-36"
NEW for us in 96
In our GARDEN 95

Excellent red choice that is always admired.

asiaticum
'Montreaux'
Asiatic Lily
Perennial, Scaled Bulb ○ ● ●
Deep mauve pink, spotted

msu 30-36"
NEW for us in 94
In our GARDEN 95

One of best strong pink lilies.

asiaticum
'Pulsar'
Asiatic Lily
Perennial, Scaled Bulb ○ ● ●
Good white

msu 28"
NEW for us in 98
In our GARDEN 99

asiaticum
'Sancerre'
Asiatic Lily
Perennial, Scaled Bulb ○ ● ●
Clear white, unspotted

msu 24-32"
NEW for us in 94
In our GARDEN

 233

asiaticum
'Science Fiction'
Asiatic Lily
Perennial, Scaled Bulb ○ ◑ ●
Deep red

msu 40"
NEW for us in 98
In our GARDEN

Red selections are always in demand.

asiaticum
'Sterling Star'
Asiatic Lily
Perennial, Scaled Bulb ○ ◑ ●
White spotted

msu 30-36"
NEW for us in 94
In our GARDEN 99

asiaticum
'Vivaldi'
Asiatic Lily
Perennial, Scaled Bulb ○ ◑ ●
Soft pink

msu 30-36"
NEW for us in 96
In our GARDEN

Strong grower and one of longest-lasting asiatics in the garden and as cut flowers.

asiflorum
L.A. 'Dani Arifin'
Asiflorum Lily, L.A. Hybrid
Perennial, Scaled Bulb ○ ◑ ●
Large pink

esu-msu 30"
NEW for us in 00
In our GARDEN

Grower calls this their best L.A. pink. It is a cross between longiflorum and asiatic lilies.

canadense, superbum, pumilum
Turk's Cap Lily
Perennial, Scaled Bulb ○ ◑ ●
Orange with black spots

msu 36-80"
NEW for us in 95
In our GARDEN

After blooming with many nodding, downward turned, small, lily-like flowers, plants gradually achieve early dormancy.

candidum
Madonna Lily
Perennial, Scaled Bulb ○ ◑
Pure white

esu-msu 36"
NEW for us in 98
In our GARDEN 98

Shallow planting in fall only.

martagon
purple

Martagon Lily
Perennial, Scaled Bulb   ○ ●
Purple

msu-lsu   36-60"
NEW for us in   00
In our GARDEN

If you are a shade gardener, you will covet tall, elegant woodland lilies and their downward turned flowers. An established colony of these is fabulous with their shiny, bright orange-red flowers. Martagons are almost impossible to find today. If you find them, order from a company that supplies large bulbs, not the tiny fragments we got one year. I'd rather order larger roots, pay more, and have them survive.

martagon
red strain

Martagon Lily
Perennial, Scaled Bulb   ○ ●
Dark burnt orange red

msu-lsu   36-60"
NEW for us in   98
In our GARDEN

Rare in the parts, shade-tolerant lily.

speciosum
'Casa Blanca'

Oriental Lily
Perennial, Scaled Bulb   ○ ○
Pure, snowy white, fragrant

msu-lsu   30-36"
NEW for us in   96
In our GARDEN

Intensely fragrant Oriental are some of the showiest lilies. In S.D. they must be sited and wintered with care, in neutral to acid soil. Winter and summer drainage is essential. Provide winter cover when in doubt of their survivability. They bloom a few weeks later than the Asiatic lilies and might require staking.

speciosum
'Stargazer'

Oriental Lily
Perennial, Scaled Bulb   ○ ○
Stunning crimson pink, edged white

msu-lsu   30"
NEW for us in   96
In our GARDEN   98

Acid soil, good drainage and winter cover will give best results with Orientals. This showy pink selection is the most asked for Oriental lily.

tigrinum
orange tiger

Tiger Lily
Perennial, Scaled Bulb   ○ ○ ●
Orange, black spots

msu   30-36"
NEW for us in   96
In our GARDEN

The famous and well known--black-spotted, orange lily.

tigrinum
pink tiger

Tiger Lily
Perennial, Scaled Bulb   ○ ○ ●
Pink, black spots

msu   34"
NEW for us in   96
In our GARDEN

The famous and well known--black-spotted, pink lily.

 235

tigrinum
red tiger
Tiger Lily

Perennial, Scaled Bulb ○ ◉ ●

Red, black spots

msu   30-36"

NEW for us in 96

In our GARDEN

The famous and well known--black-spotted, red lily.

tigrinum
yellow tiger
Tiger Lily

Perennial, Scaled Bulb ○ ◉ ●

Yellow, black spots

msu   30-36"

NEW for us in 96

In our GARDEN

The famous and well known--black-spotted, yellow lily.

LIMONIUM

Perennial and annual statice produce lovely stalks of colorful and white flowers excellent for cutting and drying, lasting for many years as plants and dried flowers. When gathering flowers for drying, harvest before they are fully open. It is sometimes recommended that they be bundled and hung upside down in dry, dark areas of good ventilation, but we have found they will easily dry in any position.

Both perennial German statice, G. tataricum, and sea lavender, L. latifolium, produce popular and common flowers found in the dried flower market. These plants grow oblong, leathery, 4-6" leaves to form a thick, basal rosette from which emerge long, thin, woody and stiff stems terminating in tiny, airy and papery, light pastel or white flowers.

When established, they require only well-drained soil, average or slightly acidic pH, average to little moisture and full sun.

The genus name for perennial German statice has been changed to Goniolinum, but for our convenience we have continued to sort it under Limonium.

latifolium (platyphyllum)
Perennial Statice, Sea Lavender

Perennial ○

Silvery blue to lavender blue

msu-lsu LB   24-36"

NEW for us in 95

In our GARDEN

Wide leaves (latifolium) emerge from the base of the plant, while thin-branched stems air well above. Provide circulation among plants, and transplant, if ever, with care. Need perfect drainage and will grow in sandy soil. The flowers cut and dry perfectly and can last for years.

 236

Goniolinum	_tataricum, dumosum_	
Perennial Statice, German Statice		msu-lsu 18-24"
Perennial ○		NEW for us in 96
White, slightest blue overtones		In our GARDEN

Plant form is similar, but smaller, than sea lavender. White appearing flower heads are dense and tight. It is cheaper to buy plants and have a yearly supply of flowers, than to buy the dried flowers at the craft store.

LINARIA

There is this old picture, taken by one of those cameras with an automatic timer, of when I escaped alone to the bike trail in northern Minnesota for two days, plant identification book in hand. It's of me and my new acquaintance, Linaria vulgaris, the little native toadflax or appropriate common name, butter and eggs, that I met on the trail. Eggs have always been one of my comfort foods, so this was the perfect description for a comforting new plant. No wonder it carried me away (or am I just getting carried away?).

The flowers look like tiny snapdragons and have a tiny columbine-like spur at the bottom. Most grow like snapdragons (the native one, L. vulgaris, does not), along tall narrow stems. They flower all season when temperatures are moderate, but will quit blooming in very hot weather. Because of our temperate climate, self-sowing Linaria are worth trying to maintain in our gardens.

The Italian native, L. purpurea occasionally can be seen naturalized in the U.S.; we've been successful with it since '97. There are several others to try, but are hard to locate in seed catalogs. Once in a while I discover another selection that can be applied to our gardens and have included some here. Most are annuals or tender perennials; we treat them as annuals that will return by self-sowing. Do whatever you can to encourage the prior year's seed to germinate the following spring. Some suggestions for the soil where they are grown: add one-third sand, and mulch with a combination of pea rock and sand.

genistifolia ssp. dalmatica

Dalmation Toadflax		msu-lsu LB 24-36"
Self Sowing Annual, Tender Perennial ○		NEW for us in
Lemon yellow snapdragons		In our GARDEN

Short spurred flowers resemble little snapdragons and cluster around the ends of wiry stems. Sometimes is looks a little shabby. It will reflower if trimmed back. Armitage calls it "a good looking weed." In western states such as Washington, it is considered a noxious weed, but our climate should keep it in-check.

 237

purpurea

Purple Toadflax | msu-lsu LB   24-36"
Self Sowing Annual, Tender Perennial   ○ | NEW for us in 97
Mixed pink, lavender pastels | In our GARDEN 97

Narrow, smooth grey-green foliage releases delicate snapdragon flowers; we love the foliage contrasts, even when flowers are not there. May not survive winter, but blooms the first year for long periods, from early to midsummer, from modestly self-sown seed. Is it annual or is it perennial? I don't know, but it works!

purpurea
Canon J. Went'

Toadflax | msu-lsu LB   24-36"
Self Sowing Annual, Tender Perennial   ○ | NEW for us in 00
Pink | In our GARDEN 00

While most toadflax are purple, here is a popular pink one. We have to depend on this to self-sow in order to see it return in our gardens. This will perform well in containers, because it will produce little tubular flowers on spikes all summer.

vulgaris

Butter and Eggs, Toadflax | msu-lsu LB   12"
Perennial, Annual   ○ | NEW for us in
Yellow | In our GARDEN

Naturalized in U.S. from European origins. Yellow miniature snapdragons bloom most of summer contrasted with gray evergreen foliage; pretty when allowed to naturalize in the lawn along curb edges. After grass is mowed, toadflax will regrow and rebloom.

 238

LINUM

Seas of blue, funnel-shaped flowers of flax are unforgettable when observed in fields along the roadside. We seldom see this plant in the sections of land around Sioux Falls, but I recently learned from a west-river (Missouri River, that is) flax grower that South Dakota is the number two state in production of flax seed. Studies have shown that eating regular amounts of flax seed can lower cholesterol and have other beneficial health effects. Glad Maria, the grand dame of our mail order herb catalog, lists flax seed among her dried herb items. Request a catalog if you are interested.

A few Linum species and cultivars provide very pretty, delicate self-sowing annuals and short-lived perennials for gardens. In addition to blue, some grow into yellow, white and red flowers. Each flower lasts only one day, but plants continue production for up to six weeks. To encourage self-sowing, provide an area of gravel or pea rock around the base of the established plant. After seeds drop into these areas, they will warm up and germinate more quickly in spring than in colder, clay soil areas. Plants are drought tolerant once established.

Flax leaves are tiny and narrow on branching stems. A few centuries ago in England the plant's foliage was grown as a rope source until a more prolific and durable material was sought in Cannabis or hemp.

narbonense
'Heavenly Blue'

Perennial Flax   esu-msu   12"
Perennial ○   NEW for us in 95
True blue   In our GARDEN

A drought tolerant dwarf for rock gardens that is slightly more adaptable than others.

perenne

Common Blue Flax   spr-esu   22"
Perennial ○   NEW for us in 95
Blue   In our GARDEN

Drought tolerant. Encourage self-sowing by incorporating pea gavel or sand into soil near plants.

perenne
'Sapphire', nanum

Perennial Flax   esu   12-15"
Perennial ○   NEW for us in 97
Blue   In our GARDEN

Drought tolerant.

LOBELIA

Most gardeners have grown annual Lobelia, the popular, trailing basket flowers in vibrant blue colors. These little gems are far removed in appearance and performance from the perennial species which grow naturally near stream banks. The hint taken, we know to grow them in the garden in rich, moist, well-drained locations in part shade, though up here in the North we can grow them in more sun. Amend soil with heavy amounts of manure and peat moss to enable moisture retentive qualities and consistent nutrition.

Blooming in mid to late season, tall stalks to four feet reveal interesting 1.5", lipped and lobed flowers. Even if we supply the necessary, light winter mulch, Lobelia will still be short lived and may require division or replacement every three years or thereabouts. Cuttings root easily, so there's no excuse not to have your own supply of replacement plants. Perennial Lobelia provide excellent container plants and cut flowers, and even the tender ones are worth growing for spectacular color and form even if they are viable for only one season. Butterflies are attracted to all.

Foliage of L. splendens or cardinalis is a rich mahogany color with rose highlights. Pungent lipstick-rosy-red flowers "compliment" the colorful foliage. The new tetraploid 'Compliment' series from a Canadian breeding program has some of the best potential for us in parts of South Dakota. Each color, 'Compliment Blue', 'Compliment Deep Red', and 'Compliment Scarlet', has received the Fleuroselect award. The 'Fan' series, many bronze-leafed types, and anything with L. fulgens in the cross may not survive South Dakota winters. Among many other cultivars and crosses, best for us are those with L. cardinalis or siphilitica added for hardiness and for producing better plants than either parent.

'Ruby Slippers'

Cardinal Flower   msu-fall   24-36"
Perennial, Water   ○ ◐ ●   NEW for us in 98
Ruby red   In our GARDEN   X

A promising hybrid of L. siphilitica and L. cardinalis indicates potential adaptability for us up here in the north. Long blooming, long spikes and lustrous rich foliage come with this promising plant. It likes wet soils, and we keep our garden on the dry side; maybe that is why we lost this the first time we tried in '98. We don't give up easily.

 240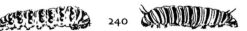

silphilitica
'Blue Select'
Big Blue Lobelia

msu-lsu   36-48"

Perennial, Water   ○ ◐ ●   NEW for us in 98

Blue   In our GARDEN

Erect adaptation of a North American woodland native for moist culture.

speciosa
'Compliment Blue'
Cardinal Flower

msu-lsu   36-48"

Perennial, Water   ○ ◐ ●   NEW for us in 97

Brilliant purple blue   In our GARDEN 97

Plants from the Complement Series may have to be grown as annuals in our state. Honors: Fleuroselect Award.

LUNARIA

Moneyplant is a good example of a biennial plant. The first year it forms basal foliage. The second year it sends up a flower stalk and blooms with large purple flowers, later setting papery thin seed discs that resemble a crisp, transparent silver dollar. They are popular as dried specimens for arrangements. When gathering, cut stems just as the green color disappears from the fruit. Leave some to self sow so you are assured of future crops. It likes moisture and a little shade during the hot times of the day.

annua (biennis)
var. 'Alba'
Money Plant, Honesty Plant, Silver Dollar Plant

msu-lsu   36"

Biennial   ○ ◐ ●   NEW for us in 95

Lavender   In our GARDEN

This biennial grows basal foliage the first year, and sets papery seed discs the second year. Popular dried, transparent, fruiting pod resembles a silver dollar. Cut it for drying just as green color disappears from the "dollars." Allow some to self-sow so it returns.

rediviva
Perennial Money Plant, Honesty Plant Silver Dollar Plant

msu-lsu   36"

Perennial   ○ ◐ ●   NEW for us in 99

Lavender   In our GARDEN

This purported perennial grows scented flowers and oval papery seed pods, and is native to Europe's moist, partially shady woodlands.

 241

Lupinus

The genus Lupinus provides a fine aura to the garden that few other flowers can surpass. Long, erect stalks rise above lovely, unusual, palmate foliage.   Aligned on these uprights are many lovely, perfectly plump, sweetpea-like flowers in June in an abundance of colors, usually to the cool side--rose-red, purple, blue, yellow, pink and combinations thereof. Mixed pastels are lovely massed. The name, Lupinus, is Latin for "wolflike", thus named in ancient times because it was believed the plants would ravage the soil. Today we understand that lupines actually boost soil fertility by enriching it with nitrogen.

Today, the most popular are the Russell Hybrids. They were bred for several decades beginning in 1911, in the hobby garden of George Russell.

Because they are categorized as perennials (there are also annual ones) and because of their unique beauty, we assume and are hopeful that lupines are long lived. Alas, they are not. We often must relay this sad message to some disappointed gardeners as they express their puzzled dismay when the longed-for form of lupines fails to color their June garden one year.

Though growing lupines is not difficult, they are short-lived perennials by nature and may persist for only three years. Follow these tips to get the most from them: provide perfect drainage in rich, neutral or slightly acid and cool soil, never allow the soil to dry out, remove spent blooms immediately so that no energy is spent on seed production, do not transplant, and mulch in winter.

polyphyllus
'Russell Strain Hybrids'

Lupine	esu-msu	30"
Perennial ○ ●	NEW for us in	94
Mixed	In our GARDEN	

Sweetpea-like blossoms are set close together on spire-like stalks.

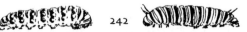

LYCHNIS

"This little light of mine; I'm gonna let it shine!" Brilliantly-colored flowers of Lychnis justifiably get their name from the Greek word for "lamp" because many species literally glow when shedding their light. The common name, "campion" is derived from "champion." Garlands of these were made for victors of early public games. The bright things occur in singles, doubles and clusters. They are a group of short-lived perennials, annuals and biennials. To coax them into longer lives, offer them plenty of sunlight with light, well-drained soil.

Many species classified in this genus overlap with other genera, Silene, Agrostemma and Viscaria. More confusion for the taxonomists. We'll let them worry; just enjoy the flowers.

arkwrightii
'Orange Gnome'

Maltese Cross		8"
Perennial ○ ●	NEW for us in	00
Red orange	In our GARDEN	

A true dwarf form of Maltese cross grows dark foliage that contrasts richly with the flowers on tight compact plants. Just think, only 8" tall compared to the usual 2-3'.

chalcedonica

Maltese Cross	msu-lsu	24-36"
Perennial ○ ●	NEW for us in	96
Intense scarlet	In our GARDEN	

Most reliable, easy to grow, and longest lived perennial species of Maltese cross that provides lovely and favorite old-fashioned cut flowers in summer.

coronaria
'Blood Red'

Rose Campion, Lamp Flower	esu	36"
Biennial, Self Sowing Annual, Perennial ○ ● ●	NEW for us in	98
Glowing dark ruby red	In our GARDEN	

Flower color: Knock-your-socks-off, intense color from early summer blooms. Foliage: Thick and fuzzy as felt and very silver in color. Flower and foliage together provide a never-to-be-ignored contrast. At best this could be called a short-lived perennial, wearing itself out in the second or third year. But in best of times, it will self-sow abundantly. Just learned that this will grow in shade too. Provide rock garden conditions. Flowers make cut specimens, too.

viscaria
'Thurnau'

German Catchfly	esu	12"
Perennial ○	NEW for us in	99
Magenta red	In our GARDEN	

Extremely bright 1" flowers are held by tufted, grass-like foliage. Sticky stems may "catch flies." This plant is also listed as the genus Viscaria.

 243

LYCORIS

Have you heard of naked lady, magic lily, resurrection lily, hardy amaryllis or surprise lily? These are all common names of an unusual and valuable plant that grows from an elongated, fat bulb from the genus, Lycoris. The strap-like foliage appears in early summer but quickly vanishes within a few days. Be sure to note the area where leaves emerge in the spring so that you do not accidentally disturb the valuable, hidden life-centers, because in August, when you have forgotten all about them. . .Surprise! Clusters of 24" stalks emerge like magic (you have been waving that magic trowel again) with lavender-pink, fragrant, trumpet-shaped flowers.

This bulb needs one to three years after planting to bulk-up or become bulb-bound before it will bloom. If you have been lucky, you may have observed large old colonies pushing up multiple blooming stalks in old neighborhoods where they've had time to become heavily entrenched.

Other than their unique rarity and beauty, what is particularly appealing to me is that the naked ladies are shade tolerant, though they do not completely object to standing, out-in-the-buff, in full sun. An interesting and unusual adaptation that one can apply to magic lilies is to naturalize them directly into patches in the lawn like you may be inclined to do with daffodils or crocus. Avoid mowing those areas while the foliage is visible to allow bulbs to refuel themselves. As soon as the leaves have withered, resume mowing. Then in August, when surprise flowering stalks seem to almost leap out of the ground, delay mowing again for a week or two until the cycle is over. I really like this idea and for over ten years have wanted to apply it, ever since witnessing such a show at a well-known public garden near Baltimore. It's time.

squamigera

Magic Lily, August Lily, Naked Lady, Hardy Amaryllis

Fall Bulb, Perennial   ○ ◐ ●

Pink

Isu   28"

NEW for us in 89

In our GARDEN 96

Strappy foliage appears in June and quickly disappears! Don't forget where you've planted their bulb-like roots, for in August, tall stalks appear with fragrant, lily-like pink blossoms. The common name, magic lily, is a perfect description. Plant as dormant fall bulbs.

LYSIMACHIA

Great diversity rules the desirable varieties in this Lysimachia genus. There are diminutive little ground covers and taller plants to three feet. Flowers can be small and subtle to unusual specimens for cutting in white and yellow. One common characteristic is their vigor and eagerness to overgrow everything nearby, though occasionally a loosestrife is recommended because it has shown some restraint. These aggressive traits become desirable when one is in need of ground covers for difficult sites.

Be forewarned and remember to site most species away from, or where they cohabit in size with, more manageable garden plants. Moisture and sun will help them run faster. To rein them in keep them dry and shady.

ciliata
'Purpurea'

Loosestrife   msu-lsu   24-30"
Perennial, Groundcover   ○ ◑ ●   NEW for us in 95
Clear, light yellow   In our GARDEN

This tough, vigorous and somewhat invasive plant provides an excellent foliage effect with deep purple leaves and later, delicate, nodding flowers.

clethroides

Gooseneck Loosestrife   msu   36"
Perennial, Groundcover   ○ ◑ ●   NEW for us in 96
Graceful white   In our GARDEN

Graceful flower spires of many tiny flowers, narrow at the tips and arch like the necks of geese. This plant is invasive; so site with caution; allow it to run in a semi shady area where it can naturalize.

nummularia

Moneywort, Creeping Jenny   1-3"
Perennial, Groundcover   ○ ◑ ●   NEW for us in 92
Foliage effect   In our GARDEN

This is the green leaved form of L. nummularia that we don't grow and don't recommend. The golden leaved form is much more attractive and effective.

nummularia
'Aurea'

Golden Moneywort, Golden Creeping Jenny   1-3"
Perennial, Groundcover, Containers   ○ ◑ ●   NEW for us in 93
Foliage effect   In our GARDEN 97

For effective dynamics of new growth in early spring, plant these small, coin-shaped (nummularia means "coin"), chartreuse leaves amongst other emerging perennials of various foliage colors and textures. Add to shady annual and herb baskets for another foliage effect. This flat spreading plant prefers moist soil, where it will be more aggressive. Occasional harsh winters set it back if it has commandeered to much of your garden space. Remove any leaves that revert to true green.

 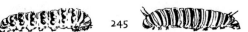

punctata

Loosestrife, Circle Flower
Perennial, Groundcover ○ ◐ ●
Yellow

esu-msu   24-30"
NEW for us in   93
In our GARDEN   93

Strong grower and strong foliage with flowers protruding from leaf axils. A relaxed pretty native, it provides cut flowers, but spreads rapidly from vigorous roots and also self-sows. Every early summer I debate--should this be allowed to stay or is really better off in a wilder garden?

punctata
'Alexander's'

Variegated Loosestrife, Circle Flower
Perennial, Groundcover ○ ◐ ●
Deep yellow

esu   12-24"
NEW for us in   99
In our GARDEN   99

Green and gold variegated foliage with deep yellow flowers from this English loosestrife, that is not as vigorous as the species. New growth emerges pink and early flowers peak out from above the leaf axils along the stems. Foliage and flower combo makes interesting cuts for fresh arrangements. This one can stay. Honors: COPF Introduction.

LYTHRUM

Lythrum was (and still really is) a much-loved and in-demand, showy perennial, once planted in abundance (prior to the last few years). And then, South Dakota, following suit of other nearby states, declared all species and cultivars of Lythrum as noxious weeds. If you plant these here, you are breaking the law! Those planted prior to the noxious designation are grandfathered in, I guess, because they are still visible all around town, in prior-established landscapes, sending up tall, relaxed, violet-purple stalks by early summer. They are showy anchors to these areas for nearly the entire remainder of the growing season.

The problem is that this non-native plant, Lyrthum, also called loosestrife, sets up a single-species dominance in marsh-like land, smothering out valuable native plants, interrupting the food chain and causing the eventual demise of the natural ecosystem which supports native plants, fish and other wildlife. Some of the cultivars are sterile, and it was supposed, at first, that these would be the solution and the route by which this lovely plant could continue in home landscapes and gardens. It was soon discovered that these cultivars, though sterile when isolated near each other, succumbed and participated in the dirty deed when planted near non-sterile varieties or the species.

'Morden's Gleam'

Loosestrife
Perennial ○ ◐
Glowing medium purple

msu-fall LB   48-60"
NEW for us in
In our GARDEN

 246

'Morden's Pink'
Loosestrife
Perennial   ○ ●
Glowing medium purple

msu-fall LB   48-60"
NEW for us in
In our GARDEN

salicaria
'Dropmore Purple'
Loosestrife
Perennial   ○ ●
Glowing medium purple

msu-fall LB   48-60"
NEW for us in
In our GARDEN

MACLEAYA

Plume poppy does not lack its share of adjectives--towering, grand, impressive, imposing. I prefer stately, relaxed attitude. All parts of this plant together create an attractive combination. Imagine large, eight-inch, deeply lobed leaves of Matisse shapes that are light green with silvery-white pubescent (hairy or felted) undersides on stalks up to eight feet and more.

In the top stories of the foliage in late summer, large, twelve-inch, fine-textured, smoky flower plumes contrast beautifully with the bold leaves and stature. Numerous individual flowers are apetalous (meaning no petals), but compelling because of prominent ornamental stamens. Counting their numbers ("get real," you might say) is the best way to differentiate between only two species in the genus.

Macleaya spreads effortlessly from rhizomatous roots and will also self-sow. These last two clues should raise a red flag to small-space gardeners. So that you won't later curse this plant, site in open spaces where it can be allowed to roam and show off its lovely self. Restrain it with infertile, dry soil and a shadier site. Give it just the opposite conditions, fertility, moisture and sunshine, to see it proliferate.

The beautifully shaped leaves of this plant take on a lovely, oat-colored glow when preserved in diluted glycerin and will last for years in this leather-like state. They add diversity and structure to dried, cut flower arrangements.

cordata

Plume Poppy, Tree Celandine   msu-lsu   72-110"
Perennial   ○ ◑ ●   NEW for us in   94
Cream clusters, showy stamens   In our GARDEN

Wonder-lobed, blue-green leaves and 12" showy cream clusters in late summer. Showier in flower, with numerous stamens, but not quite as invasive as M. microcarpa. One must still site carefully.

microcarpa

'Kelway's Coral Plume'

Small-fruited Plume Poppy, Bocconia   lsu-fall   60-72"
Perennial   ○ ◑ ●   NEW for us in   99
Coral pink fluffy clusters   In our GARDEN

Same special characteristics and role as others. Wonderful specimen plant, site carefully.

 248

MALVA

Mallows are colorful, old-fashioned flowers resembling miniature Hibiscus or hollyhocks and exude no less charm. They include annual, biennial and perennial species, most of which self-sow and bloom the first or second year from seed. Two-inch or wider, gaping, funnel-shaped flowers, pink, white, or purple, are held on a two- to three-foot vertical stalk and bloom for a long time in early to midsummer. Their self-sowing habit is a plus because they sprinkle themselves around other parts of the garden. Leave them for accidental combinations or easily weed them away. This sowing-of-their-wild-oats characteristic never was a problem in our garden until we recently had to reduce their numbers, but they were easy to pull out.

With most types the following site is preferred: neutral to slightly alkaline pH, average to dry and well-drained soil and full sun. They are drought-tolerant when established.

Malva is a Greek word meaning "soft" or "soothing" and may originate with the use of the soothing mucilage from the roots and leaves of a close relative, Althaea officianalis, the marshmallow plant. Marshmallows, originally a medicinal candy, were made of the powdered root from this plant, combined with sugar and water and purported to be an immune system stimulant and cough suppressor.

Species and cultivars of Malva are anatomically confused with those of Lavatera, Sidalcea and Althaea, which are close relatives, and I can't always tell them apart.

'Mystic Merlin'

Mallow
Perennial   ○ ⬤
Purple, mauve, blue and white blend
Silky, funnel-shaped flowers.

esu rpts LB   36-50"
NEW for us in   99
In our GARDEN

'Purpetta'

Mallow
Perennial   ○ ⬤
Rose red

esu, rpts LB   18-24"
NEW for us in   94
In our GARDEN   94

Diminutive plant, about one-half the stature of other selections, self-sows around the garden. Small blossoms adhere to upright spikes and tuck into many places that larger varieties cannot. Have had this since '94, and a new plant from a different grower we tried in '99, Malva 'Party Girl', is identical. It's not nice to fool Mother Nature.

 249

alcea
'Fastigiata'
Mallow   msu, rpts LB   36"
Perennial, Biennial   ○ ●   NEW for us in   96
Bright pink   In our GARDEN

Though this may technically be a biennial, it will perpetuate to perpetuity with abundant self-sowing. Sturdy stems, profuse, 2", chalice-shaped flowers.

moschata
'Alba'
Musk Mallow   msu, rpts   24-36"
Perennial   ○ ●   NEW for us in   94
Satin, sparkling white   In our GARDEN

Naturalizes by self-sowing.

sylvestris
'Zebrina'
Mallow   esu-msu   24-36"
Perennial, Biennial, Containers   ○ ●   NEW for us in   95
White, purple stripes   In our GARDEN

Fast-growing biennial type actually quickly blooms the first year from seed. May not return from root but will self-sow with the right conditions. Bloomed into Dec. in 1999. The leaves, but not the stalks, would freeze when temperatures dropped below 32 degrees. Then, with renewed warm weather, stalks would regrow new leaves and flowers.

MERTENSIA

Enhancing gardens as early as April, Mertensia are a much-anticipated sight, one of the year's first flowers to appear. Lovely, sapphire and porcelain blue, tubular flowers start out as pink buds on an 18" stalk, bobbing in spring breezes before tree leaves have fully emerged. It's hard to find prettier flowers than Virginia bluebells, and it's a puzzle that such an easy, unassuming plant is so often overlooked.

Mature plants are most commonly observed in older neighborhood patches, where they receive early season sun but are later shaded after leaves emerge from surrounding trees. Growing close to the ground, spreading by underground roots, they establish delightful colonies, never troublesome. Glabrous (smooth) blue leaves are four to six inches long with prominent veining, and after flowering, leaves begin a steady decline until they completely disappear by summer. Like an early hibernation, replenished plant roots then sleep in the shade until the next spring. Place them under shrubs or other areas where foliage will not be missed when dormancy takes over. There are other species that keep their foliage all summer.

The summer-dormant species are fully adaptable in northern zones, as long as good culture is provided to get them started. As with all early spring-blooming, North American wildflowers, it is best to plant dormant plants in early September. Do not plant too deep. Layer tuberous, fleshy roots near the surface of rich, organic, not-too-alkaline soil and mulch for the first two years until established. Shade, though preferred, is not necessary, but it may help to maintain a little more moisture in the soil, which they like. Do not overwater dormant plants.

asiatica

Oriental Bluebells	esu-msu	8"
Perennial ○ ●	NEW for us in	97
Pale blue flowers	In our GARDEN	97

Choice, light powdery blue leaves from an Oriental species with short stems and a sprawling habit. At first wondered how we would propagate, and then, like manna itself, silvery, soft-blue growth began to emerge from bare soil all around where seed had easily germinated! When first emerging, clumps are tidy and oh, so blue. Later, when they begin to sprawl, a bit of trimming back may help to rejuvenate them. Does not recess into summer dormancy.

ciliata

Bluebells

esu-msu   12-18"

Perennial   ◯ ●

NEW for us in 97

Lovely blue

In our GARDEN 97

One of the easiest species. Small plant, but probably too big for rock garden. Lovely light blue flowers under west office window in shade. Does not retreat to dormancy.

virginica

Virginia Bluebells, Virginia Cowslips

spr-esu   18"

Perennial   ◯ ●

NEW for us in 95

Sapphire blue, tubes on stalk

In our GARDEN 97

Most commonly grown, a popular native to U.S. Foliage goes into dormancy after flowering. A better description is given in the Mertensia summary.

 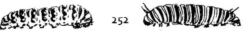

MONARDA

Every spring, while brushing away leaf cover from tiny leaves barely feeling their way out of the soil, I inhale a wonderful sweetness and immediately identify it as MONARDA! Excellent wild flowers to adapt to the garden, and magnificent when well-grown, they produce many upright stalks, enough to go around as cut flowers for you and still leave plenty for the little creatures. To prompt the plant to bloom for up to eight weeks, do this: Remove spent flowers, mulch around root zones to maintain cool soil temperature, and provide extra water during flowering.

The unusual flower of bee balm or bergamot is made up of colorful bracts and tubular parts, a sure come-on for long beaks and (dictionary, please) proboscises. If you are searching for plants that will attract hummingbirds and butterflies and deter deer foraging, these are they! Growing robustly in both sun or shade, these plants would like a little of both. In strong hot sun they would like a little more moisture and actually tolerate constantly wet soil.

The characteristic square stem is a "mint-hint"; its relationship to the mint family is a reminder of both wonderful fragrance and potential invasive qualities. The native species, M. fistulosa is native to the farther western parts of the U.S. and tends to be more drought tolerant, while the M. didyma species is native in the east and likes a little more moisture and protection from the sun.

Mildew problems depend on rainfall and humidity and usually start up after flowering. All growers provide bold assertions that their particular Monarda cultivars are mildew resistant, but with experience in growing many different varieties and reading what is published, we find the most resistant are these: 'Marshall's Delight', 'Jacob Klein', 'Claire Grace', 'Stone Throw's Pink', 'Blue Stockings', 'Violet Queen', 'Petite Delight', 'Colrain Red', 'Raspberry Wine', 'Blue Wreath', 'Gardenview Scarlet'. Avoid the two that most easily succumb to mildew, 'Croftway Pink' and 'Cambridge Scarlet'.

Monardez, botanist and practitioner of traditional medicine is Monarda's namesake. Plant parts have many therapeutic properties, and traditional uses include drinking teas to ward off gas, colds, insomnia, and stomach problems. Native Monarda is used by Native Americans in smudging ceremonies.

'Colrain Red'

Bee Balm, Bergamot, Oswego Tea
Perennial, Herb   ○ ◐ ●
Rich deep rosy red

msu LB   36"
NEW for us in   99
In our GARDEN

Consistently good growth, form and habit. One of best mildew resistant and long blooming cultivars from Colrain, Mass. Honors: Chicago study--one of best all around Monarda.

'Jacob Kline'

Bee Balm, Bergamot, Oswego Tea
Perennial, Herb   ○ ◐ ●
Large warm red

esu-lsu LB   40"
NEW for us in   97
In our GARDEN   97

One of best and biggest red flowering cultivars that really is mildew resistant. Extra long summer bloom, this one really flies out of here if butterflies don't get them first. Just barely darker than another rich red, M. 'Gardenview Scarlet'.

'Petite Delight'

Bee Balm, Bergamot, Oswego Tea
Perennial, Herb   ○ ◐ ●
Pink lavender

esu-msu LB   12-15"
NEW for us in   98
In our GARDEN

First really short cultivar of bee balm and one of the longest blooming cultivars. The Chicago Monarda study reports that the dark-green, glossy and crinkly leaf is moderately resistant to mildew. Tolerates a variety of soils, and may not spread as quickly as other bee balm. Honors: Canadian Morden's Research Center Introduction.

'Raspberry Wine'

Bee Balm, Bergamot, Oswego Tea
Perennial, Herb   ○ ◐ ●
Port red

esu-lsu LB   36-48"
NEW for us in   00
In our GARDEN

Long blooming with flowers that are raspberry look alikes. Mildew resistant. Attracts butterflies. One of longest blooming cultivars. Honors: Selected as one of best all around by Chicago study.

didyma

'Beauty of Cobham'

Bee Balm, Bergamot, Oswego Tea
Perennial, Herb   ○ ◐ ●
Pink and purple

msu LB   36-48"
NEW for us in   98
In our GARDEN

Pink and purple in unusual, showy combination of petals and calyx (group of sepals). Strong, shrubby habit has bronze cast. One of longest blooming cultivars. In Chicago Monarda study, poorly resistant to mildew.

didyma

'Blue Stocking', 'Blaustrumpf'

Bee Balm, Bergamot, Oswego Tea
Perennial, Herb   ○ ◐ ●
Dark blue lavender

esu-msu LB   30-36"
NEW for us in   94
In our GARDEN

One of longest blooming cultivars is mildew resistant, has dark-green foliage, and is strongly upright. In Chicago Monarda study, moderately resistant to mildew.

 254

didyma
'Croftway Pink'
Bee Balm, Bergamot, Oswego Tea
Perennial, Herb ○ ◉ ●
Soft, rose pink

esu-msu   30-48"
NEW for us in   95
In our GARDEN

One to avoid because of major problems with mildew. In Chicago Monarda study, poorly resistant to mildew. Substitute M. "Marshall's Delight' for a similar color.

didyma
'Gardenview Scarlet'
Bee Balm, Bergamot, Oswego Tea
Perennial, Herb ○ ◉ ●
Bright rose red

esu-msu LB   24-36"
NEW for us in   96
In our GARDEN   97

This gem has very large flower clusters and is one of longest blooming and most mildew-resistant cultivars. Use this instead of 'Cambridge Scarlet'. Only 'Jacob Klein' is slightly darker in color. Honors: Chicago study--one of best all around Monarda.

didyma
'Marshall's Delight'
Bee Balm, Bergamot, Oswego Tea
Perennial, Herb ○ ◉ ●
Clear pink

esu-msu LB   36"
NEW for us in   94
In our GARDEN

Slightly shiny foliage is mildew-resistant and contrasts with flowers. Named for Morden plantsman, Dr. Marshall. Honors: Chicago study--one of best all around Monarda, COPF introduction, Morden's Research Center introduction.

didyma
'Violet Queen'
Bee Balm, Bergamot, Oswego Tea
Perennial, Herb ○ ◉ ●
Lavender to violet

esu-msu LB   36"
NEW for us in   96
In our GARDEN

Grey-green, mildew-resistant foliage. Honors: Chicago study--one of best all around Monarda.

fistulosa
'Claire Grace'
Bee Balm, Wild Bergamot
Perennial, Herb ○ ◉ ●
Pale, soft lavender

esu-msu LB   36-48"
NEW for us in   98
In our GARDEN

In Chicago Monarda study, poorly resistant to mildew.

MYOSOTIS

sylvatica
'Victoria Dwarf Blue'
Forget Me Not
Perennial ○ ◉ ●
Iridescent blue, yellow eye

spr-esu   6"
NEW for us in   96
In our GARDEN

Unforgettable flowers are short-lived, but may continue to self-sow in good culture with moist soil.

 255

NEPETA

So taken with the successes we've experienced with Nepeta, we have planted, with confidence, several in our entrance garden. They will vary widely in height (1'- 4') and habit (sprawling or behaved), but all will billowy be, like silvery blue and green sheets hanging out to dry on a windy day. They are quickly becoming available because their value as excellent garden and landscape plants is finally being taken seriously. Many of you have already made a wise, xeric (adapted to dry habit) choice by duplicating Perennial Passion's low Nepeta 'Blue Wonder' hedge in your own gardens. Why, wise? Few plants offer more in return for the little care required.

Tough and drought-tolerant, silvery-blue foliage quickly emerges in spring for a near-immediate foliage foil, setting off and contrasting with all other textures and colors for the rest of the growing season. Blue-lavender flowers are produced abundantly, whorled around terminal stalks. It is in full bloom throughout most of June, a food supply for butterflies and bees when other perennials are just gearing up, and it is never without some flowers for the rest of the summer. If you want abundant rebloom, shear entire plant in early July (if you can manage without) as initial bloom is subsiding, and wait for its encore later in the summer.

Like most herbs, catmint tolerates poor soil but must have excellent drainage. Slightly felted leaves will languish in wet situations.

Some species have befuddled the nursery trade. Many of the species self-sow and try to colonize too much for us; in the garden we try to stick to the cultivars. Of all Nepeta species only one is the true catnip, cat aphrodisiac, N. cataria. The many remaining are lumped together under the common name catmint. Nepeta musinii species and cultivars like 'Blue Wonder' and 'Walker's Low' are supposed to be sterile; it is the N. faassenii species and selections that are not and will self sow, sometimes to dismay.

'Dawn to Dusk'
Ornamental Catmint
Perennial, Herb ○ ●
Pink with darker center on spikes

esu-lsu LB   24-36"
NEW for us in 97
In our GARDEN

Normally blue producing, Netherland's Nepeta succeeds here with tubes of pink with darker calyx (group of colored sepals). Long rosy spikes come all summer when deadheaded. Tubular flowers are full on longer spikes, and may remind one of Agastache or N. sibirica.

'Snowflake'
Ornamental Catmint
Perennial, Herb ○ ●
White

esu   10"
NEW for us in 94
In our GARDEN 94

White flowers contrast well against tidy, low clumps of grey-green.

'Walker's Low'
Ornamental Catmint
Perennial, Herb, Containers ○ ●
Blue purple

esu-fall LB   18-24"
NEW for us in 98
In our GARDEN

This recently available plant was portrayed to be nearly as compact as N. 'Blue Wonder', but it isn't. One plant covered a 3' x 3' area in one season. Tiny flowers are somewhat larger than N. 'Blue Wonder' for a more pronounced blue haze, and it has the other wonderful attributes: long blooming, drought tolerance, silver foliage strength, blue color and an herbal plant. If you have room, this is the one to use.

mussini
'Blue Wonder'
Ornamental Catmint
Perennial, Herb ○ ●
Blue lavender, abundant flowering

esu-lsu LB   12"
NEW for us in 94
In our GARDEN 94

Compact and excellent choice for hedges or edges, and still my favorite all-purpose Nepeta. Blooms throughout June along with lady's mantle. Shear, if you must, and it regrows and blooms again. It rarely needs watering. If you are interested in xeriscaping, you will want this plant.

nervosa
Ornamental Catmint
Perennial ○ ●
Blue lavender

msu-fall LB   16"
NEW for us in 97
In our GARDEN 97

Compact plant with short spikes of blue. Grey-green leaves, drought tolerance, easy care plant like the other catmints.

sibirica
'Souvenier D'Andre Chaudron', 'Blue Beauty'
Siberian Catmint
Perennial, Herb ○ ●
Deep, bright blue, long-lasting

esu-lsu LB   36-48"
NEW for us in 96
In our GARDEN 96

A tall form of catmint, great for naturalizing in difficult areas, and blooms most of summer in lax, unassuming manner. Flowers are larger and plant is taller and more vigorous than N. musinii species. Foliage is sweetly fragrant.

NIGELLA

damascena
'Miss Jekyll'

Annual, Self Sowing   O O
Bright blue

msu-lsu   12"
NEW for us in 95
In our GARDEN 95

Blue, lacy, blooms hang loosely over the plant. Seed pods ripen and resemble inflated balloons crowned with pointed caps. Seeds are aromatic and used for cooking and medicine. Leaves used to prevent moths from chewing clothing. Self-sows its bright self abundantly where the soil warms up the quickest, usually in dry, edge of walk, difficult areas.

OENOTHERA

The Oenothera group includes varied, native species representing several individual states in temperate North America. It is commonly recognized by its cheery, solitary, mostly-yellow flowers, though less-common and sometimes less-hardy white or pink-flowering species are available. Flower buds, stems or other parts may be tinged in red, a nice contrast.

Stems may trail along at four inches or stand erect to four feet. Newer cultivars of the trailing forms have showy silver leaves, which we love for foliage contrasts. Excellent fall foliage color is provided by upright forms.

There are two distinct common names given, based on the time of day that the flowers open. Sundrops have flowers that open during the day, and the evening primrose, the more popular missouriensis species (not the true Primula or primrose) flowers open in the late afternoon and evening.

Investigate those with invasive characteristics and use caution when siting them. Some are manageable in controlled garden settings, but others are best allowed to invade or self-sow in natural settings.

Culture requirements include well-drained, moisture-retentive soil in full sun, but let soil dry out occasionally between waterings. Many can be considered drought tolerant, considering their native locale.

We've tried to stick to species and cultivars that are recommended as hardy and native to the Northern Plains. Winter mulch is beneficial for the others.

missouriensis (macrocarpa)
'Fremontii'

Evening or Missouri Primrose   esu-Isu LB   6-9"
Perennial   ○ ◐   NEW for us in 99
Light yellow   In our GARDEN

Narrow silver leaves and flowers all summer on a trailing plant. Cultivars, like this one, of Missouri primrose, often offer better foliage and flowers.

missouriensis (macrocarpa)
'Missouriensis'

Evening or Missouri Primrose
Perennial ○ ◐
Large lemon yellow, fragrant

esu-msu LB 6-9"
NEW for us in 95
In our GARDEN

Large luminescent, funnel-shaped flowers last for days and are open in early morning and at the end of the day. Leathery leaves provide large textured, sprawling rock garden plant supported by deep underground tubers. Will keep blooming until enough 2-3" seed pods are set. Remove old flowers and seeds to trick it into continuing all summer. Most popular species. Provide deep, fertile soil.

missouriensis (macrocarpa), fremontii
'Lemon Silver'

Evening or Missouri Primrose
Perennial, Containers ○ ◐
Lemon yellow

esu-lsu LB 6-9"
NEW for us in 98
In our GARDEN

An evening primrose that is open during the day--shall we change its common name to "daytime primrose?" The name is <u>so</u> appropriate--silver leaves trail along the ground dragging large, lemon colored, tissue paper blossoms from early summer to fall. Rock garden, well-drained, drought conditions and hot full sun are best.

missouriensis, macrocarpa v. incana
'Silver Blade'

Evening or Missouri Primrose
Perennial, Containers ○ ◐
Large, clear yellow

esu-fall LB 6-9"
NEW for us in 00
In our GARDEN

More excellent contrasts with silvery blue leaves and large, clear-yellow flowers. One plant spreads up to 1.5'. Honors: 1999 Rocky Mountain Plant Select.

tetragona
'Fireworks', 'Fyrverkeri'

Sundrops
Perennial ○ ◐ ●
Stalks of yellow

esu-lsu LB 12-18"
NEW for us in 98
In our GARDEN 99

Bronze foliage, red stems and red buds perform beautifully while presenting the bright yellow flowers in the evenings of early summer. Similar to O. 'Summer Solstice' but with darker foliage and a tighter habit.

ORIGANUM

laevigatum
'Herrenhausen'

Oregano
Herb, Perennial, Sub-shrub ○
Cerise pink and red purple

lsu 2"
NEW for us in 96
In our GARDEN 96

One of showiest flowering oreganos cascades ten inches and can be used in hanging baskets or in front of border. Purple flowers can be used fresh or dried from July to frost. We didn't think it would be hardy at first, but this drought tolerant plant has been growing in our garden since '96, and we've done nothing more than to check on it once in a while.

BELAMCANDA, PARDANTHUS

Curious, exotic, red-spotted and splashed petals of warm, mostly bright orange colors are the distinctive mark of the blackberry lily, also known as leopard flower. The loose clusters of compelling flowers on forked stems remain for a brief period. Do not dismay; the flowers keep coming and the seed pods that follow are equally attractive. Later in the summer the pods split apart to reveal shiny black seeds arranged in neat order. Both flower and seed are excellent as cut specimens. The seed pod will dry for winter arrangements.

Sword-like leaves and tuberous roots resemble those of Gladioli or Iris.

Cultural requirements include Bach and sunshine, Monet and well-drained soil. Drought is tolerated once established. Presently, winter mulching is still recommended for this genus in our northern region, but after growing it for a few years, we may prove otherwise.

chinensis

Blackberry Lily, Leopard Flower, She Gan	msu-lsu	18-36"
Perennial ○	NEW for us in	95
Orange, maroon spotted, dried pods	In our GARDEN	99

Showy, long -asting flowers on wiry, forked stems later reveal fruit capsules that split to expose blackberry-like seed. Dry for winter arrangements. Tuberous rhizome is used in Chinese medicine as an antiviral and antifungal agent.

flava or flabellata
'Hello Yellow'

Blackberry Lily, Leopard Flower	msu-lsu	18"
Perennial ○	NEW for us in	95
Yellow, dried seed pods	In our GARDEN	

Outstanding dwarf blackberry lily that grows only to 18". Strappy leaves have a slight twist. One-day, unspotted flowers keep emerging, day after day. Shiny black seeds bulge out when seed pods split open in late summer. Cut and dry for bouquets.

261

CORYDALIS, PSEUDOFUMARIA

Corydalis is a relative of Dicentra, the bleeding hearts, and attractive, ferny foliage is similar but much daintier. Small, delicate flowers with tiny spurs are sprinkled generously throughout the plants, and they seem to be in bloom throughout the season once they begin in early summer. Yellow-flowering C. lutea is the most common; others are slowly appearing in the marketplace. One reads about varying selections of blue-flowering Corydalis advertised in catalogs, and of the few we've tried, one has reliably and abundantly returned.

They prefer cool, semi-shady, woodland conditions with excellent drainage. They perform poorly in nursery containers.

If you provide their needs, they automatically colonize by self-sowing. It is difficult to determine if the original plants return or if it is the volunteer seedlings that are maintaining the colony. I love this gentle, unassuming plant and have had lovely, naturalized stands in shady areas for many years.

x dufu Temple China

False Bleeding Heart		esu-lsu LB	6"
Perennial ○ ●		NEW for us in	97
Mostly sky blue		In our GARDEN	97

The very desirable blue Corydalis that I've mentioned before, blooms like the others for most of the summer, and self-sows from exploding seed bundles. Supposedly it is more cold hardy because of semi tuberous roots, but returns from seed, too. Germination is aided by the fact that we have the plants growing near rocks in the shade where the soil warms up more quickly in the spring. In either case, we've enjoyed it without interruption (except for winter, of course) since '97, when I was first convinced it was worth a try.

lutea

False Bleeding Heart		esu-lsu LB	15"
Perennial ○ ●		NEW for us in	94
Yellow		In our GARDEN	94

Neat, dainty foliage blooms with numerous .75" flowers for most of summer months. Seen naturalized in stone walls and among paving stones in moist shade if soil is well-drained. I was personally amazed to see this plant growing out of north facing castle walls in Scotland. I'm more familiar with it as a common companion to the variegated Solomon seal in my shaded backyard garden, where it has been self-sowing for nearly twenty years.

ochroleuca

False Bleeding Heart		esu-lsu LB	12"
Perennial ○ ●		NEW for us in	94
Creamy white		In our GARDEN	94

We've grown this near the office entrance at Perennial Passion for a few years. It doesn't appear as if the original plants return, because we wait until well into late spring or early summer to see new seedlings emerge from the seed of the former season. I've read that it tolerates slightly more sun than C. lutea. If you like to experiment with shady plants, this and C. lutea are a must.

PACHYSANDRA

Feasting your eyes on a carpet of glossy, broadleaf-evergreen Pachysandra in South Dakota (I hate the common name, spurge) makes you wonder if you are really in a more easterly or southerly geographic location. It is one of the finest ground covers available to us and provides an aristocratic touch that sometimes only glossy green can give. The angular, cut leaves are whorled around the stem, which grows eight to twelve inches tall and contrasts well with the usually ornamental foliage of other shade-loving plants. Small, creamy-white, fragrant flowers in late spring delicately enhance the overall effect. They increase gradually from underground spreading roots.

As with most broadleaf evergreens in South Dakota, it is to our and their advantage if we provide them with winter shade. This act of kindness is crucial and enables their survival without desiccation or winter burn during potentially-snowless winters. Plant them to the north of coniferous evergreens and/or provide a winter mulch of non-smothering leaves; oak leaves are best. Summer shade to part sun (east side is great), good soil conditions, consistent moisture and a couple of applications of balanced fertilizer before August will push them along nicely and ensure their longevity.

This lovely plant can be grown well in the rich soils of old neighborhoods in Sioux Falls. On the open prairie or on new construction sites that have been left in poor and compacted condition, the soil would have to be amended and/or shade supplemented.

terminalis

Spurge		spr	9-12"
Perennial, Groundcover	○ ●	NEW for us in	95
Tiny, creamy white		In our GARDEN	

One of finest evergreen groundcovers that should have winter shade. Fragrant white not-so showy flowers.

terminalis
'Green Carpet'

Spurge		spr	9"
Perennial, Groundcover	○ ●	NEW for us in	98
Tiny, creamy white		In our GARDEN	

An improved, more-compact form with darker evergreen leaves than the species.

 263

terminalis
'Green Sheen'

Spurge

Perennial, Groundcover

Tiny, creamy white

spr   9"

NEW for us in 98

In our GARDEN

Rich, very shiny, dark green leaves look as though they've just had a wax job. Spreads slower than the species. Honors: 2000 Cary Award for outstanding plants of the Northeast.

PAEONIA

Aaaah, Peonies!! That long-lived perennial, Queen of the Garden Flowers! THE best cut flower (of course there are others) and heavenly fragrance beyond description. Fat, soft buds open slowly to spectacular size and then, all at once, completely shed spent petals--kissed by a moonbeam--according to poetry from China where they have been grown since 500 BC. In Japan they could be grown only by the imperial court. As cut flowers they can be stored in a cooler at 33 degrees in a semi-dehydrated state for many weeks, and as late as late July, they can be reconstituted with water for arrangements. Ask us about a copy of a description of this process.

My homesteading great-grandparents planted peonies that are still blooming on the farm. And these "cemetery plants," now planted on their graves, will last well beyond my lifetime. Because of this longevity, special care was taken when planting the thick roots. Bushel-basket size, well-drained planting areas in full sun were amended with manure. Root buds called "eyes" were planted only a little deeper than one inch below the soil surface. If deeply submerged in the heavy, prairie-sea soil, spring growth could rot while pushing to the surface. During the growing season, average moisture was supplied but not too much when plants were dormant. Dormant plants were occasionally top-dressed in fall with the manure that was readily available. A phosphorous application was beneficial in the spring.

Now, advancing to present tense, a local peony-advocate advises that for newly planted peonies, allow only one or two flowers to develop for the first year or two, while new roots are getting well established. Cut off all other buds, hard as it may be to do. In subsequent years, never remove more than one-half the stems. And when the plants first emerge from the ground in spring, place a supporting ring around them to later hold up heavy flowers and foliage. Divide or transplant in fall, and top dress with phosphorous-based, nitrogen-free fertilizer in the spring.

Though we consider peonies to be among the most reliable plants for the Northern Plains, we sometimes hear complaints about their failure to flower. This could be from poor drainage, shade, or a fungus that causes young shoots to wilt and buds to dry or fall off. The latter problem can be treated with specific fungicides as new shoots emerge from the ground. Planting eyes too deep will also result in failure to bloom and gradual decline and rotting of roots. Discard old foliage in fall to help deter fungus leaf spot.

From the original species, which are now difficult to locate, hundreds of new plants with varying habits, colors and forms have

been introduced. They are divided into five g:oups: (If you promise never to quiz me on this, I promise the same to you.)

Single - Five or more true or basal petals around the center of pollen-bearing stamens and anthers. Japanese - Same as above, but non-pollen-bearing stamenoids are in the center rather than stamens. Anemone-flowered - Five or more true or basal petals with petal-like stamens called petaloids, the same or different color from the true petals. Semi-double - Five or more true or basal petals around a full center containing broad petals and pollen-bearing anthers on stamens. Stamens may be clustered together or mixed in with the other parts. Double - Five or more true or basal outer petals. Most of the center of the flower is made up of a mound of stamens that have been transformed into petals. Therefore, regular-looking stamens are not obvious parts of the flower. Cut the single, Japanese and anemone peonies earlier, at a firm-to-soft stage. Cut semi-double and doubles at more advanced stage, medium firm to soft.

lactiflora (double)
'Alexander Fleming'
Herbaceous Peony   esu   30-36"
Perennial   ◯ ◉   NEW for us in   96
Deep salmon, double   In our GARDEN
This blooms in spring, the mid to late peony season.

lactiflora (double)
'Kansas'
Herbaceous Peony   esu   30-36"
Perennial   ◯ ◉   NEW for us in   96
Excellent clear red, double   In our GARDEN
One of the best double red peonies. Strong stems. Honors: Peony Society 1957 Gold Medal.

lactiflora (double)
'Karl Rosenfeld'
Herbaceous Peony   esu   30"
Perennial   ◯ ◉   NEW for us in   97
Brilliant crimson, double   In our GARDEN
Free-flowering, old standby.

lactiflora (double)
'Miss Eckhard'
Herbaceous Peony   esu   30-36"
Perennial   ◯ ◉   NEW for us in   98
Pure pink double   In our GARDEN

lactiflora (double)
'Mons. Jules Elie'

Herbaceous Peony · esu · · · · 36"
Perennial · · · ○ ● · · · · · · · · · · · · · · · · · · NEW for us in · 96
Huge, silvery rose pink, double · · · · · · · · · · · · · · In our GARDEN
Early peony season. One of best cultivars for cut flowers.

lactiflora (double)
'Sarah Bernhardt'

Herbaceous Peony · esu · · · · 36"
Perennial · · · ○ ● · · · · · · · · · · · · · · · · · · NEW for us in · 95
Apple blossom pink, red flecks, double · · · · · · · · · · In our GARDEN
A popular favorite for many years with medium height, strong stems and good foliage. Flowers during the later part of the peony season, one of last to bloom. One of best cultivars for cut flowers.

lactiflora (double)
'Shirley Temple'

Herbaceous Peony · esu · · · · 40"
Perennial · · · ○ ● · · · · · · · · · · · · · · · · · · NEW for us in · 98
Blush pink fades to white, double · · · · · · · · · · · · · In our GARDEN

lactiflora (single)
'Krinkled White'

Herbaceous Peony · esu · · · 30-36"
Perennial · · · ○ ● · · · · · · · · · · · · · · · · · · NEW for us in · 96
Single white · In our GARDEN
Flaring white, crepe paper petals create large pristine flower bowls. In the center is a large fluff of yellow stamens. Strong stems for cutting. Early flowering.

smoothii

Cut Leaf Peony · 24-30"
Perennial · · · ○ ● · · · · · · · · · · · · · · · · · · NEW for us in · 98
Glowing ruby pink · In our GARDEN · 98
Similar to fern leaf peony, but has slightly finer foliage, slightly greater height, and slightly earlier flowering--by two days. Single, bright red, wide open flowers form on rigid stems that require no staking. Rescued from an old Wisconsin cemetery by R. Lysne and planted in our garden in '98, and I recently read that this plant originated in France in the mid 1800s.

tenuifolia, officinalis
'Rubra'

Fern Leaf Peony · spr-esu · · · 12-30"
Perennial · · · ○ ● · · · · · · · · · · · · · · · · · · NEW for us in · 93
Deep purple crimson · · · · · · · · · · · · · · · · · · · In our GARDEN · 93
I can picture homestead relatives carrying these to their new homes in the Northern Plains. One of first plants to emerge in spring and blooms usually by mid May. Fern-like foliage of compact tidy bush dies back in midsummer. Do not overwater. Many people complain that this is not hardy. The culprit is ill-advised planting methods--too deep in heavy soils. In fall only, plant eyes (buds) about 1" below surface of well-drained fertile soil.

PAEONIA (TREE PEONY)

Tree peonies are a class unto themselves and are not herbaceous like the lactiflora species already described, but more like woody shrubs. "Shrub peonies" describes them better since they never reach tree proportions in our region, and they have woody stems that often die back completely to the ground in winter. There are successful large specimens thriving in Sioux Falls, having survived both with and without winter protection, but I would recommend protecting new plants for a few years.

Europeans first laid eyes on the magnificent flowers of these plants in the late sixteenth century though they had been cultivated in China well before 750 AD, where they are native to mountainous regions. The cold winters and warm summers that our Plains Region have to offer suit them fine, as does our alkaline soil.

When we acquire the roots of a tree peony, we are really getting parts of two different plants--the buds of the woody tree peony and the rootstock of the herbaceous peony onto which the tree peony buds (scion) have been grafted. To force this tree peony scion to grow its own roots, Armitage recommends planting the knobby graft union six-to twelve-inches below the surface of the soil. We were misdirected a few years ago by a supplier (they actually had recommended the graft be 2" above the soil surface until we questioned them about it), so the graft of the one in our garden is planted only two inches below the surface, but it has still settled in nicely. In our heavy clay soils, a shallower depth than the Armitage recommendation is probably sufficient. Well-drained soil is essential and partial shade is a good idea. All pruning, transplanting or dividing should be carried out in the fall. If suckers grow from the rootstock below the graft, they should be removed.

suffruticosa (tree)
'Age of Gold'
Tree Peony
Perennial   ○ ●

36-48"
NEW for us in
In our GARDEN

Honos: 1973 Gold Medal Peony Award.

 268

PAPAVER

Poppies are a large group of annuals, biennials and perennials with several common traits including the color of their sap, of all things! Change "sappy" to "zappy," and you have deftly described the attention-grabbing effects their bright flowers will have in your garden! Other shared characteristics are deeply lobed leaves, long stalked, fat, nodding buds and flowers, and decorative seed capsules.

Since the Oriental poppy, P. orientale, is the most popular species and most reliable perennial, I'll dwell on it a bit. Many unusual and beautiful ranges of colors and forms have been hybridized from these strong growers from the Mediterranean. They emerge and bloom in the early season along with lupines and iris for an excellent combination. Flowers are spectacular, four-to-six inches wide, with petal consistency like that of crepe paper or the lovely, soft and wrinkly skin of my namesake grandmother, Mary Schlund. Imagine this texture in hot bright hues, highlighted by sunlight or Grandma's spirit, glowing through the thin, transparent petals. The base of each petal is punctuated with a large, dark splotch, forming a distinct wheel at the center of each flower.

Foliage becomes dormant by midsummer, providing an opportunity for later color by overplanting the area with annuals or later-emerging perennials such as Perovskia, Aster or Boltonia.

Poppies care for themselves best in rich, deep, well-drained loam and cool temperatures. Transplanting is distasteful to them, so handle with care. Place crowns one to two inches below soil surface and move or divide only during dormancy. Mulch the first couple of winters until they are well-established. Staking is sometimes necessary.

Treat the other species as annuals though many may self-sow reliably. Iceland poppy, P. nudicaule, and alpine poppy, P. alpinum, may return for a couple of years and also self-sow. Annual bread poppy, P. somniferum, gives you beautiful flowers, interesting pods for cutting and nutty-tasting seeds all in one season. They've self-sown in our garden for years on end.

nudicaule
'Pizzicato'

Iceland Poppy   esu   24"
Perennial   ○   NEW for us in 98
Mixed red, orange, white   In our GARDEN

Always-popular color range of red, orange, pink and white. Honors: Fleuro Select Gold Medal.

orientale
'Beauty of Livermore'
Oriental Poppy

Perennial ○ ●

Blood red, black blotch

esu 30-40"
NEW for us in 96
In our GARDEN

Show off colors on flaring 3-4" blossoms for early season. Bristly toothed foliage is distinct for the species. Divide or transplant after midsummer dormancy so they can recover by the following year.

orientale
'Queen Alexander'
Oriental Poppy

Perennial ○ ●

Salmon pink, black center blotch

esu 30-40"
NEW for us in 00
In our GARDEN

A reliable old favorite.

somniferum
Annual, Self Sowing ○

24-36"
NEW for us in
In our GARDEN

Self sowing showy annual flowers end up as ornamental dried pods. Only the ripe black seeds of this annual poppy are safe to eat. It gives a nutty flavor to coffee cakes, breads and rolls. A great "bite" combination is a result of adding a generous amount to tuna salad. Sometimes it is added to curry powder and acts as a thickener to sauces and stews. Showy in flower and self-sows.

PARDANCANDA X

Pardancanda is an intergeneric cross between Belamcanda and Iris dichotoma (vesper iris) producing an unusual assymmetrical bloom that resembles both genera. Plants are compact and long-flowering. Color blends and spots are unusual and compelling. Rigid, spear-shaped leaves provide good constrasts with other foliages.

norrisii x
Jungle Colors Improved
Candy Lily

Perennial ○ ●

Purple blends

esu-msu 12-18"
NEW for us in 96
In our GARDEN 97

Compact and heavy flowering cultivar of unusual and varied colors was developed by Nebraska plant people.

norrisii x
'Sangria'
Candy Lily

Perennial ○ ●

Plum purple petals, gold overlay sepals

msu LB 18"
NEW for us in 99
In our GARDEN

A new, long blooming candy lily. 3" flowers bloom for six weeks atop slightly twisted, blue hued foliage. A Nebraska introduction.

<u>norrisii</u> x
'Sunset Tones'

Candy Lily	esu-msu	12-18"
Perennial ○ ●	NEW for us in	96
Rich blend of pink, yellow, orange	In our GARDEN	

Rich blends of color, compact and heavy flowering.

PATRINIA

Patrinia is one of those genera with hard-to-duplicate plants, that, somehow, you've overlooked all these years. It's time you were introduced. It provides seldom-found, late-season color for shady sites, starting in August. Yellow blossoms on tall plants emit a lovely atmosphere, tall but unpretentious, elegant and understated, and fragrant. Foliage turns dusky brown-purple in fall. Some grow white flowers.

<u>scabiosifolia</u>

Patrinia	lsu	36-48"
Perennial ○ ● ●	NEW for us in	96
Yellow	In our GARDEN	

Wonderful beauty for late-summer, yellow flowers. Excellent tall stems and flowers for cutting and arrangements. Beautiful mahogany fall foliage color.

<u>villosa</u>

Patrinia	lsu-fall LB	36"
Perennial ○ ● ●	NEW for us in	95
White	In our GARDEN	

White flat-topped clusters form with bold, basal foliage and colonizes in a noninvasive manner.

PENSTEMON

The High Plains native Penstemon is one of the finest, though sometimes temperamental, groups of wild flowers. There are nearly 400 varieties that are native to the U.S. Every state on the continent contributes one or more species. How many have you heard from?

Desirable additions to prairie and rock gardens, many are temperamental and won't grow well beyond their places of origin. Many of the European cultivars, though developed with pollen of North American natives, are borderline in hardiness. The best Penstemon news for Northern Plains gardeners is the availability of new selections coming from the research at the University of Nebraska led by the efforts of Dr. Dale Lindgren.

Flowers are showy, bright colored tubes that open to a double-lobed upper lip and triple-lobed lower lip, five total lobes. Warm red, pink, yellow or lavender flowers attached up and down short or tall stalks are offered. (But who's actually counting?) It also has five stamens. I've read two explanations of the name, Penstemon. The first is that "penta," the prefix of Penstemon, indicates five parts. One of these stamens is actually a non-pollen producing stamen called a stamenoid. It is visible through the lips like a hairy or bearded tongue. Now for the point: the common name is beardtongue. The second explanation is that a shorter prefix "pen" means "almost" and "stamen", and we conclude that "almost a stamen" refers to that stamenoid mentioned above. (In case you wondered, my boots are knee-high; it is getting too deep in here.)

Some can be unyielding in their cultural requirements. To survive, they must have well-drained, dry soil and in many cases, high quantities of gravel or sand in the soil. Never mulch with anything but gravel; place no organic material near the crown, ever; and leave old growth on until new growth shows in spring. Never fertilize since most are short-lived, and adding fertilizer will only exhaust them more quickly.

'Prairie Splendor'

Beardtongue	msu LB 24-30"
Prairie Perennial ○	NEW for us in 94
Fabulous white, rose, lavender, pink	In our GARDEN 00

Large flowers with much detail, speckles, spots and shading, bloom for four weeks. U of Nebraska winner from North Platte area.

 272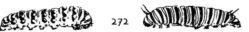

barbatus
'Elfin Pink', 'Rose Elf'

Beardtongue   esu-msu   12-15"
Perennial   ○   NEW for us in   98
Clear rose pink spikes   In our GARDEN

This long-blooming selection from the barbatus species is native to Colorado and Nevada and prefers perfect drainage in a dry western climate. Long, leafy stems rise above shiny basal leaves and carry 1" blossoms in loose panicles.

caespitosus
'Claude Barr'

Beardtongue   esu-msu   1"
Prairie Perennial   ○   NEW for us in   98
Purple   In our GARDEN

Little ground-cover plants, good for rock garden situations, hug the ground and grow rapidly. Small purplish blue trumpets tuck into dark green, glossy, prostrate foliage. Named for Claude Barr, southwestern South Dakota prairie plantsman, author of *Jewels of the Plains.*

cyananthus

Wasatch Penstemon   spr-esu   12-15"
Perennial   ○   NEW for us in   98
Brilliant blue   In our GARDEN

Beautiful 1" blue tubes on stalks bloom spring to early summer with waxy, wavy leaves. A western U.S. native.

digitalis

White Beardtongue, Smooth Penstemon   esu-msu LB   48"
Prairie Perennial   ○ ●   NEW for us in   98
White clusters   In our GARDEN

Parent plant of popular P. 'Husker Red' and most-hardy of white beardtongue. this stately, native prairie plant has glossy foliage and stalks of loose, elegant, inflated, pure white clusters of flowers in early summer. More tolerant of moisture compared to most Penstemon but is also drought tolerant.

digitalis
'Husker Red'

White Beardtongue, Smooth Penstemon   esu-msu LB   24-36"
Perennial, Containers   ○ ●   NEW for us in   95
White with pink blush   In our GARDEN   95

Entire plant has mahogany red color for great foliage contrasts, and abundant white flowers are held on many spikes. Drought-tolerant introduction by S.D. neighbor, Dale Lundgren of U of Nebraska. Seed-grown plants may look more like the green leaved species. Insist on red foliage or vegetatively propagated plants. Honors: 1996 Perennial Plant of the Year.

 273

fruticosa
'Purple Haze'

Rock Penstemon   spr-esu   9"
Perennial, Subshrub   ○   NEW for us in   98
Bright lilac purple   In our GARDEN   99

Hundreds of bright flowers completely cover this cascading evergreen subshrub in early season. Prefers rock garden culture, dry and well-drained. A native introduction from British Columbia Botanic Gardens. Honors: Canadian Ornamental Plant Foundation (COPF) introduction.

grandiflorus

Beardtongue, Shell Leaf Penstemon   esu   18-24"
Prairie Perennial   ○   NEW for us in   94
Pale pink   In our GARDEN

Large flowers on spikes with ascending blue-green, thick and waxy leaves. Good cut flower, though a short-lived plant. Cut all flowers or deadhead after flowering to keep them living longer. Drought tolerant, grows in sandy soil, and is native to S.D. Honors: Rocky Mountain Plant Select.

grandiflorus
'War Axe'

Beardtongue, Shell Leaf Penstemon   esu   24-48"
Prairie Perennial   ○   NEW for us in   97
Mixed warm colors   In our GARDEN   97

Steel blue, glaucous foliage, a cultivar of native shell-leaf penstemon in mixed warm colors of pinks, maroon, purple and red. So far, we've seen the pink flowers of the species dominate this seed-grown selection.

mexicale
'Pike's Peak Purple'

Penstemon   esu-lsu LB   15"
Prairie Perennial   ○   NEW for us in   99
Purple violet   In our GARDEN   99

Same description as P. 'Red Rocks', this time in purple. Honors: 1999 Rocky Mountain Plant Select.

mexicale
'Red Rocks'

Penstemon   esu-lsu LB   15"
Prairie Perennial   ○   NEW for us in   99
Bright rose red   In our GARDEN   99

Cross between Mexican and American native species. Narrow, dark green leaves. Provide good drainage and moderate watering. Honors: 1999 Rocky Mountain Plant Select.

pinifolius

'Mersea Yellow'

Beardtongue, Penstemon	esu LB	12"
Prairie Perennial ○	NEW for us in	98
Soft yellow tubes	In our GARDEN	

Hundreds of little yellow tubes on stalks emerge from fluffy, shrubby little plants over a long period in midsummer. They are vigorous, heat tolerant and easy to grow in well-drained soil. They may appear dainty but by late March in 2000, after a very' mild winter, the fluffy bright green mounds were still intact, rearin' to go. A rare, yellow flowering species detected in English garden in 1980.

strictus

'Prairie Dusk'

Rocky Mountain Penstemon	esu LB	18-24"
Prairie Perennial ○	NEW for us in	98
Rosy purple	In our GARDEN	

Early-summer, richly hued flowers bloom for over a month. The species is native over a wide range of western U.S. and is one of the easiest, most adaptable and longest lived Penstemon. Stout stalks and narrow, glossy green leaves increase slowly into clumps on well-drained soil. This cultivar is another of the U of Nebraska selections.

PERILLA, SHI-SO

frutescens

'Crispa'

Beafsteak Plant, Shi-So		8-16"
Herb, Tender Perennial, Self Sowing Annual, ○ ●	NEW for us in	95
White	In our GARDEN	94

Elegant leaves of this plant are reddish purple with metallic overtones. I've included this annual here, because it reliably returns every year by self-sowing all over our garden, providing chance snapshots of foliage contrasts and excellent backgrounds for brighter annuals. Small, white flowers are best pinched off to limit self-sowing. The leaf is popular in Japanese and Thai cooking, used to wrap sushi, and to flavor and color vinegar, pickles, and pasta.

PEROVSKIA

Always on my top ten list, Russian sage is one of the best plants available for ease-of-care, long-flowering, foliage contrast and drought-tolerance. Could one ask for more? In my home garden this plant has been growing since 1985, and we have long proclaimed its value and dreamed what we thought was impossible: that it would replace the ubiquitously planted potentilla and spirea. Now, finally, it is catching-on in Sioux Falls. Dreams really do come true!

This plant is actually classified as a sub-shrub. Woody stems will die completely in late fall; leave them for winter interest. By late spring, in the lower part of the plant, a few inches above the soil line or below winter-snow levels, buds will begin to swell. At this time, prune away old wood, just above the buds.

New aromatic, woody, branching, silvery-green stems will begin soon. Rabbits and deer avoid the camphor-like odor of the foliage. After regrowing to full height, up to five feet by early July, it will begin to bloom and continue for the rest of the growing season. Many small, two-lipped, lavender-blue flowers are whorled around the stem on terminal branches. An excellent description I once heard referred to Perovskia as a "lavender on steroids." Get the picture?

Though growing very tall and often equally as wide, the open and airy form provides opportunity to intermingle other tall plants like coneflowers and tall Asiatic lilies into the foliage. Spring bulbs can be planted close to its roots and later not be noticed as their foliage dies back. It could be a support to a shrubby or vining Clematis. Creeping sedum or yellow moneywort make excellent ground covers beneath it. There is a recent introduction that has a more compact habit, and I'm glad that small gardens can now include this plant, too.

Provide full sun, dry conditions and good drainage, especially in winter. If in any shade, it will flop and lean toward the light. Plant them two to three feet apart so they can support one another. You are welcome to observe eight year old specimens in Perennial Passion's entrance garden.

'Little Spire'

Russian Sage	msu-fall LB	25"
Perennial, Sub-shrub ○	NEW for us in	00
Blue lavender	In our GARDEN	

I can think of a dozen different ways to use a short Russian sage. Too often, the big ones just won't fit into a small-scale scheme. The same desirable attributes of the others are retained.

atriplicifolia

Russian Sage
Perennial, Sub-shrub   ○
Blue lavender

msu-fall LB   36-48"
NEW for us in   92
In our GARDEN   93

One of ten best plants for long flowering, foliage contrast and near-blue color. Honors: 1995 Perennial Plant of the Year, Penn State Top 20 Perennial Performers, Pennsylvania Gardener Select.

atriplicifolia
'Filigran'

Russian Sage
Perennial, Sub-shrub   ○
Violet blue spikes

msu-fall LB   36-60"
NEW for us in   95
In our GARDEN

This cultivar of the '95 Perennial Plant of the Year is new from Germany, selected for upright habit, long-flowering and filigree foliage. Is it possible to garden in S.D. without Perovskia? I don't think so!

atriplicifolia
'Longin', 'Blue Spire'

Russian Sage
Perennial, Sub-shrub   ○
Blue lavender

msu-fall LB   36-48"
NEW for us in   95
In our GARDEN

Russian sage, a pillar of my sunny garden, is hard to improve upon, but here's another cultivar that is more branched and upright. Leaf edges are not as lacy as the shrubby forms.

Persicaria (Polygonum)

The genus formerly named Polygonum has been rechristened as Persicaria. The two most common names of this plant, fleeceflower and knot weed, are aptly chosen, but describe two entirely different anatomical parts. Fleeceflower tells of attractive spikes of pink or red flowers that appear hazily over the foliage in late season. Knotweed refers to the obvious swollen areas where leaves join stems.

These plants make up a group of aggressive ground covers and bank stabilizers; avoid them like the plague in a garden or mixed shrub situation! With or without a proper root barrier, they will eventually invade your lawn or any adjoining plantings. They are most effective as large sweeps of ground cover away from most other plants. Though somewhat shade tolerant, for fastest and thickest cover, provide plenty of sunshine and moisture.

To add variety and a new look to large, old established colonies of fleeceflower, I've had pretty good luck interplanting very tall daylilies, asters, Russian sage and yarrow. These seem to be able to hold their own in spite of this normally-dominating, new neighbor.

amplexicaule
'Speciosa'

Mountain Fleeceflower

msu-Isu LB   38"

Perennial   ○ ◑ ●

Bright red pokers

NEW for us in

In our GARDEN

By late summer, flower spikes glow among clumps of foliage that will grow stronger with consistent moisture. When Latinized,"leaves clasp the stem" means "amplexicaule".

filiformis (virginianum)
'Painter's Palette'

Fleeceflower, European Bistort

24"

Perennial   ○ ◑ ●

Rosy red

NEW for us in   98

In our GARDEN

Fabulously variegated foliage is splashed and striped in green, ivory, and reddish tones. Suggested as hardy, but we've avoided planting it in our garden where we have limited space, because of potential invasiveness. A beautiful plant, but best kept isolated. Cut stems and leaves for arrangements.

microcephela
'Red Dragon'

Fleeceflower, Knotweed

Isu   24"

Perennial   ○ ◑ ●

White flower sprays

NEW for us in   00

In our GARDEN

Tall mounds of arching red stems that yield to red petioles and leaf veins. Silver arrow shapes fill the center of arrow-shaped, red purple leaves. Really spectacular foliage then combines with sprays of white flowers all summer. Site this carefully, because it spreads fairly rapidly, especially in moist soils.

 278

PETALOSTEMON (DALEA)

purpureum

Purple Prairie Clover
Prairie Perennial ○
Glowing blue purple, yellow highlights

msu   24"
NEW for us in 97
In our GARDEN 97

We love this native, pea-leaved, nitrogen-fixing legume. Intriguing flower clusters whorl around elongated small cones of tiny ray flowers, and showy yellow stamens make colors glow! Like many tap-rooted Northern Plains plants, they do not fare well in small pots and grow better once planted in the ground. The root is used for medicinal, native teas.

PETASITES

japonica
'Giganteus'

Giant Butterbur
Perennial, Water ○ ●
Mauve to white

spr-esu   36-42"
NEW for us in 96
In our GARDEN

Bold, I mean HUGE, rhubarb-like leaves to 2' across. Large, I mean HUGE, buds emerge and flower before leaves unfold in spring. Spreads by creeping rhizomes and very hard to eliminate, so site carefully. Excellent in large areas around bogs or streams.

PETRORHAGIA (TUNICA)

saxifraga
'Rosette'

Tunic Flower
Perennial ○
Double pink

esu-lsu LB   8-10"
NEW for us in 98
In our GARDEN 97

Finest of texture and wiry, low stems and leaves are laden with double pink, baby's-breath-like flowers. Low mounds barely reach 8-10", and bloom for most of the summer. This long lived, rock garden plant is new to most gardeners, but once observed, is very much admired.

PHLOX

Phlox is a large genus that everyone is familiar with, offering a wide range of selections to all levels of gardeners. If you haven't grown any yet, your initiation is probably not far off. The common name for the genus Phlox is phlox. Don't you wish it were this easy for all plants?

Plants in this group are predominantly North American natives. Phlox is just one of many genera that was "discovered" and sent back to England as the new American colonies were established. The overseers of our foremothers and fathers, quickly recognized the plants' potential as fragrant garden and cut flowers. Phlox subulata, creeping phlox, excited English horticulturists as early as 1745. Remember this as you shake yourself loose from the bondage of unnecessarily granting superiority to England's gardening realm. Please, American gardeners, no more twinges of garden inferiority. The Revolution was over 200 years ago!

Locally common, sun-loving, rock garden plants are called creeping phlox, P. subulata; the tall garden phlox we are mostly familiar with, P. paniculata, prefer full sun; P. maculata, mildew-resistant meadow phlox, are for part shade to sun. The low, creeping, ground-cover species of P. stolonifera and P. divaricata tend to be shade lovers.

Anyone who has ever grown Phlox paniculata, tall garden phlox, has looked on helplessly as powdery mildew transformed an entire plant to downy white stalks during hot humid days of summer. Lynne, a gardening quick-study, runs her pinched forefinger and thumb down the stalk and in one fell swoop, detaches all leaves and discards them. She is left with bare stalks, but still-beautiful flowers. Somehow her plants still manage to thrive year after year, sans leaves for half the summer.

To lessen mildew effects, promote ventilation by thinning clumps and allowing space between plantings, water only in the morning, and, my least favorite, follow a rigid fungicide program. To avoid the last suggestion of regular fungicide use, choose the newer mildew-resistant cultivars of tall garden phlox or the meadow phlox, also resistant. All prefer sun or part shade with a little extra moisture. Butterflies feed from the flowers in summer.

arendsii x paniculata
'Miss Jill'

Phlox, Spring Pearl Hybrids   esu-msu   18-24"
Perennial   ○ ●   NEW for us in   99
White, small pink eye   In our GARDEN

Fragrant hybrids of tall garden phlox are half the height while maintaining the same large, full flower heads. Christened the Spring Pearl Hybrids, they bloom a little earlier in the summer that do Phlox paniculata cultivars.

arendsii x paniculata
'Miss Karen'

Phlox, Spring Pearl Hybrids   esu-msu   22"
Perennial, Containers   ○ ●   NEW for us in   00
Dark rose, dark red eye   In our GARDEN

These crosses with tall garden phlox have very full heads of fragrant flowers and shorter, stronger stems. Use them in containers or the garden.

arendsii x paniculata
'Miss Mary'

Phlox, Spring Pearl Hybrids   esu-msu   20"
Perennial   ○ ●   NEW for us in   00
Clear red   In our GARDEN

We picked this one for the Marys-quite-contraries. Dark, nearly mildew-resistant foliage contrasts well with red flowers.

maculata
'Alpha'

Meadow or Spotted Phlox   esu-msu   24-36"
Perennial, Water   ○ ●   NEW for us in   95
Lavender rose   In our GARDEN

Turn to this species for glossier leaves and mildew resistance. Will tolerate consistently moist or boggy sites.

maculata
'Natascha'

Meadow or Spotted Phlox   esu-msu   24-30"
Perennial, Water   ○ ●   NEW for us in   97
Rose and white pinwheels   In our GARDEN   97

Sweet, mildew-resistant meadow phlox with rose and white pinwheel flowers. I love this unusual and charming plant.

maculata
'Omega'

Meadow or Spotted Phlox   esu-msu   24-36"
Perennial, Water   ○ ●   NEW for us in   95
White tinged violet with pink eye   In our GARDEN

Another powder-proof (mildew-proof) cultivar. Glossy leaves of meadow phlox cultivars help deter mildew. Bred in Europe. A little more water, please.

maculata x carolina
'Miss Lingard'

Meadow or Spotted Phlox
Perennial ○ ◐
Pure white, slight yellow eye

esu-msu   36"
NEW for us in 96
In our GARDEN

Large, fragrant flower trusses. Usually good rebloom if flowers and foliage are removed after first flowering. Mildew-resistant leaves; dark, sturdy stems. Prefers a little shade and moist soil.

paniculata
'Bright Eyes'

Tall Garden Phlox
Perennial ○ ◐
Pink, red eye

msu-lsu   24"
NEW for us in 97
In our GARDEN

Purplish foliage tinted with green is mildew resistant. Large heads of pink flowers have contrasting eye. Honors: Chicago Botanic Garden rates as one of best Phlox for disease resistance and ornamental qualities.

paniculata
'Cecil Hanbury'

Tall Garden Phlox
Perennial ○ ◐
Salmon orange

msu-lsu LB   36-48"
NEW for us in 96
In our GARDEN 97

Really a warm pink trying to reach orange.

paniculata
'David'

Tall Garden Phlox
Perennial ○ ◐
Clear white, fragrant

msu-lsu LB   36-42"
NEW for us in 94
In our GARDEN 96

The best, new white introduction with mildew-resistant foliage and wonderfully fragrant and long-blooming flowers. What more can I say? Honors: Chicago Botanic Garden rates as one of best Phlox for disease resistance and ornamental qualities.

paniculata
'Dodo Hanbury Forbes'

Tall Garden Phlox
Perennial ○ ◐
Clear pink with red eye

msu-lsu LB   36"
NEW for us in 96
In our GARDEN 96

Huge, pyramidal, weather-resistant flower heads may reach 16" across.

paniculata
'Eva Cullum'

Tall Garden Phlox
Perennial ○ ◐
Clear pink with maroon eye

msu-lsu LB   24-30"
NEW for us in 96
In our GARDEN 96

Always looks good, blooms long and strong, and carries its space in the garden for the rest of the season once it begins in midsummer. One of the most-preferred Bloom of Bressingham introductions that has large flower heads, strong stems, compact habit and mildew-resistant foliage.

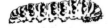 282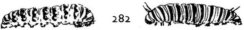

paniculata
'Franz Shubert'

Tall Garden Phlox

Perennial ○ ●

Cool, lilac blue, contrasting crimson eye

msu-lsu LB   24-36"

NEW for us in 96

In our GARDEN 97

Unique cool color combination with huge petals and flower clusters. Plant is sturdy and compact with excellent mildew resistance. One of the best introduced by the noted English Blooms of Bressingham Nursery. Honors: Chicago Botanic Garden rates as one of best Phlox for disease resistance and ornamental qualities.

paniculata
'Mt. Fujiyama'

Tall Garden Phlox

Perennial ○ ●

Pure white

msu-lsu LB   36"

NEW for us in 94

In our GARDEN

We've replaced this mildew-prone cultivar with newer freer P. 'David'.

paniculata
'Nicky'

Tall Garden Phlox

Perennial ○ ●

Darkest magenta purple

msu-lsu LB   36-48"

NEW for us in 98

In our GARDEN 00

New, berry bright and very mildew-resistant.

paniculata
'Nora Leigh'

Variegated Tall Garden Phlox

Perennial ○ ●

Pale lilac, dark centers

msu-lsu LB   18-24"

NEW for us in 96

In our GARDEN 96

One of few variegated selections and a highlight in the garden. Leaves have broad creamy edges and midsummer flowers are pale lilac with dark centers. Hard to differentiate from another tall variegated phlox, P. 'Darwin's Choice'.

paniculata
'Orange Perfection'

Tall Garden Phlox

Perennial ○ ●

Bright, salmon orange, red eye

msu-lsu LB   24-36"

NEW for us in 96

In our GARDEN 96

The Phlox flower that is closest in color to true orange and vigorous, heavy flowering, early, and mildew resistant.

paniculata
'Robert Poore'

Tall Garden Phlox

Perennial ○ ●

Vibrant magenta pink

msu-lsu LB   48-60"

NEW for us in 99

In our GARDEN

Outstanding mildew resistant selection has iridescent flowers and is very, very tall. Honors: U of Georgia Athens Better Performer; 1999 Georgia Gold Medal Plant.

paniculata
'Sandra'
Tall Garden Phlox
Perennial ○ ●
Magenta pink with punch

msu-lsu LB   24-36"
NEW for us in   99
In our GARDEN   00

A very showy pink with a punch, a perfect match to Rosa 'Winnipeg Parks'.

paniculata
'Shortwood'
Tall Garden Phlox
Perennial ○ ●
Glowing pink

msu-lsu LB   24-36"
NEW for us in   00
In our GARDEN

A sport of mildew resistant P. 'David'. New in the market in 2000. Honors: COPF Introduction.

paniculata
'Snow White'
Tall Garden Phlox
Perennial ○ ●
Snow white, green center

msu-lsu   23"
NEW for us in   00
In our GARDEN

Bright white individual flowers have tiny green hearts. Mildew resistant and shorter than usual paniculata types. We're hoping this is as mildew resistant as the other excellent white, P. 'David'.

paniculata
'Spitfire'
Tall Garden Phlox
Perennial ○ ●
Rose red

msu-lsu   30"
NEW for us in   95
In our GARDEN   96

One of most-colorful garden phlox that is noted for strong, bright midsummer color.

paniculata
'Starfire'
Tall Garden Phlox
Perennial ○ ●
Brightest, rose red

msu-lsu LB   36"
NEW for us in   95
In our GARDEN   97,

Attractive maroon foliage in early spring changes to deep green and is mildew resistant. Always in demand because of foliage/flower contrasts, vivid color, vigor and early flowering. Now that we've introduced this bright color-anchor to our garden, we can never be without it.

paniculata
'The King'
Tall Garden Phlox
Perennial ○ ●
Dark purple

msu LB   48"
NEW for us in   99
In our GARDEN

The very tall and very new garden phlox.

paniculata x stolonifera
'Spring Delight'
Woodlan Phlox
Perennial ○ ●
Rose pink clusters

esu-lsu LB   12-15"
NEW for us in 97
In our GARDEN 97

Another rare-find with abundant, long-lasting flower clusters that could be a cross between creeping phlox and woodland phlox. Give partial shade with sandy, rich soil-- tolerates dry shade. Honors: U of Georgia Athens Better Performers.

pilosa
Downy Phlox
Prairie Perennial ○ ●
Pink

spr-esu   12-18"
NEW for us in 98
In our GARDEN

A drought tolerant, early flowering, long blooming, butterfly plant and a Great Plains native, too.

subulata
'Candy Stripe', 'Tamanonagalei'
Creeping Phlox
Perennial, Groundcover ○ ●
Bold, pink stroke on white petal

spr-esu   6-9"
NEW for us in 94
In our GARDEN 94

New engaging flowers with unusual pinwheel-like color pattern on a compact grower that reblooms in fall. Tiny, needled leaves are evergreen and benefit from even slight winter cover.

subulata
'Emerald Blue'
Creeping Phlox
Perennial, Groundcover ○ ●
Glowing blue lavender

spr-esu   6-9"
NEW for us in 95
In our GARDEN

A gem of a groundcover that is a mass of color in spring. Moss-like foliage forms evergreen mats.

subulata
'Emerald Pink'
Creeping Phlox
Perennial, Groundcover ○ ●
Rose pink

spr-esu   5"
NEW for us in 00
In our GARDEN

subulata
'Oakington Blue Eyes'
Creeping Phlox
Perennial, Groundcover ○ ●
Lavender blue

spr-esu   36-60"
NEW for us in 99
In our GARDEN

Profuse flowering creeping phlox with clean, neat foliage. Blooms Nursery introduction from England. Honors: U of Georgia Athens Better Perfomers Selection, high ratings in field trials.

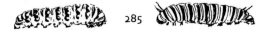

subulata
'Red Wing'
Creeping Phlox
Perennial, Groundcover ○ ●
Red with darker eye

spr-esu   6-9"
NEW for us in   98
In our GARDEN

Brilliant, striking color on early flowering, creeping plant. What would May be like without mats of creeping phlox spilling onto walks and drives and tumbling over steps and walls?

subulata
'White Delight'
Creeping Phlox
Perennial, Groundcover ○ ●
Pure white

spr-esu
NEW for us in   00
In our GARDEN

PHYSALIS

The common name, Chinese lantern, is a right-on description of this ground-cherry relative. The lanterns are really the sepals that join together to form an inflated, two inch husk that protects a small fruit within. The Greek word "phusa" is translated as "bladder" and refers to this inflated structure. The color is magnetic, an illuminating vermillion-red-orange, complete with prominent veins that appear as applied ridges. They are in demand by cut and dried-flower enthusiasts.

Described as a perennial, tender perennial, or grow-as-an-annual genus, it spreads by underground runners and can be invasive. Be careful. Plant it in rich, well-drained soil in sun in areas where they will not compete with tamer perennials. Provide constant moisture while lanterns are forming. Traditional medicine prescribed the use of the fruit as a relief for gout.

alkekengi (Franchetti)
Chinese Lantern
Perennial ○ ●
Papery orange husks, white flowers

24"
NEW for us in   97
In our GARDEN

 286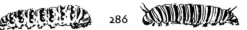

PHYSOSTEGIA

The common name for this genus, obedient plant, is an excellent example of an oxymoron, strictly defined as "sharply stupid". To get to the point, this plant is anything but obedient; it is highly invasive! But quickly spreading clumps do not always need to be viewed in a negative light or preclude the value of a plant. They are an excellent choice when applied to difficult site problems. Use them as a tall ground cover anywhere that you can allow free roaming, or as a bank stabilizer in partially shaded sites.

One-inch, tubular flowers are arranged up and down rigid stems, and the common name really describes the obedience of these blooms, not the habit of the plant itself. Flower spikes of the lavender-pink cultivars provide long-lasting cuts until very late in the season. White-flowering ones bloom a few weeks earlier in mid to late summer. Foliage offers thick, glossy, dark-green, toothed leaves of exceptional quality.

Not that Physostegia needs much encouragement; it will be most vigorous in moist, slightly acid soil with light shade, though it won't object to sun. Give it opposite culture to keep in check.

My appreciation for this plant was solidified late one fall. After several nights of below-freezing temperatures, the dragonheads (the other common name) continued to bloom, covered with early winter snow. We had cut flowers from the garden clear into October.

'Miss Manners'

Perennial   ○ ◐ ●

esu-fall LB
NEW for us in   00
In our GARDEN

Clumping form of usually invasive false dragonhead.

virginiana
'Pink Bouquet'

Obedient Plant, False Dragonhead
Perennial, Groundcover   ○ ◐ ●
Beautiful, bright pink

msu-lsu   36-48"
NEW for us in   94
In our GARDEN

Slightly less-invasive than others but one must still site with care. Taller cultivars may require staking. Site these in out of the way, troublesome areas where grass or other plants are hard to grow.

virginiana
'Snow Crown', 'Crown of Snow'

Obedient Plant, False Dragonhead
Perennial, Groundcover   ○ ◐ ●
Bright white

msu   24-36"
NEW for us in   94
In our GARDEN

Blooms earlier than pink varieties but valuable still for late summer flowering. Not quite as aggressive as others.

 287

virginiana
'Summer Snow'

Obedient Plant, False Dragonhead

msu   24-30"

Perennial, Groundcover   ○ ◐ ●

NEW for us in 94

Pure white

In our GARDEN

Midsummer flowering, slightly less invasive than the pink varieties. Plants eventually colonize providing abundant and perfect cut flower stalks.

virginiana
'Variegata'

Variegated Obedient Plant, False Dragonhead

msu-lsu LB   18-24"

Perennial, Groundcover   ○ ◐ ●

NEW for us in 94

Lavender pink

In our GARDEN

This is a not-as-invasive, uncommon variegated form. The foliage upstages the flowers.

PHYTEUMA

scheuchzeri

Rampion

esu   8-15"

Perennial   ○ ◐

NEW for us in 94

Deep blue

In our GARDEN 94

Early summer bright-blue spheres on a tufted, compact plant that has returned in my garden year after year. Could be used as rock garden plant for it likes dry feet and non-acid soil. Though unsure of the species and knowing of no present source for this plant, I still had to include this.

PLATYCODON

Balloon flowers are one of the easiest perennials to grow and have long been popular with gardeners. Compelling to children and adults alike, puffed or inflated, balloon-shaped buds open to flaring, cup-shaped flowers in beautiful blue, pink or white. When open, the flowers resemble Campanula (bellflowers), to which they are related, but balloon flowers bloom later, usually in July, and are a great help to extend desirable blue hues throughout the season.

Plant form is narrow and restrained; it will never show aggression towards its neighbors. As individual stems elongate and become heavy with buds and blossoms, they may sometimes flop. Clumps, though somewhat slow to develop, settle in for the long-haul and don't like to be moved. Be sure to site it with this in mind and provide it well-drained soil in full sun or light shade. It is one of the last flowers to emerge in spring; mark its location so you don't unintentionally injure its roots during spring cleanup.

This plant provides overall ease to the garden and gardener alike as it effortlessly produces cut flowers and is without pest or disease problems.

'Fuji Pink'

Balloon Flower	msu-lsu	24"
Perennial ○ ◐	NEW for us in	98
Shell pink	In our GARDEN	

Pink color holds up best in part shade.

'Komachii'

Balloon Flower	msu-lsu	24"
Perennial ○ ◐	NEW for us in	00
Glowing blue	In our GARDEN	00

This unusual variety impressed us in '99 at the Minnesota Landscape Arboretum, and then we went searching for it. Double puffed-up flowers never seem to open.

apoyama
'Misato Purple'

Balloon Flower	msu-lsu	6-9"
Perennial ○ ◐	NEW for us in	98
Blue hued purple	In our GARDEN	

A dwarf form of purple balloon flower, tough and versatile.

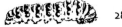 

grandiflorus
'Mariesii Blue'

Balloon Flower

msu LB 12-18"

Perennial ○ ◉

NEW for us in 94

Rich blue

In our GARDEN

This low-maintenance, long-lived plant might be the choicest blue form. of balloon flower. It is a compact plant with 2" flowers. Be patient in early spring because it is one of the last perennials to emerge from the ground.

grandiflorus
'Sentimental Blue'

Balloon Flower

msu-lsu 6"

Perennial ○ ◉

NEW for us in 98

Intense blue

In our GARDEN

Another dwarf plant with balloons of blue.

POLEMONIUM

Jacob's ladder is a highly desirable, long-lived and often overlooked garden plant for somewhat moist soil, shade or part sun. Glossy leaves grow opposite one another on a stalk, representing bushy ladders, stairways to heaven for some tiny insect or animal. As you look to the top rungs of these "ladders," leaves become smaller and give way to beautiful, mostly blue flowers, clustered at the top. Uncommon white, pink, and yellow colors are also attainable, with difficulty. Flowers are tube shaped and sharply accentuated by color-wheel-complement, orange stamens, which hang out immodestly. Semi-shady areas are brightened by Polemonium flowers for long periods in early summer and lovely foliage holds its position ever after.

'Silver Leaf'

Jacob's Ladder

esu-msu 18"

Perennial ○ ◉ ●

NEW for us in 98

Yellow trumpets

In our GARDEN

Catalog description: "Yellow clusters of 2" long, trumpet-shaped flowers, fern-like, silvery foliage, summer-long bloom. Moist shade." We grew from seed in 1998 and now my description: "Dull green leaves with maybe a silver cast if you squint.
Weak-stemmed foliage seems to be slightly hairy and tends to cling when brushed. Uncommon yellow, but not showy, Jacob's ladder flowers. Plant has a disagreeable odor." I don't think we'll grow this again.

Brise d'Anjou
'Brise d'Anjou'
Variegated Jacob's Ladder

esu-msu   24"

Perennial ○ ◐ ●

NEW for us in 98

Blue clusters

In our GARDEN

Ladder-like arrangement of cream edged leaves makes this plant most unusual. It shows vigor too, not always the case with variegated plants. Provide reliably moist, rich woodland soil in shade to part sun. A French connection but an English Blooms Nursery introduction, first available in '98. Honors: Penn State Impressive Performance, COPF Introduction.

caeruleum
Jacob's Ladder

18-24"

Perennial ○ ◐ ●

NEW for us in 93

Lovely rich blue, obvious orange stamens

In our GARDEN

Requiring moist shade like the others, this flowers later than P. reptans.

caeruleum
'Blue Whirl'
Jacob's Ladder

esu-msu   24"

Perennial ○ ◐ ●

NEW for us in 98

Blue clusters

In our GARDEN

A compact selection.

POLYGONATUM

Watching Solomon seal emerge and unfurl in spring is like watching a graceful dancer with one green foot securely anchored to the forest floor. I love this plant and it brings most pleasant feelings--subtle, elegant, gently-aristocratic, mysterious and . . . creative. Single tiny tusks of tight unfurled leaves first pierce the air, and as several in the colony or "herd" emerge, I can imagine a group of tiny rhinos just below the earth's surface. Soon, piercing yields to thrusting as tusks enlarge and elongate. And then, magically, the two-to-four inch, alternate leaves untwine, and the uppermost part of the plant begins to arch forward. As plants colonize in groups, they parallel one another, all arching gracefully in the same direction. Small ivory-colored, bell-like flowers dangle from the overhanging stems at every leaf node. Delicate purple-black fruits follow the flowers, never dominating the plant's overall presence.

These wildflowers, native to South Dakota and related to the lily family, add an aristocratic touch to a shady, woodland garden and are very easy to grow. With consistent moisture, they gradually set up non-invasive colonies, but in our old neighborhood they have naturalized and thrive in many areas that have unreliable moisture. Fall color is effective, even in the shade, a yellowish-gold color. Foliage alone or combined with flowers provides lovely stems for cut flower arrangements.

The Latin word "polygonatum" refers to the many small joints that are found in the roots. Early healers believed roots could hasten the healing or sealing of broken bones, hence the common name of Solomon seal.

commutatum, canaliculatum

Giant Solomon Seal
esu   36-48"
Perennial   O ●
NEW for us in
Creamy dangling bells
In our GARDEN

The giant among Solomon seal with up to 4' arching stalks with dangling white bells.

humile

Dwarf Solomon Seal
6-8"
Perennial   O ●
NEW for us in   90
Creamy dangling bells
In our GARDEN

Wonderful woodland dwarf species that I garden-gifted until it was gone. Those of you who received a division, would you share some back?

multiflorum

Solomon Seal
Perennial ◐ ●
Creamy dangling bells

esu-msu   24"
NEW for us in 80
In our GARDEN

First, arching flower stalks and white dangling bell-shaped flowers, and later, dangling blue berries. Nearly every shade garden can accommodate this species.

odoratum (falcatum)

'Variegatum'

Variegated Solomon Seal
Perennial ◐ ●
Creamy white

esu   24"
NEW for us in 95
In our GARDEN 96

Light-green leaves with subtle white margins attract attention without dominating it. White bells hang from leaf nodes. Brightens up dull, shady spots and provides beautiful material for arrangements. I've had the same colony for nearly two decades. Honors: 1999 Arkansas Select.

PORTERANTHUS, GILLENIA

Porteranthus or Gillenia is another native American plant that was "rediscovered" after it had emigrated to Europe. With natural elegance, a-girl-or-boy-next-door plant, its light, airy texture belies its easiness.

Foliage and flower work together to produce an interesting growth and blooming habit. Its flower show is like a flight of small white butterflies. In midsummer, observe masses of bright, white, starry, one-inch flowers; red calyces (group of sepals); long, wiry, red stems; and intricate leaf structure. Interesting seed heads look good into the winter along with fall-colored foliage.

I read that one must provide moist, acid to neutral soil in partial shade for this plant or it will languish. But, here again, we have it planted near our prairie plants that receive very little supplemental moisture. We have planned for some future shade by planting a nearby conifer, so it may be awhile before it gets to cool off in our garden! Now you can understand why we view this as an easy plant to grow.

stipulata, trifoliata

Bowman's Root, Indian Physic
Perennial ○ ◐ ●
White, pink blush

esu   18-36"
NEW for us in 97
In our GARDEN 97

New England native for the border or naturalizing. Grows in sun and shade with real wildflower appearance.

 293

POTENTILLA

The pretty foliage of the herbaceous cinquefoil displays strawberry-like leaves. Flowers are round and shaped like tiny roses in bright, showy colors of yellow, red, pink, rose and white. There are hundreds of both herbaceous and woody species, mostly trailing and prostrate or upright to two feet. Some are native to South Dakota.

Instead of choosing the potentially weedy and invasive species Potentilla for your garden, try the better behaved cultivars. The taller ones are showy in early summer; if they later grow leggy, a quick pruning will take care of them and induce more flowers. The trailing ones are excellent rock garden choices.

Easy to grow and reliable in our climate, they perform best with cool nights and non-fertile, lean soils. All need sharp drainage and are usually drought tolerant.

These herbaceous cinquefoils are related to the more common, woody Potentilla shrubs that seem to have dominated nearly every, newly installed landscape in Sioux Falls for the last two or three decades.

The Latin word "potens" means "powerful" or "potent." Early physicians believed in Potentilla's medicinal potency and advised this plant for a number of therapeutic treatments, including colds and toothache.

atrosanguinea x
'Gibson's Scarlet'

Red Cinquefoil	msu-lsu LB	18"
Perennial ○	NEW for us in	96
Brilliant red	In our GARDEN	

Plants for well-drained sites. Compact and long blooming.

atrosanguinea x
'William Rollisson'

Cinquefoil	msu-lsu LB	12-15"
Perennial ○	NEW for us in	97
Red orange with yellow centers	In our GARDEN	97

Showy, semi double flowers, strawberry foliage. Red petals are reversed in yellow.

nepalensis
'Miss Wilmott'

Nepal Cinquefoil	esu-lsu LB	12"
Perennial, Groundcover ○	NEW for us in	97
Carmine red, dark centers	In our GARDEN	97

Strawberry-like leaves, long leafy stems and clusters of 1" flowers all summer. Short-lived plant that may come true from seed.

<u>reptans</u>
'Pleniflora'

Cinquefoil   esu-lsu LB   3-6"
Perennial, Groundcover   ○   NEW for us in   94
Yellow   In our GARDEN

Spreads rapidly as a dense, mat-like groundcover. Introduced by Royal Botanical Garden.

PRIMULA

The early blooms of Primula announce the arrival of spring and last for several weeks if temperatures remain cool. Flowers are tube or funnel shaped, flaring from stalks of a few inches to 1' or 1.5' tall. Rainbows of color in many combinations are displayed. The yellow or white eye or margin of the flower is often contrasted with the primary color of red, yellow, orange and pink.

Basal leaves emerge at soil level, forming low mounds from which flower stalks emerge, sometimes simultaneously. The small, nubby texture on leaves and stalks is sometimes referred to as farina which indicates a mealy-like texture.

Of hundreds of primrose species, there are bound to be some that can be adapted to South Dakota if correct growing conditions are provided. We've begun to investigate the following species that are worth trying: P. auricula, denticulata, polyantha, and sieboldii.

The secret to their adaptability, as with any plant, is not only the test of winter temperatures. As natives to bogs, woodlands and meadows of North American climates, fluctuating moisture levels, from wet to dry during summer, is the single most important cause of their demise. For this reason, summer mulching is as important as winter mulching. Some are more heat tolerant than others, but all prefer cool soil and air temperatures. Plant them in semi-shade in organically amended soil. Winter mulch to keep freeze-thaw cycles from heaving them out of the ground in spring.

<u>auricula</u>
<u>mix</u>

Auricula Primrose   spr-esu   6-9"
Perennial   ○ ●   NEW for us in   97
Mixed   In our GARDEN

Requires rich well-drained soil with shaded afternoons and will yield 1" fragrant bells and thick, long leaves. Many cultivars of this exist, but the species is hard to improve upon and easy to grow.

denticulata
mix
Drumstick Primrose   spr   8"
Perennial   ◐ ●   NEW for us in   99
Mixed colors   In our GARDEN   99

Early to flower, round heads are held by fragile-appearing stems. Toothed and flat, elongated leaves continue to expand after flowering until they reach 12".

pubescens x
Primrose   spr   8"
Perennial   ◐ ●   NEW for us in   99
Lavender rose, white eye.   In our GARDEN   99

One of oldest-cultivated hybrids and a cross between P. auricula and rubra.

saxatilis, cortusoides
Primrose   spr-lsu LB   6"
Perennial   ◐ ●   NEW for us in   97
Rosy pink to lavender   In our GARDEN   ·

Another species to try in Dakota climes. Looks like a small P. sieboldii with quilted leaves and scalloped leaf edges. If kept moist and active with woodland conditions, it will flower from spring until late fall. Native to Siberia, this is an easy to grow Asian primrose.

PRUNELLA, BRUNELLA

Butterflies are attracted to the short, bright, flower spikes of self-heal in early summer. Flowers have both upper and lower lips with a hood-like appearance. Mat-forming, semi-evergreen foliage can be used as a groundcover under shrubs or as a rock garden plant in sun or partial shade. Provide humus-rich soil and consistent moisture. If plants dry out, they will decline rapidly. They will increase by self-sowing and spreading stems. Prunella is sometimes referred to as the German genus, Brunella. Do not use Prunella vulgaris, a common lawn weed.

grandiflora
mix
Self-heal, Bigflower   esu-msu   9-12"
Perennial   ○ ◐   NEW for us in   96
Lavender, pink, rose, white   In our GARDEN

Short blooming stalks of hooded flowers appear for long periods from spreading mats of attractive, oval leaves. Moist alkaline soils are necessary in sun to partial shade; plants will die if allowed to dry out. This can be invasive in ideal conditions.

 296

PSEUDOSCABER

'Veil of Lace'

Hardy Asparagus Vine   24-36"
Perennial   ○ ●   NEW for us in 93
Foliage effect   In our GARDEN 94

Though not really a vine for us, relaxed upright shrubby asparagus has
returned year after year. Finest, thread-like, bright green foliage is a foil for
other plants.

PULMONARIA

Transfer the spotted rump of an Appaloosa horse to the wide and elongated leaf of a woodland plant, and abracadabra, make-believe plants appear. I'll name the new species Appaloomonaria, Pulmonaroosa, Rumpalaria, and Pulmonorumpa. And we'll use easier-to-remember, common names, like lung-rump and rump-lung or rump-wort, and apply them to the plants that resemble like body parts!

Kidding aside, rumpworts, I mean, lungworts, are compelling, unusual and unassuming plants for shade gardens. Their main attraction is their gray, silver, and white-splashed green foliage. The best species for showy foliage are P. saccharata, P. longifolia and P. officinalis. The species P. angustifolia and P. rubra have no or few spots but redeem themselves by producing distinct, showy flowers. In addition to the common name lungwort, other common names are given--spotted dog, soldiers and sailors, Joseph and Mary, and Bethlehem sage.

Flowers are also quite different. Borage-like, tubular forms dangle from stems held aloft about one foot high and are pink, blue, white or red. Some cultivars' flowers come in as one color, often pink, and go out as another, often blue. They may open before or at the same time as the foliage unfurls.

Lungworts are easy to care for, returning and increasing gradually year after year if you provide them well-drained soil, partial shade and consistent moisture. Wilting will set in quickly in direct sun even when ample moisture is there. Consistent shade from deciduous trees is best, where plants can fulfill roles as eye-catching focal points or ground covers.

The Latin word "pulmo" relates to the lungs. In early traditional medicine, diagnosticians would use a method called the Doctrine of the Signatures. Because a diseased lung resembled the spotted leaf of lungwort, it was believed that medicating with parts of this plant would help the related organ.

longifolia
'Bertram Anderson'

Lungwort, Joseph and Mary, Spotted Dog	spr-esu	12"
Perennial, Groundcover ○ ●	NEW for us in	98
Dark violet blue	In our GARDEN	

Silver spots on narrow, long and pointed, dark green leaves. One of largest lungwort plants, this could be used as a groundcover.

saccharata
'British Sterling'

Lungwort, Soldiers and Sailors	spr-esu	12"
Perennial O ●	NEW for us in	99
Magenta merging to blue	In our GARDEN	99

Large spotted leaves appear as a green periphery around white blended center. Will perform well in S.D. when proper culture is provided.

saccharata
'David Ward'

Lungwort, Spotted Dog	spr-esu	12"
Perennial O ●	NEW for us in	00
	In our GARDEN	

White margins narrowly edge green leaves along with the typical white blotches. According to Armitage, "Will take the gardening world by storm."

saccharata
'Highdown'

Lungwort	spr-esu	18-24"
Perennial O ●	NEW for us in	00
Thick blue	In our GARDEN	

An outstanding taller cultivar and earlier emerging flowers. Hairy, soft green leaves with silver speckles, called "the finest flowering Pulmonaria" from the few who are acquainted with this plant. Honors: U of Georgia Athens Better Performers.

saccharata
'Janet Fisk'

Lungwort, Bethlehem Sage	spr-esu	12"
Perennial, Groundcover O ●	NEW for us in	98
Pink buds and flowers turn blue	In our GARDEN	

Abundant, cloud-like, white blotches create marbled leaves.

saccharata
'Little Star'

Lungwort, Bethlehem Sage	spr-esu	9-12"
Perennial O ●	NEW for us in	00
Dark blue	In our GARDEN	

Narrow leaves spotted silver and cobalt blue flowers in early spring with a nice, compact plant. Pulmonaria culture for all--reliably moist soil in shade or part sun.

saccharata
'Margery Fish'

Lungwort, Bethlehem Sage	spr-esu	9-18"
Perennial O ●	NEW for us in	
Pink buds and flowers turn blue	In our GARDEN	

Vigorous blue-green foliage with large silvery blotches. Prized and sought after in Europe.

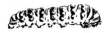 299

saccharata
'Mrs. Moon'

Lungwort, Bethlehem Sage	spr-esu	9"
Perennial, Groundcover, Containers ○ ●	NEW for us in	95
Pink flowers turn to blue	In our GARDEN	

Still one of most popular, but old cultivar. Silver spots are clearly defined.

saccharata
'Roy Davidson'

Lungwort, Joseph and Mary, Spotted Dog	spr-esu	9-12"
Perennial, Containers ○ ●	NEW for us in	00
Pink turns heavenly blue	In our GARDEN	

An American cultivar of silver blotched elongated leaves and early blooming flowers. Honors: U of Georgia Athens Better Performers.

saccharata
'White Wings'

Lungwort, Bethlehem Sage	spr-esu	12"
Perennial ○ ●	NEW for us in	
Large white	In our GARDEN	

Larger flowers, longer in bloom, and a strong, vigorous grower results in an improvement over 'Sissinghurst White'.

saccharata, officinalis
'Sissinghurst White'

Lungwort, Bethlehem Sage	spr-esu	12"
Perennial ○ ●	NEW for us in	95
Large, white, showy	In our GARDEN	

Large white flowers outshow the more subtly spotted foliage and contrast well with blue and pink forms.

PULSATILLA

patens
violet blue

Pasque Flower, Anemone	spr	9-12"
Prairie Perennial ○	NEW for us in	95
Violet blue	In our GARDEN	

Laying eyes on this flower strikes a memory string for most of us natives. Very dark lavender, cup-shaped blooms appear while hairy and feathery, silver foliage is still emerging and stretching. No Dakota garden should be without this showy and delightful, drought-tolerant spring flower and season-long foliage effect. Pulsatilla was formerly including in the Anemone genus.

vulgaris

Pasque Flower, Anemone	spr	9-12"
Perennial, Containers ○	NEW for us in	95
Violet blue	In our GARDEN	94

One of first spring flowers, the commonly requested, blue pasque flower. Not the true, native pasque but lovely and showy. Fine, silvery hairs, lovely for petting, cover young foliage as blossoms emerge. Give well-drained soil and keep it dry.

 300

vulgaris
'Alba'

Pasque Flower, Anemone
Perennial   ○
White

spr   9-12"
NEW for us in 98
In our GARDEN

The drought tolerant, white form.

vulgaris
'Papageno'

Pasque Flower, Anemone
Perennial   ○
Mixed colors

spr   9-12"
NEW for us in 98
In our GARDEN

Seed-grown strains may bloom in yellow, red or white but are still dominated by traditional lavender blue colors, but I'm not complaining. Flowers are distinctly fringed and semi double. I can't get you out of my mind. Honors: Penn State Top 20 Perennial Performers.

vulgaris, patens
'Rubra'

Pasque Flower, Anemone
Perennial, Prairie   ○
Dark, ruby red

spr   9-12"
NEW for us in 95
In our GARDEN

In spring, blossoms emerge first, protected simultaneously by silver haired, feathery foliage. Foliage later elongates and fills-in to make an ethereal shrublet. Vivid colors. Drought tolerant.

RANUNCULUS

My neighbor Ann has found the ideal application for the aggressive little buttercup. Every late spring to early summer, I admire the double form tumbling over her front brick steps. The small bright-yellow flowers create a lovely combination with lavender-blue true geraniums and large unfurling Hosta leaves. As pretty as a picture, it's a perfect little garden setting in which all plants work equally well together and one that takes care of itself year after year.

Years back I planted this little tyrant in a rock garden of collected plants over which it quickly dominated. I had to give it and everything nearby, lethal injections of Round-up to eradicate it. With this plant and most invasive plants, choose the right application and work magic; place carelessly and reap disaster.

Besides yellow-flowering species there are white or red, single or double, anemone-like flowers. Foliage is shiny and dark, or flat and spotted. All spread from creeping roots and stems that root at every leaf node. They will grow in sun or shade but will be most aggressive in moist, sunny sites.

'Buttered Popcorn'

Buttercup   6"
Perennial, Water   ○ ◐ ●   NEW for us in 00
Yellow buttons   In our GARDEN

The metallic glow of these buttercup leaves is more yellow in sun, chartreuse green in the shade. It makes a good cover for under tall shrubby perennials or shrubs; but I would keep it out of the primary gardens. Save it for difficult sites or large scale landscaping, wherever you can live with its invasiveness. This tenacious thing will root and increase from every node. Tolerates shade and wet feet and will survive in shallow water. Button yellow flowers reflect a cheery attitude.

 302

repens, pleniflorus
'Flore Pleno', 'Multiplex', 'Pleniflorus'

Buttercup   esu   18"
Perennial   ○ ◑ ●   NEW for us in   97
Double yellow buttons   In our GARDEN

Button flowers with long stems are held above creeping foliage and make excellent cut flowers. Vigorous, like invasive, spreader can stand drought but can really take off and root at every leaf node if moist. I'm looking for the white buttercup (is this an oxymoron?) that Armitage says is a better behaved plant.

RATIBIDA

columnifera
'Buttons and Bows'

Mexican Hat, Coneflower   msu   30"
Prairie Perennial   ○   NEW for us in   99
Rust, edged in gold   In our GARDEN

Drooping ray flowers (petals to most of us) are suspended from the lower end of an elongated upright pistil. This plant grows strong and erect in rich, well-drained soil.

columnifera
red

Mexican Hat, Coneflower   msu-fall   48"
Prairie Perennial   ○   NEW for us in   94
Red orange   In our GARDEN

Bright-red petals create a broomstick skirt around the lower end of a cone-body that is long, narrow and upright. The common name, Mexican hat, is most descriptive. Native Americans made dye and tea from blossoms and leaves of this big bushy plant.

columnifera
yellow

Mexican Hat, Coneflower   msu-fall   48"
Prairie Perennial   ○   NEW for us in   94
Yellow   In our GARDEN

Bushy plant has flowers of drooping petals around elongated, erect cones of tiny ray flowers. The exposed cone is easily accessed and has a great surface area compared to the size of the flower. These are clues that this is a plant that would attract butterflies.

RHEUM

There are some plants that will change your "edible-only" rhubarb attitude. My awareness of the ornamental potential of the pie plant was heightened by the practices of my neighbor. Some springs she would faithfully gather the stalks (actually leaf petioles) for herself and her grateful neighbors until there was little left for decoration. Luckily, Dee occasionally faltered in her resourcefulness and didn't get around to using the fresh stalks every spring. By summer the plants were able to achieve their natural form and gloat in their I'll-show-you ornamental value.

The ornamental value of plants has mostly been discussed in this book, but may I digress a bit. While growing up in the 50's in a small rural German/Scandinavia community, there were two schools of profound thought regarding methods of gathering the long, juicy and tasty leaf petioles from a rhubarb plant: the cut-clean-with-a-knife school or the grab-hold-and-yank-hard school. A person could be psychologically evaluated based on his or her methods. I know, because I recall eavesdropping on adults as they discussed this very thing!

Large, two-to-three feet wide, elephant-ear leaves created imposing mounds, three to four feet across and as high. Sturdy, tall stalks stretched upward as if they would never stop, like Jack's beanstalk to a low heaven. Flower heads and seed heads bolted to a commanding post, five to seven feet beyond the crip sheared edge of a fine-textured hedge, a perfect, though accidental, example of stunning foliage contrast.

The rhubarb species that are selected for their ornamental value may, or may not, provide the sour-so-good taste of the old-fashioned pie plants we grew near the shelter belt. Taste is sacrificed for the beautiful red and green leaf color, bold red flowers, and form. They are not quite as flexible in their growing requirements as the old-fashioned edible types either, requiring constant moisture while being well-drained. Provide deeply cultivated, fertile soil and full sun. Once established, plants will persist for years.

palmatum
'Red Select'

Ornamental Rhubarb
Perennial, Containers ○
Deep red

esu 48-60"
NEW for us in 00
In our GARDEN

Size and color of foliage and flower contrasts well with Aquilegia 'Corbet' or other tall yellow columbines, lady's mantle and other June flowering plants.

RODGERSIA

One will choose with difficulty which parts of Rodgersia are the most elegant, the flowers or the foliage. Flowers resemble the plumes of Astilbe. Soft, feathery, lush, branched panicles are dense with tiny, individual, rosy-red or white, petal-less flowers.

Bronze-green, huge and handsome leaves, upon casual observation, appear to be palmate but are really compound. They are at the end of long petioles that emerge from around the lower, basal part of the plant. Wonderful ornamentals, they grow three-to-five feet tall and as wide; allow them plenty of room.

All require a moist, rich soil and are adaptable to bog gardens. Plant them in light shade. Varying sources rate Rodersia for zone five; we have easily wintered them here in zone four in containers under leaf cover and in our garden. Provide winter mulch in your garden if you want extra protection.

henricii
hybrids

Rodger's Flower, Fingerleaf Rodgersia	spr-esu	36-72"
Perennial O ●	NEW for us in	99
Red lavender	In our GARDEN	

Elongated leaves taper and are sharper at the tips. Deep reddish seed capsules contrast with dusky, deeply textured, bold leaves.

pinnata

Rodger's Flower, Featherleaf Rodgersia	spr-esu	30-36"
Perennial O ●	NEW for us in	95
Creamy, dense, rose pink spikes	In our GARDEN	97

Excellent foliage plants of heavy substance, these bloom in late spring over palmately compound leaves and petioles that have a type of hairy texture. Two inch flower panicles, not as showy as the leaves, top out at the same height as does the foliage. Siting should be done in areas that receive reliable moisture.

RUBUS

arcticus

Trailing Blackberry, Arctic Bramble	esu	6"
Perennial, Containers O O	NEW for us in	99
Pink with red berries	In our GARDEN	

Edible and ornamental hybrids of R. arcticus and R. stellatus are thornless. They bear pink flowers in spring, later sweet-tart berries. I've read claims that a pound of fruit can be produced per plant, per season, but I can't confirm that. For alpine, trough, containers or rock gardens, it tolerates sun, wind and temperatures to -50, and spreads by underground stolons. Foliage turns to beautiful colors in fall. With a description like this how could one resist?

RUDBECKIA

Black-eyed Susans or coneflowers are awesome natives with a shining meadow attitude that exudes continuous bloom from midsummer to frost. They can be annuals, biennials or perennials, all adapting very well to gardens and landscapes. There are many superior cultivars available, and it's hard to imagine a sunny garden without at least one. They can easily be cut for bringing indoors and they are enjoyed by butterflies.

Daisy-like heads, large, small and every size in-between, can be ruffled and fluffy, or blunt and smooth. They are excellent examples of composite flowers. What appears to be a single, daisy-like flower is really a composite of thousands of two, very-different types of flowers. The disk flowers, packed tightly together, make up the often-raised, cone-like center. The ray flowers appear to be the petals, encircling the center cone of disk flowers.

Showy, warming colors of yellow and gold develop from all Rudbeckia. Centers are dark, usually black, brown or green. Foliage may be rough-feeling or hairy but not unattractive.

Culture is not difficult. This is one of the easiest plants there is to grow. Moisture requirements vary from species to species, but most are drought tolerant; in fact they are more sturdy and upright when kept on the dry side. They spread easily but not invasively from spreading rhizomatous roots. Plants can grow in a few short weeks into large, shrubby clumps from two-feet to as tall as seven-feet.

Although the popular R. hirta cultivars are usually listed as annuals or tender perennials, some may survive more than one year because of mild winters or by self-sowing; don't bank on them entirely.

fulgida
'Goldsturm', 'Gold Storm'

Black-eyed Susan   msu-fall LB   30-36"
Prairie Perennial   ○ ●   NEW for us in   95
Yellow with dark centers   In our GARDEN

Yes, Susan, you honor us with such outstanding, long blooming plants for gardens and landscaping. Our showy, late summer gardens would never be the same without you and your reliable, floriferous, pest-free, black-eyed, daisy-like blossoms! Thank you also, for the excellent cut flowers and your tough constitution, which allows you to withstand drought. Honors: 1999 Perennial Plant of the Year.

fulgida
var. fulgida

Black-eyed Susan ⁣   msu-fall LB   24-30"
Prairie Perennial   ◯ ⬤   NEW for us in   96
Rich, golden yellow, brown cone   In our GARDEN

True, Susan, you do have smaller form, finer texture, and two or three weeks more bloom. As cold days begin, thanks for hanging around after your cousin, 'Goldsturm', has packed it in for the season. In S.D. we'll blanket you for severe winters.

hirta
'Goldilocks'

Black-eyed Susan   msu-fall LB   15"
Perennial   ◯ ⬤   NEW for us in   00
Yellow with dark centers   In our GARDEN

Neat, compact 15" plant covered with 3-4" double flowers all summer. Honors: Fleuroselect Award.

laciniata
'Goldquelle'

Green Headed Coneflower   msu-fall LB   30-36"
Prairie Perennial   ◯ ⬤   NEW for us in   96
Shaggy lemon yellow   In our GARDEN   99

From August to frost you are spectacular! You give us wonderful, shaggy garden flowers to brighten up the outdoors, and after we snip you from your mounts, we enjoy you indoors too.

maxima
'Maxima'

Dumbo's Ears, Great Rudbeckia   msu-fall LB   60-72"
Prairie Perennial   ◯ ⬤   NEW for us in   96
Deep gold   In our GARDEN   97

Incredible, truly wild flower reaches a spectacular 5-7' height. Plants form thick, powder-blue leaves up to 12" across. High centered, large, cone-shaped disks hold relaxed ray petals. Deep moist soil is recommended, but it has grown and repeated well in our dry garden for four years. The flowers, when finished, have fat, high centered, brown cones and are still showy throughout fall and winter.

nitida
'Herbstsonne', 'Autumn Sun'

Black-eyed Susan   msu-fall LB   90"
Prairie Perennial   ◯ ⬤   NEW for us in   96
Large single yellow   In our GARDEN   97

Exceptionally large aren't you, Susan? We like the new you that seldom needs propping. You make it look so easy as those bright, golden, daisy buds keep unfolding all summer from beneath the protective sheath of your branches.

subtomentosa

Black-eyed Susan, Midwest or Sweet Coneflower   msu-lsu LB   36-72"
Prairie Perennial   ○ ◐   NEW for us in 99
Tall yellow   In our GARDEN

Loads of black eyed flowers come from this North American prairie native.
Keep soil dry so plant will stand erect.

RUMEX

sanguineus

Sorrel   msu-lsu   12"
Tender Perennial?   ○ ◐   NEW for us in 97
                                                           In our GARDEN

The word "sanguineus" again the clue, blood red veins through rich dark green
leaves. These outstanding basal leaves form into clumps. Small flowers
terminate pink-tinged stems. Evergreen in mild climates, herbaceous here in
S.D. Provide winter protection at first.

SAGINA

subulata

Pearlwort | spr-esu | 1"
Perennial, Containers ○ | NEW for us in 94
White | In our GARDEN

Tight little mossy mounds can be used in containers or between stepping stones. Little white flowers are held above on little stalks. Moisture gets trapped in the foliage tufts, and plants must be planted in extremely well-drained areas. They will rot if they cannot quickly dry out. This is true during winter, too.

SAGITTARIA

latifolia

Arrowhead | msu | 24-36"
Prairie Perennial, Water ○ ● | NEW for us in
Simple white, lovely | In our GARDEN

This is a lovely water plant, native to S.D. shallow streams and lake edges. Leaves are deeply lobed, pointed and arching like those of Philodendron. Lovely white flowers, along with their reflections, are best viewed at dusk. It is a perfect plant for Japanese style gardens, a subtle aristocrat with architectural foliage that doesn't compete, but rather, enhances other foliage schemes in the garden. It is a welcomed treat whenever I discover arrowhead still thriving naturally at the edges of Covell Lake in the Terrace Park Japanese Garden of Sioux Falls.

SALVIA

This is one humongous diverse genus and we've barely made a dent in our trials with many. It includes over 800 varieties and cultivars, which fill many ornamental and culinary needs. Where should I begin to coordinate the description of its members?

First, there is the finest of culinary plants, Salvia officinalis, and its many variations and variegations, so indispensable in pork and meat dishes (1 tsp. fresh per pound at least).

Second, there are the very ornamental plants, the Salvia superbum and Salvia nemerosa crosses that are mostly mainstay early- and long-blooming perennials for us in the north. These emerge quickly from the ground in spring, ready to bloom through June and longer. If June is a wet month, mounded foliage will relax and open up in the center. We get complaints about the lack of neatness this flopping displays. If this laxity happens, one can cut the stems all the way to the ground and they will regrow. If it is a typical summer, moisture levels will taper off and the new clump will look complete for the rest of the summer. If your irrigation system is watering this plant regularly, you might as well move it to a drier spot.

Third, there are the new and different forms being introduced to the U.S. from southern countries of Mexico and Central and South America. Some of these are ancient herbs used in native ceremonies, being "rediscovered" for abilities to induce hallucinatory experiences (if that's your bag). Most of these south-of-the-border plants are tender for us but provide ornamental tender perennial or annual plants that grow into large specimens in our summer heat. They may flower through the summer if purchased as large plants in spring or put on spectacular late season shows. Most have potential as xeriscaping landscape plants for the southwestern regions of the U.S.

Since all love heat, full sun, and dry conditions, you can understand the dream we have of finding new ones with potential for South Dakota summers. Hummingbirds, bees, butterflies, all are attracted to these plants, which also provide abundant cut flowers.

This genus does not include Russian sage, Perovskia, or Jerusalem sage, Phlomis.

 310

azurea

Azure Sage
Perennial ○
Azure blue

lsu-fall   48-72"
NEW for us in 93
In our GARDEN 93

Come every autumn, when azure sage finally begins to flower, we are so glad that we didn't weed away this plant earlier in the summer. Very tall and willowy, it will stand up best with some support; or keep it on the dry side so it doesn't flop too much. This has been a self-sowing perennial in our garden since we started it from seed in early '90's.

nemerosa

'Viola Klose'

Meadow Sage, Perennial Salvia
Perennial ○
Dark blue spikes

esu-msu LB   12-18"
NEW for us in 00
In our GARDEN

This is one of the newest cultivars of meadow sage from Europe. It has a dense compact form and blooms for long periods throughout the summer. If this plant is overwatered, it cannot maintain a tight clumping habit, and will flop open.

nemerosa x superba

'Lubeca'

Meadow Sage, Perennial Salvia
Perennial ○
Violet blue

esu, rpts   18-36"
NEW for us in 96
In our GARDEN

This improved, drought tolerant meadow sage blooms three weeks longer and is superior to its predecessor, S. 'East Friesland'. Like other cultivar cousins, it starts blooming in June, when few other perennials have really cranked-up. Remove spent flowers to encourage new side shoots and longer blooming.

nemerosa x superba

'Plumosa'

Meadow Sage, Perennial Salvia
Perennial ○
Dense lavender purple spikes

esu-lsu LB   12-18"
NEW for us in 97
In our GARDEN 97

Fluffy, fat and velvety, flower spikes in lavender blue hold up for weeks in summer, never seeming to fade. We planted this first in '97 and we are still impressed, especially with how it complements blue-flowering Erigeron and silvery lamb's ears.

nemerosa x superba

'Snow Hill', 'Schneehuegel'

Meadow Sage, Perennial Salvia
Perennial ○
Pure white

esu, rpts   18"
NEW for us in 98
In our GARDEN

This is supposed to be the first compact white form of meadow sage that has no reported problems. Another great drought tolerant plant, it blooms throughout June; remove spent flowers for rebloom. Keep dry so shoots stand upright, and mounds stay intact.

 311

nemerosa x sylvestris
'May Night', 'Mainacht'

Meadow Sage, Perennial Salvia

Perennial ○

Dark, blue violet, red purple bracts

esu-msu LB   18"

NEW for us in   95

In our GARDEN

Flowers of rich blue, bloom for a longer period than other meadow sages. Keep removing spent flower stalks for continuous bloom. Keep dry and plants stand more erect. This plant is an outstanding hybrid of S. nemerosa and S. pratensis, bred by German plantsman, Karl Foerster. Honors: 1997 Perennial Plant of the Year, Penn State Top 20 Perennial Performers.

sclarea
var. Turkestanica

Clary Sage

Tender Perennial, Biennial   ○

Blue, I think

LB   18"

NEW for us in   00

In our GARDEN

Over the years we've tried from seed, various plants called clary sage. None really ever turned out the way I had once seen them. This one promises to be the elusive found. Honors: Penn State Impressive Performance.

verticillata
'Purple Rain'

Ornamental Sage

Perennial, Tender, Containers   ○

Smoky purple

esu-fall LB   18-24"

NEW for us in   97

In our GARDEN   97

Lush blossoming plant, introduced from Holland, has smoky-purple flowers that carry through the entire season. It is carefree, pest resistant and drought tolerant. The gray, pebbly leaves create a plant with bolder texture than the nemerosa, superba crosses, and combine well with other silver leaved plants. Usually listed for zone 5, and we had recommended mulching this plant; but it has been reliable through '99 and self-sown too.

 312

SANGUINARIA

It's easy to detect why the common name bloodroot has been given to this plant. Break a fragile stem and red-orange latex flows from the wound. Native Americans used this poisonous red sap as a dye. This lovely creation is one of the earliest native woodland wildflowers to bloom in South Dakota. Very undulating leaves emerge with unopened blossom clasped between them. As leaves release the blossom, the white petals fold outward.

The sanguinarea alkaloid of this red sap is very poisonous and has been harvested in the eastern U.S. as an anti-placque agent. Plume poppy is now cultivated to provide another source for the same alkaloid, and one can hope that the native crops of bloodroot will be left alone and not harvested to extinction.

Plant dormant rhizomes in fall only. Lay them laterally, parallel with soil, with buds barely below the soil surface. They are a little bit stubborn to establish. Provide them perfect S.D. woodland soil conditions, mulch with oak leaves by late fall, keep an eye on them for a couple of years, and from then on they will make it on their own.

canadense
'Multiplex'
Double Bloodroot
Perennial ○ ● ●
White double

spr 9-12"
NEW for us in 92
In our GARDEN

This is the rare and pricey, double variety of bloodroot, one of the earliest of lovely woodland flowers. We recommend planting the dormant rhizomes in fall only.

canadensis
Bloodroot, Puc
Perennial ○ ●
White

spr 12"
NEW for us in 81
In our GARDEN 97

Undulating, deeply lobed pairs of Matisse inspired leaves emerge erect with a single, unopened blossom clasped between them. As leaves open, they release the white petals and fold outward. In my yard, these leafless stalks of flowers are the blooming vanguard of early spring, open exactly at the same time that Magnolia 'Royal Star' is in flower, providing early pollen-food for insects. S.D. native woodland plants are available in fall only as dormant rhizomes. Woodland, rich soil conditions are imperative.

 313

SAPONARIA

One of the few things I remember from organic chemistry is the word "saponification." The word is remembered, yes, but I must look up the exact meaning since I've forgotten the chemical explanation. (I'm not sure I understood it back in class either.) The hydrolysis of an ester (like pig fat) by an alkali (like cookstove ashes) results in free alcohol and an acid salt otherwise known as soap. The root word of both saponification and Saponaria is the Latin word "sapon."

Saponaria plants contain a glucoside that can form a soapy solution used in detergents, emulsifiers, foaming agents and synthetic sex hormones. The instructions for making soap from the plants of Saponaria (sorry I don't have recipes for those other uses) are much easier to understand: Boil chopped rhizomes or leaves of this plant for five minutes or steep in water for several hours; then agitate until suds appear.

Now, what about their uses as garden plants? The best known is S. ocymoides, a trailing, rock garden plant for sun or part shade in well drained soils. Bouncing Bet, S. officinalis, is the naturalized, best-for-soap plant, a favorite Shaker herb and an old and valuable, gentle cleanser for antique fabrics, furniture and pictures. It recently has become popularized as an "in" cut flower for modern "with-it" florists, probably because old-fashioned charm is also "in."

lempergii x
'Max Frei'

Soapwort   esu-fall LB   4"
Perennial   ○ ◉   NEW for us in 94
Light pink sprays   In our GARDEN

Site near plants that won't overpower this lovely, long blooming plant. Best combined with dark or silver leaves of substance such as Sedum 'Matrona', sieboldii, or 'Vera Jameson' and Antennaria, Cerastium or lamb's ears.

ocymoides
'Rubra Compacta'

Soapwort   esu-msu   6"
Perennial, Herb   ○ ◉   NEW for us in 93
Rosy pink   In our GARDEN

This choice, drought tolerant plant creeps and cascades over walls or rocks in full sun or part shade. Broad, leafy, sprawling forms erupt to a profusion of delicate pink flowers. It will not tolerate overly moist, slow-to-drain soils. Prune spent flowers to neaten it up.

officinalis
'Rosea Plena'

Soapwort, Bouncing Bet	esu	12-24"
Perennial ○ ●	NEW for us in	97
Double pink	In our GARDEN	

From this creeper we get double fluffffy (this is not a typo) flowers in white to soft pale or rich lavender colors clustered in bunches at ends of stems, and delicious fragrance one can inhale down deep. May naturalize by self-sowing.

SCABIOSA

The common name, pincushion flower, is tailor-made for Scabiosa (pun intended.) Charming annual and perennial flowers, they've been popular for decades in the garden and as cut flowers and butterfly magnets. The blue hues are some of the finest provided for gardeners' palettes and butterflies' palates. Pink, white and yellow hues can also be located.

Since we've observed that these charmers will noticeably languish on poorly drained soil, provide elevated, even rock garden sites. Since they are drought tolerant, keep soils dry. Bed preparation is another key to success, especially with the highly acclaimed 'Butterfly Blue' and 'Pink Mist' cultivars. Along with well-drained, fertile soil, provide neutral or alkaline pH and full sun to light shade. The cooler summers of northern climes cater to pincushions, but they suffer in the far south.

Cutting old stems and dead-heading old flowers keep the flowers coming and the plants looking their best. These plants are finicky about having their crowns disturbed. Protect them and never tear away old stems. Always use scissors for a clean cut. Avoid disturbing the crown during fall or spring cleanup as well. Divide every three or four years if crowded.

alpina, nana
nana

Dwarf Pincushion Flower	esu-lsu LB	6-8"
Perennial ○ ●	NEW for us in	90
One of truest blues	In our GARDEN	98

In '98, I rediscovered this delightful, dependable, continually blooming little pincushion, that I had for years in my old garden at home. I must have lost it from neglect. There was always some to share from self-sown seedlings.

caucasica
'Fama'

Pincushion Flower	esu-msu LB	12-18"
Perennial ○ ●	NEW for us in	97
Periwinkle blue, silver center	In our GARDEN	99

From another pincushion plant we get beautiful, long-lasting, and large--not to leave out--lovely and desirable, blue flowers.

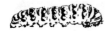 

caucasica
'Perfecta Alba'
Pincushion Flower   esu-msu LB   12-18"
Perennial   ○ ●   NEW for us in   94
Pure white   In our GARDEN

This time we are granted white pincushions, popular, old-fashioned, fringed flowers for cutting,

caucasica
'Pink Mist'
Irish Pincushion Flower   esu-fall LB   12-18"
Perennial, Containers   ○ ●   NEW for us in   95
Lavender pink   In our GARDEN

This companion to S. 'Butterfly Blue' blooms even a little more! Excellent in containers and loved by butterflies and hummingbirds, but not really as pink as the name implies. Good culture is imperative if it is to perennialize. Follow instructions under genus description, protect crown in all ways, and mulch for our winters. Once in a while, a candid plantsperson will acknowledge that this is really a short-lived perennial.

columbaria
'Butterfly Blue'
Irish Pincushion Flower   esu-fall LB   12"
Perennial, Containers   ○ ●   NEW for us in   95
Pale, soft blue   In our GARDEN

Semi evergreen plants grow pincushion flowers in abundance, as many as 400 on one plant in one season. This is a fine, fine plant, but must be mulched for our winters and planted in well-drained sites or containers. Pinch for fullness, but never remove foliage at crown of plant, or it will die. This registered cultivar originated in Ireland. Honors: 2000 Perennial Plant of the Year.

lucida
Pincushion Flower   esu-fall LB   18"
Perennial   ○ ●   NEW for us in   97
Pale yellow   In our GARDEN

Smooth leaves and stems produce lovely plants, excellent when sited at the front edge of the flower border. Will continue in flower for eight weeks when happy.

ochroleuca
Cream Pincushion Flower   esu-fall LB   24-36"
Perennial   ○ ●   NEW for us in   98
Pale yellow pincushions   In our GARDEN

Willowy stems float with air currents and support delicate, 1-2", rotund, yellow flowers all summer long, and can colonize by self-sowing. Flowers and seed heads both provide excellent cut ornamentals. The plant is more branched and shorter in stature than Cephalaria,which is resembles. Cephalaria, giant scalehead, also goes by the common name yellow scabiosa.

SCHRANKIA

nuttalii

Catclaw, Sensitive Briar | esu | 18-24"
Perennial ○ | NEW for us in 99
Bright pink puffy balls | In our GARDEN

Ferny foliage sprawls 3', and in early summer, bright pink balls appear. Leguminous, Great Plains plant is nitrogen-fixing, and long enjoyed by range animals for its high protein content.

SCILLA

Some twenty years ago, beneath a small naturalized grove of black locust trees, I poked a handful of little half-inch Scilla bulbs into well-drained soil. Now there are hundreds of them, the seeded offspring of the earlier ones, scattered over several hundred square feet. They intermingle with evergreen Vinca minor, which will soon thicken and cover them. They might be alert long enough to look up and see the unfurling of Hosta leaves and the opening of late spring flowers and leaves of the deciduous trees. After that they will begin another ten month sleep.

bifolia

Catclaw, Sensitive Briar | spr | 3-6"
Perennial, Fall Bulb ○ ● | NEW for us in 82
Blue | In our GARDEN 82

The flowering stalk and slate-blue buds of beautiful, six-petaled, blue flowers emerge just a step behind the twin leaves. The little bulbous plants, which I'm describing here from my garden, may be S. sibirica. I haven't been able to key them exactly from the books I've been using. No matter; they provide a quick flower fix almost as soon as winter retires, and I've grown accustomed to the pleasure.

numidica

Fall Blooming Scilla | 12"
Perennial, Fall Bulb ○ ◑ | NEW for us in 98
Lavender pink spikes | In our GARDEN 97

This is a very unique bulb based plant, because leaves and 1' stalks of foamy flowers emerge and bloom in August. Mark site carefully to not disturb colonies of dormant bulbs during busy, earlier gardening season. This native of Africa was introduced to Minnesota by Dr. Leon Snyder, former director of Minnesota Landscape Arboretum, and a gift of many years ago from mentor Betty Ann Addison and Rice Creek Gardens.

SCUTELLARIA

Previously ignored as a genus that could contribute to flower gardens, Scutellaria selections are always mentioned in herbal catalogs because of centuries-old knowledge of their sedative and antispasmodic properties. Maybe they should take some of their own medicine, since so many tend to have short lives. The common name comes from the flower's resemblance to the military helmet of early colonists, called a skullcap. Flower stalks have the square stems and alternate leaves and hooded flowers as do Salvia and mints, but the foliage doesn't have the fragrance of either.

This true native to North America likes dry, well drained conditions, alkaline soil and full sun in S.D. Their habits are usually low growing and spreading, although some taller selections can be found.

alpina

'Rainbow', 'Arcobaleno'

Alpine Skullcap, Helmet Flower   12"

Perennial, Herb   ○   NEW for us in 98

Mixed lavender, pink, yellow   In our GARDEN

Whorled, lipped flowers crowd around short stalks over mats of handsome foliage. This plant has medicinal applications at home in Asia, and this species provides some of the more handsome rock garden plants in this genus.

orientalis

Skullcap, Helmet Flower   esu-fall LB   8-12"

Perennial, Herb   ○   NEW for us in 98

Yellow   In our GARDEN

This plant mounds to 10" and produces abundant spikes of dragonhead flowers. It has ferny, fine foliage, a mat-like Chinese native. Texture and color of plant is outstanding in summer over a long period. Still for-trial in S.D. in '98.

resinosa

Prairie Skullcap, Helmet Flower   esu   10"

Perennial, Herb   ○   NEW for us in 98

Periwinkle blue   In our GARDEN

Wonderful Great Plains native has blue-violet spring flowers and mounded bluish foliage. Resilient plants keep blooming if deadheaded. We still consider this a for-trial plant in '00.

SEDUM

Too large, too diverse; I'm too tired to tackle this. OK, a synopsis: succulent, dynamic foliage effects from spring to late summer; well-drained, drought-tolerant, easily-divided xeriscaping plants; many attracted to butterflies and bees; some good as cut flowers; all manner of heights; wide range of leaf sizes and color; sun through light shade--easy. Read the following species and cultivar descriptions for more. A new genus name, Hylotelephium, will soon be commanding some of the species and cultivars that are now categorized as Sedum.

'Arthur Branch'

Stonecrop | msu-lsu | 24"
Perennial ○ ● | NEW for us in 00
Dusty rose pink | In our GARDEN

Dark red-purple leaves and stems provide foliage backbone to the garden. Shiny red stems and flowers are like those of S. 'Mohrchen', but plant form doesn't require support.

'Autumn Fire'

Stonecrop | msu-lsu | 30-36"
Perennial ○ ● | NEW for us in 01
| In our GARDEN

Newly patented plant from Quebec has leaves of thicker consistency than S. 'Autumn Joy' and could overtake it in popularity. We'll watch.

'John Creech'

Stonecrop | esu, rpts | 4"
Perennial, Containers ○ ● | NEW for us in 96
Pink | In our GARDEN

One of best groundcovers for sun. Uniform green rounded leaves grow into prostrate mounds.

'Matrona'

Stonecrop, Sedum | lsu-fall | 30-36"
Perennial, Containers ○ ● | NEW for us in 97
Soft pink | In our GARDEN

Smoky grey-green foliage has strong reddish tints and red stems. Stiff upright habit can be maintained by minimal watering. "Matrona" in Deutsch bedeutet "grandmotherly." Honors: 2000 International Perennial of the Year.

'Mohrchen'

Stonecrop | lsu-fall | 12-18"
Perennial, Containers ○ ● | NEW for us in 94
Reddish pink | In our GARDEN 94

This is a striking succulent with shiny, burgundy foliage, and contrasts excellently with nearly every other plant. Continuously changes from first emerging foliage in spring to bloom in late summer.

'Rosy Glow', 'Robustum'

Stonecrop — esu — 9"
Perennial, Containers ○ ● — NEW for us in 99
Rosy red — In our GARDEN

Very low mounds of lovely blue-green foliage have rosy highlights and are always admired.

aizoon
'Aurianticum'

Stonecrop — esu — 12-18"
Perennial ○ ● — NEW for us in 98
Yellow orange — In our GARDEN

Dark-green, thick and large, succulent foliage plus reddish, upright stems complement the warm tempered flowers clusters of this tall sedum. We've never seen this anywhere else.

cauticola
'Lidakense'

Stonecrop — msu-lsu — 6-10"
Perennial, Containers ○ ● — NEW for us in 00
Rosy red — In our GARDEN 00

Low mounded plants of very nice, dusty blue leaves and rosy red highlights, in late summer come rosy pink flowers. Resembles Sedum sieboldii but has smaller foliage and lighter texture.

floriferum
'Weihen Stephaner Gold', 'Acre'

Stonecrop — esu — 4"
Perennial, Containers ○ ● — NEW for us in 97
Yellow — In our GARDEN

Pale green, serrated leaves provide quick cover. Bronze color in fall.

kamtschaticum
'Variegatum'

VariegatedStonecrop — esu, rpts — 6-9"
Perennial, Containers ○ ● — NEW for us in 93
Yellow — In our GARDEN

Interesting, variegated green and white, succulent creeper is an excellent groundcover in sun or to add to annual containers. Cut out any leaves that revert to plain green.

lineare
'Golden Teardrop'

Stonecrop — esu — 1"
Perennial, Containers ○ ● ● — NEW for us in 96
Yellow — In our GARDEN 97

Fast-covering, tiny leaves trail and cling to the ground and mound up near hot rocks. Use in baskets or rock gardens. A plant becomes invasive if it outlasts easy winters, and we find ourselves frequently pulling it out to keep it in one place.

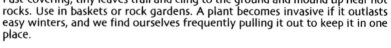 320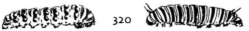

sieboldii (populifolium)

Stonecrop, October Daphne,
Perennial, Containers ○ ●
Bright pink

msu-lsu   8"
NEW for us in   96
In our GARDEN

Thick blue, scalloped leaves and arching stems reach back to the ground forming lovely mounded ground cover. This and other low growing sedum fill in well in the spaces among daylilies. Flowers in late summer.

spectabile
'Brilliant'

Tall Stonecrop
Perennial ○ ●
Rosy pink

lsu-fall   12-15"
NEW for us in   94
In our GARDEN

Flowers grow in flat headed clusters on clumped upright stalks. Loved by bees. Can grow in light shade and is drought tolerant.

spectabile
'Neon'

Tall Stonecrop
Perennial ○ ●
Dark rose

lsu-fall   24"
NEW for us in   00
In our GARDEN

Deep rose colored flowers are compared to the color and form of S. 'Brilliant'. Vibrant color is easy to spot from a distance when in bloom.

spectabile, telephium
'Autumn Joy"

Tall Stonecrop
Perennial ○ ●
Dusty pink

lsu-fall LB   18-24"
NEW for us in   95
In our GARDEN   95

Fine upright plant, fine foliage, fine late bloom, fine everything. Excellent plan-first-in-green plant has long been popular for landscapes and gardens. Contrasts well with everything else and provides weight and landing points for one's eye as a view is scanned.

spectabilis
'Frosty Morn'

Tall Stonecrop
Perennial ○ ●
Pink

lsu-fall LB   12-24"
NEW for us in   00
In our GARDEN

Flowers finally come in late summer on upright plants, after we've had the entire season to admire bright silver, white and light green foliage. The variegated foliage of this plant is stable, that is, doesn't revert to plain green. If it does, I want to be the first to know.

spurium
'Dragon's Blood', 'Schorbuser Blut'

Creeping Stonecrop, Dragon's Blood Sedum
Perennial, Containers ○ ●
Purplish red

esu, rpts   6-9"
NEW for us in   95
In our GARDEN

Common and easy, yet still outstanding, creeping plant and groundcover for sun. The foliage color is a glossy dark-green and burgundy.

spurium
'Fulda Glow', 'Fuldeglut'

Creeping Stonecrop
Perennial, Containers ○ ●
Rose pink

esu, rpts 4"
NEW for us in 98
In our GARDEN 99

This improved dragon's blood sedum has excellent foliage that keeps its intense red-bronze color all summer. Rosy flowers are a perfect and bright contrast to the foliage.

spurium
'Red Carpet', 'Elizabeth'

Creeping Stonecrop
Perennial, Containers ○ ●
Rosy pink

esu, rpts 4"
NEW for us in 93
In our GARDEN

Red bronze and green foliage blends, and is pretty, with pink flowers. Very nice color retained all summer and another excellent groundcover for sun.

spurium
'Tricolor'

Creeping Stonecrop
Perennial, Containers ○ ●
Purplish red

esu, rpts 6"
NEW for us in 95
In our GARDEN 96

Sparkling sunny groundcover with pink and white variegation that makes a striking contrast plant. We really like this as another foliage contrast spilling over the rims of hanging baskets and other containers.

telephium
'Vera Jameson'

Stonecrop
Perennial, Containers ○ ●
Dusty pink

lsu-fall 12"
NEW for us in 94
In our GARDEN 99

Deep purple, blue and green blended leaves contrast well with all others. Dynamic, season long interest from foliage effects. Low mounds will not fall apart if kept dry.

ternatum
'Larinem Park', 'Shale Barrens',

Stonecrop
Perennial ○ ● ●
White

esu 6"
NEW for us in 99
In our GARDEN 99

Delicate appearing white flowers sparkle in early summer. This cultivar, formerly known as 'Shale Barrens', has larger leaves, and a tighter and more compact habit than the species. This is a little known, shade tolerant sedum that continues to be drought tolerant.

 322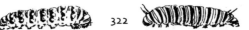

SEMPERVIVUM

mixed

Hens and Chicks	esu	3"
Perennial ○ ◐	NEW for us in	96
	In our GARDEN	

Excellent rock garden plants, little baby chicks cluster around the mother rosette made up of concentric rings of succulent leaves. Do you remember these from the gardens of the "old crones" of your young lives? Keep dry and slightly protected for winter.

SENECIO

doria

Groundsel	lsu-fall	48"
Perennial ○ ◐ ●	NEW for us in	98
Yellow daisies	In our GARDEN	

The late season feature of this plant provides large heads of daisy-like blossoms. Low light or sun with moisture are ideal.

plattenensis

Prairie Ragwort, Groundsel	spr-esu	8-20"
Prairie Perennial ○ ◐ ●	NEW for us in	98
Yellow daisies	In our GARDEN	

Versatile, self-sowing, gray foliage plants have clusters of daisies in spring and early summer. Give moist shade and or sun.

SENNA (CASSIA)

This North American native provides pretty texture with relaxed, large, glossy, dark-green pinnate leaves on woody stems while maintaining a sturdy, erect shrub form. Yellow, pea-like flowers develop in clusters at the ends of terminal stems. As members of the greater pea family, Senna plants are nitrogen fixers and drought tolerant when established.

hebecarpa (marylandica)

Wild Senna	msu-lsu	36-72"
Perennial, Sub-shrub ○ ◐	NEW for us in	97
Yellow pea flowers	In our GARDEN	97

Useful as an accent plant, site this at the back of perennial borders or as a substitute for woody shrubs. For years we've admired a large clump at SDSU's McCrory Gardens. Grows in partial shade or full sun.

SIDALCEA

'Party Girl'

Checker or Prairie Mallow	msu	24-48"
Perennial ○ ◐	NEW for us in	99
Rosy pink	In our GARDEN	

To my eyes, this supposed new perennial looks identical to S. 'Purpetta', which has self-sown in our garden for many years. Small bright flowers on upright stalks are dwarf compared to common false mallow. If typical false mallow is one-half the size of regular hollyhocks, then this has been reduced times two.

'Purpetta'

Checker or Prairie Mallow   msu   24-36"
Perennial   ○ ◐   NEW for us in   94
Magenta pink   In our GARDEN   94

Delicate magenta malva appears dwarfed compared to larger M. 'Brilliant'. Self-sows in just the right numbers along our flagstone paths. It seems to me that this is identical to a recently available plant, S. 'Party Girl'.

'Rosy Gem'

Mallow   esu-msu   36"
Perennial   ○ ◐   NEW for us in   00
Clear energetic pink   In our GARDEN

oregana
'Brilliant'

False Mallow, Malva   esu, rpts LB   30"
Perennial   ○ ◐   NEW for us in   94
Dark rose red   In our GARDEN

False mallows have flowers similar to hollyhocks but plants and flowers are smaller in scale. Divided and lobed leaves will reappear after self-sowing, sometimes abundantly, but it is easy to maintain and pull up unwanted seedlings.

SILPHIUM

laciniatum

Compass Plant   msu   48-84"
Prairie Perennial   ○   NEW for us in   97
Bright yellow   In our GARDEN   97

A single tall flower stalk from this native plant may unfold 100 flowers over a one-month period. Leaves have deeply incised, Matisse-like shapes and reptilian texture, and seem to emerge directly from the ground without plant stalks. They align their surfaces parallel with north/south direction to avoid direct sunlight in the middle of the day. In winter, weathered copper leaves curl and twist. This automatic bird feeder is slow to establish but long lived. Unusual and unappreciated in prairie area gardens, it's time you've been introduced.

perfoliatum

Cup Plant, Carpenter Plant   msu   72-96"
Prairie Perennial   ○   NEW for us in   97
Bright yellow   In our GARDEN   97

Opposite leaves clasp very thick, up to 1" or greater in diameter, segmented, square stems, creating water-holding pockets. Little prairie animals take advantage of this water source. The dried cut stems alone make it worth growing this plant. They offer tall, dried, uniquely square stems, substitutes for bamboo in arrangements (we're always looking for such new and different material). Remove self-sown seedlings early; tap rooted plants are difficult to dig out later. Moist locations are advised, but they perform gallantly in the dry native end of our garden at Perennial Passion.

 324

SMILACINA

racemosa

False Solomon's Seal — msu — 24"
Perennial ○ ● — NEW for us in 98
White, red fruit — In our GARDEN

This beautiful woodlander has stalks of alternate leaves that grow up from horizontal rhizomes. Terminal clusters above arching stems show fluffy white flowers and eventually, bright-red spheres of fruit. Differs from P. biflorum, true Solomon's seal that has fruit and flowers that hang from beneath arched stalks.

SOLIDAGO

Again we have North American natives that have achieved popularity in European gardens before gaining acceptance in American ones. Common prairie plants, goldenrods provide excellent cut flowers and are drought tolerant when established. A number of them can tolerate a certain amount of dry shade, although I most often think of them as sun-loving plants. Choose hybrids, instead of the species, as the superior and manageable garden forms.

These are the showy plants that are often blamed by hay fever sufferers for allergic attacks in late summer and fall. But goldenrods produce mostly sticky pollen, which attaches to insect bodies, especially butterflies and bees, to be carried from flower to flower. The non-showy ragweed has no need to show off flowers and attract insects because its pollen is dry and fine in order to allow the wind and breezes to carry it into the atmosphere and drift over to your eyes and nostrils....Ah Ahh Ahhh CHOO!

caesia

Bluestem or Wreath Goldenrod — lsu-fall — 24-36"
Prairie Perennial ○ ◑ ● — NEW for us in 99
Golden yellow — In our GARDEN

Wavy flower spikes provide a cloud-like effect in late summer or fall. Flowers line the entire length of arching, blue-purple stems and do not cluster only at the top. Tolerates dry shade. Allow to self-sow for large colonies.

canadensis
'Crown of Rays', 'Strahlenkrone'

Goldenrod — msu-lsu LB — 24"
Perennial ○ ◑ ● — NEW for us in 99
Bright yellow gold — In our GARDEN

Large, bright yellow, sterile flowers last longer because they've been tricked out of setting seed. They think they have to keep-on, bloomin'-on. These dry shade tolerant plants never need staking and bloom mid to late summer. Called best goldenrod by "those who know".

ohioensis

Ohio Goldenrod
Perennial ○ ●
Gold domes

msu-fall   36-48"
NEW for us in   00
In our GARDEN

Imposing, forward goldenrod with solid gold domed flowers. It looks so big and substantial, you'd think it was a tetraploid (chromosomes x 2).

sphacelata
'Golden Fleece'

Goldenrod
Perennial ○ ● ●
Golden yellow wands

lsu-fall   18"
NEW for us in   96
In our GARDEN   97

One of finest and dependable, shorter garden goldenrods with distinct flowering habit. Bright and tiny, numerous and spritzy flowers grow into unusual wands of effervescence. Drought tolerant when established and tolerates dry shade. Will not self-sow, but will establish nice clumps from traveling roots. Native to eastern U.S.

SOLIDASTER

Solidaster is an intergeneric cross, a result of the mating of two different genera, Aster and Solidago. The new plant, golden aster, reveals fine, subtle differences from each of the parents. In general, this plant blooms at a shorter height and a little earlier in summer than its goldenrod parent. Hundreds of tiny, aster-like flowers on full, broad heads are excellent as cut flowers. What a lovely surprise in our '97 garden--its atmospheric presence reminds one of a yellow baby's breath.

Culture is similar to that required by the parents: sunshine and well-drained soils. These combine well with Russian sage and purple coneflower as drought-tolerant members of a xeriscape.

'Lemore'

Golden Aster
Perennial ○ ●
Bright lemon yellow

lsu-fall   30"
NEW for us in   97
In our GARDEN   97

The original hybrid cross of Aster and Solidago, from a French nursery.

luteus
hybrids

Golden Aster, Asterago
Perennial ○ ●
Yellow

msu   24"
NEW for us in   95
In our GARDEN

Dense heads of tiny yellow daisies, turn to pale-yellow from July to September. In some areas, the excellent cut flowers are used year-round as a floral crop.

 326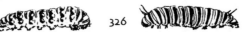

SPHAERALCEA

coccinea

Red False, Lobeleaf, Copper or Prairie Mallow   msu LB   36-48"
Perennial, Containers   ○   NEW for us in   98
Mixed colors, orange, pink, magenta, lavender.   In our GARDEN   98

Flowers most of the summer with little 1" hollyhock-like flowers. Silver leaved plants are drought tolerant, increase by rhizomes, and may be invasive. The long tap root supposedly descends 10'! Good in containers. For-trial in '98.

SPIGELIA

marilandica

Indian Pink   esu-lsu LB   12-24"
Perennial   ○ ●   NEW for us in   99
Scarlet tubes   In our GARDEN   99

Showy, abundant, upright facing, tubular flowers grow from a plant that is native to edges of woods and desires consistently moist soil. It establishes slowly but is worth the wait, because it is an unusual magnet for hummingbirds.

SPIRANTHES

cernua

var odorata

Nodding Ladies' Tresses   esu   12"
Perennial   ○ ●   NEW for us in   99
White stalks   In our GARDEN   99

From the orchid family, mats of foliage remain at 3-4", while fragrant flowers spiral around 12" stalks. Hardy here but needs reliable, constant moisture in organic, well-drained soils. Excellent cut flower lasts long time in a vase.

STACHYS

grandiflora, spicata
'Superba', 'Purpurea'

Big or Smooth Betony   msu   12-18"
Perennial   ○ ●   NEW for us in   94
Lavender   In our GARDEN

A neat and glossy, crinkled leaved betony is totally unlike woolly lamb's ears. Drought tolerant.

lanata
'Cotton Ball'

Lamb's Ears, Woolly Betony   24"
Perennial   ○ ● ●   NEW for us in   00
Cottony balls   In our GARDEN

This plant has the same silver woolly foliage as do the other lamb's ears. Flowers are camouflaged by small cottony balls or tufts of growth. They grow in sun and also in shade, provided they are kept dry.

lanata
'Helene Von Stein', 'Big Ears'

Lamb's Ears, Woolly Betony

Perennial, Containers ○ ◐ ●

Fuzzy white

msu   6-12"
NEW for us in 94
In our GARDEN 94

Rapidly growing, large leaved lamb's ear stands up better to damp, humid conditions, but needs perfect drainage; provide mulch or gravel under fuzzy silver leaves. When they bloom, wonderful fuzz-cocooned flowers are whorled on cottony stems. These interesting flowers cut and dry well, and look like nothing else you will ever put into an arrangement. This drought tolerant, deer resistant plant grows rapidly in sun and moderately in partial shade. A hit combo in our June garden is this plant with dark-blue lavender Erigeron and fuzzy light lavender Salvia 'Plumosa'.

lanata
'Silver Carpet'

Lamb's Ears, Woolly Betony

Perennial ○ ◐ ●

Foliage effect

esu   12"
NEW for us in 93
In our GARDEN

Silver-grey, fuzzy mats form few to no flowers, and are excellent in rock gardens or as groundcovers in hot and dry, well-drained sites. Fuzzy leaves are red flags (don't take this literally), and will easily rot if not kept dry with mulch or gravel beneath leaves. Drought tolerant.

monieri, densiflora
'Hummelo'

Betony

Perennial ○ ◐

Rosy purple

esu-msu   12-24"
NEW for us in 99
In our GARDEN

Very shiny, oblong leaves form basal clumps from which flower stalks emerge, and spread by creeping stolons.

officinalis
'Alba'

Wood or Smooth Betony, Woundwort

Perennial ○ ◐

White spikes

msu   18"
NEW for us in 93
In our GARDEN

Clump forming plant produces sturdy spikes from rosettes of blue-green, crinkled and scalloped foliage. It is totally unlike fuzzy, silvery lamb's ears, but similar to S. macrantha or betonica. Drought tolerant.

STOKESIA
'Purple Parasols'

Stoke's Aster

Tender? Perennial ○

Simultaneous mixed blue to lavender

12-18"
NEW for us in 99
In our GARDEN

Though many Stokes' fringed asters are pretty much regimented to winter mulching, even in zone 5, we will try again with this patented, super floriferous northern recommendation. Depending on the age of the flowers, they change in color, and can range from light blue to magenta on the same plant. The plant is drought tolerant, and the source of a cut flower crop. Honors: Penn State Top 20 Perennial Performers

laevis

'Klaus Jelitto'

Stoke's Aster · Perennial ○ · Dark blue lavender

msu-lsu LB 12-18"
NEW for us in 00
In our GARDEN

This selection grows larger flowers than others, up to 4", over a long period from mid to late summer. They have the same beautiful fringes.

STYLOPHORUM

diphyllum

Yellow Wood, Celandine or Golden Poppy · Perennial ◑ ● · Glossy, deep yellow

spr, rpts LB 12-24"
NEW for us in 95
In our GARDEN

This handsome plant produces large mounds of deeply cut leaves and single, yellow, 2 inch, poppy-like blossoms throughout the summer. An outstanding woodland native, it is common in eastern forests, and prefers a humus rich, woodland soil on the acidic side. Deadheading the old blossoms serves two purposes: plants will bloom more, and fewer seeds will germinate. To naturalize, collect seed and spread immediately where you want them to come up. Germination will occur the next spring after a cold stratification.

SYMPHYANDRA

hoffmannii

Ring Bellflower · Perennial, Tender ○ ◑ · White bells

esu-msu LB 18"
NEW for us in 99
In our GARDEN 99

This Campanula cousin produces wide white bells for a long period during summer. Deadheading helps to keep it in bloom. Seldom seen here, in fact, '99 from seed was the only way we could find it. We didn't sow it early enough, and witnessed no flowers before winter; but by spring, 2000, after a mild winter, they were back. Maybe these aren't as tender as I thought they were.

SYMPHYTUM

grandiflorum

'Hidcote Variegated'

Large Flowered Comfrey · Perennial ○ ◑ ● · Light blue

12"
NEW for us in 00
In our GARDEN 00

Brighten up shade with the large cream and green leaves and light blue tubular flowers of this uncommon plant. Plants colonize quickly with sandpaper stems and shiny leaves. As a dry-shade-tolerant groundcover this can hold its own against weeds and will be even stronger if moist. It grows in sun with ample moisture, but variegated foliage seldom has the impact in sun that it does in shade.

TALINUM

calycinum

Fame Flower
12"

Annual, Containers   O   NEW for us in   99

Purple pink   In our GARDEN

Succulent leaves on a zone 4 plant that is a Great Plains Native. Brilliant flowers.

TELLIMA

grandiflora

Fringe Cups
12-24"

Perennial, Tender   O ●   NEW for us in   99

Yellow green fade to red hues   In our GARDEN   99

Hairy and pretty, heart-shaped (cordate) leaves for shady and preferably moist, wild garden. 1-2' spikes of flowers begin lime green and fade into red hues. It is native to Pacific Northwest, where it is considered a perennial. We germinated this late in '99, and it didn't bloom from seed; but according to Armitage it should be hardy. It was back in the spring of 2000 after a first, mild winter.

TEUCRIUM

chamaedrys

Germander   msu   12"

Perennial   O O ●   NEW for us in

Pink   In our GARDEN

Compact, evergreen sub-shrub often used for low growing hedges in herb gardens, actually looks and performs better when allowed its natural form. It did not return in my garden many years ago. I should give it a better shake; grow several from seed; line them out for observation; select the strong plants that survive the winter; propagate those with rooted stem-cuttings; then grow those in full sun and ample moisture so they can better survive the next winter. So many plants; so little time!

THALICTRUM

A long, long time ago I transplanted some native meadowrue from northern Minnesota to my garden. After all, there was plenty to spare; it was growing everywhere. (Sorry, neighbor. I claim youth and naivete for not knowing this was an illegal move.) The foliage was so pretty; I thought it was maidenhair fern. But unlike the lovely maidenhair, the meadowrue gave me extra prizes and surprises.

Little flowers in abundant, puffy clusters were so compelling that these were some for which I needed the magnification glass. Then I caught-on. What I observed with my naked eye was really their "naked" flowers. I was attracted, not by nonexistent petals, but by magnificently-colored stamens and pistils. As I voyeured (well, not exactly) even closer, eyeball to boldly-exposed, sexy parts, I learned that flowers may be female on one plant and male on another. I now refer to the area where they grow as the "nudists' colony." There they thrive and procreate, happily self-sowing. Lack of petals excludes landing platforms for any larger pollinating insects.

Many lovely forms of Thalictrum are native to parts of North America, including South Dakota, and additional ones have come from Japan. They are diverse in height and form, all provide beautiful and unusual cut flowers.

After rabbits girdled the trunk of one of our PG Hydrangea trees to a new low, 2.5' height, the depth of snow cover at mealtime, we had an accidental and favorite discovery after we planted Thalictrum at the northeast side of its trunk. Hydrangea branches now shade meadowrue roots and provide support to stalks and flowers which can find a little more sun. Both Hydrangea and Thalicturm give their best performance with ample moisture.

aquilegifolium

Meadowrue   spr-esu   24-36"
Perennial   ○ ●   NEW for us in   95
Fluffy lilac heads   In our GARDEN

I am always captivated by the fluffy pink and white panicles of meadowrue. This is one of the last plants to emerge in spring, so be patient as you wait for them to appear. Prefers light shade, but can tolerate some sun when provided with even moisture. Use in garden or naturalized with other woodland plants.

 331

delavayi

'Hewitt's Double'

Meadowrue		esu-msu	36-48"
Perennial	O ●	NEW for us in	96
Double lilac with yellow stamens		In our GARDEN	97

Airy puffs of flowers resembling those of baby's breath are enjoyed over long periods. On this excellent selection the exposed stamens, though still small, are broader and more like petals than the stamens of single flowered meadowrues. This characteristic lends them an even puffier and showier appearance. Provide some shade and humus-rich, moist soil.

flavum

ssp. glaucum

Meadowrue		msu-lsu	36-72"
Perennial	O ●	NEW for us in	96
Puffy pale yellow		In our GARDEN	97

Large, this time, yellow flower sprays, make lovely unusual cuts. Blue-green foliage is fabulous on its own. Spreads 2' to good sized, excellent specimen after emerging in late spring. Provide partial shade and extra moisture with amended soil for this easy and rewarding plant.

kiusianum

Meadowrue, Kyushu		esu-lsu LB	4"
Perennial	O ●	NEW for us in	98
Lavender		In our GARDEN	00

Purple tinged leaves and arching stems show off airy clusters of small flowers all summer. A diminutive plant, sweet and loverly, use it as a shady garden edger tucked in near other small shade plants such as dwarf Hosta to create a shady garden. of miniatures. Native to Japan.

rochebrunianum

'Lavender Mist'

Meadowrue		msu-lsu	48-72"
Perennial	O ●	NEW for us in	96
Pale purple, yellow stamens		In our GARDEN	96

Mist-like flower clusters with showy stamens can reach tall heights in partial shade. To support blue, smooth foliage, stake with bamboo for visual effect. It emerges very late, and blooms at the same time as Oriental lilies.

THERMOPSIS

caroliniana (villosa)

False or Carolina Lupine, Bush Pea, Aaron's Rod		spr-esu	48"
Perennial	O O	NEW for us in	95
Canary yellow, showy		In our GARDEN	

We've spent too many years overlooking this plant and its 10" spikes of lupine-like flowers that can last up to four weeks. Growing tall and vigorous in sun or shade, it is disease-, pest-, and care-free, and drought-tolerant when established. Cut back after flowering as it begins to deteriorate.

 332

fabacea

False Lupine, Yellow Bush Pea

Perennial ○ ⬤

Bright yellow

msu-lsu   36"

NEW for us in   98

In our GARDEN

Large foliage and pea-like flowers grow from tall colonizing plants. Cut flowers are provided too.

lupinoides, lanceolata

False Lupine

Perennial ○ ⬤

Yellow pea flowers on stalks

spr-esu   12"

NEW for us in   98

In our GARDEN

Pea-like flowers are densely whorled around 18" stalks, and later, interesting recurved pods show up. Tolerates heat poorly, but likes it in cooler northern climates.

THYMUS

It's easy to get enthusiastic about all the different species and cultivars of Thymus, and we've collected and experimented with a few over the years. We have learned that thymes, like many herbs and other plants, are generally adaptable to South Dakota, provided educated gardeners provide exactly the right culture for them. Think of growing them in the sparest of conditions. Where many plants would be parched, thymes will thrive. Like many herbs, they require strict drainage, hot, dry conditions, and elevated growing areas. Languishing in heavy wet soil in winter or summer where their roots cannot find quick reprieve, they will quickly rot. They love hot rocks! They rarely need water. Provide winter shade or a very light, non-compacting cover, like oak leaves, that is raked away in spring. If they do dehydrate in winter sun, most will return from the established roots of heavy stands, provided they have been properly sited and drained.

I've elected to include this genus here, because there are hordes of cultivars, ecotypes, and naturally occurring crosses that provide a few design functions in addition to their culinary uses. Use them creeping between flagstones, hanging over rocky outcroppings, tucked into dry-set stone walls, or planted along the edges of container plantings. Their names are sometimes mixed up among growers.

Their flavors and scents range from lemon, to mint, to caraway and camphor. Thymes are one of the main ingredients of the centuries-old recipes for bouquet garni and herbs of provence. Use whenever a recipe calls for slow cooking with wine, and add to soups, stuffing, sauces and any beef, chicken, fish, and hot vegetable recipes. Harvest the soft growth at the tips; older stems become woody.

According to old herbal guides: Thyme tea could be chosen to make a hangover more tolerable; relieve insomnia, poor circulation, and muscle pain; and boost the body's defense mechanisms. Add to honey, and use for cold symptoms of cough and sore throat. Ancient Egyptians valued thyme's very strong properties as an antiseptic, antibacterial and preservative in their embalming processes. The Greek word "thymon" means "courage," and thyme water baths gave vigor to Roman soldiers. Sprigs of thyme were given to knights on their journeys during the Crusades. Thyme tea was drunk by Scottish Highlanders for strength and courage. And--a soup of thyme and beer was eaten to overcome shyness!

'Citriodorus'

Lemon Thyme   esu   6"
Perennial, Herb   ○   NEW for us in   89
Pale lavender, foliage effect   In our GARDEN   95

Excellent among flagstones in full sun; may spread 18". A few thymes have come to us that share the name T. citriodorus, but they have all had slight differences.

'Porlock'

Thyme   esu   2"
Herb, Perennial   ○   NEW for us in   97
Pink   In our GARDEN

For pathway uses and culinary uses: neat and low, fluffy specimens and wonderful flavor.

'Wedgewood'

Thyme   esu   6-8"
Herb, Perennial, Containers   ○   NEW for us in   98
Lavender   In our GARDEN

Tiny, dark-green leaves have a gold stripe.

citriodorus
'Aureus'

Thyme   esu   48-72"
Perennial, Containers   ○   NEW for us in   92
Palest lavender   In our GARDEN   92

Excellent between flagstone in full sun. Requires sharp drainage provided by rocks or sand. This is my favorite thyme for chartreuse foliage color, fluffy vigor and fragrance. This is just one, of several, thymes that have included in their name, the species or cultivar 'Aureus'. .

citriodorus x
'Mayfair'

Thyme   esu   6"
Herb, Perennial   ○   NEW for us in   95
   In our GARDEN

Vigorous and choice for landscaping, herb gardens and culinary uses.

dzevenarski

Russian Thyme   esu   1"
Herb, Perennial   ○   NEW for us in   92
Pink   In our GARDEN   93

Tiny and pointed, needle-like, grey-green leaves hug the ground with a flat profile. This was trampled to death in our garden after living out many winters, and is worth trying again.

praecox
albus

Thyme   esu   24-36"
Herb, Perennial   ○   NEW for us in   94
White   In our GARDEN

praecox
'Pink Chintz'

Thyme	esu	48-72"
Herb, Perennial ○	NEW for us in	95
Pink	In our GARDEN	

Dark-green, low growing and pretty in flower.

praecox pseudolanuginosus
'Pseudolanuginosus'

Woolly Creeping Thyme	esu	1"
Herb, Perennial ○	NEW for us in	92
Pink	In our GARDEN	X

Fuzzy, woolly foliage requires the driest of conditions. Ours was tread upon, eventually rotted, and died. Provide hot rocks for all thymes and this one for sure. Most thymes can take foot traffic when grown under proper conditions, but I wouldn't recommend it for woolly thyme.

praecox (serphyllum)
'Coccineum'

Creeping Red Thyme	ESU-MSU	1-2"
Herb, Perennial ○	NEW for us in	92
Wine pink	In our GARDEN	93

Creeping ornamental thyme, one of showiest in bloom. Sheets of bright, rose-pink cover the foliage in early summer.

praecox, serphyllum
'Rosea'

Creeping Thyme	esu	1-2"
Perennial ○	NEW for us in	93
Bright rose	In our GARDEN	96

Another showy pink flowering thyme. Excellent between flagstones in full sun.

TIARELLA
'Skeleton Key'

Foamflower		6-10"
Perennial, Groundcover ○ ●	NEW for us in	01
	In our GARDEN	

Tolerates dry shade.

cordifolia

Foamflower	spr-esu	6-9"
Perennial, Groundcover ○ ●	NEW for us in	95
White, foamy stalks	In our GARDEN	

Great woodland groundcover for humus rich soil in shade has deeply cut leaves. Flower stalks are on display in early spring.

 336

cordifolia
'Dark Eyes'

Foamflower
Perennial, Groundcover ○ ●
Delicate pink

spr-esu   6-12"
NEW for us in
In our GARDEN

Vigorous, dry shade tolerant, little plant will fill in quickly. Heart-shaped leaves have a dark center splotch. Sepals, stamens, and petals all work together to produce the lovely long-lasting flowers held on short stalks.

cordifolia
'Winterglow'

Foamflower
Perennial, Groundcover ○ ●
Delicate white

spr-esu   6-12"
NEW for us in
In our GARDEN

Interesting leaves of this cultivar have red flecks on green. The leaves continue the show in autumn, when they turn yellow. Delicate flowers are held carefully above the foliage in early season.

wherryi (collina)

Foamflower
Perennial, Groundcover ○ ●
White, foamy with pink tints.

spr-esu   6-9"
NEW for us in 95
In our GARDEN dis

This woodland garden, groundcover classic tolerates dry shade and grows in clumps. Heart-shaped foliage with bronze tints turns a reddish color in fall.

TRADESCANTIA
'Blue Stone'

Spiderwort
Perennial ○ ◐
Medium blue

esu-lsu LB   12-24"
NEW for us in 00
In our GARDEN

Flower buds group and dangle at the end of the flower stalk where they take turns starring in the show, each opening for one day. So many buds are produced that they can maintain the daily appearances for almost eight weeks. We find spiderwort naturalized along the rough, dry area of the railroad right-of-way behind us, and the cultivars like the same culture.

'Concord Grape'

Spiderwort
Prairie Perennial ○ ◐ ●
Rick dark purple

msu-lsu LB   12"
NEW for us in 99
In our GARDEN

Flowers open in mornings throughout entire summer on this vigorous cultivar. Silvery blue colored foliage is distinct and fine among spiderworts. Trim back leaves if they deteriorate.

337

TRICYRTIS

By the time I saw Tricyrtis in Ann's garden, they had completed a two-year residency and were colonizing nicely, as predicted, in her moist-shade garden (but not always expected with certainty in Northern Plains gardens.) Since then we have read about nearly 20 different named cultivars and have grown a half a dozen. It's been easy to get absorbed in this intriguing plant.

As if its common name, toad lily, isn't enough to pique your interest, the plant's appearance invites you to pull up a stump, to inquire deeply, to touch and press or scratch and sniff, and look into every angle and crevice of leaf, stem and--oh! those exotic and fascinating flowers!

Subtle, long-lasting, late-summer and fall flowers appear, growing from the axils (the angle between the stem and the upper surface of a leaf or flower stalk) of arched or upright stems that grow from clumps or large stoloniferous (spreading by stolons), non-invasive patches. These flowers can be white, yellow, purple and tricolored. Many are neatly spotted and so, so compelling. They are simpler than most flowers--six tepals (non-differentiated petals or sepals) with six stamens. Because of their thick and wax-like substance, individual flowers can last for six weeks in the shade garden and for a long time as a cut flower as well. Plain glossy-green or speckled foliage is rated high even when not in flower. Most T. formosa and T. hirta species are hardy to zone four. Some of the recently "discovered" species brought from Japan and China, like T. macropoda and T. macranthopsis, are worth experimenting with. Note that many of the species and cultivars are sometimes confused in the trade.

'Golden Gleam'

Toad Lily	Isu-fall 24"
Perennial ○ ●	NEW for us in
White with lavender spots	In our GARDEN

Golden foliage and flowers spotted with lavender.

formosana
'Togen'

Toad Lily	Isu-fall 24-36"
Perennial ○ ●	NEW for us in 98
Lavender, yellow centers, speckles	In our GARDEN

We've loved all the toad lilies with their unusual speckled flowers. This one is native to wet forests of Taiwan and has had great success in gardens. Large shiny leaves have no spots and clasp tall stems.

 338

formosana, stolinifera

Toad Lily | Isu-fall | 24"
Perennial | NEW for us in 97
Lavender, yellow centers, speckles | In our GARDEN

The T. formosana and stolinifera are now considered the same species. As it has become more available, its popularity has increased proportionately. The formosana cultivars have leaves that only partially clasp around the stem. T. hirta leaves are closer together and fully clasp the stem.

hirta

Toad Lily | Isu-fall | 12-36"
Perennial | NEW for us in 96
White, spotted with purple | In our GARDEN 97

Overall effect creates wonder and curiosity. Unusual, thick and glossy foliage contrasts with lovely waxy flowers which are borne from the axils of fully clasping leaves.

hirta
'Moonlight'

Toad Lily | Isu-fall | 24"
Perennial | NEW for us in 97
Waxy white and lilac | In our GARDEN

Gold trim on glossy chartreuse leaves gives lively, but not overpowering contrasts. This cultivar and the one called T. hirta 'Variegata' may be the same plant.

hirta
'Variegata'

Toad Lily | Isu-fall | 24"
Perennial | NEW for us in 99
Light pink, spotted | In our GARDEN

Hairline cream margins on bright green leaves show off a plant that may be the same as T. 'Moonlight'. Lavender-pink flowers have toady spots.

hirta
'White Towers'

Toad Lily | Isu-fall | 24"
Perennial | NEW for us in 94
Creamy yellow | In our GARDEN

Axil-borne flowers are waxy and lasting for up to three weeks.

hirta x formosa
'Miyazaki Hybrids'

Toad Lily | Isu-fall | 24-36"
Perennial | NEW for us in 96
Blush, spotted purple and black | In our GARDEN 97

Natural, rich appearing plant has flowers forming in leaf axils along long arching stems. Encourage it into individual clumps or to spread for a groundcover effect.

 339

TRILLIUM

If you garden in shade, you'll find these lovely woodland wildflowers as indispensable as do I. I will never garden without them; they uplift and waken my spring spirit! Trillium foliage and simple flowers emerge in spring and last for weeks in cool May soils and temperatures.

The leading syllable, "tri-" of Trillium, explains it all. The most obvious three parts of this plant, the petals, sepals and leaves, are each divisible, but once, by the number three. Would that be "a trinity of triads," "a triune of triplets" or "a trio in triplicate"? Three whorled leaves present three outer sepals which, in turn, stage a single flower that has three petals. (The flower does have six stamens, but that would really mess up what I've got going here.)

In my old shade garden, these little wakerobins have the woodland stage to themselves until the resurrected leaves of Hosta and other shade-loving plants begin to unfurl. Then the triads peek from larger, newly emerged plants, as their flowers and leaves slowly begin to shrivel and retreat into dormancy. Their performance is over; we had waited all year for them to return; and now our wait begins again. I have a fond memory of spring walks in a Virginia forest amongst vast natural drifts of various native Trillium species in full bloom.

Culture is important for these little guys; one must duplicate their natural requirements--well-drained, humus-rich, woodland soil, kept moist while they are actively growing. If dug or transplanted while visible, they most surely will die. Plant thick, budded rhizomes only in autumn when fully dormant. Place them horizontally with small eye-buds facing upward, an inch or so below soil surface.

I often recommend sprinkling beautiful wakerobins throughout the evergreen groundcover, Vinca minor, with which it cohabits splendidly. Other spring flowers that share the month of May include Virginia bluebells, Lamium, species and other tulips, daffodils and Allium.

cernuum

Trillium, Nodding; Wakerobin	spr	6"
Perennial, Wildflower ○ ●	NEW for us in	92
White	In our GARDEN	

Flowers with reflexed petals, resembling shooting stars, are barely visible above the leaves. Plant dormant roots in fall only.

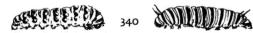 

340

erectum

Wakerobin, Purple Trillium, Stinking Benjamin

Perennial, Wildflower ○ ●

Red purple

spr   6"

NEW for us in   96

In our GARDEN

Flowers are held erect. The purple ones have a slightly disagreeable odor. The occasional white and yellow hued ones have no odor. Fall planting.

grandiflorum

Wakerobin, Great White Trillium

Perennial, Wildflower ○ ●

Large white

spr   9-12"

NEW for us in   95

In our GARDEN   96

Blooms seem to last an eternity in early spring on this showiest-of-Trillium. Large white, three-petal flowers are held well above three whorled leaves. As flowers slowly retire, they fade from bright white to faint pink. Plant only in fall.

luteum

Wakerobin, Lemon Trillium

Perennial, Wildflower ○ ●

Pale yellow

spr   6"

NEW for us in   95

In our GARDEN

Glossy, mottled foliage and small, palest-of-yellow, sweetly scented flowers exude a lovely, understated elegance. This little wakerobin has the same growth habit of some others, holding flowers above whorled leaves. Fall planting.

recurvatum

Wakerobin, Toad Trillium

Perennial, Wildflower ○ ●

Maroon

spr   6"

NEW for us in   92

In our GARDEN

Sepals curve back and clutch the stem. Petals curve and reach inward toward the center of the flower. Fall planting.

sessile

Wakerobin, Toad or Sessile Trillium

Perennial, Wildflower ○ ●

spr   6"

NEW for us in   92

In our GARDEN

Short petaled flowers are sessile, having no flower stalk, and sit down amongst the whorled leaves. Foliage is mottled green and darkest green. Fall planting

TROLLIUS

Trollius is a very attractive, early summer flower, appearing when color and brightness is always at a premium in South Dakota. The tangerine, gold and yellow hues of the brightly pigmented sepals, not petals, are unique and vivid. The smaller, true petals and showy stamens both emerge upright from the center of a two- to three-inch wide, saucer shaped arrangement of these showy sepals. The pollen-bearing stamens are easily accessible to early butterflies and other hungry insects. Humans want these flowers too, for they provide unusual cut flowers in addition to their garden appeal.

Differing from most perennials, globeflowers prefer wet, heavy soils and can even withstand boggy conditions. But in our garden they don't get an abundance of extra moisture and still have been quite reliable considering they aren't supposed to tolerate heat or drought. We probably supplement with just-enough water to maintain roots and foliage adequately. Trollius is also shade tolerant, though partial shade with some sun is best. Thick, dark green, glossy foliage is deeply divided and always attractive until late summer.

The genus contains native species and cultivars originating from three continents, Europe, Asia and North America. They bloom simultaneously with the flowers of coral bells, catmint and lady's mantle.

ledebourii
'Golden Queen'

Ledebour Globeflower   esu LB   24-48"
Perennial   ○ ◑ ●   NEW for us in 94
Tangerine gold   In our GARDEN

This popular cultivar has long-lasting, showy sepals and flowers later than some of the other globeflowers.

 342

UVULARIA

grandiflora

Merrybells, Large Flowered Bellwort   spr   12-18"
Perennial   ◐ ●   NEW for us in   95
Bright yellow   In our GARDEN

Graceful woodland perennial is a good choice for naturalized shade garden. As it slowly colonizes, slightly twisted flowers and leaves appear to weep from lax, arched, forked stems.

VALERIANA

Having been christened with the common name, garden heliotrope, attests to the fragrance of this flower. Though this old fashioned plant has been returning for decades in old Sioux Falls' neighborhoods, most June visitors to Perennial Passion's garden are not familiar with "that wonderful fragrance with the ferny foliage." One cool and moist June, abundant little flowers wafted their scent and looked fabulous for weeks. The tiny and long-lived flowers appear by the hundreds atop branched umbels, similar to the flower form and habit of carrot or queen anne's lace. The deeply divided foliage provides a texture similar to that of Jacob's ladder. These tough plants like moist soil, but perform splendidly in our full sun, on-the-dry-side garden.

Valerian is an ancient, herbal medicinal plant. You may have tried the sleep tea made from Valerian roots; they are described as a "nervine". Old books relate that the Pied Piper of Hamlin carried pieces of Valerian in her pocket to entice the rats to follow to their deaths. This herb, catnips and mints are all in the same family and have varying success of luring kitties to their fragrances.

officinalis

Garden Heliotrope, Vervain	esu LB	36-60"
Herb, Perennial ○ ◐ ●	NEW for us in	94
White with hint of pink	In our GARDEN	94

Deeply toothed leaves emerge early in spring and form a basal rosette from which emerge tall, leafy stems. Umbels of sweetly fragrant, tiny tubular blossoms can be detected from several feet away.

officinalis

'Arterner Zuchtung'

Garden Heliotrope, Vervain	esu LB	36-60"
Herb, Perennial ○ ◐ ●	NEW for us in	97
White with hint of pink	In our GARDEN	98

Very interesting to contrast with the old species Valerian we've been growing. This Deutscher hast at least double the leaf and flower size as the species we've been growing; and double the length of internodes, results in twice as tall, too. Very definitely a keeper. Same fabulous fragrance this genus is known for.

VERBASCUM

Of all the flowers in our garden at perennial passion, the dramatic spikes that arise from Verbascums' bold rosettes of basal leaves receive as many inquiries as any. I couldn't garden without them and am eager to try any that appear to be new on the market. The most diminutive I tried from seed in my home garden fifteen years or more ago. From then on, they self-sowed in modest fashion until I lost them from neglect during the time I was devoting all my energy to starting my business, the nursery Perennial Passion.

The wild species common in S.D. is V. thapsus, not native though, but spread throughout the U.S. from Europe. Sometime during its history the stems of this widely spread plant have been used as candles, the leaves as shoe liners and the seeds as narcotics and other traditional medical uses.

The boldest we've grown were from seed several years ago, and these very tall dramatic yellow flowering spikes are still self-sowing about in our garden and now, enhancing the railroad right-of-way behind us. I've lost record of what the actual species was that we grew that year. I know it was either V. blattaria or olympicum. Since Verbascum cross breeds and hybridizes willingly, I probably don't have the original genetic base we started with. Our plants have huge, thick and velvety leaves with 18" long and 1/4" thick not uncommon. I recently heard that some people still use the leaves from this species as a comforting bandage.

Now some people eschew them, thinking they look too native, and call them pasture flowers. They mean this statement to be disparaging. It is funny that we don't appreciate the greener pastures that are in our own back yard and still encounter the attitude that what is brought in is better. But the truth is, I believe that valuing what is here and now and not what is always strange is better philosophy. True, you will see them naturalized along fences, even along the bike trail here in the city. (I like to think they blew in from our garden.) They seem more abundant as one travels west toward the Missouri River; the climate is drier out there. You've seen them, the erect tall brown sentries that dot the pastures out west. If you find them after seed has been developed in tall brown stalks, cut them and use them like a magic wand, waving them or laying them in your garden. You will soon have their dramatic forms and flowers to enjoy firsthand.

'Silbercandelaber', 'Silver Candelabra'

Mullein	esu	48-72"
Biennial, Perennial ○ ●	NEW for us in	97
Yellow spires	In our GARDEN	97

Large and woolly, basal rosettes the first year, and tall spikes of flowers come the second year.

chaixii

Nettle Leaved or Chaix Mullein	esu-msu	36"
Biennial, Perennial ○ ●	NEW for us in	94
Yellow or white with purple stamens	In our GARDEN	97

Showy candelabra spikes of yellow flowers have violet centers. Leaves are smaller and not as velvety, flower stalks are shorter, and it blooms slightly earlier than the bold and naturalized mullein, V. thapsus. We get both white or yellow flowers with purple stamens. Bold! New! Look!

nigrum

Dark Mullein	esu-msu LB	48"
Biennial, Perennial ○ ●	NEW for us in	99
Yellow with lavender centers	In our GARDEN	99

Center stamens are purple, and petals are yellow. Foliage is less pubescent than most of the others. We grew this from seed in 1999, and upon this writing, have not yet seen the flowers. If they are anything like the other mulleins we've grown, we are eagerly anticipating the blessed event. Similar to V. chiaxii but grows taller, and flowers for up to six weeks in summer.

phoenicium

Mullein	esu	24"
Biennial, Perennial ○ ●	NEW for us in	95
Mixed pinks, whites, lavenders	In our GARDEN	

On a nearly true biennial, phantasmagoric colors captivated me during their second year and have filled my mind forever. This plant filled an important niche with June bloom, between spring bulbs and full-blown summer flowers, for years at my home garden, and I miss her now. I've had trouble establishing purchased plants at Perennial Passion's garden, and I'm beginning to think this would be best started directly from seed in alkaline soil. Poor soil will do but it must be well-drained; spikes will flop in rich moist soil. Learn to identify first year, self-sown, basal foliage rosettes, so that the second year you can enjoy the hues.

thapsus

Mullein	esu-msu LB	48-60"
Prairie Biennial, Perennial ○ ●	NEW for us in	94
Yellow towers	In our GARDEN	

This European native has naturalized throughout North America. There are many other species and some new hybrids that offer less-wild plants for the garden, but we still love the boldness of this plant. Visitors, even native South Dakotans who have grown up with this plant, always ask what it is.

 346

VERBENA

bonariensis

Peruvian Verbena, Purple Top

Annual, Self Sowing, Tender Perennial, Containers   O

Violet purple

msu-fall LB   36-48"

NEW for us in   92

In our GARDEN   92

Fabulous tender perennial from Peru that we treat as an annual that self-sows abundantly from year to year. By late June or early July dense clusters of punchy violet-purple flowers appear at the top of tall, strong, branching stems. Plants, narrow and wiry, take up tiny amounts of lateral space as they weave through other perennials, rose bushes and other shrubs. Unexcelled as cut and dried flowers. Remember, in the spring, do not cultivate around these plants until you see tiny seedlings appear. Butterflies adorn in late summer. Use in container plantings, too. Wouldn't be without this and Tithonia in late summer.

hastata

Blue Vervain, Simpler's Joy

Prairie Perennial   O O

Blue lavender

msu-lsu LB   24-48"

NEW for us in   96

In our GARDEN   96

No one brought this plant to us; it moved in all by itself. Now it continues to germinate and return, a permanent member of the family. We occasionally weed it away to leave room for those who were here first. A pretty native plant, stiff, narrow, candelabra spikes grow blue lavender, tubular flowers. It is drought tolerant but, during moist humid summers, susceptible to powdery mildew.

VERNONIA

noveboracensis

Ironweed

Perennial   O

Purple

lsu-fall   36-80"

NEW for us in   96

In our GARDEN   96

First saw this blooming in North Carolina at its projected maximum height, a towering eight feet. I had to have it. Well, it has grown for us since then, and returns after winters; but it has never reached over three feet, a fraction of that height first witnessed. If we grew it in wet soil, which it prefers, it would probably grow taller.

347

VERONICA

If I ever have to choose one genus, it would be Veronica. It provides chlorophyll and color for nearly any sunny garden situation. Its namesake is St. Veronica because blossom markings resemble her sacred handkerchief. She gives us the most versatile plant selections that are rewarding and easy to grow.

All V. spicata crosses have spiked flowers of varying lengths on plants from six- inches to five-feet. They offer long lasting cut flowers, and many are grown as patented cultivars for the cut-flower market. Then there are many, many creeping forms that perform well in rock gardens, there preferring hot, sunny, well-drained situations. Most are drought tolerant and attractive to butterflies.

Fungus problems sometimes affect the leaves of the spicata selections, and the ones closest to the ground turn crisp and brown. They can be removed without affecting the plant, and bare lower stems can be screened with other perennials. Systemic fungus diseases occasionally strangle a plant by clogging the main stem.

'Bergen Blue'

Speedwell		esu	6-9"
Perennial ○ ●		NEW for us in	96
Bright blue		In our GARDEN	

Vivid small flowers and leaves grow from a mat forming cultivar. Try it in rock gardens or any sunny well-drained site.

'Giles Van Hees'

Speedwell		msu-lsu LB	6"
Perennial ○ ●		NEW for us in	96
Bright pink spikes		In our GARDEN	96

This plant forms basal mats or rosettes of leaves with short upright spikes, and blooms all summer. The dwarf cultivar can be used as rock garden plant or perennial garden edger.

'Noah Williams'

Variegated Speedwell		msu-lsu LB	12-24"
Perennial ○ ●		NEW for us in	96
White spikes		In our GARDEN	X

Grey-green foliage with toothed edges is lined with silvery margins. Abundant white flowers attach to spikes. This is the only variegated Veronica that I am acquainted with, and we lost this patented specimen after our first try. I've noticed that the Minnesota grower, from whom we purchased it, is not listing it in his catalog this year. However, I'd like to try it again. One loss is usually not enough to warrant giving up entirely.

 348

alpina x spicata
'Goodness Grows'

Speedwell	msu-lsu LB	12"
Perennial ○ ◐	NEW for us in	96
Penetrating blue violet	In our GARDEN	96

New, long-blooming, mat forming hybrid for edgings and rock gardens withstands heat and drought. Deadhead long lasting flower spikes after they turn green, and they will continue from mid spring to autumn. One of the best low growing cultivars, a cross between V. alpina and V. incana.

hybrida x
'White Icicle'

Speedwell	msu-lsu LB	18"
Perennial ○ ◐	NEW for us in	96
Pure white spikes	In our GARDEN	96

Masses of pure white blossoms on erect stalks bloom over a long period. One of best for wonderful cut flowers. Plant has a neat, compact habit. So many choices of Veronica; so little time.

incana
'Silbersee'

Speedwell	esu	12-15"
Perennial ○ ◐	NEW for us in	98
Blue spikes	In our GARDEN	

Both this and the straight species, incana, provide indispensable silver foliage contrast. Cut flowers are nice too.

liwanensis

Creeping Speedwell	esu-msu LB	2-5"
Perennial ○ ◐	NEW for us in	95
Sparkling blue	In our GARDEN	95

Covered in sparkling, small blue flowers for a long period in spring and early summer, these plants are mat-forming, with tiny and shiny green leaves for rock gardens. First introduced to us by P. Kalaidas, rock garden curator of Denver Botanic Garden. Honors: 1997 Rocky Mountain Plant Select.

longifolia
'Blauriesin', 'Blue Giantess'

Spike Speedwell	msu-lsu LB	24"
Perennial ○ ◐	NEW for us in	96
Bright, deep blue	In our GARDEN	96

Excellent patented form for cut flowers. Honors: Cut Flower Association special designation.

longifolia
mixed

Long Leaf Speedwell	esu-lsu LB	18"
Perennial ○ ◐	NEW for us in	00
Mixed blue, pink, white	In our GARDEN	

Long blooming spikes of mixed colors are looking for spaces to fill in cutting gardens.

longifolia x
'Sunny Border Blue'

Spike Speedwell   msu-fall LB   24-30"
Perennial   ○ ●   NEW for us in 92
Near perfect blue   In our GARDEN 93

Strong spikes of dark blue keep coming all summer. Side branches quickly develop when first blooms are spent and pinched off. Drought tolerant and well-drained conditions preferred. Remove the lower dry brown leaves that are affected by fungus, and hide the bared stalks with lower growing perennials. Honors: 1993 Perennial Plant of the Year.

oltensis

Thyme Leafed or Creeping Speedwell   esu   1"
Perennial   ○ ●   NEW for us in
Dark azure blue   In our GARDEN

This flat plant has many uses--growing in rock gardens, in between flagstones, and as a xeric groundcover. Carpets of tiny dark-green leaves of lacy texture always look good. One must look and smell closely to discern difference between this and thyme. It is a drought tolerant, slow growing and long lived evergreen from Turkish mountains.

pectinata
'Rosea', 'Rubra'

Woolly Creeping Speedwell   1"
Perennial   ○ ●   NEW for us in 94
Rose pink   In our GARDEN

Silvery-grey, fuzzy foliage needs absolutely perfect drainage. Provide rocky mulch or one-half sand blended into the soil to keep foliage dry. As with all woolly or tomentose foliage, plants will quickly rot if allowed to languish upon muddy under girth.

peduncularis
'Georgia Blue' ·

Speedwell   esu   12"
Perennial, Containers   ○ ●   NEW for us in 96
Round sky blue, white eye   In our GARDEN 96

An evergreen perennial, collected in Soviet Georgia, forms low spreading clumps of carpet, and blooms over long period in spring and early summer with white-centered, near-perfect blue flowers. It is drought tolerant and wants well-drained soil. Jagged margins outline pointed small leaves, compared to the rounded leaves of another low grower, V. 'Waterperry Blue'. It has wintered well, planted in our garden, since '96, but hasn't wintered as well in containers above the ground. I suspect they rot in the containers, after being exposed too long to cold damp soil.

prostrata, rupestris
'Heavenly Blue'

Creeping Speedwell   esu, rpts   4"
Perennial   ○ ●   NEW for us in 81
Sapphire blue   In our GARDEN

Mats of foliage with 4" spikes of flowers creep and cover in early summer. They are easy to maintain and control in well-drained rock gardens or as edgings. All forms of V. prostrata provide brilliant color in early summer.

prostrata, rupestris
'Mrs. Holt'

Creeping Speedwell · esu-msu LB · 6"
Perennial ○ ● · NEW for us in 95
Bright pink · In our GARDEN 95

For a unique pink application, this great little creeping cultivar has short, 6" spires in May and June.

prostrata, rupestris
'Trehanii'

Speedwell · esu · 6"
Perennial, Containers ○ ● · NEW for us in 91
Bright, near to true blue · In our GARDEN 93

This is one of my favorite plants with which to introduce chartreuse colored foliage. Bright cobalt-blue flowers work magical contrast with the bright leaves. Foliage color is most intense in early summer or when flowers are showing, and is a perfect combination with the chartreuse flowers of lady's mantle. Once flowers are gone, foliage loses some of its punch.

spicata
'Blue Bouquet'

Speedwell · LB · 12-15"
Perennial, Containers ○ ● · NEW for us in 97
Wedgewood blue · In our GARDEN

Developed in England to flower the first year from seed, this versatile plant could be categorized as an annual, cut flower, perennial, and container plant. Tapered feathery spikes last up to two weeks as cut flowers. Foliage is dark, rich green. We still don't know how well this plant will adapt to our climate.

spicata
'Minuet'

Spike Speedwell · msu-lsu LB · 15"
Perennial ○ ● · NEW for us in 94
Pure pink · In our GARDEN 96

This time-honored favorite produces pink spikes for a long period in summer and provides excellent cut flowers. Foliage has silver highlights. So reliable and so diverse--but then, I've never met a Veronica that I didn't like. Honors: COPF introduction in 1972.

spicata
'Red Fox', 'Rosenrot', 'Rotfuchs'

Spike Speedwell · msu-lsu LB · 12-18"
Perennial ○ ● · NEW for us in 94
Dark rose pink · In our GARDEN 97

One of best, long blooming cultivars, compact and best in front of border or in rock gardens of large scale.

 351

spicata nana
'Blue Carpet', 'Blau Teppich'

Spike Speedwell	esu	6"
Perennial ○ ◉	NEW for us in	97
Blue spikes	In our GARDEN	96

Short groundcover is excellent for edging and in rock gardens. As a strong performer, it spreads evenly and reliably.

spicata, subsp incana

Speedwell	esu-msu LB	12"
Perennial ○ ◉	NEW for us in	82
One of best blues	In our GARDEN	

Very silver foliage needs a prop rock. Drought tolerant plants stand up better if kept dry. They provide excellent cut flower as do all spiky Veronica.

spicata x
'Waterperry Blue'

Spike Speedwell	esu	6"
Perennial ○ ◉	NEW for us in	96
Sky blue	In our GARDEN	96

First introduced to me by P. Kalaidas, rock garden curator of Denver Botanic Garden. Let this one spread to produce dozens of flowers in rocky areas in early summer.

VERONICASTRUM

One of South Dakota's most lovely native plants, Culver's root, is strongly vertical and tall, and seldom needs staking. Graceful, mostly white pointed spires top four foot or taller plants. Other colors are showing up such as rosy and blue lavender. Leaves whorl around the stems, which is one way to differentiate it from the Veronica genus.   This perennial is always one of my first-choice garden plants, selling itself displayed in our garden. Why? It is drought-tolerant, easy and reliable, and provides an old-fashioned, understated elegance that many of the newer introductions and imports can't match. It contrasts well in our garden with the black seed pods of Baptisia and the golden foliage of golden hops vine, Humulus aurea. Allow three years for large and mature plants to become established.

virginicum
'Rosea'

Culver's Physic, Bowman's Root	msu	48-60"
Prairie Perennial ○ ◉	NEW for us in	95
Delicate pink white	In our GARDEN	

Great plant, with tinge-of-pink flowers, that fulfills the best attributes of this genus.

 352

virginicum
'Temptation'
Culver's Physic, Bowman's Root   msu   40-50"
Perennial   ○ ●   NEW for us in   99
Glowing rose purple   In our GARDEN

Long loose flower wands, up to 15", make excellent cut flowers from plants that grow much taller. Leaves are whorled around stems.f

virginicum
white
Culver's Physic, Bowman's Root   msu-lsu LB   48"
Prairie Perennial   ○ ●   NEW for us in   94
White spires   In our GARDEN   94

Pure white form and stunning in our garden. For a study in white hues and textures, plant with Hydrangea paniculata 'Grandiflora'. They bloom at the same time. The tall white spires of Veronicastrum contrast beautifully with the large fluffy, rose-creamy panicles of Hydrangea.

VINCA
minor
Periwinkle, Vinca   spr-esu   6-12"
Perennial, Groundcover   ○ ●   NEW for us in   88
Periwinkle blue   In our GARDEN   92

Luscious quality of glossy, dark-green, broadleaf evergreen groundcover is perfect for shade in good soil. Without winter shade from leaf cover or evergreen trees, it is susceptible to freezer burn. Blooms with "periwinkle" blue flowers from new growth in spring. Interplant with larger, upright shade lovers like Hosta, variegated Solomon seal, Astilbe or monkshood. Once mature patches are established, the plant-growth tangle can deepen to 10".

minor
'Blue and Gold'
Periwinkle, Variegated Vinca   spr-esu   6"
Perennial, Groundcover, Containers   ○ ●   NEW for us in   98
Periwinkle blue   In our GARDEN

A variegated vinca, this time with yellow margined leaves, is also a good plant to add to hanging baskets or containers for shade. Give evergreen culture--winter shade, snow or leaf cover, and good soil, and this will reward you well.

minor
'Miss Jekyll'
Periwinkle, Vinca   spr-esu   3-4"
Perennial, Groundcover   ○ ●   NEW for us in   90
Crisp white   In our GARDEN

This crisp, white-flowering, glossy broadleaf evergreen is very prostrate and ground hugging, and the growth tangle doesn't thicken to the depths of other Vinca. Leaves are slightly smaller, too. Provide non-compacted, humus rich soil, and winter shade.

 353

minor
'Ralph Shugert'

Periwinkle, Variegated Vinca
Perennial, Groundcover, Containers ○ ●
Dark periwinkle blue

spr-esu   6"
NEW for us in   98
In our GARDEN

Dark green leaves have a pretty and distinct, thin white border. We've used in them hanging baskets and container gardens in shade for foliage effects. We haven't wintered in the garden as of '99, and are uncertain of hardiness of this Bowles type.

VIOLA

corsica

Corsican Violet
Perennial   ○ ●
Bright periwinkle blue, cream and yellow

spr-fall LB   6"
NEW for us in   99
In our GARDEN

First violet to bloom in spring and continue through to fall, with large violet, 1.25" flowers. Individual plants may not live for many years, but will further themselves by self-sowing.

labradorica, purpurea

Labrador Violet
Biennial   ○ ●
Blue violet

esu   6"
NEW for us in   98
In our GARDEN

This unusual violet has distinctive purple leaves that hold their color. Plant in shade in good soils in partial shade that do not dry out, and allow them to naturalize there. Plants will spread by both underground rhizomes and seed. This may be the same as the species, V. purpurea.

pedata

Bird Foot Violet
Perennial   ○ ●
Blue purple

esu LB   6"
NEW for us in   98
In our GARDEN

Probably the showiest of violet species (though none are truly bold), this is a lovely and desirable wildflower and part of a butterfly food chain. It displays 1" wide, flat, blue-purple flowers, one of the largest violet flowers in nature. Deeply incised leaves are shaped like the form of a bird's foot, so it is easy to identify. Though it will self-sow, it will never be weedy in moist and well-drained soil.

WALDSTEINIA

ternata

Siberian or Barren Strawberry

Perennial ○ ◐ ●

Yellow

spr-esu 6"

NEW for us in 97

In our GARDEN

Shiny and pretty, semi evergreen, strawberry-like foliage seems to reflect a glint, like that of dew, from slightly hairy leaves. Adapts to many soils, even dry ones, in sun to shade. More ornamental but not as aggressive as strawberry-like cousin, Duchesnea; spreads by stolons. I had forgotten about this plant, until I recently rediscovered it in a garden we had planted a few years back.

YUCCA

Dramatic upright thrust, architectural and historical interest is why we want Yucca in our gardens. Native Americans used its fibrous leaves for baskets and in sewing. The roots produce a soapy lather. It also provides a unique lesson in pollination. A single insect, the yucca moth, is vital for pollinating yucca flowers. Their symbiotic relationship provides resulting fruit on which the moth larvae can feed. Instinct and timing are everything; one cannot live without the other!

Yucca leaves are usually thick and spiny; flowers are bell shaped attached to candle-like spires. Yucca glauca is the primary native to the upper Northern Plains, and the species, Y. filimentosa and filifera, can be adapted here. They like to root into dry, gravelly upper slopes. Because of its drought tolerance, Yucca is an excellent example of a xeriscaping plant, one that can adapt to an extremely dry habitat. Both flowers and foliage provide interesting plant material for cut-flower arrangements.

filamentosa

Adam's Needle, Dagger Plant	msu 60-72"
Perennial ○	NEW for us in 93
Creamy bells	In our GARDEN

Stiff sword-like, bright-green foliage reaches a height of 3', while tall flower stalks of dangling white bells, can loom several feet above. Grow plants as stately, architectural accents. Some protection might be needed this far north.

filamentosa, flaccida
'Bright Edge'

Adam's Needle, Dagger Plant	msu 48-60"
Perennial ○	NEW for us in 95
Creamy white	In our GARDEN

Gold-edged, sword-like leaves seem to fray as thread-like filaments pull away from leaf edges. Stunning flower spires are architectural and contemporary in appearance, and were favored by Gertrude Jekyll in early twentieth century. Use as single specimen or grouped.

356

glauca

Soapweed, Desert Candle
Prairie Perennial ○
Creamy white stalks, fragrant bells

msu   48-60"
NEW for us in 94
In our GARDEN

Native plant culminates with bold flower spikes of fragrant white bells. Blue-green, sword-like foliage provides architectural delight with strong upright thrust. (Dirk Diggler, eat your heart out!) Nearly indestructible while growing, but resents transplanting. Both cut flower and dried foliage work in arrangements.

GRASS, ACORUS

calamus

Sweet Flag
msu   36-60"

Grass, Perennial, Water   ○ ◐ ●
NEW for us in 98

Tiny, greenish flowers on spadex
In our GARDEN

These are shade and water-tolerant, Iris-like plants, not true grasses. Tiny, creamy flowers are borne abundantly on an interesting spadex, the short and narrow reproductive stalk. Grows naturally in shallow water; do not let this dry out. Recommended by U of Minnesota grass study.

calamus
'Variegatus'

Variegated Sweet Flag
msu   24-36"

Grass, Perennial, Water, Houseplant   ○ ◐ ●
NEW for us in 98

Tiny, greenish flowers on spadex
In our GARDEN

Tolerates standing water; provide extra moisture in garden, or plant in low area that dries out slowly. This serves as excellent and uncommon house plant in cool sunny windows with its clean and long-lasting, green and cream variegation. Recommended by U of Minnesota grass study.

gramineus

Golden Sweet Grass
spr-esu   6"

Grass, Perennial, Water, Houseplant   ◐ ●
NEW for us in 98

Foliage effect
In our GARDEN 98

Develops a thick, low clump, less than 6" tall, of thin gold and green strappy leaves, but barely spreads at all. Great dish plant or house plant and has wintered over two seasons in our garden. Requires some shade.

gramineus
'Ogon'

Dwarf Sweet Flag
spr-esu   8-10"

Grass, Perennial, Water   ◐ ●
NEW for us in 99

In our GARDEN

Popular chartreuse and cream variegated cultivar for water gardens or consistently moist, perennial garden niche.

GRASS, ALOPECURUS

pratensis
'Aureus'
Yellow Foxtail Grass

Grass, Perennial ○

Foliage effect, grassy plumes

12-24"

NEW for us in 96

In our GARDEN 97x

Clumping, cool season grass has dense, yellow and green variegated foliage. Recommended by U of Minnesota grass study but rated low by Canadian Morden grass evaluation.

GRASS, ANDROPOGON

Big bluestem, a deep-rooted bunchgrass, was predominant in the Great Plains ecosystem. Before early settlers first broke the virgin sod and still today this essential prairie grass has many uses as animal forage, soil stabilizer, and soil nutrition booster. These and other prairie grasses are responsible for the organic content of the great croplands of the Midwest and Great Plains that we cultivate today to feed nations. Today it is also used ornamentally in gardens, landscapes and prairie restoration. It survives in evenly wet or dry situations making it an excellent drought tolerant or xeriscaping grass. Navaho and other Native Americans use the ashes of this grass in religious ceremonies. Seed selections have been made for foliage color, flower color and height. Special ecotypes are gathered and distributed through the USDA Plant Materials Center, 3308 University Drive, Bismark, ND 58504.

gerardi
Big Bluestem, Beardgrass, Turkeyfoot

Grass, Prairie Perennial, Containers ○ ●

Foliage effect, grassy plumes

msu 48-60"

NEW for us in 96

In our GARDEN

Native to northern Great Plains, important in prairie restorations or prairie landscaping. Rated high by Canadian Morden grass evaluation. Use massed or as specimens in the garden or as container plants.

gerardi
'Pawnee'
Big Bluestem, Beardgrass, Turkeyfoot

Grass, Prairie Perennial ○ ●

Foliage effect

msu 60-72"

NEW for us in 98

In our GARDEN

Drought-tolerant, hearty grower has definitive three-fingered seed clusters and light rosy-red fall color. Rated high by Canadian Morden grass evaluation.

GRASS, ARRHENATHERUM

elatius, bulbosum
'Variegatum'

Bulbous Oat Grass   msu   9-12"
Grass, Perennial   ◯ ◉   NEW for us in   98
Foliage effect   In our GARDEN

Tolerating poor, dry soil, little bulbous oat grass offers season-long interest with neat, bladed tufts of cream and green stripes. Prefers well-drained rock garden conditions in sun or part shade. Recommended by U of Minnesota grass study.

GRASS, BOUTELOUA

curtipendula
'Trailway'

Side Oats Grama Grass   msu-lsu   12-18"
Grass, Prairie Perennial   ◯   NEW for us in   98
Foliage effect   In our GARDEN

Warm season, fine-bladed grass. Distinct "side oats" dangle from sides of stems.

GRASS, BRIZA

maxima

Large Quaking Grass   msu   12"
Grass, Perennial, Containers   ◯ ◉   NEW for us in   97
Foliage effect   In our GARDEN

Heart-shaped seed heads flutter in summer breezes atop low green tufts. Seed heads dry well.

GRASS, BUCHLOE

Buffalo Grass   msu   6" +
Grass, Prairie Perennial, Containers   ◯ ◉   NEW for us in   96
Foliage effect   In our GARDEN

Native warm season prairie grass takes traffic and has few pests and diseases. A sod-forming spreader, it is a soft blue green color requiring minimal mowing and no fertilizers or chemicals. It needs just 2" of rain per month to stay green, and is an excellent xeriscaping plant. The predominant tan color in spring, before soil warms; in fall, as soil cools; and during prolonged periods of drought, is too much dormancy for many who are accustomed to the quick greening in spring of cool season grasses such as bluegrass. Different ecotypes are available--short mat-formers or taller range grasses.

GRASS, CALAMAGROSTIS

With powerful, upright thrust, the reed grasses make a stately foliage statement in all seasons, especially striking in winter. They blend well with our prairie environment. Of all the reed grasses, the Calamagrostis genus is one of the most ornamental and carefree. Narrow and upright, they show their decorative, sterile seed heads on 4-7' tall clumps before the end of June, and they are there to enjoy through winter. A bronze to rosy cast develops on feathery clumps in late summer that are beyond description when covered with frost. Culture requirements are not demanding - average to moist soils, sun to part shade, and well-drained, non-compacted, wide range of soil mixtures. One could even classify them as drought tolerant when established. If you love grasses you won't want to be without the following selections.

acutiflora x
'Karl Foerster', 'Stricta'

Feather Reed Grass
Grass, Perennial, Containers   ○ ●
Delicate buff, foliage effect

esu-fall LB   48-72"
NEW for us in 94
In our GARDEN 94

One of the most versatile, attractive and indispensable of all ornamental grasses, and one of the best for northern gardens. Need I say more? Ok, I will. Attractive, sterile seed heads appear before the end of June, and this showy part can be enjoyed for the rest of the season until colors fade to a fall bronze. Narrow, tall, upright form maintains its shape even through the winter, and is effective with broad, airy Molinia (purple moorgrass) and Panicum (switchgrass) cultivars. Recommended by U of Minnesota study and a high rating by Canadian Morden evaluation. Use massed or as specimen or container plantings.

acutiflora x
'Overdam'

Feather Reed Grass
Grass, Perennial, Containers   ○ ●
Delicate buff, foliage effect

esu-fall LB   36-48"
NEW for us in 95
In our GARDEN 94

Subtle, delicate, cream edge on green foliage and rosy fall foliage color with creamy seed heads. Same upright thrust and June flowering as C. 'Karl Foerster', but with shorter stature. Carefree, as are all hardy reed grasses, and can be used as container plants. Tanacetum corymbosum's white daisy flowers complements the fresh June foliage of this grass.

 361

brachytricha
'Brachytricha'

Korean Reed Grass   esu-fall LB   36-48"
Grass, Prairie Perennial, Containers   ○ ◐ ●   NEW for us in   95
Rosy lavender   In our GARDEN

A good northern selection with beautiful smoky pink and purple flowers and fluffy seed heads in late season. Outstanding strong upright blends well with prairie environment as container, specimen or massed plantings. The most dry-shade tolerant reed grass. This species is not sterile and will moderately self-sow. Recommended by U of Minnesota grass study.

GRASS, CAREX

Sedges are similar to grasses but differ in triangulated or three sided leaf bases. Reproductive parts have three sections and seeds occur in starlike formations. Differing from most grasses, most sedges like partial to full shade and moist sites, but we can still grow them in sun with extra moisture. There are many Carex with beautiful foliages that can be grown as annuals in container combinations. Some of the starry seed heads are great for cut and dried flower arrangements.

elata
'Bowles Golden', 'Aurea'

Bowle's Golden Sedge   30"
Grass, Perennial   ◐ ●   NEW for us in   00
           In our GARDEN   00

A marginally hardy sedge, but one I wanted to try because of finest-of-gold foliage to grow in light shade and moist soil. The dark yellow edged leaves have a green stripe that runs parallel to the leaf margin.

flacca, glauca, nigra

Blue Sedge   msu   6-10"
Grass, Perennial, Containers   ○ ◐ ●   NEW for us in   94
Foliage effect, grassy plumes   In our GARDEN   94

Lovely, very soft, narrow, steel blue foliage from a sedge, not a true grass, creates excellent groundcover; creeps, but is not overly invasive in sun or shade. In my yard for eight years it has remained evergreen in most severe, open winters. It is dry-shade tolerant. We have been encouraging the use of this Carex as an alternative turf grass or lawn substitute; we'll have to develop a demonstration patch at Perennial Passion. Excellent groundcover, it forms mats that could be mowed once or twice a year or after flowering to keep them healthy and fresh looking. Recommended by U of Minnesota grass study.

grayii
'Morning Star'

Morning Star Sedge   msu   30"
Grass, Perennial, Water   ○ ◐ ●   NEW for us in   96
Star-shaped seed   In our GARDEN   97

Conspicuous, 1", star-shaped seeds for cutting and drying naturalize in shady, wet areas, but sun is ok, too. Recommended by U of Minnesota grass study.

montana

Mountain Sedge

Grass, Perennial ○ ◐ ●

Foliage effect

msu   9-12"

NEW for us in 98

In our GARDEN

Dense, fine mounds grow from a versatile sedge for sun or shade. Recommended by U of Minnesota grass study.

muskingumensis

Palm Sedge

Grass, Perennial, Water ○ ◐ ●

Foliage effect

msu   18-24"

NEW for us in 95

In our GARDEN 97

Little miniature papyrus tree shapes grow at ends of sedge stems. Bright green, graceful, unusual. Rated as one of best ornamental sedges for our climate. Good in difficult, moist, shady or partially sunny areas. Excellent performance in our sometimes dry and very sunny display garden. Recommended by U of Minnesota grass study. Shallow water gardens.

muskingumensis
'Oehme'

Variegated Palm Sedge

Perennial

24"

NEW for us in 00

In our GARDEN 00

We've been really happy about the performance of the C. muskingumensis species, so thought we shouldn't pass up on trying this variegated form. Palmate leaf tips provide rich texture and the color glows with yellow margins of shiny green blades. At the '00 PPA, Wolfgang Oehme told me he found it growing in his garden.

GRASS, DESCHAMPSIA

'Northern Lights'

Variegated Tufted Hair Grass

Grass, Perennial, Containers ○ ◐ ●

Variegated foliage

msu-fall   12-18"

NEW for us in 98

In our GARDEN

Finely textured foliage is highly variegated with white and green and gold, pinkish tips in cool weather. Container or specimen plantings for sun or shade.

caespitosa

Tufted Hair Grass

Grass, Perennial, Containers ○ ◐ ●

msu-fall   40-48"

NEW for us in 94

In our GARDEN 94

Strong clumping grass has airy sprays of delicate green flowers in early summer. Fine sprays mature to deeper colors as summer develops; eventually foliage clump is completely hidden. Good for partially shaded woodland or in the mixed perennial border as specimen, container or massed plantings. Tolerates a wide range of soil types and moisture. Recommended by U of Minnesota grass study.

caespitosa
'Fairy's Joke'

Tufted Hair Grass   msu-fall   24-36"
Grass, Perennial,Containers   ○ ◑ ●   NEW for us in   94
Pale green, tinged purple   In our GARDEN

As plants mature in middle to late summer, little plantlets form where seeds would normally develop, and their weight causes the blades to droop. Interesting texture. Sun or shade. Container or specimen plantings. Recommended by U of Minnesota grass study.

GRASS, FESTUCA

Needless to say, there are plenty of blue fescue cultivars to go around. The time-honored effects of foliage strength is the number one reason to grow this plant. Beautiful glaucous blue or blue green tufted mounds provide both texture and color contrasts to any garden or landscape setting. Most bear tan or beige flowers above the foliage. Flower heights range from 6-24" but for most cultivars remain around one foot. They are short lived and need periodic dividing or replacement. The blue color and leaf texture provided by these grasses are the perfect variations and contrasts that make container plantings work.

cinerea
'Sea Urchin'

Fescue   msu-fall   9-12"
Grass, Perennial, Containers   ○ ◑   NEW for us in   96
Foliage effect   In our GARDEN

Container or specimen plantings. Recommended by U of Minnesota grass study.

glauca (ovina)

Sheep Fescue   msu-fall   9-12"
Grass, Perennial, Containers   ○ ◑ ●   NEW for us in
Foliage effect   In our GARDEN

Cool-season, drought-tolerant, bunch-forming grass for a green lawn alternative. Fine blades clump and arch gracefully. Tolerant of soil types and partial shade. Easy to establish from seed. 3-5 lb/1000 sq. ft. Container or specimen plantings.

glauca (ovina)
'Elijah Blue'

Blue Fescue   msu-fall   9-12"
Grass, Perennial, Containers   ○ ◑   NEW for us in   95
Foliage effect, grassy plumes   In our GARDEN

Best blue fescue for ornamental garden use, vigor, heat and drought tolerance. Supposedly longer lived. Divide clumps every few years to maintain longer in landscape. Use in containers or hanging baskets for brilliant foliage contrasts. Recommended by U of Minnesota grass study.

 364

glauca (ovina)
'Glauca', 'Dwarf'

Blue Fescue   msu-fall   12"

Grass, Perennial, Containers   ○ ◐   NEW for us in   96

Foliage effect, grassy plumes   In our GARDEN

Very blue-green foliage on tufted, small, drought-tolerant plant. Divide periodically to extend life. Container or specimen plantings.

tenuifolia

Fine Leaved Fescue   msu-fall   6-10"

Grass, Perennial, Containers   ○ ◐   NEW for us in   96

Foliage effect   In our GARDEN

Tiny drought-tolerant plant with finely textured leaves. Container or specimen plantings. Recommended by U of Minnesota grass study.

GRASS, HELICTOTRICHON

'Sparkling Sapphire', 'Saphirsprudel'

Blue Oat or Blue Avena Grass   lsu   24-36"

Grass, Perennial, Containers   ○ ◐   NEW for us in   98

                                     In our GARDEN

Improved blue oat grass from Germany has more vigor, better hardiness, and best blue color that always stands out. Many uses either as isolated single specimen, grouped with other grasses, massed by itself in the garden, or in containers. Moist soils in sun or light shade.

GRASS, HIEROCHLOE

odorata

Sweet Grass   msu   15"

Grass, Perennial, Herb   ○ ◐   NEW for us in   94

Fragrant foliage   In our GARDEN

Fragrant native grass is used in smudging ceremonies by Native American tribes for grounding, for protecting and making sacred. Has similar fragrance to vanilla grass when dried. Use as a perfume or burn as incense. Can be an invasive grower.

GRASS, HYSTRIX

patula

Bottle Brush Grass   msu   36"

Grass, Perennial   ○ ◐ ●   NEW for us in   92

Buff colored, bottle brush shape   In our GARDEN   97

Unusual among grasses because tolerant of shaded woodlands. Graceful to 3' with bottlebrush effects. First grown here in 1992 after PPA convention that same year. Recommended by U of Minnesota grass study. Native to eastern U.S.

 365

GRASS, JUNCUS

effusus
Common or Soft Rush   30"
Grass, Perennial, Water   ○ ●   NEW for us in 96
Foliage effect   In our GARDEN   X
Native to marshes and wetlands, this tolerates standing water and shade.
Recommended by U of Minnesota grass study.

effusus
'Spiralis'
Corkscrew Rush   12"
Grass, Perennial, Water, Containers   ○ ●   NEW for us in 96
Foliage effect   In our GARDEN   X
Individual blades are wavy, some in distinct corkscrew shapes that shoot out
in all directions. Tolerates moist or boggy conditions. Did not winter in our dry
garden.

GRASS, KOELERIA

brevifolia, cenisia
Blue Hair Grass   6-12"
Grass, Perennial, Containers   ○ ●   NEW for us in
Foliage effect   In our GARDEN
Narrow blue-green leaf blades in dense clumps that may have a short life
span. Recommended by U of Minnesota grass study.

GRASS, LEYMUS (ELYMUS)

arenarius
'Glaucus'
Lyme or European Dune Grass, Wild Rye   msu-lsu   24-36"
Grass, Perennial, Containers   ○ ●   NEW for us in 96
Foliage effect, grassy plumes   In our GARDEN
Metallic foliage of shimmering, solid, blue-gray blades up to one-half inch wide.
Drought-tolerant, invasive groundcover for difficult sites, or decorative in
large containers.

GRASS, LUZULA

sylvatica
Greater Woodrush   12-24"
Grass, Perennial, Water, Containers   ● ●   NEW for us in 96
Small brown   In our GARDEN   96
Dense, clump-forming rush, prefers moist, shady site, but tolerates occasional
dry shade. Not invasive. Recommended by U of Minnesota grass study.
Container, specimen, or water plantings.

 366

GRASS, MISCANTHUS

With so many Miscanthus selections to choose from, where does one begin? We rely on three sources: The "Minnesota Grass Study" by Hockenberry Meyer; the "Morden Grass Study Report" from Canada; repeat observation visits to SDSU's McCrory Gardens at Brookings, S.D. and the University of Minnesota Landscape Arboretum at Chanhassen, Minnesota; and last, but not least, our own experiences with wintering them in Perennial Passion's garden and containers. From all this information we know that only a small percentage of available Miscanthus are recommended as hardy for us without protection, and we have most listed here. Without a doubt, more will be forthcoming in upcoming years. But for now, this is what we know.

Beautiful, feathery, fan-like seed plumes are distinctive for the genus. When choosing it is important to select cultivars that will bloom within our short growing season. Many do not. Read on for more details. Many of the unusual striped foliaged Miscanthus, though borderline hardy, make excellent container plants, or grow foliage for cuttings to add to flower arrangements.

Miscanthus tolerate a wide range of soil moisture conditions.

floridulas, giganteus

Giant Silver Grass   96-120"
Grass, Perennial, Water   ○ ●   NEW for us in 96
Silver fan-like plumes   In our GARDEN

Towering, 3-4' wide clumps of long, wide, foliage rustles continuously in the breeze. Flowers usually don't develop in our short season. Spreads slowly, not invasive. Tolerates poorly drained, wet soils and standing water. Unforgettable for their immense size, and rarely seen in these northern parts. Use old stems as bamboo-like stakes. Recommended by U of Minnesota grass study.

oligostachyus, sinensis
'Purpurescens', Autumn Red'

Purple Maiden, Red Silver, Flame Grass   lsu-fall   48-60"
Grass, Perennial   ○ ●   NEW for us in 95
Rose, silvery fan-like plumes   In our GARDEN

Pronounced reddish foliage begins in late June with ample moisture. Earlier flowering in full sun. Rusty-orange by Sept. with rosy-silver plumes. Tolerates poorly drained, wet sites. Excellent choice for northern climes. Recommended by U of Minnesota grass study.

sacchariflorus

Chinese Silver, Amur or Hardy Pampas Grass
Grass, Perennial   ○ ◐
Silvery, fluffy, fan-like plumes

msu-fall   48-72"
NEW for us in 92
In our GARDEN 93

This invasive, though sterile, non native grass can occasionally be seen naturalized in regional ditches, because it tolerates poorly drained, wet sites. Lovely silver, fluffy, fan plumes are showy in late summer, and hard to miss. Recommended by U of Minnesota grass study. Also called hardy pampas grass but is not the true pampas.

sacchariflorus
'Robustus'

Giant Silver Banner Grass
Grass, Perennial   ○ ◐
Silver flag-like plumes

msu-fall   72-96"
NEW for us in 98
In our GARDEN

Stronger than the more common species of silvergrass.

sinensis

Japanese Silver, Hardy Pampas Grass, Eulalia
Grass, Perennial   ○ ◐ ●
Silver flag-like plumes

lsu-fall   72-96"
NEW for us in 95
In our GARDEN

Quickly forms an effective architectural clump. Somewhat invasive and good for naturalizing in troublesome areas such as poorly drained, wet sites. Effective bloom in late season. Not the true pampas grass, which is tender in S.D. Hardiness is rated marginal by U of Minnesota grass study.

sinensis
'Bluttenwunder'

Maiden Grass, Eulalia
Grass, Perennial   ○ ◐
Rose pink and silver flag-like plumes

lsu-fall   48-72"
NEW for us in 99
In our GARDEN

Excellent burgundy rose-colored flowers and seed heads blooming easily by Sept. 1. The gorgeous red fall color exceeds that of M. 'Purpurescens'. Distinct red stalks emerge. Seed heads begin with silver tones and then turn a burgundy color. When choosing grasses for northern climates, choose for earliest bloom.

sinensis
'Graziella'

Maiden Grass
Grass, Perennial   ○ ◐
Foliage effect, silver, fan-like plumes

lsu-fall   48-70"
NEW for us in 96
In our GARDEN

Rich-green, arching, medium fine leaves and large, shimmering, white panicles in September. Marginally hardy rating by U of Minnesota grass study.

 368

sinensis
'Juli'

Maiden Grass
Grass, Perennial   ○ ●
Silver fan-like plumes

Isu-fall   60"
NEW for us in 00
In our GARDEN

Silver midrib in leaves topped with rosy, relaxed and pendulous flowers. Colonizes quickly. We admired this and several other plants during our annual visit to the Minnesota Landscape Arboretum, and we have followed up by getting some for 2000.

sinensis
'Morning Light'

Silver Maiden Grass
Grass, Perennial   ○ ●
Silver fan-like plumes

Isu-fall   48-60"
NEW for us in 95
In our GARDEN

Fine blades on shorter maiden grass show distinct green and white stripes. Flowers late; sometimes too late. Hardiness is rated marginal by U of Minnesota grass study. Introduced by the USNA.

sinensis
'Red Silver', 'Rotsilber'

Maiden Grass
Grass, Perennial   ○ ●
Rose pink fan-like plumes

Isu-fall   4-7'
NEW for us in 00
In our GARDEN

Red-tinted green foliage turns orange-red in fall and supports silver-pink flowers well above. Much admired during our '99 visit to the Minnesota Landscape Arboretum.

sinensis
'Sarabande'

Maiden Grass
Grass, Perennial   ○ ●
Silver fan-like plumes

Isu-fall   60"
NEW for us in 94
In our GARDEN 94

Silvery, narrow foliage; one of finest but marginally hardy in S.D. Pronounced white stripe on leaf midrib. Hardiness is rated marginal by U of Minnesota grass study.

sinensis
'Silver Arrow', 'Silberfeil'

Maiden Grass
Grass, Perennial   ○ ●
Silver fan-like plumes

Isu-fall   60-72"
NEW for us in 99
In our GARDEN

Variegated silver highlights. Hardiness is rated marginal by U of Minnesota grass study.

sinensis
'Silverfeather', 'Silberfeder'

Maiden Grass   lsu-fall   60-72"
Grass, Perennial   ○ ●   NEW for us in 94
Silver fan-like plumes   In our GARDEN 94

Shimmering, feathery flower panicles are showy, refined and beautiful in the late summer breeze. Silver midrib in green, grassy blade. One of grandest maiden grasses for our region because it blooms a bit earlier than others. Sunnier sites encourage earliest blooming. Recommended by U of Minnesota grass study.

sinensis
'Zebrinus'

Zebra Grass   lsu-fall   60-72"
Grass, Tender Perennial, Containers   ○ ●   NEW for us in 99
Silver fan-like plumes   In our GARDEN

Distinct yellow horizontal variegation is perpendicular to the edge of the blade. Lovely and showy. We know this is not completely adaptable, but people are often willing to try it anyway for the distinct foliage effects. Our mild winters don't effect it at all, but the tough ones will. Use in containers and winter indoors when dormant and carry over year to year, or mulch heavily in garden.

GRASS, MOLINIA

caerulea ssp. arundinacea
'Skyracer'

Purple Moor Grass   msu-fall   84-96"
Grass, Perennial   ○ ●   NEW for us in 96
Buff, airy plumes, foliage effect   In our GARDEN 94

Allow sunlight to beam through the broad, arching, architectural form of one of our favorite grasses. Specimen plantings or those massed on large sites are topped with airy flower heads in fall when foliage color is yellow, turning gold. Recommended by U of Minnesota grass study.

caerulea ssp. arundinacea
'Transparent'

Tall Moor Grass   msu-fall   72-96"
Grass, Perennial   ○ ●   NEW for us in 96
                                              In our GARDEN

Exciting graceful grass is similar to the species. Recommended by U of Minnesota grass study.

caerulea ssp. arundinacea
'Variegata'

Variegated Purple Moor Grass   msu-fall   36-60"
Grass, Perennial   ○ ●   NEW for us in 92
Purplish buff, airy plumes   In our GARDEN 93

One of best variegated grasses. We are trying this, though so far not recommended by U of Minnesota grass study.

caerulea ssp. arundinacea
'Windplay', 'Windspiel'

Tall Moor Grass
Grass, Perennial   ○ ●

msu-fall   72-96"
NEW for us in   94
In our GARDEN

Upon its strong, architectural form, foliage is tall and arching, and turns a golden yellow in the fall. A contrasting background or back lighting is especially effective with this grass. Cut the purplish-buff flower heads for fall bouquets, or leave in the landscape for pleasing winter effects. Recommended by U of Minnesota grass study.

GRASS, PANICUM

One of the stalwarts of the northern prairie, a reliable grazing crop, switchgrass is just as handsome in the garden or landscape. European plant hybridizers, especially in Germany, selected distinct characteristics in the seedlings and upgraded their selections to many that are outstanding ornamentals. You will notice that many have cultivar names provided in both German and English. It seems as if new ones are added every year.

Once established it provides excellent material for xeriscaping, drought-tolerant gardening. Special ecotypes are gathered and distributed through the USDA Plant Materials Center, 3308 University Drive, Bismark, ND 58504.

clandestinum

Deerstongue or Switch Grass
Grass, Prairie Perennial   ○ ●

msu-fall   30-36"
NEW for us in
In our GARDEN

Invasive. Recommended as hardy by U of Minnesota grass study.

virgatum
'Cloud Nine'

Blue Switch Grass
Grass, Prairie Perennial   ○ ●

msu-fall   72-96"
NEW for us in   98
In our GARDEN

Tallest and strongest hardy switch grass. Spectacular in fall as clouds of flowers reach their place in the skies. Light blue-green foliage. Average to moist soils. First admired at '97 PPA symposium.

virgatum
'Dallas Blues'

Switch Grass
Grass, Prairie Perennial   ○ ●

7'
NEW for us in   00
In our GARDEN

Steel-blue foliage takes on purple overtones. Abundant flowering from early fall onward. Wide blades, full form, and long-lasting, heavy flower heads offer better winter interest compared to other switch grass. Little to no viable seed set, so self-sowing is at a minimum.

   371 

virgatum
'Prairie Sky'
Switch Grass   msu-fall   48-60"
Grass, Prairie Perennial   ○ ●   NEW for us in   99
                                         In our GARDEN
Stronger grower, quicker out of dormancy, and better color than P. 'Heavy Metal'. Discovered in Wisconsin. Most powder-blue colored switch grass.

virgatum
'Shenandoah'
Switch Grass   36-48"
Grass, Prairie Perennial   ○ ●   NEW for us in   00
                                         In our GARDEN
Brightest red-leaf switch grass, a shorter cultivar. Slow growing habit attributed to lack of chlorophyll. Sometimes mistaken for a tall blood grass.

virgatum, virginicum
Switch Grass   msu-fall   48-72"
Grass, Prairie Perennial   ○ ●   NEW for us in   94
                                         In our GARDEN   96
Native and prominent grass of tall grass prairie. Great winter interest in sweeps or groups. Tolerates wide range of soils, wet to dry. Recommended by U of Minnesota grass study.

virgatum, virginicum
'Haense Herms'
Red Switch Grass   msu-fall   48-60"
Grass, Prairie Perennial   ○ ●   NEW for us in
Suffused, rosy red cloud   ' In our GARDEN
Nearly identical to 'Rotstrahlbusch'. Excellent selection for fall color. Flowers on plants to 4', produce the overall effect of a finely textured, rose-red cloud with purple and bronze foliage. Full sun required for this color effect. Tolerates temporary standing water. Recommended by U of Minnesota grass study.

virgatum, virginicum
'Heavy Metal'
Switch Grass   msu-fall   60"
Grass, Prairie Perennial   ○ ●   NEW for us in   95
Suffused, pink red cloud   In our GARDEN
Foliage is a stiff steel-blue that holds throughout the season until fall when it turns a bright yellow. Plants have delicate, misty pink flowers in summer at about 5' on upright forms.

virgatum, virginicum
'Rehbraun'
Red Switch Grass   msu-fall   36-60"
Grass, Prairie Perennial   ○ ●   NEW for us in   95
Foliage effect   In our GARDEN
One of best German selections of a native plain's plant. Leaves have red-brown tinges and a good fiery glow in fall, fading to bronze in winter. Similar to P. 'Haense Herms'. One of best to stand against wind. Recommended by U of Minnesota grass study.

 372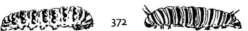

virgatum, virginicum
'Rotstrahlbusch'

Switch Grass, Red Rays
Grass, Prairie Perennial   ○ ●
Suffused pink red cloud

msu-fall   60"
NEW for us in 94
In our GARDEN 94

One of best for red fall color. Sturdy upright form. Purple bronze tints in late season with red, cloud-like seed heads in late summer. Nearly impossible to discern between this and P. 'Haense Herms'. Recommended by U of Minnesota grass study.

virgatum, virginicum
'Squaw'

Switch Grass
Grass, Prairie Perennial   ○ ●
Suffused pink red cloud

msu-lsu   60"
NEW for us in
In our GARDEN

Similar to P. 'Haense Herms' except this selection has a grey-green cast. Fall color is also reddish. Recommended by U of Minnesota grass study.

virgatum, virginicum
'Strictum'

Tall Switch Grass
Grass, Prairie Perennial   ○ ●

msu-lsu   48-60"
NEW for us in
In our GARDEN

Slightly shorter and stiffer, blue-gray leaves. Recommended by U of Minnesota grass study. Tight, strong, upright habit, use where a sentry would be needed--rows of marching soldiers.

GRASS, PENNISETUM

Of many fountain grass selections we have found few that can survive South Dakota winters. Those that are listed here are worth trying. We have also listed here some of the excellent, ornamental, tender Pennisetum, such as red fountain grass, that we can grow as annuals.

alopecuroides
'Hameln'

Dwarf Fountain Grass
Grass, Perennial   ○ ●
Buff, bottlebrush plumes

lsu-fall   24-36"
NEW for us in 95
In our GARDEN

At best, only a handful of fountain grass varieties can be depended on to survive our winters. On a scale of 1-100%, I regard this as 80% adaptable. The U of Minnesota gives a marginal hardiness rating. Drought tolerant. Honors: Arkansas Select 1998, 2000 Mich Growers Choice Award.

 373

orientale

Oriental Fountain Grass   esu-fall   24-36"
Grass, Perennial   ○ ●   NEW for us in   99
Silver pink   In our GARDEN 99x

Beautiful, distinct flowering habit is showy from early to late summer. Blue-green foliage supports many distinct spritzy plumes held well above that could provide cut flowers or seed heads for arrangements. If planted early in season for better establishment before winter, it has a better chance of adapting. Hardiness is rated marginal by U of Minnesota grass study.

GRASS, PHALARIS

arundinacea
'Picta'

Ribbon Grass, Gardener's Garters   msu-fall   24-36"
Grass, Perennial   ○ ● ●   NEW for us in   90
Foliage effect   In our GARDEN   94

Pretty variegated foliage has white margins, green and white centers, an old, old garden plant. Though it could solve many difficult garden situations, keep in mind that it is invasive. Tolerates poorly drained, wet sites. Recommended by U of Minnesota grass study. Sun or shade. The reverse coloration of P. 'Feesey's Variety'.

arundinaceae
'Feesey's Variety', 'Strawberries and Cream'

Ribbon Grass, Gardener's Garters   msu-lsu   24-36"
Grass, Perennial   ○ ● ●   NEW for us in   93
White, green, pink highlights   In our GARDEN

Foliage is nearly white when mature, with narrow green margins and white center leaf. It has strong pink shades when first emerging in spring. It can be invasive but somewhat less than other selections. Plant in a bucket submerged in soil to contain it. Tolerates poorly drained, wet sites; actually grows anywhere. Recommended by U of Minnesota grass study. The reverse coloration of P. 'Picta'.

GRASS, SACCHARUM (ERIANTHUS)

ravennae

Ravenna, Hardy Pampas, Plume or Northern Grass   lsu   72-112"
Grass, Perennial   ○ ●   NEW for us in   97
Silver plumes   In our GARDEN

Architectural colonizer produces beautiful silvery show in late summer throughout the winter until time for pruning in late spring. Called northern pampas grass but doesn't look at all like true pampas (which is really the genus, Cortaderia).

GRASS, SCHIZACHYRIUM

Little bluestem, deep-rooted bunchgrass, was predominant in the ecosystem of the Great Plains before the homesteaders arrived. Then and now it has many uses as animal forage and soil stabilization and today is used as an ornamental grass for the xeric garden or landscape and for prairie restoration. They can tolerate a wide variation of soil conditions, evenly wet or dry, and are drought tolerant when established. Some of the selections are from indigenous areas of South Dakota and have distinct blue-green foliage color. Special ecotypes are gathered and distributed through the USDA Plant Materials Center, 3308 University Drive, Bismark ND 58504. Navaho Indians used ashes in ceremonies.

scoparium
Little Bluestem   msu-fall   36-48"
Grass, Prairie Perennial   ○ ●   NEW for us in   95
                                      In our GARDEN   97
Honors: Honors: Nebraska Great Plants for the Great Plains selection.

scoparium
Badlands Ecotype
Little Bluestem   msu-fall   24-30"
Grass, Prairie Perennial   ○ ●   NEW for us in   98
                                      In our GARDEN
Blue-green leaves create upright forms that turn red when mature. Silvery beard on seed stalks in fall. Joint-release, warm-season grass by USDA Plant Materials Center in Bismark, N.D. and S.D. Agriculture Experiment Stations. A composite of native plants of N.D. and S.D. Badlands gathered from 68 sites. Prefers full sun, adapts to gravel soils, drought tolerant, yet will tolerate some extra moisture. Xeriscaping plant.

scoparium
'Blaze'
Little Bluestem   msu-fall   36-48"
Grass, Prairie Perennial   ○ ●   NEW for us in   95
Foliage effect, grassy plumes   In our GARDEN   96
Native, finely leaved grass shows its russet-red color through fall and winter. Excellent as accents in borders or massed with clump forming, compact habit. Ripening plumes contrast well with fall foliage. Recommended by U of M grass study. Drought tolerant.

scoparium
'The Blues'
Little Bluestem   msu-fall   36"
Grass, Prairie Perennial   ○ ●   NEW for us in   99
                                      In our GARDEN
Very blue selection of prairie standby. Foliage melts into fall burgundy colors.

GRASS, SESLERIA

autumnalis

Autumn Moor Grass — msu-fall — 18"

Grass, Prairie Perennial ○ ● — NEW for us in 94

Silvery white to light brown — In our GARDEN

Exceptional in mass plantings. Yellow-green foliage and good contrasts with all other plants. Marginally hardy according to U of Minnesota study.

caerulea

Blue Moor Grass — msu-fall — 12-18"

Grass, Prairie Perennial ○ ● — NEW for us in 99

In our GARDEN

Provides striking, yellow-green foliage and a form that contrasts well with nearly every other type of plant. It is especially effective in the landscape with fall-blooming perennials, or used in the foreground of dark, dense trees or shrubs such as evergreens. Marginally hardy in 4a. Recommended by U of Minnesota grass study.

heufeliana

Blue Moor Grass — msu-fall — 15-20"

Grass, Prairie Perennial ○ ● — NEW for us in 98

In our GARDEN

Light green, clumping form is recommended by U of Minnesota grass study.

GRASS, SORGHASTRUM

nutans
'Bluebird'

Indian Grass — lsu-fall — 48-60"

Grass, Prairie Perennial ○ ● — NEW for us in 94

In our GARDEN

Wide, sturdy, blue-leaved selection has golden, seed plumes. Recommended by U of Minnesota grass study. Drought tolerant.

nutans
'Sioux Blue'

Indian Grass — lsu-fall — 48-60"

Grass, Prairie Perennial ○ ● — NEW for us in 95

Bronze yellow — In our GARDEN 96

Very blue and upright, a knock-out plant in all seasons. Distinct anthers protrude obviously from grass flowers. Later they turn into golden seeds and remain for winter effect. Excellent cut or dried. Drought-tolerant when established. Though Indian grass is one of our best native grasses, this cultivar shows slight tenderness. Easy to identify in winter because of deep gold to orange color.

 376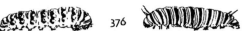

GRASS, SPARTINA

pectinata

Prairie or Freshwater Cord Grass
Grass, Perennial, Containers ○ ●

msu-fall   48-72"
NEW for us in 96
In our GARDEN

Tall, invasive, prairie native tolerates many soil types, but performs best in wet, poorly drained soils. Recommended by U of Minnesota grass study. Use as submerged plant in 1-6" of water in containers. Graceful form turns rich golden color in fall. Honors: 1999 Rocky Mountain Plant Select.

GRASS, SPODIOPOGON

sibiricus

Silver Spike Grass
Grass, Perennial ○ ●
Purple shades

msu-fall   48-54"
NEW for us in 98
In our GARDEN

Bronze color in fall on thick, clumping, bamboo-like foliage. Purple spikes from July onward. Recommended by U of Minnesota grass study. Drought tolerant.

GRASS, SPOROBOLUS

heterolepsis

Prairie Dropseed
Grass, Perennial ○ ●

lsu-fall   30"
NEW for us in 94
In our GARDEN

Hair-fine, glossy, dark-green blades sweep in spiral mounds as tips dust the ground's surface. This drought-tolerant upland grass is one of finest prairie grasses. Flowers in late summer. Fall foliage is the color of a glossy pumpkin.

Fern, Adiantum

pedatum, aleuticum

Northern Maidenhair Fern   12-18"

Fern, Perennial   ○ ●   NEW for us in   90

Foliage effect   In our GARDEN

This is a well-behaved fern that is a popular and peaceful plant for shade gardens. Lacy, light-green, circular leaves attach to feathery, fan-shaped fronds that have a polished, dark stalk. Fall color is yellow . Fine northern woods native, for planting in moist, rich soil, is non-invasive, pest and disease-free.

Fern, Athyrium

filex-femina

Northern Lady Fern   36"

Fern, Perennial   ○ ●   NEW for us in   94

Foliage effect   In our GARDEN

One of best and easy, medium sized fern. 36" feathery, lacy, bright-green fronds are beautiful in floral arrangements. Because this one will eventually colonize, site for massing or groundcover in rich, moist soil.

goeringianum, nipponicum
'Metallicum Pictum'

Japanese Painted Fern   12-18"

Fern, Perennial, Containers   ○ ●   NEW for us in   85

Foliage effect   In our GARDEN   85

One of the most beautiful and valuable foliage plants for shade. Smaller in stature compared to familiar fern. Fabulous silver and green foliage and pink-stemmed combination on individual plants, one wishes it would increase much faster than it does. Grown in our home garden for 15 years, and it has spread very little.

Fern, Cystopteris

bulbifera

Berry or Bladder Fern   24-48"

Fern, Perennial   ○ ●   NEW for us in   94

Foliage effect   In our GARDEN

Small, moisture-loving fern for tucking into shady, rocky niches or near the shady garden path. Little bulblets fall from undersides of fronds to form new plants. Fronds can be added to cut-flower arrangements. Likes alkaline soil, and lime is a suggested additive for the soil; but in the already alkaline soils of S.D., do not add lime (not the green-skinned fruit).

 378

FERN, DRYOPTERIS

dilatata
'Recurvata'
Recurved Broad Buckler Fern | 18-24"
Fern, Perennial ◐ ● | NEW for us in 99
Foliage effect | In our GARDEN

Thin, delicate, dark-green, deciduous fern has pinnate margins that curve downward (recurve) giving a lacy appearance. Plant beneath acidic conifers and in woodland locations.

erythrosora
Autumn Fern | 24"
Fern, Perennial ◐ ● | NEW for us in 98
Foliage effect | In our GARDEN

New fronds emerge with rusty browns of autumn, later changing to dark green. In fall, rusty browns return. Like most ferns, grows best with some morning sun and afternoon shade.

felix mas undulata
'Linearis Polydactyla'
Male or Many Fingered Fern | 24"
Fern, Perennial ◐ ● | NEW for us in 99
Foliage effect | In our GARDEN

Finely textured, semi evergreen fronds terminate with crisp and lacy, forked tips like that of the crested lady fern.

felix mas undulata
'Robusta'
Male Fern | 36"
Fern, Perennial ◐ ● | NEW for us in
Foliage effect | In our GARDEN

Strong, semi evergreen fern colonizes willingly. Site for robust growth and allow plenty of room.

marginalis
Eastern, Marginal Wood or Leatherwood Fern | 12-24"
Fern, Perennial ◐ ● | NEW for us in 94
Foliage effect | In our GARDEN

FERN, MATTEUCCIA

struthiopteris, pennsylvanica
Ostrich Fern | 36"
Fern, Perennial ○ ◐ ● | NEW for us in 95
Foliage effect | In our GARDEN

One of the biggest and most popular fern grown in upper Great Plains. Vegetative fronds are dark green, tall and gracefully arching. They freeze and whither with first sign of cold weather. By late summer the stiff and woody, 1-1.5' fertile fronds have developed. They are glossy brown in color, covered with spore cases. These make excellent contributions to dried arrangements. I always use them for our rustic, forest-floor twig wreaths that we make from scratch in the fall.

 379

Fern, Onoclea

sensibilis

Sensitive or Bead Fern 12-18"
Fern, Perennial, Water NEW for us in 95
Foliage effect In our GARDEN

This fern is compact in stature and frond leaflets (frondlets?) are blunt and wavy, "sensitive" to early frost. Sterile fronds freeze-out in fall, while fertile fronds remain viable. Thrives even in standing water, yet grows well in my dry-shade garden. Typical of most fern, it creeps by rhizomes.

Fern, Osmunda

cinnamomea

Cinnamon Fern 36-48"
Fern, Perennial NEW for us in 95
Foliage effect In our GARDEN

Doubly cut, pinnate fronds are an untoothed, dark-green with a wavy, heavy texture. Center fertile fronds emerge first and appear as if coated with "cinnamon" as spores mature on them., Spiraled tips of newly emerging fronds are called fiddleheads or crosiers. They are delicious when eaten in salads and added to stir fry. This fern will colonize quickly in moist shade and turn a brilliant gold color in fall.

claytonia

Interrupted or Clayton Fern 36-48"
Fern, Perennial NEW for us in 96
Foliage effect In our GARDEN

Early in spring the new sterile fronds are somewhat easy to identify, because they are wider in the center of growth, narrower at the ends, and arch outwardly. The fertile stems do not arch, but grow upright. Leaflets of fertile stems are "interrupted" by pairs of brown sporangia (this is a new word for me, too. I think it means "spore cases"). This will colonize a large area in moist shade.

regalis

Royal Fern 48-72"
Fern, Perennial NEW for us in 95
Foliage effect In our GARDEN

Royal in stature, leaf margins are finely toothed, nearly smooth, and the leaves are doubly pinnate. Distinct appearance; one of my favorites for good cover in shade. Center fertile fronds stand upright, and are surrounded by a ring of non-fertile arching fronds. Excellent yellow fall color. Prefers moist soil and will spread rapidly.

Fern, Polystichum

acrostichoides

Christmas Fern 24"
Fern, Perennial NEW for us in 95
Foliage effect In our GARDEN

Leathery, dark-green leaves make up easy, dependable evergreen fern, and provide winter cover, or at least winter shade. Prefers acid to neutral, lime-free soils, Fronds can grow to 5" across, and are an excellent source of cut specimens for floral arrangements.

 380

FERN, PTERETIS

nodulosa

Ostrich Fern

36-48"

Fern, Perennial ○ ◑ ●

NEW for us in 94

Foliage effect

In our GARDEN 83

A bold grower and very showy, the ostrich-of-fern is tolerant of most conditions, even sun and temporary dryness. This is the old-fashioned fern commonly found around older homes in Sioux Falls. This is one of those vigorous and quick colonizers. Why not harvest and eat edible fiddleheads (crosiers) to maintain control? Fern provide a peaceful, airy, cooling effect in the woodland or shady landscape.

Common Name Cross Reference

Adam's Needle *Yucca*

Ageratum, Hardy *Eupatorium*

Alkanet *Brunnera, Anchusa*

Alum Root *Heuchera*

Alyssum *Aurinia, Alyssum*

Anemone, Grape Leaf *Anemone tomentosa*

Anemone, Japanese *Anemone hybrida*

Angelica *Angelica*

Anise Hyssop *Agastache foeniculum*

Anise Mint *Agastache foeniculum*

Arctic Bramble *Rubus*

Arrowhead *Sagittaria*

Asparagus Vine *Pseudoscaber*

Aster, Blue Wood *Aster cordifolius*

Aster, Calico *Aster lateriflorus*

Aster, Frikart's *Aster frikartii*

Aster, Golden *Solidaster*

Aster, Heath *Aster ericoides*

Aster, New England *Aster novi angliae*

Aster, New York *Aster novi belgii*

Aster, Prairie *Aster fendleri*

Aster, Smooth *Aster laevis*

Aster, Thousand Flowered *Boltonia asteroides*

Aster, White Wood *Aster divaricata*

Asterago *Solidaster*

August Lily *Lycoris*

Aztec Indian Berry *Duchesnea indica*

Baby's Breath *Gypsophila*

Baby's Breath, Creeping *Gypsophila repens*

Bachelor Button *Centaurea*

Balloon Flower *Platycodon*

Barrenwort *Epimedium*

Basket of Gold *Alyssum, Aurinia*

Beafsteak Plant *Perilla*

Beardtongue *Penstemon*

Beardtongue, Smooth *Penstemon digitalis*

Bearsfoot *Helleborus foetidus*

Beautyberry *Callicarpa*

Bedstraw *Galium odoratum*

Bee Balm *Monarda*

Belladonna *Delphinium belladonna*

Bellflower *Campanula*

Bellflower, Dalmatian *Campanula portenschlagiana*

Bellflower, Milky *Campanula lactiflora*

Bellflower, Peach Leaf *Campanula persicaria*

Bellflower, Ring *Campanula hoffmannii*

Bellflower, Spotted *Campanula punctata*

Bellflower, Willow *Campanula persicaria*

Bellwort, Large Flowered *Uvularia grandiflora*

Bergamot *Monarda*

Bethlehem Sage *Pulmonaria*

Betony, Big *Stachys grandiflora, spicata*

Betony, Smooth *Stachys officinalis*

Betony, Wood *Stachys officinalis*

Bigflower *Prunella grandiflora*

Bigleaf *Ligularia*

Bishop's Weed *Aegopodium*

Bistort, European *Persicaria, Polygonum*

Black Cohosh *Cimicifuga*

Black Eyed Susan *Rudbeckia fulgida*

Blackberry Lily *Belamcanda, Pardanthus*

Blackberry, Trailing *Rubus arcticus*

Bladder Pod *Alyssoides utriculata*

Blanket Flower *Gaillardia*

Blazing Star *Liatris*

Bleeding Heart, False *Corydalis*

Bleeding Heart, Fern Leaf *Dicentra eximia*

Bleeding Heart, Fringed *Dicentra eximia*

Bleeding Heart, Old Fashioned *Dicentra spectabilis*

Bleeding Heart, Pacific *Dicentra formosa*

Bloodroot *Sanguinarea*

Blue Spiraea *Caryopteris*

Bluebeard *Caryopteris*

Bluebells of Scotland *Campanula rotundifolia*

Bluebells, Oriental *Mertensia asiatica*

Bluebells, Virginia *Mertensia virginica*

Bluestar *Amsonia*

Bocconia *Macleaya*

Boneset *Eupatorium*

Bouncing Bet *Saponaria officinalis*

Bowman's Root *Porteranthus, Gillenia*

Bowman's Root *Veronicastrum virginicum*
Brown Eyed Susan *Rudbeckia fulgida*
Bugbane *Cimicifuga*
Bugleweed *Ajuga*
Burst Wort *Herniaria glabra*
Bush Clover *Lespedeza*
Bush Pea, Carolina *Thermopsis caroliniana, villosa*
Bush Pea, Yellow *Thermopsis caroliniana, fabacea*
Butter and Eggs *Linaria vulgaris*
Butterbur, Giant *Petasites japonica*
Buttercup *Trollius*
Butterfly Bush *Buddleia*
Calamint *Calamintha*
Campion *Lychnis chalcedonica*
Candylily *Pardancanda x*
Candytuft *Iberis*
Cardinal Flower *Lobelia cardinalis*
Carnation, Hardy *Dianthus grenadin, caryophyllus*
Carpenter Plant *Silphium perfoliatum*
Catchfly, German *Lychnis viscaria*
Catclaw *Schrankia nuttalii*
Catmint *Nepeta*
Catmint, Siberian *Nepeta sibirica*
Catnip *Nepeta cataria*
Celandine or Golden *Stylophorum*
Celandine, Tree *Macleaya*
Chameleon Plant *Houttuynia*
Chinese Lantern *Physalis*
Chives *Allium schoenoprasum*
Chives, Garlic *Allium tuberosum*
Cinquefoil *Potentilla*
Cinquefoil, Nepal *Potentilla nepalensis*
Cinquefoil, Red *Potentilla atrosanguinea*
Circle Flower *Lysimachia punctata*
Cohosh, Blue *Caulophyllum thalictroides*
Columbine *Aquilegia*
Columbine, Clematis *Aquilegia clematifolia*
Flowering
Columbine, Japanese *Aquilegia flabellata*
Fan
Columbine, Nosegay *Aquilegia hybrids*
Columbine, Rocky *Aquilegia caerulea*
Mountain
Comfrey *Symphytum*
Compass Plant *Silphium laciniatum*

Coneflower *Echinaceae purpurea*
Coneflower, Green *Rudbeckia laciniata*
Headed
Coneflower, Pale *Echinaceae pallida*
Purple
Coneflower, Purple *Echinaceae*
Coral Bells *Heuchera*
Coreopsis, *Coreopsis verticillata*
Threadleaf
Cornflower *Centaurea*
Cornleaf Restharrow *Ononis rotundifolia*
Cowslips *Mertensia virginica*
Cranesbill, Bloody *Geranium sanguineum*
Cranesbill, True *Geranium*
Geranium
Creeping Jenny *Lysimachia nummularia*
Crownvetch *Coronilla*
Culver's Physic *Veronicastrum virginicum*
Cup Plant *Silphium perfoliatum*
Curly Garlic Chives *Allium senescens 'Glauca'*
Daffodil *Narcissus*
Dagger Plant *Yucca*
Daisy, English *Bellis perennis*
Daisy Fleabane *Erigeron*
Daisy, Hungarian *Leucanthemum serotina, uliginosum*
Daisy, Marguerite *Anthemis*
Daisy, Meadow *Leucanthemum vulgare*
Daisy, Ox Eye *Leucanthemum vulgare*
Daisy, Painted *Tanacetum coccineum*
Daisy, Shasta *Leucanthemum x superbum*
Daisy, Willowleaf *Telekia speciosa, salicifolium*
Dame's Rocket *Hesperis*
Daylily *Hemerocallis*
Desert Candle *Yucca*
Dong Quai *Angelica*
Double Dropwort *Filipendula vulgaris, hexapetala*
Dragon's Blood *Sedum spurium*
Dumbo's Ears *Rudbeckia maxima*
Dusty Miller, Hardy *Artemisia stellerana*
Edelweiss *Leontopodium alpinum*
Elephant Ears *Ligularia*
Eulalia *Miscanthus sinensis*
Fairy Candles *Cimicifuga*
Fairy Flower *Digitalis*
False Dragonhead *Physostegia*

Featherleaf Rodgersia *Rodgersia pinnata*

Fern, Autumn *Dryopteris erythrosora*

Fern, Bead *Onoclea sensibilis*

Fern, Bladder *Cystopteris bulbifera*

Fern, Christmas *Polystichum acrostichoides*

Fern, Cinnamon *Osmunda cinnamomea*

Fern, Clayton *Osmunda claytonia*

Fern, Eastern Wood *Dryopteris marginalis*

Fern, Interrupted *Osmunda claytonia*

Fern, Japanese Painted *Athyrium goer., nipponicum*

Fern, Lady Northern *Athyrium filex-femina*

Fern, Leatherwood *Dryopteris marginalis*

Fern, Maidenhair *Adiantum pedatum, aleuticum*

Fern, Male *Dryopteris felix mas, affinis*

Fern, Many Fingered *Dryopteris felix mas, undulata*

Fern, Marginal Wood *Dryopteris marginalis*

Fern, Ostrich *Matteuccia*

Fern, Recurved Broad Buckler *Dryopteris dilatata*

Fern, Royal *Osmunda regalis*

Fern, Sensitive *Onoclea sensibilis*

Fern, Shaggy Shield *Dryopteris cycadina*

Feverfew *Chrysanthemum parthenium*

Fingerleaf Rodgersia *Rodgersia henricii*

Flag, Sweet *Acorus calamus*

Flag, Variegated Sweet *Acorus gramineus 'Variegatus', 'Argenteostriatus'*

Flax *Linum*

Fleeceflower *Polygonum (Persicaria)*

Fleur De Lis *Iris*

Foamflower *Tiarella*

Foamy Bells *Heucherella*

Forget Me Not *Brunnera, Anchusa, Myosotis*

Four O'clock *Mirabilis jalapa, multiflora*

Foxglove, Fairy or Finger *Digitalis*

Foxglove, Rusty *Digitalis ferruginea*

Foxglove, Strawberry *Digitalis mertonensis*

Foxglove, Willow *Digitalis obscura*

Fringe Cups *Tellima grandiflora*

Funkia Lily *Hosta*

Gas Plant *Dictamnus*

Gayfeather *Liatris*

Gentian, Autumn or Everyman's *Gentiana septemfida var. lagodechiana*

Gentian, Bottle or Closed *Gentiana andrewsii*

Geranium, Bigroot *Geranium macrorrhizum*

Germander *Teucrium chamaedrys*

Ghengis Khan Aster *Kalimeras, Asteromoea*

Giant Heartleaf *Crambe cordifolia*

Giant Scalehead *Cephalaria*

Gilia, Scarlet *Ipomopsis, Gilia*

Ginger, Canadian *Asarum canadense*

Ginger, European *Asarum europeaum*

Globe Centaurea *Centaurea macrocephala*

Globe Flower *Trollius*

Globe Thistle *Echinops*

Goatsbeard *Aruncus dioicus*

Golden Alexander *Zizia*

Golden Ray *Ligularia*

Goldenrod *Solidago*

Grass, Amur *Miscanthus sacchariflorus*

Grass, Avena *Helictotrichon sempervirens*

Grass, Banner *Miscanthus sacchariflorus*

Grass, Blue Fescue *Festuca cinerea*

Grass, Blue Hair *Koeleria glauca*

Grass, Blue Oat Grass *Helictotrichon sempervirens*

Grass, Buffalo *Buchloe*

Grass, Bulbous Oat *Arrhenatherum elatius*

Grass, Chinese Silver *Miscanthus sacchariflorus*

Grass, Dune *Leymus (Elymus) arenarius*

Grass, Dwarf Fountain *Pennisetum alopecuroides*

Grass, Feather Reed *Calamagrostis*

Grass, Fineleaf Fescue *Festuca tenuifolia*

Grass, Giant Silver *Miscanthus sacchariflorus*

Grass, Golden Sweet *Acrous gramineus*

Grass, Hardy Pampas (not true) *Miscanthus sinensis*

Grass, Indian *Sorghastrum nutans*

Grass, Japanese Silver *Miscanthus sinensis*

Grass, Job's Tears *Coix lachryma*

Grass, Lyme *Leymus (Elymus) arenarius*

Grass, Maiden *Miscanthus sinensis*

Grass, Moorgrass, *Sesleria caerulea,*
Blue *heufeliana*

Grass, Moorgrass, *Molinia caerulea ssp.*
Purple or Tall *arundinaceae*

Grass, Northern *Saccharum (Erianthus)*
Pampas *ravennae*

Grass, Oriental *Pennisetum orientale*
Fountain

Grass, Plume *Saccharum (Erianthus)*
ravennae

Grass, Prairie Cord *Spartina pectinata*

Grass, Prairie *Sporobolus*
Dropseed

Grass, Quaking *Briza*

Grass, Ravenna *Saccharum (Erianthus)*
ravennae

Grass, Sea Oats *Chasmanthium*

Grass, Silver Grass *Miscanthus sinensis*

Grass, Silver Spike *Spodiopogon sibiricus*

Grass, Sweet *Hierochloe odorata*

Grass, Switch *Panicum*

Grass, Tufted Hair *Deschampsia caespitosa*

Grass, Yellow Foxtail *Alopecurus pratensis*
'Aureus'

Grass, Zebra *Miscanthus sinensis*
'Zebrinus'

Grasswort, Starry *Cerastium arvense*

Groundsel *Senecio, Ligularia*

Hakone *Hakonechloa macra*

Harebell *Campanula carpartica*

Harebell, Carpathian *Campanula carpatica*

Harebell, Clustered *Campanula carpatica*

Hawkweed *Hieracium aurantiacum*

Helen's Flower *Helenium*

Heliotrope, Garden *Valeriana officinalis*

Hellebore *Helleborus*

Helmet Flower *Aconitum, Scutellaria*

Hens and Chicks *Sempervivum*

Hollyhock *Alcea (Althaea) rosea*

Honesty Plant *Lunaria*

Horsetail *Equisetum*

Hyacinth, Feather *Muscari plumosum*

Hyacinth, Grape *Muscari comusum*

Hyssop *Hyssopus officinalis,*
Agastache

Indian Physic *Porteranthus, Gillenia*

Indian Pink *Spigelia*

Indigo, False *Amorpha nana, Baptisia*
australis

Inula *Inula, Buphthalmum*

Iris, Alaska *Iris setosa*

Iris, Arctic *Iris setosa*

Iris, Bristly *Iris setosa*

Iris, Butterfly *Iris spuria*

Iris, Dwarf Crested *Iris cristata*

Iris, Flag *Iris pseudacorus*

Iris, Florentine *Iris pallida*

Iris, Seashore *Iris spuria*

Iris, Siberian *Iris sibirica*

Iris, Sweet *Iris pallida*

Ironweed *Vernonia*

Italian Bugloss ~~Brunnera~~, *Anchusa*

Jack In the Pulpit *Arisaema*

Jacob's Ladder *Polemonium*

Joe Pye Weed *Eupatorium*

Joseph and Mary *Pulmonaria*

Jupiter's Beard *Centranthus ruber*

Knapweed *Centaurea dealbata*

Lacy Veil *Asparagus, Pseudoscaber*

Ladies' Tresses *Spiranthes*

Lady's Mantle *Alchemilla*

Lady's Mantle, *Alchemilla alpina*
Mountain

Ladybells *Adenophora*

Lake Oswego Tea *Monarda*

Lamb's Ears *Stachys lanata*

Lanceleaf Coreopsis *Coreopsis lanceolata*

Larkspur *Delphinium*

Lavender *Lavandula*

Leadplant *Amorpha canescens*

Lemon Lily *Hemerocallis*
lilioasphodelus (flava)

Lenten Rose *Helleborus*

Leopard Flower *Belamcanda, Pardanthus*

Leopard Plant *Ligularia przewalskii*

Lily, Asiatic *Lilium asiatica*

Lily Leek *Allium moly luteum*

Lily, Martagon *Lilium martagon*

Lily of the Valley *Convallaria*

Lily, Oriental *Lilium orientale*

Lily, Tiger *Lilium tigrinum*

Lilyleaf *Adenophora*

Liverleaf *Hepatica Americana*

Lobelia, Big Blue *Lobelia siphilitica*

Loosestrife *Lythrum*

Loosestrife, *Lysimachia clethroides*
Gooseneck

Lungwort *Pulmonaria*

Lupine *Lupinus*
Lupine, False *Thermopsis caroliniana*
Madonna Lily *Lily candidum*
Madwort *Aurinia, Alyssum*
Magic Lily *Lycoris*
Mallow *Malva, Lavatera*
Mallow, Checker *Sidalcea*
Mallow, False *Sidalcea oregana, coccinea*
Mallow, Musk *Malva moschata*
Mallow, Prairie *Sidalcea*
Mallow, Rose *Hibiscus moscheutos*
Maltese Cross *Lychnis chalcedonica*
Malva *Sidalcea*
Marshmallow Plant *Malva officinalis*
Mary's Tears *Pulmonaria*
Masterwort *Astrantia*
Meadowrue *Thalictrum*
Meadowsweet *Filipendula*
Merrybells *Uvularia grandiflora*
Mexican Hat *Ratibida*
Michaelmas Daisy *Aster novi angliae or novi belgii*
Milfoil *Achillea*
Milk Vetch *Astragalus crassicarpus*
Milkweed, Pleurisy *Asclepias tuberosa* Root
Milkweed, Swamp *Asclepias* or Butterfly
Mistflower *Eupatorium*
Money Plant, Silver *Lunaria* Dollat Plant
Moneywort *Lysimachia nummularia*
Moneywort, Golden *Lysimachia nummularia 'Aurea'*
Monkshood *Aconitum*
Monkshood, *Aconitum anthora* Pyrenees
Monkshood, Yellow *Aconitum lamarckii, lycotocum*
Morning Glory, Bush *Ipomoea leptophylla*
Morning Widow *Geranium phaeum*
Mountain Bluet *Centaurea*
Mugwort *Artemisia*
Mullein *Verbascum*
Mum, Cushion *Dendranthema*
Mum, Hardy *Dendranthema zawadskii or x rubella*
Obedient Plant *Physostegia*
October Daphne *Sedum spurium*

Old Man of the *Ipomoea leptophylla* Prairie
Old Woman *Artemisia stellerana* Wormwood
Onion, Downy *Allium christophii, albopilosum*
Onion, Drumstick *Allium spherocephalum*
Onion, Egyptian *Allium cepa proliferum*
Onion, Mountain *Allium oreophilum, ostrowskianum*
Onion, Persian *Allium aflatunense*
Onion, Treetop *Allium cepa proliferum*
Orchid, Chinese *Bletilla striata* Ground
Oregano *Origanum*
Orphanage Plant *Kalimeras, Asteromoea*
Orris Root *Iris pallida*
Pasque Flower *Pulsatilla patens*
Patrinia *Patrinia*
Pearlwort *Sagina*
Pearly Everlasting *Anaphalis*
Peony, Common *Paeonia lactiflora*
Peony, Fern Leaf *Paeonia tenuifolia, officinalis*
Peony, Tree *Paeonia suffruticosa*
Periwinkle *Vinca minor*
Persian Cornflower *Centaurea dealbata*
Peruvian Verbena, *Verbena boniarensis* Purple Top
Phlox, Creeping *Phlox subulata*
Phlox, Downy *Phlox pilosa*
Phlox, Meadow or *Phlox maculata, carolina* Spotted
Phlox, Spring Pearl *Phlox paniculata x arendsii* Hybrids
Phlox, Tall Garden *Phlox paniculata*
Phlox, Woodland *Phlox stolonifera*
Pigsqueak *Bergenia*
Pincushion Flower *Scabiosa*
Pink, Border *Dianthus*
Pink, Cheddar *Dianthus gratianopolitanus*
Pink, Maiden Rock *Dianthus deltoides*
Plantain Lily *Hosta*
Plumbago *Ceratostigma plumbaginoides*
Plume Poppy *Macleaya*
Poppy, Iceland *Papaver nudicaule*
Poppy, Oriental *Papaver orientale*
Prairie Ragwort *Senecio plattensis*
Prairie Smoke *Geum triflorum*

Primrose, Evening *Oenothera macrocarpa, missouriensis*

Primrose, Missouri *Oenothera macrocarpa, missouriensis*

Primrose, True *Primula*

Purple Poppy Mallow *Callirhoe*

Purple Prairie Clover *Petalostemon purpureum*

Pussy Toes *Antennaria*

Pyrethrum *Tanacetum coccineum*

Queen Anne's Lace *Daucus*

Queen of the Meadow *Filipendula rubra*

Rabbit Bush *Chrysothamus nauseosus*

Rabbit Ear Iris *Iris laevigata*

Rattlesnake Master *Eryngium yuccafolium*

Rhubarb *Rheum*

Rock Cress *Arabis*

Rose of Sharon *Hibiscus moscheutos*

Rudbeckia, Great *Rudbeckia maxima*

Rue *Ruta graveolens*

Rue Anemone *Anemonella thalictroides*

Rush *Juncus*

Rush, Scouring *Equisetum*

Russian Sage *Perovskia*

Sage *Salvia*

Sage, Meadow *Salvia nemerosa x superba*

Saxifrage *Bergenia*

Scabiosa, Perennial *Knautia*

Scarlet Rocket *Ipomopsis, Gilia*

Scilla, Fall Blooming *Scilla numidica*

Sea Holly *Eryngium*

Sea Kale *Crambe maritima*

Sea Lavender *Limonium latifolium*

Sea Pink *Armeria maritima*

Sedge *Carex*

Sedge, Blue *Carex flacca, glauca*

Sedge, Finger *Carex digitata*

Sedge, Morning Star *Carex grayii*

Sedge, Mountain *Carex montana*

Sedge, Palm *Carex muskingumensis*

Self Heal *Prunella*

Senna, Wild *Cassia, Senna*

Sensitive Briar *Schrankia nuttalii*

She Gan *Belamcanda, Pardanthus*

Sheep Fescue *Festuca glauca (ovina)*

Shell Leaf Penstemon *Penstemon grandiflora*

Shi-So *Perilla*

Shooting Star *Dodecatheon*

Side Oats Grama *Bouteloua curtipendula*

Simpler's Joy *Verbena hastata*

Skullcap, Prairie *Scutellaria resinosa*

Smokeweed *Eupatorium*

Snakehead *Chelone*

Snakeroot *Cimicifuga*

Sneezeweed *Helenium*

Sneezewort *Achillea ptarmica*

Snow In Summer *Cerastium tomentosa*

Snow on the Mountain *Aegopodium*

Snowdrop *Anemone sylvestris*

Soapweed *Yucca glauca*

Soapwort *Saponaria officinalis*

Soldiers and Sailors *Pulmonaria*

Solomon Seal *Polygonatum*

Sorrel *Rumex*

Southernwood *Artemisia ludov., abrotanum*

Speedwell *Veronica*

Speedwell, Creeping *Veronica prostrata, rupestris*

Speedwell, Spike *Veronica spicata or longifolia*

Spiderwort *Tradescantia*

Spiraea, False *Astilbe*

Spotted Dead Nettle *Lamium*

Spotted Dog *Pulmonaria*

Spurge *Euphorbia*

Spurge *Pachysandra*

Spurge, Cypress *Euphorbia cyparissias*

Spurge, Donkey *Euphorbia myrsinites*

Standing Cypress *Ipomopsis, Gilia*

Star of Persia *Allium christophii, albopilosum*

Statice, German Perennial *Goniolinum (Limonium) tataricum*

Stinking Benjamin *Trillium*

Stoke's Aster *Stoke's Aster*

Stonecrop *Sedum*

Strawberry *Fragaria*

Strawberry, Barren *Waldsteinia*

Strawberry, False *Duchesnea*

Strawberry, Siberian *Waldsteinia*

Sun Wheels *Inula, Buphthalmum*

Sundrops *Oenothera tetragona*

Sundrops, Dwarf *Calylophus serrulatus*

Sunflower *Helianthus*

Sunflower, False *Heliopsis*

Sunflower, *Helianthus maximillianii*
Maxmillians

Surprise Lily *Lycoris*

Sweet Pea *Lathyrus*

Sweet Woodruff *Galium odoratum*

Swordleaf *Inula, Buphthalmum*

Tarragon, True *Artemisia dracunculus*
French

Thrift *Armeria maritima*

Thyme, Creeping *Thymus*

Tickseed *Coreopsis*

Toad Lily *Tricyrtis*

Toadflax *Linaria*

Tulip *Tulipa*

Tulip, Botanical *Tulipa species*

Tulip, Lily Flowered *Tulipa*

Tulip, Species *Tulipa species*

Tunic Flower *Petrorhagia, Tunica*

Turk's Cap Lily *Lily Canadense,*
                 superbum, pumilum,
                 martagon

Turtlehead *Chelone*

Valerian *Valeriana officinalis*

Valerian, Red *Centranthus ruber*

Veil of Lace *Pseudoscaber*

Vervain, Blue *Verbena hastata*

Vinca *Vinca minor*

Violet, Bird Foot *Viola pedata*

Violet, Corsican *Viola corsica*

Violet, Labrador *Violoa labradorica,*
                  purpurea

Wakerobin *Trillium*

Wall Cress *Arabis*

Wandflower *Cimicifuga*

Wasatch *Penstemon cyananthus*

Waxbells, Yellow *Kirengeshoma*

Willow Amsonia *Amsonia tabernaemontana*

Willow Herb *Epilobium*

Wine Cups *Callirhoe*

Wintercreeper, *Euonymus kewensis*
Dwarf

Wintercreeper, *Euonymus coloratus*
Purpleleaf

Woadwaxen *Genista*

Woodrush *Luzula*

Woolly Betony *Stachys grandiflora,*
               spicata

Wormwood *Artemisia*

Wormwood, *Artemisia absinthium*
Absinthe

Wormwood, Roman *Artemisia pontica*

Wormwood, Silver *Artemisia schmidtiana*
Mound

Wormwood, White *Artemisia ludoviciana*
Sage

Woundwort *Stachys officinalis*

Yarrow *Achillea*

Yellow Archangel *Lamiastrum*

Yellow Scabiosa *Cephalira*

How Our Garden Grows

Resources

There are so many many writers, lecturers and educators who have contributed to my horticulture and experience. My apologies if I have mistakenly omitted someone from this list.

Books About Perennials
Armitage, Allan A. 1997. *Herbaceous Perennial Plants. A Treatise on Their Identification, Culture, and Garden Attributes.* Varsity Press, Inc., Athens, Georgia.

Claussen, Ruth Rogers and Nicolas H. Ekstrom. 1989. *Perennials for American Gardens.* Random House, New York, NY.

Cox, Jeff and Marilyn. 1985. *The Perennial Garden. Color Harmonies Through the Seasons.* Rodale Press, Emmaus, PA.

Helmer, M. Jane Colman, Karla S, Decker Hodge. 1998. *Pictorial Guide to Perennials.* Merchants Publishing Co., Kalamazoo, MI.

Phillips, Roger and Martyn Rix. 1991. *The Random House Book of Perennials,* Volumes 1 and 2. Random House, New York, NY.

Snyder, Leon C. 1983. *Perennials For Northern Gardens.* University of Minnesota Press, Minneapolis, MN.

Still, Steven. 1982. *Herbaceous Ornamental Plants.* Department of Horticulture, Ohio State University. Stipes Publishing, 10-12 Chester Street, Champaign, Illinois 61820.

Valleau, John. 1995. *Perennial Gardening Guide.* Canada. Published by Valleybrook Gardens Ltd., Abbotsford, BC Canada.

Books About Herbs
Bremness, Lesley. 1988. *The Complete Book of Herbs.* Dorling Kindersley Limited, London.

Ody, Penelope. 1993. *The Complete Medicinal Herbal.* Dorling Kindersley Limited, London.

Tyler, Varro. 1993. *The Honest Herbal.* The Pharmaceutical Products Press, Haworth Press, New York, NY.

Books About Native Plants
Barr, Claude A. 1983. *Jewels of the Plains.* University of Minnesota Press, Minneapolis, MN.

Johnson, James R. and James. T. Nichols. 1982. *Plants of South Dakota Grasslands.* Bulletin 566. Agricultural Experiment Station, SDSU, Brookings, SD 57007.

Johnson, James and Gary Larson. 1999. *Grassland Plants of South Dakota and the Northern Great Plains,* Bulletin 566. SDSU College of Agriculture and Biological Sciences, Brookings, SD 57007.

Niering, William and Nancy Olmstead. 1979. *Audubon Society Field Guide to North American Wildflowers, Eastern Region.* Alfred A. Knopf, New York, NY.

Rogers, Dilwyn J. 1980. *Edible, Medicinal, Useful and Poisonous Wild*

Plants of the Northern Great Plains, South Dakota Region. Biology Department, Augustana College, Sioux Falls, SD. Published by Buechel Memorial Lakota Museum, St. Francis, SD 57572.

Van Bruggen, Theodore. 1992. *Wildflowers, Grasses and Other Plants of the Northern Plains and Black Hills.* Badlands Natural History Ass., Interior, SD. 57750. Fenske Printing, Rapid City, SD.

Books About Shrubs and Trees

Ball, John and David Graper. *Trees for South Dakota.* Ext. Bulletin 903. Horticulture, Forestry, Landscape and Parks Dept, SDSU. Distributed by Cooperative Extension Office, Brookings, SD.

Dirr, Michael. 1983. *Manual of Woody Plants.* Dept. of Horticulture, University of Georgia, Athens, GA. Stipes Publishing, Chicago, IL 61820.

Phillips, Roger and Martyn Rix. 1989. *Random House Book of Shrubs.* Random House, New York, NY.

Sabuco, John. 1985. *The Best of the Hardiest.* Plantsman Publications, Box 1, Flossmoor, IL 60422.

Books About Grasses

Brown, Lauren. 1979. *Grasses, An Identification Guide.* Houghton Mifflen, New York, NY.

Hockenberry Meyer, M, D.B. White, H. Pellet. 1995. *Ornamental Grasses for Cold Climates.* North Central Regional Publication 573, Department of Horticultural Science, University of Minnesota, St. Paul, MN.

Davidson, Dr. Campbell. Morden Research Center Grass Study. 101 Route 100, Morden, MB, Canada R6M 1Y5.

Books About Roses

Osborne, Robert. 1991. *Hardy Roses.* Gardenway Publishing, Vermont.

Zuzec, Richard, McNamara, Pellet. 1995. *Roses of the North, Shrub Roses For Northern Gardeners.* University of Minn. Agriculture Experiment Station, St. Paul, MN.

Miscellaneous Books

Brady, Nyle C. *Nature and Properties of Soils, Eighth Edition.* McMillan Co., New York, NY.

Browne, Roland A. 1964. *For Better Gardens.* Doubleday and Co., Garden City, NY.

Johnson, A. T. and H. A. Smith. 1976. *Plant Names Simplified, Their Pronunciation, Derivation and Meaning.* 1986 Edition. Landsmans Bookshop LTD, Buckenhill, Bromyard, Herefordshire, England.

Krischik, Vera. 1996. *Butterfly Gardening.* Minnesota Extension Service, University of Minnesota, St. Paul, MN.

Patent, Dorothy Hinshaw and Diane E. Bilderback. 1991. *Book of Garden Secrets.* Camden House Publishing, Charlotte, VT.

Stephens, Pamela Gehn. 1994. *Deer Resistant Ornamental Plants for the Northern United States.* 7555 Northwest Oak Creek Drive, Corvallis, OR 97330.

National Geographic Society. 1957. *The World in Your Garden.* Washington, D.C.

Staff of the L. H. Bailey Hortorium. 1976. *Hortus Three.* Cornell University, Macmillan Publishing, New York, NY.

Morris Editor, William. 1975. *American Heritage Dictionary of the English Language.* Houghton Mifflen Co. New York, NY.

Periodicals

Fine Gardening. The Taunton Press, Inc., Newton, CT 06470.

Garden Design. 100 Avenue of the Americas, New York, New York 10013.

Gardens Illustrated. John Brown Publishing LTD, The New Boathouse, 136-142 Bramley Road, London, England W10 6SR.

Horticulture The Magazine of American Gardening. Horticulture Inc., 98 No. Washington Street, Boston, MA 02114.

Minnesota Horticulture. Minnesota State Horticulture Society, 1755 Prior Avenue North, Falcon Heights, MN 55113.

Perennial Plants, Quarterly Journal of the Perennial Plant Association. Steven Still, Editor, Perennial Plant Association, 3383 Schirtzinger Road, Hilliard, OH 43026. The Chicago Botanic Garden Clematis Study and The Chicago Botanic Garden Monarda Study.

Nursery Retailer.

Nursery Management and Production. Branch Smith Publishing. 120 St. Louis Ave., Ft. Worth, TX 76104.

Sunset Magazine. Sunset Publishing Company, 80 Willow Road, Menlo Park, CA 94025.

The Herb Companion. Herb Companion Press, LLC., 741 Corporate Circle, Suite A Box 4101, Golden, CO 80401.

Writers and Lecturers

Addison, Betty Ann. Rice Creek Gardens, Blaine, MN.

Appleton, Bonnie Lee. Virginia Cooperative Extension, VA.

Ball, John. Forestry Dept., SDSU, Brookings, SD.

Buus, Rick. former instructor for Horticulture Program at Southeast Technical Institute, 2301 Career Place, Sioux Falls, SD 57107.

Evers, Norm. Horticulture Dept., SDSU, Brookings, SD.

Gerwing, Jim. Extension Specialist, Brookings, SD.

Hammernink, Harlan and Mrs. Bluebird Nursery, Clarkson, NE.

Heger, Mike. Ambergate Gardens, Chaska, MN.

Josko, Don. Former instructor for Horticulture Program at Southeast Technical Institute, 2301 Career Place, Sioux Falls, SD 57105.

Lindgren, Dale. Nebraska State Extension Horticulturist, West Central Research Station, North Platte, NE.

Maca, Martin. Landscape Design, SDSU, Brookings, SD.

Metli, Steve. Sioux Falls City Planning, Sioux Falls, SD.

Munk, Steve. Minnehaha County Extension Agent, 220 West Sixth St., Sioux Falls, SD 57104.

Prosser, Tom. Minnesota Horticulturist. May, 1990. Minnesota State Horticulture Society, 1755 Prior Avenue North, Falcon Heights, MN 55113.

Raulston, Dr. J. C. North Carolina State University Professor and former director of NCSU Arboretum, Dept. of Horticulture Science, NCSU, Raleigh, NC 27695.

Tatroe, Marcia. Denver Botanic Garden, Denver, CO.

Newsletters

COPF Newsletter. Canadian Ornamental Plant Foundation, North Bay, Ontario, Canada.

From the Ground Up. Minnehaha County Extension Newsletter, Steve Munk, Minnehaha County Extension Office, 220 W 6Th St., Sioux Falls, SD 57104.

Homeground. Allen Lacy, PO Box 271, Linwood, NJ 08221.

Minnesota Rock Plant Notes. Newsletter of the Minnesota Chapter of the North American Rock Garden Society. c/o Steve Roos, 311 Sunnydale Ln. S.E., Rochester, MN 55904.

The Avant Gardener. Horticultural Data Processors, Box 489, New York, NY 10028.

The Business of Herbs. Northwind Publication, 439 Ponderosa Way, Jemez Springs, NM 87025.

Woody Plant Society Newsletter. (dissolved and entered with the Landscape Plant Development Center, U of Minnesota Landscape Arboretum, Chanhassen, MN).

Mayo Clinic Health Letter. April 1999. Mayo Clinic, Rochester, MN.

Landscape Plant News. Landscape Plant Development Center, University of Minnesota Landscape Arboretum, P.O. Box 39, Chanhassen, MN 55317.

Landscape Plant News. Volume 9. 1998. Susan Barton. University of Delaware.

McCrory Gardens Newsletter. Horticulture Department, SDSU, Brookings, SD.

South Dakota Horticulture Society Newsletter. Dave Graper, Extension Horticulturist, NPB201 Box 2140A, SDSU, Brookings, SD 57007.

Other

Minnesota Landscape Arboretum. PO Box 39, Chanhassen, MN 55317.

Murschel, Casey, Sioux Falls City Commissioner.

Geyer, Dr. Caroline for primary editing. Other reading by Mary Pat Sweetman, Lori Kiesow, Suzanne Theophilus, Kristi Heinert, Marianne Larsen, Linda and Gary Pashby, Kris Egger, Marlene Billion, Dr. Lucy Fryxell.

Numerous notes from lectures, symposia, interviews, trade journals and catalogs collected over the past several years.

Ideas and word images from Sue Evans, Lori Kiesow, Jeff Krambeck and all the other people I've been blessed to know and work with over the past twelve years.